Praise for
PHILOSOPHERS ON RACE

"Skeptical scrutiny of the many ways in which Western philosophy has been enmeshed with the practices of slavery, dispossession of indigenous peoples, and anti-Semitism is, with the publication of *Philosophers on Race*, reaching its maturity. It is bringing into focus the inadequacy of our philosophical tradition's efforts to achieve self-consciousness about its own racism and about the deep meaning of being anti-racist. This book sets the terms for serious discussion of racism in the future."

Anatole Anton, San Francisco State University

"In this distinguished collection, noted authorities explain how the idea of race informed the philosophies of Aristotle, Hobbes, Locke, Rousseau, Kant, Mill, Sartre, and others. It deepens our understanding not only of race, but also of Western philosophy."

Bernard Boxill, University of North Carolina at Chapel Hill

"This collection makes a splendid contribution to our understanding of the history of thinking on race and racism in the history of philosophy. It goes far to remedy what now appear as the thundering silences about racial and anti-racist thinking characteristic of standard histories of philosophy, and to counter prevalent simplistic reactions and generalizations on all sides of the issues."

Sandra Harding, University of California, Los Angeles

"This book offers a highly sophisticated, well-thought-out, and balanced treatment of a very delicate but much downplayed subject, namely, the role and significance of the views of celebrated Western philosophical forebears in shaping the discourse on race, racism, and oppression. As such, it provides a variety of very powerful critical lenses through which to re-examine the epistemological, metaphysical, and ethical claims of those philosophical icons whose views on race are interrogated."

Clarence Shole Johnson, Middle Tennessee State University

"Critical race theory in philosophy has until now lagged behind the comparable feminist revisionist project on gender. This landmark collection of essays, ranging in scope from Plato to Dewey, represents a dramatic step forward in theoretically engaging the role of race in the work of central figures of the canon. After reading this text, no one will be able to claim in good faith that race is irrelevant to Western philosophy."

Charles W. Mills, University of Illinois at Chicago

PHILOSOPHERS ON RACE

Critical Essays

Edited by
Julie K. Ward
and
Tommy L. Lott

Blackwell Publishers

© 2002 by Blackwell Publishers Ltd
a Blackwell Publishing company

Editorial Offices:
108 Cowley Road, Oxford OX4 1JF, UK
Tel: +44 (0)1865 791100
Osney Mead, Oxford OX2 0EL, UK
Tel: +44 (0)1865 206206
Blackwell Publishing USA 350 Main Street, Malden, MA 02148-5018, USA
Tel: +1 781 388 8250
Iowa State Press, a Blackwell Publishing company, 2121 State Avenue, Ames, Iowa 50014-8300,
USA
Tel: +1 515 292 0140
Blackwell Munksgaard, Nørre Søgade 35, PO Box 2148, Copenhagen, DK-1016, Denmark
Tel: +45 77 33 33 33
Blackwell Publishing Asia, 54 University Street, Carlton, Victoria 3053, Australia
Tel: +61 (0)3 9347 0300
Blackwell Verlag, Kurfürstendamm 57, 10707 Berlin, Germany
Tel: +49 (0)30 32 79 060
Blackwell Publishing, 10, rue Casimir Delavigne, 75006 Paris, France
Tel: +331 5310 3310

First published 2002 by Blackwell Publishers Ltd

Library of Congress Cataloging-in-Publication Data

Philosophers on race: critical essays / edited by Julie K. Ward and Tommy L. Lott.
p. cm.
Includes bibliographical references and index.
ISBN 0-631-22226-X (alk. paper)—ISBN 0-631-22227-8 (pb. : alk. paper)
1. Race. I. Ward, Julie K., 1953– II. Lott, Tommy Lee, 1946–
HT1523 .P48 2002
305.8—dc21
2001043230

A catalogue record for this title is available from the British Library.

Set in 10.5 on 12.5 pt Garamond 3
by Best-set Typesetter Ltd., Hong Kong
Printed and bound in Great Britain by Antony Rowe

For further information on
Blackwell Publishers, visit our website:
www.blackwellpublishers.co.uk

Contents

Contents

Contributors

Robert Bernasconi is Moss Professor of Philosophy at the University of Memphis. He is the editor of *Race* (Blackwell, 2001) and co-editor with Tommy L. Lott of *The Idea of Race* (Hackett, 2000). In addition to his work in race theory, he writes on Hegel, twentieth-century continental philosophy, and social and political philosophy.

Daniel W. Conway is Professor of Philosophy and Director of Graduate Studies in Philosophy at Pennsylvania State University. He is the author of *Nietzsche and the Political* (Routledge, 1997) and *Nietzsche's Dangerous Game* (Cambridge University Press, 1997), and has published widely on topics in political philosophy, contemporary European philosophy, and the history of philosophy.

David Theo Goldberg is the Director of the Humanities Research Institute, University of California, Irvine, and Professor of African American Studies and Criminology, Law, and Society, University of California, Irvine. Formerly Director and Professor of the School of Justice Studies, a law and social science program, at Arizona State University, he is author of *The Racial State* (Blackwell, 2001), *Racist Culture: Philosophy and the Politics of Meaning* (Blackwell, 1993), *Racial Subjects: Writing on Race in America* (Routledge, 1997), and *Ethical Theory and Social Issues* (Holt, Rinehart, and Wilson, 1990/1995). He edited *Anatomy of Racism* (University of Minnesota Press, 1990) and *Multiculturalism: A Critical Reader* (Blackwell, 1994) and co-editor of *Race Critical Theories* (Blackwell, 2001), *Relocating Postcolonialism* (Blackwell, 2001), *The Blackwell Companion on Racial and Ethnic Studies* (Blackwell, 2001) and *Between Law and Culture* (Minnesota, 2001). He is the founding co-editor of *Social Identities: Journal for the Study of Race, Nation, and Culture*.

Lewis R. Gordon is Director of Afro-American Studies and Professor of Afro-American Studies, Religious Studies, and Modern Culture and Media at Brown. He is author of numerous books and articles, including: *Bad Faith and Anti-Black Racism* (Humanities Press, 1995), *Fanon and the Crisis of European Man: An Essay on Philosophy and the Human Sciences* (Routledge, 1995), and editor of *Existence in Black: An Anthology of Black Existential Philosophy* (Routledge, 1997).

Paul-A. Hardy is a New Yorker who received his BA/MA from Oxford University, and his Ph.D. in Islamic Thought at the Oriental Institute at the University of Chicago. For the past five years, he has lectured on Islamic thought at the School of Oriental and African Studies at the University of London. Forthcoming publications include *Avicenna on Self-Knowing; Traditions In Islam*, editor; a contribution to *Cambridge Companion to Islam*.

Rachana Kamtekar works on ancient philosophy, in particular on ancient ethical theory, moral psychology, and political philosophy. She has published articles on Plato and Stoicism and in 1998–9 was a Solmsen Fellow at the University of Wisconsin, Madison. She is currently Assistant Professor of Philosophy at the University of Michigan, Ann Arbor; she has previously taught Philosophy at Williams College, MA.

Berel Lang is Professor of Humanities at Trinity College. He has been a professor of philosophy at the University of Colorado and the State University of New York at Albany, and a Visiting Professor at the University of Connecticut, Wesleyan University, and the Hebrew University. His books include *Act and Idea in the Nazi Genocide* (University of Chicago Press, 1990), *The Future of the Holocaust* (Cornell University Press, 1999), *Race and Racism in Theory and Practice* (Rowman & Littlefield, 2000), and *Holocaust Representation: Art within the Limits of History and Ethics* (Johns Hopkins University Press, 2000).

Tommy L. Lott is Professor of Philosophy at San Jose State University. He is author of *The Invention of Race* (Blackwell, 1999), and *Like Rum in the Punch: Alain Locke and the Theory of African American Culture* (University of Massachusetts Press, forthcoming). He is editor of *Subjugation and Bondage: Critical Essays on Slavery and Social Philosophy* (Rowman & Littlefield, 1998) and co-editor of *The Idea of Race*, with Robert Bernasconi (Hackett, 2000), and of *A Companion to African-American Philosophy*, with John Pittman (Blackwell, forthcoming).

Francis Moran III is an Assistant Professor of Political Science at New Jersey City University. He received his doctorate from New York University and his research has concentrated on the role and uses of nature in political thought. His work has appeared in the *Journal of the History of Ideas*, *The Review of Politics*, *Commonwealth*, and *Politics and the Life Sciences*. He has also contributed to the edited collection *Recent Research in Biopolitics, Volume V* (JAI Press, 1997), which is part of his current project exploring the affinities between Marxism and biopolitics.

Julien Murphy is Professor of Philosophy at the University of Southern Maine, Portland. She is the author of *The Constructed Body: AIDS, Reproductive Technology and Ethics* (State University of New York, 1995), a feminist book in bioethics, and editor of *Re-Reading the Canon: Feminist Interpretations of Jean-Paul Sartre* (Pennsylvania State University Press, 1999). Her work has appeared in numerous collections in bioethics and continental philosophy.

Gregory Fernando Pappas is an Associate Professor of Philosophy at Texas A&M University. He has been the recipient of a Ford Foundation Fellowship and the William James Prize. His area of specialization is American and Latin American philosophy. Most of his publications are on John Dewey and William James, and he is currently working on a book-length manuscript on the ethics of John Dewey.

Margaret A. Simons, Professor in the Department of Philosophical Studies at Southern Illinois University Edwardsville and Co-Director of the Society for Phenomenology and Existential Philosophy, is author of *Beauvoir and The Second Sex: Feminism, Race, and the Origins of Existentialism* (Rowman & Littlefield, 1999) and numerous articles on Beauvoir's philosophy. A founding editor of *Hypatia: A Journal of Feminist Philosophy*, she co-edited, with Azizah al-Hibri, *Hypatia Reborn: Essays in Feminist Philosophy* (Indiana University Press, 1990), as well as *Feminist Interpretations of Simone de Beauvoir* (Pennsylvania State University Press, 1995) and "The Philosophy of Simone de Beauvoir," a special issue of *Hypatia* 14:4 (fall 1999). She is currently co-editing, with Sylvie Le Bon de Beauvoir, a six-volume series of Simone de Beauvoir's philosophically significant texts.

Kathy Squadrito received her doctorate from Washington University, and is currently Associate Professor of Philosophy at Purdue University, Fort Wayne, Indiana, where she specializes in Locke, and epistemology. She has published papers in Locke's epistemology, and environmental ethics.

William Uzgalis is an Associate Professor at Oregon State University. Uzgalis has published several papers on various aspects of the philosophy of John Locke. He also has an interest in philosophy and computers and is currently serving as a member of the APA Committee on Computers and Philosophy and as Associate Editor of the APA Computer Use in Philosophy newsletter.

Julie K. Ward is Associate Professor of Philosophy at Loyola University, Chicago. She has published papers both in ancient philosophy and in feminism, and has edited an anthology entitled *Feminism and Ancient Philosophy* (Routledge, 1996), to which she contributed a chapter on Aristotle's theory of friendship. She has also written an essay on Equiano and eighteenth century anti-abolitionist arguments in *Subjugation and Bondage: Critical Essays on Slavery and Social Philosophy*, ed. Tommy L. Lott (Rowman & Littlefield, 1998).

Acknowledgments

The foundation for the essays presented in this anthology originated in papers presented at three sessions of the American Philosophical Association (APA) meetings sponsored by the Committee on the Status of Blacks in the Profession that were devoted to the topic "Traditional Philosophers on Race" held between 1998 and 1999. These sessions were planned with the help of the APA Committee. Julie Ward would like to thank her co-editor, Tommy Lott, for originating these sessions and for suggesting a consideration of the topic of race among classical Western philosophers from Plato to the present time.

Many friends and colleagues helped us during the time period these various papers became a book manuscript. Julie Ward would like to thank members of the Philosophy Department at Loyola University, and especially Corinne Painter and Michael Silva for their assistance at various stages in production. In the latter regard, a summer grant from Loyola University supported critical and editorial work on the manuscript undertaken during the summer of 2000. Tommy Lott would like to thank Dorothy Whitman and Rebecca Wolpinsky for valuable assistance with the research for this volume. Both of us wish to thank Beth Remmes, editor at Blackwell Publishing, for her assistance during the production of this volume, and finally, our families for their encouragement and support.

The editors and publishers gratefully acknowledge the following for permission to reproduce copyright material:

Gordon, Lewis R., "Sartrean Bad Faith and Antiblack Racism" from Crowell (ed.) *The Prism of the Self.* Dordrecht, The Netherlands: Kluwer Academic Publishers, 1995. Reproduced by permission of Kluwer Academic Publishers;

Moran Francis, III, "Between Primates and Primitives: Natural Man as the Missing Link in Rousseau's *Second Discourse*" from *Journal of the History of Ideas.* Copyright © 1993 Johns Hopkins University Press;

Pappas, Gregory Fernando, "Dewey's Philosophical Approach to Racial Prejudice" *Social Theory and Practice* 22:1 (Spring 1996), reprinted by permission of Florida State University, Department of Philosophy and the author.

Introduction

Until recently, the history of Western philosophy has been devoted exclusively to the ideas of a select group of European men. However, with the recent development of a substantial body of feminist criticism of this tradition, the presuppositions and claims about women have come to be discussed in their own right by historians of philosophy.[1] The critical appraisal of the views held by traditional philosophers regarding women has sought to provide more than simply an alternative perspective. The goal has been to incorporate women's issues into discussions within the history of philosophy. This collection of essays inaugurates a similar examination of questions regarding race and racism in the history of Western philosophy from the Greeks to twentieth-century thinkers. The essays cover a wide range of topics including the *Greek–barbarian* opposition remarked upon by Plato and Aristotle, the religious notion of race in Islamic philosophy, the concurrent development of social contract theory and racist discourse in Hobbes, Locke, Hume, and Kant in the modern period, the modifications of this Enlightenment tradition in the more ambiguous views of Nietzsche, Mill, Carlyle, and Heidegger, and the critical reflections of progressive twentieth-century thinkers such as Dewey, Beauvoir and Sartre.

It is no coincidence that questions regarding race began to receive growing attention in the Renaissance and throughout the Enlightenment period. Various ideas regarding the inferiority of non-Europeans, often based upon Europeans' accounts of non-Europeans both in colonial accounts in the Americas and travel journals from abroad, emerged alongside a growing scientific interest in the subject.[2] The writings of prominent thinkers such as François-Marie Voltaire, Isaac La Peyrere, and Comte de Buffon also fostered critical reflection on race. Thus, a sharpened awareness of race is introduced into the modern period, as is illustrated in the classic debates about slavery and race between Bartolome de Las Casas and Juan Gines de Sepúlveda in the sixteenth century, Immanuel Kant and Johann Herder in the eighteenth century, and John Stuart Mill and Thomas Carlyle in the nineteenth century. Modern thought was influenced by its development within the context of a global expansion of European colonialism. Yet some of the theoretical bases for modern racism had earlier roots. The enslavement of African people in the medieval period found support in certain aspects of Islamic thought. In turn, Islamic social philosophy was largely influenced by two aspects of Greek thought: a climate theory of racial differences, and Aristotle's theory of natural slavery. The fact that early Enlightenment philosophers such as Hobbes were preoccupied with a need to break with Aristotle's teachings attests to the magnitude of the latter's influence in the modern period.

Considering Greek philosophical thought with an eye to issues of race, the first two essays in the volume critically examine the concept of "barbarians" in classical Greek thought. Rachana Kamtekar's essay, "Distinction Without a Difference? Race and *Genos* in Plato," undertakes three tasks: first, to discuss the cogency of investigating the concept of *race* in Plato's thought; second, to examine Plato's actual texts for indications of race, or racialist thought; third, to determine whether Plato's philosophy is supportive of, or antithetical, to race, or racialist thinking. On the first point, Kamtekar concludes that while the idea of race involving biological determinism is undoubtedly a modern invention, one may, nonetheless look for similar constructions in the ancient period. In this sense the investigation of race in ancient Greek philosophy is not misplaced. On the second point, she concludes that although Plato makes use of "racial" stereotypes in various dialogues – such as that Phoenicians and Egyptians love money (*Republic*, 435e–36a) – in some of his other statements on the issue, he openly criticizes the standard division of humanity into Greeks and "barbarians" as unjustified. According to Plato in *Politicus* (262b–63a), since those the Greeks commonly call "barbarians" share neither a common culture nor a common language, the term fails to name an existing category of human beings, and is thus incorrect. For Plato, when it comes to human beings the only kind of distinction that is meaningful is the ability to demonstrate moral virtue.

But there are two other respects in which it is less obvious where Plato's thought stands in relation to modern racism. He is well known for his advocacy of inegalitarianism that rests on the idea that society ought to be arranged to accord with inequalities in "natural" capacities. To some extent, he shares ideological territory with contemporary inegalitarian thinkers such as David Herrnstein and Charles Murray, authors of the *The Bell Curve*, even though for Plato classifications based on race or ethnicity are irrelevant. What keeps Plato's inegalitarianism from being racist in the modern sense is his view that the virtue is not inherited by one's family or, more broadly, by biological means, as is illustrated by Socrates' claim that when morally deficient sons are born to parents of high virtue, the two must belong to different kinds, or *gene*, given the difference in virtue (*Cratylus*, 393c–94e). For Plato, the basis for proper membership in a *genos* – here meaning what it is to belong to the same kind based on moral virtue – does not imply biological, or inherited, criteria.

Plato's position on what constitutes a *genos* is inconsistent with the aspect of contemporary racist thinking regarding heredity, but whether ethnic or racial categories correlate with virtue categories remains undetermined: his view is compatible with some forms of racialist thought, even though it does not logically imply them. While Kamtekar is cautious in her appraisal, the idea that a certain ethnic or national group would in principle be marked out for moral virtue apart from its actual achievement remains implausible for Plato, and in this respect, Plato's thought is anti-racist.

While Aristotle's doctrine regarding natural slaves was prominent in the racist discourse of apologists for New World slavery, it remains unclear whether Aristotle's political work itself assumes racial categories. In her essay, "*Ethnos* in the *Politics*: Aristotle on Race," Julie Ward focuses on this issue by re-identifying the terms of the question: she suggests that the question may be answered by substituting the terms "Greek" and "barbarian" for their modern counterparts. Yet Aristotle's views as a whole remain difficult to assess since he makes inconsistent comments on "barbarians" and natural slaves. On the one hand, he finds that some "barbarians" are dispositionally prone to becoming enslaved, and yet he fails to identify them as slaves by nature. In addition, he refrains from endorsing the idea that a person's moral virtue is due to natural inheritance, through familial lines or generally, biological descent, as some modern racists have. For Aristotle, moral excellence is a permanent state of character requiring experience and practical reasoning, among other factors. The view on moral virtue thus conflicts with Aristotle's claims in *Politics*, VII. 7 that some "barbarians" have a tendency to servility that make them easily enslaved. Of Aristotle's various "barbarian" nations, he identifies two, Europeans and Asians, as differing widely in disposition: Europeans are unsociable, unintelligent, and wild, while Asians are intelligent, docile and able to be enslaved.

For some scholars, Aristotle's comments about "barbarians" constitute the cornerstone for the connection between his theory of "natural" slaves in Book I and his remarks about Asian barbarians in Book VII. Yet the question whether Asians can be Aristotle's "natural" slaves is complicated by the fact that he also thinks that they possess intelligence and skill in craft-making, claims which do not support the description of so-called natural slaves from Book I. Another factor confounding the connection between Asian "barbarians" and natural slaves involves Aristotle's remarks on moral education, which suggest that natural or innate tendencies can be modified or replaced by social training, political institutions, and by individual rational control. Thus, prior to reaching a final assessment of Aristotle's view, these passages on moral education should be considered as well as those claiming that Asian "barbarians" have the kind of nature suitable for slavery. Ward concludes that since the account of natural slaves specifies a docile nature combined with deficient intelligence, Asians are not "natural" slaves because they are intelligent. This finding, coupled with the discussion concerning moral training, does not fit with the claim that Aristotle held a view of biological determinism concerning racial inheritance. But while his views about national groups (Greeks, Europeans, Asians) is not identical with biological racism, other textual evidence suggests that his use of *ethnos*, or "nationality," especially used in contrast with *polis*, implies a cultural concept of race.

According to some thinkers, the spread of Islam in Africa during the Middle Ages was a by-product of the Arab slave trade.[3] In his essay "Medieval Muslim Philosophers on Race," Paul Hardy recognizes the presence of slavery in the medieval Muslim world as a context for Islamic thought regarding race. Hardy begins his examination by nothing that in Islam itself, the notion of Oneness with God seems to lead to that of the equality of all believers. Furthermore, he observes that in the period of classical Islamic philosophy (from the ninth to the fourteenth centuries CE), race appears to be absent as a category. Nonetheless, in spite of certain tendencies within Islam itself, the culture supported slavery, and this practice led to ideas of exclusion of certain groups, such as Africans, Slavs, and Turks. So, while Islamic law required that "conspecifics" or things having the same genus and species be treated as having the same value and in the same way, slaves were not treated as equal to other human beings with souls. Thus, a basic conceptual problem was reached: either slaves were not the same in species as other humans like Muslims, and so, could be used for commercial exchange, or they were the same in species, and so, slavery should be legally prohibited. On this issue, Islamic legal scholars and philosophers often disagreed. Ibn Sīnā, the Islamic philosopher, held that while the specific difference of humans in general was the rational soul, this was not an actual reality, but an ideal or norm that humans were supposed to move towards. In contrast, some Islamic jurists thought that the human soul was not one in species, but allowed for different kinds, specifically, that some humans possess servile souls. On this view, human souls might form a hierarchy, from the most perfect Islamic believers and prophets down to those who denied Islam, and so, would be considered to be justly enslaved.

The Islamic acceptance of slavery received theoretical support, in large part, from its use of the Aristotelian theory of natural slaves. In addition, the Islamic philosopher Ibn Sīnā employed the "climate theory" found in Aristotle's *Politics*, Book VII as suggesting that certain groups of people, those whom he termed "Turks" and "Negroes," were destined for slavery on the basis that their climate prevented them from inheriting the balanced temperament that was required for virtue. This position on climate and natural slaves is echoed by other thinkers such as Maimonides in the twelfth century, and Ibn Khaldūn, an historiographer, in the fourteenth century. The thought of some Islamic philosophers thus bears a similarity to that of Greek thinkers who, though they did not strictly classify people on the basis of race, endorsed theories that led to marking human differences along racial and ethnic lines.

The debt Modern European thought owes to Greek philosophy is also evident in the social and political philosophy of Thomas Hobbes, an influential proponent of the social contract theory and ardent critic of Aristotle. In his essay, "Patriarchy and Slavery in Hobbes's Political Philosophy," Tommy Lott investigates the question of whether Hobbes maintained a biased view of gender and race and finds that Hobbes's detractors have not fully appreciated the extent to which he acknowledges the social construction of patriarchy and, as a consequence, have overlooked his important insight regarding subordination based on gender, race, and class. Lott points out that Hobbes was constrained by his political theory to acknowledge the artificial nature of male authority in the household and in the commonwealth. With reference to Hobbes's account of the political-economic structure of the household, Lott critically examines his natural rights justification of a patriarchal civil society. Although, on Hobbes's account, a radicalized patriarchy is justified, Lott insists that Hobbes does not employ gender or race as criteria on which to ground the authority of a father, husband, master, or sovereign. Even though there is virtually no discussion of race, Hobbes's various remarks in his political writings suggest an anthropological view of Native Americans, Africans, and the people of India as culturally different. Lott situates Hobbes's anthropological view within his political theory. With regard to the different social positions occupied by wives, servants and slaves, Lott points out that, on Hobbes's account, important distinctions among various forms of subordination based on gender, race, and class can be maintained.

The question of whether Hobbes viewed Native Americans as inferior is generated by his use of the term " savages" to refer to them. One source of the charge of racial bias is his ambiguous use of terms such as "barbarian" and "savage" to refer to groups of people in some early stage of social development. Although he also used these terms to refer to Europeans, his silence on the matter of New World colonialism and slavery adds greater weight to the suspicion. On Lott's interpretation, Hobbes's political theory did not require a racist view of Native Americans to offer a justification of their dispossession. But unlike Hobbes, whose political doctrine was complicit with colonial expansion, but which has gone largely unremarked by scholars, John Locke's view of Native Americans has generated heated debates.

Much of the debate over Locke's view has been devoted to the question of whether his political theory justifies the appropriation of lands belonging to the Native Americans. In her essay, "Locke and the Dispossession of the American Indian," Kathy Squadrito challenges the received view that accords Locke's *Second Treatise* (1690) a prominent role in policy that resulted in Native American dispossession. She draws attention to Locke's *Essay* (1690) as having a more lasting influence for Native Americans. Squadrito focuses on the image of Native Americans in the *Second Treatise* and the *Essay* to provide an assessment of the sources from which Locke derived his view. She argues that in his account of the state of nature, he selectively employs images that support a view of Native Americans as uncivilized savages. She points out that Locke never argues, as Hobbes does, that land acquisition is justified by conquest. Instead, he relies on a view of tacit consent involving the exchange of goods for land. Nonetheless, his just war theory applies to Native Americans who oppose such exchanges. According to Squadrito, Locke's remarks regarding the right to develop a wasteland have been misinterpreted to provide evidence that he supported the dispossession of Native Americans by force. The source of this misinterpretation can be traced to an important ambiguity in his view, both sides of which are represented in the debate between Las Casas and Sepúlveda regarding slavery and the status of Native Americans as humans. Squadrito points out that Locke's description of Native Americans as morally inferior is similar to Sepúlveda's, but like Las Casas (and unlike Sepúlveda), Locke rejects the ideas of innate inferiority and natural slavery. She adds the fact that Locke, as well as his employer, William Shaftsbury, favored peaceful relations to show that Locke would not have endorsed a just war against Native American resistance to conquest.

Squadrito accounts for the tension between Locke's view in *The Constitution of the Carolinas* and the view he presents in the *Second Treatise*. She considers the question of whether Locke proposed Native American land grants on the condition that Native Americans consent to adopting European cultural values. Although Locke does not approve of genocide in the physical sense, he failed to appreciate Native American values and cultivates a view that supports cultural genocide. Squadrito criticizes Locke scholars who have attributed too much weight to the influence of Locke's argument for appropriating wasteland. She maintains that Locke's racism was "soft" in the sense that he believed Native Americans were inferior, but also that this inferiority could be remedied by assimilation. Squadrito surveys the major views regarding the role of Christian teaching in the dispossession of Native Americans to highlight the greater influence of Locke's *Essay* on the policy of forced assimilation.

Along with questions regarding his view of Native Americans, the question of whether Locke subscribed to a view of black people as inferior also has been a matter of heated debate. In his essay, "'An Inconsistency not to be Excused': On Locke and Racism," William Uzgalis enters this debate. Beginning with the apparent inconsistency between the Enlightenment doctrine of equality advocated by Locke and his contemporaries and their support of the institution of slavery, Uzgalis defends Locke against the charge that he was a proponent of modern racism – a theory of the permanent inferiority of a group of people due to biology or climate. Uzgalis discusses H. M. Bracken's influential argument that Locke held a racist view of black people. Bracken's argument turns on how we understand Locke's view of nominal essences. Uzgalis cites Locke's inconsistent claims that leave unclear whether shape is to count as a nominal essence, to indicate that Locke thought shape alone is neither necessary, nor sufficient, to decide what things can be called human. Uzgalis contends that the major thrust of Locke's view of race is cultural. Although Locke mentions the Mayan and Aztec civilizations in the *Second Treatise*, he refuses to recognize Native Americans as having a civilization. Uzgalis examines Locke's comparison of Native Americans with animals to propose a line of thought (available to Locke) that responds to the question of whether Locke's comparison implies a racist view of Native Americans. Uzgalis concludes that Locke's belief that Native Americans failed to use the land properly is certainly Eurocentric, but that this is not necessarily racist. Rather than suppose that Locke believed that Native Americans are inferior, and therefore, the appropriation of their land is justified, Uzgalis argues that we should understand his theory regarding land use to entail a view of cultural development. On this reading, Locke's stipulation should be understood as a policy designed to encourage Native Americans to give up their Native-American culture and enter a more advanced Western society. Uzgalis is critical of this Eurocentric bias, pointing out that, unfortunately, it led Locke to insist that Native Americans assimilate European cultural values, ruling out the possibility of Europeans learning anything from Native Americans regarding the environment and living in harmony with nature.

Jean-Jacques Rousseau's discussion of "Natural Man" contains a critique of European racial superiority. In his essay, "Between Primates and Primitives: Natural Man as the Missing Link in Rousseau's *Second Discourse*," Francis Moran explores the question of whether Rousseau's account in the *Discourse on Inequality* (1755) points to a kind of "proto-human." Commentators have suggested that Rousseau thought of "natural man" as a "midpoint" between primates and humans, anticipating later developments in evolutionist thought. Instead, Moran suggests that Rousseau conceives of "natural man" as a genuine human modeled after the eighteenth-century conception of the "missing link" connecting humans and animals in the "chain of being" (p. 126). Previous explorations in Africa, the South Pacific, and the Americas had provided new discoveries that were employed by European naturalists to show similarities between certain non-European cultures and other primates. For example, they drew frequent comparisons in terms of facial structure, gesture, body posture, and level of intelligence between the "Hottentots" of South Africa and monkeys, or baboons. Rousseau's speculations were situated within this racialized "scientific" context, and it influenced his decision to accord "natural man" an ambiguous human status. Like most European naturalists of the period, Rousseau characterized "natural man" as having low intelligence, little foresight, and bad memory, but unlike other speculative thinkers of the period, he characterized natural man as being strong, healthy, well coordinated, and self-reliant. More importantly, Rousseau deviated from the racist views of his contemporaries by refraining from attributing moral deficiencies and vices to "natural man." In contrast to them, he argued that because they lacked great intelligence, these so-called primitive people were unable to develop common human vices like jealousy and vanity, nor to fall prey to mutual exploitation and slavery. In effect, Rousseau turned the tables on European naturalists and their "chain of being" model by arguing for a continuity of traits between "natural man" and present humans, rather than maintaining a subdivision and ranking of human groups with one race or culture at the apex. Contrary to the dominant view of his time, Rousseau made it clear that he thought that Europeans were a "corrupt form of the species and [that] the inequity inherent in [their] societies should not be taken as the standard for assessing either other cultures or other species" (p. 140).

In the essay by Robert Bernasconi, "Kant as an Unfamiliar Source of Racism," Kant's political writings are drawn into question as a source of his racism. The proposition that Kant's political philosophy should contain more than a germ of racist thinking might strike us as surprising given Kant's avowed allegiance to universalism and cosmopolitanism. But Bernasconi's examination of Kant's writings demonstrates that Kant's thought not merely accommodated racist thinking but furthered and contributed to its development in three areas. First, Kant's essays on race from 1775, 1785 and 1788 show that he not only subscribed to a fixed, biological notion of race and a hierarchy of races, but that he was opposed to "racial mixing." Predictably, Kant held to "European superiority" of race and culture, finding blacks and Native Americans at the lowest levels. For evidence of his beliefs about racial inferiority, he turned to a pro-slavery tract by James Tobin, paraphrased into German, to support his claim about the persistence of racial characteristics. Kant used the dubious testimony about Africans afforded by such works as those authored by plantation owners, even when these views about race were being strongly contested. Since Kant himself had no direct experience of Africans or Native Americans, there was no reason for him not to have been skeptical of one-sided reports offered by slave owners, but he chose otherwise. The second relevant aspect of Kant's thought concerns his remarks about racial mixing. While Kant supported a monogenetic origin of race, maintaining that all races are derived from a single set of parents, he nonetheless held that existing racial differences were fixed and determinate. Neither Africans nor Native Americans would ever be susceptible of attaining culture, and in this way, they were dependent upon European culture and mastery. Furthermore, the fact that this was so demonstrated the teleology of nature for Kant, since on his view each race was specially suited by nature to a certain part of the globe. Thus, he opposed racial mixing on the grounds that it was "against nature" and led to the "degradation" of the higher races by the lower ones.

Finally, Kant failed to oppose the African slave trade, even though slavery surely contradicted his moral principles concerning treating other persons never merely as means, and his claim that all are born free since none has yet committed a crime. And it might also be noted that even the commission of a crime only reduces the person to a kind of "bondsman" who, though being "the tool" of his owner, nonetheless retains the right to his life and his body. Hence, Kant would seem to have had no recourse but to condemn the enslavement of Africans and the dispossession of Native Americans. Once it is noted that Kant also held that these same peoples were "born slaves," meaning they were unable to govern themselves by nature, that he did not do so is less puzzling. If we interpret Kant's view to be that these races were destined by nature to serve, it would follow that they would possess no natural rights and so would be exempt from the provisions protecting "persons" from chattel slavery.

The assessment of Nietzsche's influence on German racist thinking, specifically, on the anti-Semitic views of the Nazi regime, has been plagued by years of misinterpretation and poor scholarship that have obscured what he actually wrote. To begin with, Nietzsche's sister, Elizabeth Forster, contributed to the confusion by claiming her brother's philosophy as the foundation for her own anti-Semitism, a distortion which the Nazis found useful to cultivate for their own purposes. As early as 1950, Walter Kaufman tried to correct the then standing conception of Nietzsche as "the Nazi philosopher" by re-examining the full complexity of his philosophical thought. Yet it must be admitted that such misinterpretation was facilitated by Nietzsche's remarks about race and eugenics which were phrased in the current racist, pseudo-scientific jargon, and could be used to support anti-Semitic and racist movements such as Aryanism. Consequently, the reassessment of Nietzsche's contribution to modern racist thought provided by Dan Conway in his essay "The Great Play and Fight of Forces: Nietzsche on Race" attends to a pressing issue among scholars.

Apart from the distortions committed by Elizabeth Forster, Conway finds a systematic strain of racism in Nietzsche's philosophy. In Nietzsche's writing that dealt with conceptions of "race," "nation," and "people," he distinguishes between innate and acquired racial traits, holding that Jews as a race embodied the highest level of cultural achievement. By acquiring a distinct cultural identity and character that persisted over time, Nietzsche praises the achievement of Jews, ranking them as the highest European race, far surpassing Germans, whom he thinks are decadent. While praising Jews, Nietzsche speaks of the racial "improvement" of inferior races, such as the Aryans. But he is less than clear concerning the means by which racial improvement is accomplished, for he identifies "blood" and "spirit" as critical components, giving more weight to "spirit," a cultural factor. Employing a metallurgical analogy for the "forging" of well-formed races, Nietzsche suggests that "superior" races can be made, and not simply found. He maintains that races can be improved by forging new ones from existing ones, but cultural order must be imposed on the process, otherwise the result will be a proliferation of decadent races. Two problems arise here: first, the process becomes akin in Nietzsche's mind to the "breeding" of animals, and second, it requires the role of an animal "overseer" who tends to the breeding of the "healthy" races and weeds out the "unhealthy" types. As to which person might be capable of such a role, Nietzsche simply nominates himself.

The British debate over slavery and colonialism in the mid-nineteenth century was fueled by an exchange between Thomas Carlyle and John Stuart Mill in a series of articles on "The Negro Question." David Goldberg critically examines this exchange in his essay, "Liberalism's Limits: Carlyle and Mill on 'The Negro Question.'" The politically conservative Carlyle used the economic problems faced by curtailment of subsidies to Caribbean sugar plantation owners as an occasion to voice his view of the inherent inferiority of Africans, arguing that they were destined by nature to serve whites. By employing standard racist images such as that of the idle black laborer, dubbed "Quashee," Carlyle attempts to blame increases in sugar prices on those whom the plantation owners oppressed. In response, Mill offers the view of an enlightened Victorian abolitionist, arguing against the notion that some peoples are "born to serve," and insisting upon the abolishment of slavery by citing its social disutility. Although Mill's position on slavery and abolition is progressive, especially in comparison to that of Carlyle, some of his assumptions and his ideas about the relative value of cultures are less than progressive. In particular, Mill assumes that while Africans should not be enslaved, nonetheless they are culturally inferior to Europeans, a line of thinking that was perhaps affected by his own work as an examiner for the English East Indies Company from 1823 to 1856. This experience appears to have contributed to his ideas about the need for colonial intervention in "undeveloped" countries so that they might achieve a level of culture required for "progress." The further problem here is that for Mill, some nations are capable of "development" with the intervention of a wealthy, industrial state, while others lack this potential, and in this conclusion, Mill displays a more subtle form of racism than one would suspect to find situated within his classical liberalism.

Dewey's pragmatism is often associated with the support of a progressive social policy on educational issues, but hardly any attention has been devoted to his view of race. In his essay, "Dewey's Philosophical Approach to Racial Prejudice," Gregory Pappas maintains that Dewey was the most involved of the American pragmatists with combating racism, even though he addressed the topic only once in a lecture delivered in China in 1922. Dewey nonetheless sought an overall philosophical understanding of the nature of racial prejudice.

Dewey found the concept of race to be generally a fiction, but he also realized that it was a "useful fiction" (p. 287) that society utilized for a number of reasons. First, its origin in America is due to certain historical factors leading to the privilege of white people, who have sought to maintain their dominance through legally enforced processes of exclusion. Dewey understands racism to be, at a deeper psychological level, caused by an innate human tendency to dislike and distrust what seems new or different to a group. For Dewey, racism is an expression of a defensive posture toward that which is experienced as different from what is taken to be the norm. Economic and political factors support racial prejudice in America, making it impossible for oppressed groups, particularly African Americans, to extricate themselves from these problems.

As Dewey saw it, all of these factors mutually contribute to racial prejudice, which becomes intransigent as the factors reinforce one another.

Dewey's generic notion is designed to cover all forms of racial prejudice. Pappas criticizes Dewey's analysis for its inability to explain the cause of anti-black racism in particular. Pappas also thinks that some racists might be what he terms "naive racists," i.e., people who think and act like racists, but do not have the aversive response that Dewey maintains is fundamental to racial prejudice. Finally, Pappas considers the suggestion that Dewey accounts for what it is to be an individual racist, but that he does not go far enough in explaining racism as a collective set of practices, or as an institution. Nonetheless, Dewey's contextualist method of analysis, which considers racial prejudice as an organic whole, lends itself to a nonreductive explanation of racism that Pappas finds promising.

When Herbert Marcuse wrote to Heidegger requesting an explanation of his seemingly complicitous status in Germany under Nazi rule, he raised an important question regarding Heidegger's anti-Semitism – a question that has since been the subject of several books. In his essay, "Heidegger and the Jewish Question: Metaphysical Racism in Silence and Word," Berel Lang examines the evidence for the charges concerning Heidegger's anti-Semitism. The issue is fraught with difficulties, partly due to the fact that Heidegger said relatively little about Jews before, during, or after the Holocaust. Nonetheless, Lang makes a persuasive case that in choosing to say next to nothing about the genocide of Jews, even years after the war, Heidegger supported anti-Semitic and racist thought. To come to this conclusion, first Lang examines the actual written material found either in the published work, or in his personal letters, and second, he evaluates the significance of Heidegger's silence, that is, his lack of writing on a subject that seems to require comment, if not during the war, at least afterwards. On both considerations, Heidegger appears to be notably oblique if not reticent in his comments regarding the Jews, Nazi policy, and concentration camps. Lang points out that in some of his few remarks, the implications are often disquieting, as in one of the post-war lectures – the second Bremen Lecture in 1949 – in which he compares the mechanization of the food industry to the production of corpses in Nazi concentration camps. Heidegger's reference to the extermination of Jews along with the comparison he draws to modern agricultural practice is particularly unsettling in that here Heidegger glosses over an important difference between the two cases, viz., the greater immorality of human genocide to animal slaughter. Heidegger's response to Herbert Marcuse, a reply that wholly avoids the issue, is equally suggestive. Marcuse had requested that Heidegger publicly disavow any anti-Semitic sympathies. Heidegger instead compared the Nazi genocide of Jews to the Russian deportation of East Germans. Lang points out that the effect of the comparison is to diminish the Nazi crime. According to Lang, "one way to attempt to make something disappear is to place it – like a grain of sand in the desert – in the midst of a mass of supposed likeness" (p. 213–14). For Lang, Heidegger's silence, before and after the war, suggests that he was, throughout the period of National Socialism and following the end of the war, unconcerned with the plight of Jews in Germany. His lack of engagement with the political events in Nazi Germany, and his subsequent failure to address the issue of genocide following the war, even when invited to do so by Marcuse, implies a tacit agreement with some aspects of Nazi anti-Semitism.

Heidegger's failure to come to grips with racism and anti-Semitism stands in sharp contrast with Simone de Beauvoir and Jean Paul Sartre, who, as social activists, were directly involved in combating these issues. Julien Murphy's essay, "Sartre on American Racism," provides an assessment of Sartre's understanding of American anti-black racism. Murphy analyzes a number of lesser known works by Sartre, including a play written in 1946 entitled *The Respectful Prostitute*, which concerns the racially motivated collusion of a poor white woman with a rich man involving the framing of an innocent black man with a false accusation of interracial rape. In his writings during this period, some of which appeared in the French newspaper *Le Figaro*, Sartre demonstrates that he is a strong supporter of anti-racist views, speaking out against all forms of racism in France and abroad.

But arriving at a final conclusion concerning Sartre's overall position on race remains difficult on two counts. The first concerns Sartre's commitment to Marxism, and its interpretation of political struggles largely in terms of class. Although Sartre shows great interest in disclosing the existence of racism, and makes astute observations about the relation of American racism to urban black poverty, he tends to explain American racism in terms of class rather than racial differences. The second difficulty relates to the uneven character of Sartre's thinking on race throughout various works. For example, his earlier travel writing in America (1945–9) tends to reflect a kind of obliviousness to race that reflects what Murphy terms "class profiling." This tendency causes Sartre to neglect the specificity of racial oppression in his analysis. However, in some of his later writing, such as the essay "Revolutionary Violence" from the posthumously published *Notebooks for an Ethics* (1992), he presents a new phenomenological analysis of racist consciousness that avoids a Marxist reduction of race to class oppression, reflecting his theoretical attempt to comprehend race as a distinct ground of social and economic oppression.

In his essay, "Sartrean Bad Faith and Antiblack Racism," Lewis Gordon is more broadly concerned with the potential of the Sartrean notion of "bad faith" to illuminate elements of anti-black racism. Although Sartre's early writings seem to lack a social theory, and thus appear to be irrelevant to a political analysis of oppression, according to Gordon, his concept of alienation, by implication, presupposes a social context. To highlight its relevance to the analysis of racial consciousness, Gordon defines Sartre's notion of bad faith in terms of an evasion of the body. Sartre's notion presupposes a mutual recognition of the body, and through this social process, a recognition of its racial significance. Thus, the concept of embodiment becomes a "perspective on others." According to Gordon, Sartre lays the groundwork for "a transcendental existential phenomenology." Sartrean bad faith elucidates anti-black racism through the understanding it provides of the manner in which black people are interpreted as "material embodiments of inferiority – objective anti-values in the world" (p. 246). By placing existential notions of situation and choice within the social and political context of oppression, the Sartrean analysis explains how something institutional like racism can nevertheless involve individual choice. Since our choices do not occur apart from, but only within institutional meanings, bad faith consists in lying to oneself about the inferiority of black people, even when one is black oneself.

Gordon agrees with Franz Fanon's criticisms of Sartre's analysis of racism, particularly in *Anti-Semite and Jew*. Sartre argues that Jews are constructed from the sadistic look of the anti-Semite. Gordon disputes Sartre on this point, adopting Fanon's view that Jews existed prior to there being anti-Semites, and, by extension, maintaining that the black man pre-exists the advent of slavery and race exploitation. Gordon quotes Fanon's remark that, "not only must the black man be black; he must be black in relation to the white man."[4]

Margaret Simons critically assesses Simone de Beauvoir's position on racism in her essay, "Beauvoir and the Problem of Racism." In her essay, Simons examines the textual evidence of concern about race from Beauvoir's unpublished early diaries, extending her recent work concerning the influence of Richard Wright on Beauvoir's analysis of gender in *The Second Sex* (1949).[5] She also considers the charges leveled by some recent scholars regarding Beauvoir's anti-Semitic, and generally, ethnocentric biases and finds that the evidence is not unambiguous. On the one hand, some evidence from Beauvoir's pre-war diaries suggests that she uses anti-Jewish stereotyping, but the diaries also document several close friendships with Jewish students, including Georgette Levy and Simone Weil, among others. More importantly, a turning point comes for Beauvoir when, during the war, a Jewish student who is a close friend of hers and Sartre's is apprehended and killed by the police. This event apparently changed her thinking on racism and anti-Semitism altogether. Together with her travel writing about America based on her visit to the US in 1947, and her friendship with novelist Richard Wright, Beauvoir began to develop a theoretical basis for the analysis of oppression based on gender oppression that was rooted in her knowledge of anti-Semitic and anti-black racism. The conceptual framework for such analysis emerges through the use of the notion of *situation* that Beauvoir begins to develop in her work *America Day by Day* (1948), and which she comes to expand and refine in *The Second Sex* (1949). Relying on her travel writing, Beauvoir first makes use of a parallel between anti-Semitism in Europe and anti-black racism in America. She then goes on to employ a similar framework in her analysis of the oppression of women: she compares the situation of blacks and Jews to that of women. The influence of W. E. B. Du Bois's notion of "double consciousness" is reflected in Beauvoir's view of the difficulty of women's situation as partly involving the idea of "being other to oneself" in a variety of social contexts. By comparison with the standard Marxist analysis in terms of class that Sartre typically employed, Beauvoir found the analytical tool of *situation* to be more flexible as a means of accounting for the multiple forms of oppression.

Overall, the fifteen essays we have included in this volume serve either as contributing to an existing debate about race and racial thinking, or as raising anew the discussion of these issues among historians of philosophy. With this collection of essays, we hope to stimulate further interest in examining the views of other canonical Western philosophers who have written about race, allowing that these texts afford much room for alternative readings. We are in fact encouraged to find that a growing body of literature appears to be replacing the previous scholarly evasion of, or lack of interest in, the subject of race in the history of philosophy. As progress is made in broadening the scope of the field, we suggest that new thought should be given to restructuring the way in which the history of philosophy is studied, and our aim is to assist students and colleagues in following some new paths in the analysis of historical thinkers.

Notes

1. See, for example, Charlotte Witt and Louise Antony (1993), Bat-Ami Bar On (1994), Julie K. Ward (1996), as well as the various volumes (e.g., Plato, Aristotle, Hegel) in the ongoing Pennsylvania State University Press series in the history of philosophy, *Re-Reading the Canon*, under Nancy Tuana, general editor.
2. Consider, for example, the racist work by sugar-plantation owner and polygenist Edward Long (1774), and critical replies by James Ramsey (1784), Thomas Clarkson (1788), Antony Benezet (1788), and in contrast, Thomas Jefferson (1785).
3. For example, Edward W. Blyden (1967), and W. E .B. Du Bois (1970).
4. Frantz Fanon, (1967, p. 110).
5. Margaret Simons (1999).

References

Bar On, Bat-Ami 1994: *Engendering Origins: Critical Feminist Readings in Plato and Aristotle.* Albany: State University of New York Press.

Benezet, Antony 1788: *Some Historical Account of Guinea.* London.

Blyden, Edward W. 1967: *Christianity, Islam and the Negro Race.* Edinburgh: Edinburgh University Press.

Clarkson, Thomas 1788: *An Essay on the Slavery and Commerce of the Human Species.* London: Phillips.

Du Bois, W. E. B. 1970 [1915]: *The Negro.* Reprint. Oxford: Oxford University Press.

Fanon, Frantz 1976: *Black Skin, White Masks.* Tr. Charles Markmann. New York: Grove Press.

Jefferson, Thomas 1955 [1785]: *Notes on the State of Virginia.* Chapel Hill: University of North Carolina Press.

Long, Edward 1774: *The History of Jamaica.* London: T. Lowndes.

Ramsey, James 1784: *Essays on the Treatment and Conversion of African Slaves in the British Sugar Colonies.* London.

Simons, Margaret 1999: *Beauvoir and The Second Sex: Feminism, Race and the Origins of Existentialism.* Lanham, MD: Rowman and Littlefield.

Ward, Julie K. (ed.) 1996: *Feminism and Ancient Philosophy.* New York and London: Routledge Publishing.

Witt, Charlotte, and Louise Anthony (eds) 1993: *A Mind of One's Own: Feminist Essays on Reason and Objectivity.* Boulder: Westview Press.

CHAPTER 1

Distinction Without a Difference?
Race and *Genos* in Plato

RACHANA KAMTEKAR

1

This paper investigates Plato's views about what we today call race, the classification of human beings according to supposedly hereditary physical and/or psychological traits. I begin by considering and setting aside an objection to this investigation on the grounds that race is a modern concept about which Plato could have had no views (section 2). I go on to examine Plato's ways of classifying people. Plato divides up people in some ways that resemble racial classifications, observing the distinction commonly observed in his time between Greeks and barbarians, and subscribing to ethnic stereotypes about such groups as the Thracians, Phoenicians, and Egyptians. However, the only classification of people he considers significant is according to the capacity for virtue. This leaves it open to Plato to hold that the capacity for virtue is correlated with certain ethnicities, but it does not commit him to such a view (section 3). Whatever he may think about correlations between ethnicity and virtue, however, Plato requires that the allocation of social goods and responsibilities reflect natural inequalities in virtue and that these natural inequalities be assessed directly, rather than via any correlated physical traits. I examine Plato's reasons for holding this position and locate it within some contemporary debates on racial discrimination (section 4).

2

Before turning to Plato, then, let us consider the objection to looking for race or its counterparts among the ancients on the grounds that the concept of race is a peculiarly modern concept. Now one might think that because of the modernity of the concept,

1

what "race" means cannot be understood outside of its modern historical context – outside, for instance, of the role it has played in the justification of racist institutions such as slavery, colonialism, and segregation. On this basis, one might conclude that looking for an ancient philosopher's views on race or its counterparts is a hopelessly ahistorical and confused task.

This objection may be thought to follow from the general context-dependence of meaning,[1] or from a special dependence of the concept of race on a modern context. But in the first case, cross-cultural comparisons are not made impossible or wrong-headed just by the context-dependence of meaning – that would require a stronger (and extremely unlikely) condition, namely that any difference in meaning results in incommensurability.[2] Further, the stronger condition makes nonsense of our practices of translating between cultures and tracking social forms across cultures.[3] These practices depend on our judging concepts or social forms to be closer to or more distant from each other. Of course, it is always possible that a particular concept is not translatable by a given ancient counterpart, or indeed, by any ancient counterpart. But whether or not this is the case should be determined not by a theory of meaning or translation, but rather by our judgment about the historical and analytical contexts in which that concept makes sense. (Not that the question is entirely empirical, either, for whether "race" can be translated by some ancient term such as "*genos*" or "*ethnos*" is also partly determined by the analytical hypotheses imposed on the translation by the investigator.[4] And these in turn depend on the investigator's purposes.)

But then might the concept of race in particular be new in, and especially dependent on, the modern context? Here, we may contrast the purely scientific character of such concepts as transfer-RNA or the neutrino with the folk character of the concept of race. In his history of the concept of race, Michael Banton shows how this folk concept has been successively modified by scientists' attempts to give it analytical precision.[5] Thus from the sixteenth to the nineteenth centuries, race was understood as a lineage or stock, that is, a race was thought to be a group of humans with the same original ancestors, but differentiated from other humans as a result of dispersion, adaptation to different environments, and reproductive isolation. In the nineteenth century, the prevailing idea of race was of a variety or type with each race having its own original ancestor.[6] Finally, Darwinism synthesized the notions of lineage and type in the idea of an evolving subspecies, in which typical traits are not instantiated in every member, but are instead distributed across a population as a result of genetic variability, random mutation, and natural selection in the competition among individuals. Darwin's idea of a population gave the notion of race scientific respectability by providing a mechanism for heredity and accounting for the absence of law-like generalizations about racial characteristics. But why do we think that the idea of race is new in the early modern period but is only given new scientific sophistication in the nineteenth century? How do we conclude that in one case we have a new concept, in the other an extension of the old concept? It is true that the word "race" first appears in English in the early modern period, but the first occurrence of a word is not the same as the first occurrence of a concept. It is relatively easy to see how a concept like transfer-RNA or the neutrino can have a first occurrence, a time before which people did not and could not think about it: at some point in inquiry, a new explanatory gap requires investigators to posit a new entity; the character of this entity is partly determined by its explanatory role within an investigative context, by the theory informing the investigation. Outside of these contexts, transfer-RNA or the neutrino make little sense and play no explanatory role. But this is not how a folk concept like race works. The condition for using and making sense of the concept of race is not a specific scientific theory or investigative context, but rather, the rough idea that people who are related by birth resemble one another. This notion is clearly available to the ancients in general and to Plato in particular.[7]

In what follows, I examine Plato's ways of classifying people, treating his term *"genos"* as a rough equivalent to our "race", but remaining sensitive to differences between the two concepts. Once the data on Plato is in, we will be better able to judge what, if any, significance there is to these differences between Plato's classification of people and modern racial classifications.

3

To begin with the ethnic distinction most common in his time, Plato follows common parlance in treating "Greek" and "barbarian" as an exhaustive classification, using "Greek and barbarian" to mean "everyone, all of humanity."[8] In *Inventing the Barbarian*, Edith Hall argues that the notion of the barbarian as a social or ethnic type (rather than simply as any non-Greek-speaker) was constructed in fifth-century public discourse as part of panhellenic and anti-Persian propaganda. Some of Plato's writings seem to contribute to or at least reflect this construction of the barbarian: the *Menexenus*, the mock funeral oration allegedly composed by Aspasia, describes Athens' legendary war against the Amazons as of a piece with the wars against the Persians, part of the history of Greek self-defense against barbarian hubris (239b); the speech attributes Athenian war policies to the special Athenian hatred of barbarians, which it in turn explains by the Athenians' purely Greek blood – the other Greeks have mixed blood, being descendants of Aegyptus, Danaus, Pelops or Cadmus, being "by nature barbarians" (245de).

Plato's purpose in the *Menexenus* may be to parody the funeral oration and criticize the sentiments to which it panders. But the Athenian in the *Laws* echoes the sentiment about purity, praising the Athenians and Spartans among the Greeks for saving their races (*genê*) from being mixed with the Persians – but surprisingly, also from being mixed with other Greeks (692e–93a). In the *Republic*, Socrates describes Greeks and barbarians as natural enemies, and Greeks and other Greeks as natural friends; he recommends that the Greeks, when they are at war with each other, not enslave war captives, strip corpses, ravage fields or burn houses – for this would prolong resentment between them, and they should regard each other as people who will one day be reconciled (469b–71b). But what is natural here might be that Greeks would ally with Greeks and against Persians – *given* the Greeks' and Persians' perceptions of each others' interests, or likenesses and differences. That is, Plato may be recognizing a political actuality rather than asserting a scientific necessity. In the *Theaetetus*, Socrates ridicules claims to noble descent on the grounds that the philosopher knows that everyone's ancestors include both rich and poor, kings and slaves, and Greeks and barbarians (175a).

Although this sampling of cites suggests that Plato's attitude towards the Greek–barbarian distinction varies with rhetorical context,[9] we may privilege the *Theaetetus'* attitude, since it is said to be the philosopher's. In general, when Plato is by his own characterization speaking from the philosopher's point of view, he seems to discard the distinction between Greek and barbarian, as, for example, in the *Statesman*, when the Eleatic Visitor makes the point that not every division into a part is a *genos* or real division in nature:

> Let's not take off one small part on its own, leaving many large ones behind, and without reference to real classes [*genê*]; let the part bring a real class with it . . . it's as if someone tried to divide the human race into two and made the cut in the way that most people here carve things up, taking the Greek away as one, separate from all the rest, and to all the other races together, which are unlimited in number, which don't mix with one another, and don't share the same language – calling this collection by the single appellation "barbarian". Because of this single appellation, they expect it to be a single family or class too. Another example would be if someone thought that he was dividing number into two real classes by cutting off the number ten-thousand from all the rest, separating it off as a single class, and in positing a single name for all the rest supposed here too that through getting the name this class too came into existence, a second single one apart from the other. But I imagine the division would be done better, more by real classes and more into two, if one cut number by means of even and odd, and the human race in its turn by means of male and female, and only split off Lydians or Phrygians or anyone else and ranged them against all the rest when one was at a loss as to how to split in such a way that each of the halves split off was simultaneously a real class and a part. (262b–63a)

In the dialogue, Young Socrates has just divided the arts of collective herd rearing into the art concerned with rearing humans and the art concerned with rearing animals (262e). But, the Eleatic Visitor argues, in a scientific investigation one may not separate the art of rearing human beings from that of rearing animals merely because one commonly distinguishes the human species from other herd animals. Real *genê* may be contrary to, and may correct, common sense. And as it turns out, humans are quite close in kind to pigs (266c). The Eleatic Visitor illustrates his point with the example of the common Greek division of human beings into Greeks and barbarians. The Greek–barbarian division misleadingly suggests that barbarians, having one name, are a single *genos* when in fact they are "unlimited in number" or heterogeneous, not sharing the same language and not mixing with one another. Of course, this does not mean that Greek or any other national or ethnic grouping is not a real *genos*, for the explicit criticism is only against treating barbarian as a *genos*, but it does show Plato to be critical of classifications that serve no intellectual purpose other than dividing people up into "us" and "them". A possible target here would be someone like Euripides, who treats all non-Greeks as exotic and alike in their exoticism.[10]

What then are the natural kinds of human beings? If we consider Plato's use of the term *genos*, we find him using it in a variety of received senses but also to challenge commonsense classifications by means of a philosophical or scientific classification. Examples of *genê* include the elements or principles (*Timaeus*, 48e ff, *Philebus*, 23d ff), the branches of expertise (*Sophist*, 223cff, *Statesman*, 263e), kinds of perception (*Theaetetus*, 156b) or capacities in general (*Republic*, 477cd). A person's *genos* also comprises his descendants and/or ancestors (*Cratylus*, 395c; *Alcibiades 1*, 120a–21b), his ethnic group (*Phaedrus*, 237a; *Republic*, 469c). There is also a male *genos* and a female *genos* (*Republic*, 453a–57a), an androgynous genos, a lesbian genos and an "entirely masculine" one (*Symposium*, 191e, 193c). A *genos* may also be a species (*Protagoras*, 321c), for example, there is the *genos* of the cicada (*Phaedrus*, 259c), dog (*Republic*, 459b), or a still more inclusive class, such as the winged *genos* (*Sophist*, 220b) or the *genos* of tame and herd-living creatures (*Statesman*, 266a). Finally, there is the *genos* of gods and that of humans (*Hippias Major*, 289ac; *Charmides*, 173c).

Plato's use of *genos* is revisionary when he classifies people according to their virtue. According to the *Cratylus*, a person's *genos* depends on his character and conduct rather than his descent. As Socrates puts it, ". . . when a good and pious man has an impious son, the latter shouldn't have his father's name but that of the kind [*genos*] to which he belongs . . ." (394de). He also interprets Hesiod's *genê* as describing distinctions in virtue:

> Well, I don't think he [Hesiod] is saying that the golden race is by nature made of gold, but that it is good and fine . . . don't you think that if someone who presently exists were good, Hesiod would say that he too belonged to the golden race? (398ab)

In the ideal city of the *Republic*, people are divided up into the *genê* of philosopher, military auxiliary, and money-maker, according to the kind of virtue they are capable of achieving (434c, 519e). Their membership in these different groups according to their different capacities for virtue is represented in the Myth of Metals' classification of citizens into gold, silver, or bronze and iron races (*genê*) (414b–15d).[11] The myth of the *Phaedo* also divides up people according to the type of virtue or vice their life has exhibited, representing these divisions by the different species into which people are reincarnated: gluttons, violent persons and drunks are reincarnated as donkeys; the unjust as wolves, hawks and kites; and the type who practice social virtue are reincarnated into the social *genê* of wasps, ants, or humans. Only the philosophically virtuous end up in the *genos* of the gods (81e–82b). These reincarnation outcomes show people for what they are.[12]

There is some ambiguity here in whether it is one's capacity for virtue, realized or not, or one's actual achievement or non-achievement of virtue, that determines one's *genos*.[13] This question does not arise for the ideal society, where capacities for virtue are always realized, but since they are not so realized in ordinary societies, we might well ask: are Socrates and Alcibiades the same *genos* even though Socrates fulfilled his capacity for virtue whereas Alcibiades was corrupted (assuming that Alcibiades had the capacity for philosophical virtue)? Modern racial thinking would group Socrates and Alcibiades together, since it classifies people according to their supposedly innate capacities.[14] But the *Cratylus* passage puts father and son – whose capacities we may reasonably expect to be the same, because it is "according to nature" for a horse to give birth to a horse, a king to a king, and a good man to a good man (393c–94a) – in different *genê* on the basis of their actual piety and impiety. To the extent that Plato classifies people by achievement rather than capacity, and acknowledges that capacities may not be realized, his classifications are distanced from racial classifications.

Now Plato might have thought that distinctions among people on the basis of virtue cut across ethnic distinctions, rendering ethnicity morally and politically irrelevant; alternatively, he might have thought that virtue, by nature, belongs, or is more likely to belong, to certain ethnicities than others. These interpretive possibilities are underdetermined by the textual evidence: Plato's inegalitarianism does not by itself commit him to the racialist view that different ethnicities or races have different psychological capacities, but it is compatible with racialism.

On the one hand, Plato's subscription to standard ethnic stereotypes might incline him to think that different peoples are predisposed to virtue or vice, or to particular virtues and vices. For example, Socrates says that Thracians, Scythians and other northerners are high-spirited, Greeks love learning,[15] and Phoenicians and Egyptians love money (*Republic*, 435e–36a); Plato may think that this means Europeans can have the virtue of military auxiliaries, Greeks that of philosophers, and Phoenicians that of money-lovers. In the *Republic* these ethnic stereotypes illustrate the principle that the forms and qualities characteristic of a state are characteristic of individuals in that state. However, the "same forms and qualities" principle only tells us that there is a relationship between individual and state characteristics; it says nothing about the ultimate cause of those characteristics. Are the individual characteristics natural and inherited or themselves the result of the political constitution in which these people live? In the case of the Phoenicians' and Egyptians' love of money, the Athenian in the *Laws* wonders whether this quality is due to defects in their legislators, incidental misfortune, or some other natural circumstance.[16] Certainly Plato's favorite explanation for morally significant character-traits is political constitution, including education. So, for example, Persian rulers tend to be tyrannical because their education has been neglected: they have grown up in the care of women and eunuchs, fabulously wealthy and learning that wealth is to be honored – instead of learning to value virtue most, bodily goods second and property last of all (694c–96, 697ac). This explains why they do not rule in the interests of their people, and that in turn explains why the Persian people are unwilling to fight for their rulers (or cowardly, as many Greeks think); finally, the rulers' need to hire mercenaries to fight for them confirms the high value they place on wealth (697d–98a). Thus, even though he subscribes to various ethnic stereotypes, Plato does not posit a natural link between ethnicity and virtue.[17]

Plato may, however, be perpetuating a morally loaded stereotype in his characterization of the tyrant. Plato's tyrant is licentious, fond of luxury, a slave to his desires; he brooks no criticism and surrounds himself with flatterers. This characterization both resembles the popular stereotype of the Persian, and fits into the classical literary practice of "barbarizing" vicious characters – representing their vices in barbarian garb.[18] But even if this accurately describes Plato's characterization of the tyrant, it is countered by his remarks about Persians themselves, as when he has Socrates remind Alcibiades that he must compete with the noble birth and cultivated virtue of Persian rulers (*Alcibiades 1*, 120d–24a) and when he praises the Persian king Darius (*Laws*, 695cd; *Letter VII*, 332ab).

On the other hand, one might think the opposite – that Plato's ranking of people according to the psychological criterion of virtue makes him unlikely to discriminate on the basis of bodily criteria. In that case, Plato's attitude would confirm Harry Bracken's thesis that dualism has historically provided a "modest conceptual barrier to treating race, color, sex, or religion as other than accidental" because it defines a human being by a non-bodily essence.[19] But suppose we take as evidence for Plato's position on the relevance of bodily criteria to virtue his position on sex-discrimination. In this case, Plato argues on the one hand that the socially valuable capacities of individual women and men must be determined individually, by sex-blind methods, and on the other hand, that the distribution of socially valuable capacities is sex-related. As Socrates puts it in the *Republic*, "it's true that one sex is much superior to the other in pretty well everything, although many women are better than many men in many things" (455d). By analogy, Plato might think that there is some natural correlation between ethnicity and virtue (whether as a result of inheritance or some other condition, such as climate). There is a hereditary component to virtue – it is "according to nature" for good men to have good sons (*Cratylus*, 393c–94a), which is presumably why the ideal city seeks to improve its citizens by arranging their mating and breeding (*Republic*, 459a–61b).[20] However, it would seem that, with ethnicity as with sex, virtue is too important, and the body too unreliable, to be depended on to sort people. Even with the controlled breeding in the ideal city, parents of one *genos* sometimes give birth to children of another (*Republic*, 415bc, 460c, 546bd).

Plato's position on the relationship between bodily characteristics and virtue is best stated in the terms of a view Socrates airs in the *Cratylus*:

> some people say that the body [*sôma*] is the tomb [*sêma*] of the soul, on the grounds that it is entombed in its present life, while others say that it is correctly called 'a sign' [*sêma*] because the soul signifies whatever it wants to signify by means of the body. I think it is most likely the followers of Orpheus who gave the body its name, with the idea that the soul is being punished for something, and that the body is an enclosure or prison in which the soul is securely kept [*sôzetai*] – as the name '*sôma*' itself suggests – until the penalty is paid . . . (400c)

Elizabeth Spelman has suggested that something like this is Plato's view in the case of sex. Although the soul–body distinction allows Plato to look beyond a person's sex in judging her abilities, Spelman argues, Plato treats a person's body as something that nevertheless does or ought to say something about her nature, if not in this life then in its reincarnation. Thus, vicious men are reborn as women (*Timaeus*, 42bc, 90e–91a); the most appropriate punishment for cowardly men is to be turned into women (*Laws*, 944e).[21] And as we saw in the *Phaedo*, unjust men are reborn as hawks, wolves or kites, socially just men as wasps, ants or humans, and so on (81e–82b). Obviously, such a sign is not infallible, and so is not usable for assigning people to their various civic roles, the performance of which requires different types and levels of virtue. Thus, Plato requires a scrupulous body-blindness of his guardians when it comes to casting people into civic roles. On the other hand, if the only problem with using bodily criteria to identify psychic criteria is reliability, then it would seem that Plato would not frown on this type of discrimination for situations in which mistakes are more tolerable.

4

What makes even a slight unreliability in physical criteria for identifying virtue intolerable, for Plato, is the magnitude of the moral and political implications of the differences in virtue. Happiness depends on virtue (*Gorgias*, 470e; *Phaedo*, 69bd, 80d–82c, 113d–14c; *Euthydemus*, 278e–82e; *Republic*, 587ce). In the *Republic*, people's different capacities for virtue determine what sort of work they may do in their society – whether rule it, guard it morally or physically, or just fill its breadbasket (412be, 433e–34c, 453b–6b). In the *Laws*, citizenship itself depends on virtue (846d–47a). Since capacities for virtue are set by nature (*Republic*, 580bc, 442be), nature itself sets ceilings on the civic roles people may occupy and the happiness they may achieve.

But underlying Plato's judgment that mistakes in identifying virtue are intolerable is a deeper moral principle that entirely rules out racial and sexual discrimination, as well. In the *Republic*, Socrates says that the aim of the law in the ideal city is the maximization of all the citizens' happiness:

> in establishing our city, we aren't aiming to make any one group outstandingly happy but to make the whole city so, as far as possible. We thought that we'd find justice most easily in such a city . . . We take ourselves, then, to be fashioning the happy city, not picking out a few happy people and putting them in it, but making the whole city happy . . . you mustn't force us to give our guardians the kind of happiness that would make them something other than guardians. We know how to clothe the farmers in purple robes, festoon them with gold jewelry, and tell them to work the land whenever they please. We know how to settle our potters on couches by the fire, feasting and passing the wine around, with their wheel beside them for whenever they want to make pots. And we can make all the others happy in the same way, so that the whole city is happy. Don't urge us to do this, however, for if we do, a farmer wouldn't be a farmer, nor a potter a potter, and none of the others would keep to the patterns of work that give rise to a city . . . In this way, with the whole city developing and being governed well, we must leave it to nature to provide each group with its share of happiness. (*Republic*, 420b–21c, cf. 519e–20a)

Discrimination on the basis of anything that is even slightly imperfectly correlated with virtue violates the injunction to maximize happiness. For since happiness depends on virtue, a socially misassigned citizen would not only not do her job well and so harm or impede the pursuits of those dependent on her work, she would herself not be realizing her own best capacities and so would be living a less happy life.

Thus, even though Plato posits deep differences in virtue, resulting in great differences in civic role and happiness among citizens, he considers all the citizens' happinesses equally (the law aims at the happiness not of one class, but of the city as a whole). Differences in citizens' happiness and virtue are meant to be the result of nature alone, not of any social arrangements. But racial discrimination would involve inequality at the level of the consideration of citizens' interests.[22]

It will be useful, at this point, to contrast Plato's views with those of some modern inegalitarians, for superficial similarities between the two may be misleading. Indeed,

Stephen Jay Gould credits Plato with one hereditarian commitment crucial to modern racism: "that social and economic roles accurately reflect the innate construction of people."[23] I take Herrnstein and Murray in *The Bell Curve* as typical modern spokesmen for inequality. They claim that there are intellectual differences between the races (and classes), which result in the less intelligent races' economic backwardness, but that this fact should not affect how individuals are treated because a given individual may fall anywhere on a "bell curve" distribution for the population of which he is a member.[24] How close are these views to Plato's?

Plato shares with the modern inegalitarians the view that there are important natural inequalities among people which social planning should attend to and perpetuate, in a good society. But Herrnstein and Murray think that cognitive stratification is inevitable, that in any society the stupid are generally poor and the smart generally rich – although this is most true in modern "rational" societies. So in their view, the society in which we live is the best or near-best society. By contrast, Plato thinks that stratification by intellectual qualities is very difficult to achieve, because societies tend not to value intellectual qualities (philosophers *should* be rulers, but they are not in fact). For the same reason, he rejects wealth as evidence of superiority. Further, while he believes that the capacity for virtue is hereditary, he also recognizes that people as a whole have not been bred for virtue. Modern "invisible hand" type theories according to which environmental pressure or natural selection just happens to result in a naturally superior group's social ascendancy would surely seem like mumbo-jumbo to Plato. For Plato would not accept that any group that comes out on top in any social competition is for that reason superior: the criterion for superiority is virtue, and virtue is not valued except in a society designed to value it. In the *Gorgias* Socrates undermines Callicles' might-based conception of natural superiority on just these grounds – by questioning the criteria on which he bases his claims about superiority (488bff). Thus, while Plato does consider just and desirable an order in which roles reflect the innate construction of people, on his view such an order must be brought about by rational planning, which involves great effort, understanding, calculation, supervision – not just natural and social selection. On Plato's view social and economic roles *should* reflect the innate construction of people but in ordinary societies they *do not*. Thus, his inegalitarianism does not legitimate existing inequalities as does the moderns'.

These observations lead us to note another difference: Plato's ranking of people is hyper-elitist. Virtue is too rare to belong to a whole race or ethnicity; even with a lot of attention given to breeding and education in the ideal city, true virtue belongs to the smallest class (*Republic*, 429a–30c), namely philosophers (*Phaedo*, 69bd, 80d–82c).[25] The idea of racial superiority is, ironically, far too egalitarian for Plato.[26]

Finally, there is the issue of exactly how social planners are to treat natural inequalities. Here, Plato may seem to be quite close in spirit to Herrnstein and Murray, for they too claim that a just social order will reflect natural inequalities as social inequalities. Herrnstein and Murray ask, "How should policy deal with the twin realities that people differ in intelligence for reasons that are not their fault and that intelligence has a powerful bearing on how well people do in life?" Their recommendation is cash supplements for hardworking but cognitively deficient persons so that they can achieve a minimal standard of living, and the revitalization of family and community to help these cognitively deficient persons get on with their lives and to give them the feeling of being valued.[27] In short, they propose charity for those they consider the stupid and poor, acknowledging that their stupidity, and thus their poverty, is not their fault.

Plato shares Herrnstein's and Murray's basic pessimism about the lots that fall to people but he does not seem to judge this apportioning unfair and attempt to compensate for it when it is undeserved. This is because Herrnstein and Murray seem to think that goods ought to be apportioned according to merit – hence their concern with fault. This contrasts with Plato's principle of justice in the *Republic*, which, as we have seen, simply apportions both goods and responsibilities so as to maximize happiness. Citizens' shares of goods in the ideal city are unequal not because of differences in merit, but when different shares are required by their work[28] (thus philosophers and military auxiliaries may not own private property, although farmers and householders may [416d–17b]), or when they serve as an incentive to virtuous behavior (like kissing rewards in the military to encourage brave performances in battle [468bc]), or when they are suited to their different natures and capacities to be benefited (thus the philosophical class is given an education in dialectic, but the lower classes are not [535a–39d]). In principle, the lower classes of the ideal city are given no less than the ruling class – they are all given what makes them as happy as possible.

We have found that while there is no conceptual impossibility in Plato's having views about race, he considers moral distinctions between people more significant than ethnic ones – although the two might be related. But while Plato's views about a possible relationship between virtue and race are underdetermined, his criteria of moral superiority undermine, rather than legitimate, existing inequalities, and his principle of justice rules out the meritocratic intuitions that are the basis of modern racism.[29]

Notes

1. Proponents of meaning holism might hold this. Thomas Kuhn (1962), p. 128, writes: "neither scientists nor laymen learn to see the world piecemeal or item by item. Except when all the conceptual and manipulative categories are prepared in advance – e.g. for the discovery of an additional transuranic element or for catching sight of a new house – both scientists and laymen sort out whole areas together from the flux of experience. The child who transfers the word 'mama' from all humans to all females and then to his mother is not just learning what 'mama' means or who his mother is. Simultaneously he is learning some of the differences between males and females as well as something about the ways in which all but one female will behave toward him. His reactions, expectations, and beliefs – indeed, much of his perceived world – change accordingly."
2. This point is made by Dudley Shapere (1981), p. 55.
3. Donald Davidson (1984), p. 197, argues that conceptual schemes and languages are necessarily translatable, because to interpret a speaker at all one must accept most of his utterances as true, which makes it impossible for one to say that his beliefs and concepts are radically different from (or for that matter, the same as) one's own.
4. W. V. O. Quine (1960), ch. 2.

5. Michael Banton (1987), pp. xi–xiv, 1–97.
6. On the modern debate between proponents of monogenesis and polygenesis, see Richard Popkin (1980), pp. 79–102.
7. To the extent that this notion is deeply embedded in our beliefs, Davidson's argument against incommensurability, from the possibility of interpretation, applies: we are bound to find equivalents for the notion when we translate from another culture.
8. See, e.g. *Symposium*, 209e, *Alcibiades 1*, 105b, 124b, *Lysis*, 210b, *Republic*, 423a, 544d, *Laws*, 814a, 886a. Plato uses a similar pairing, of citizen and foreigner (*xenos*) in the same way (*Theaetetus*, 145b, *Apology*, 30a, *Meno*, 94e). But the citizen–foreigner distinction is purely political: in the *Laws*, where Plato distinguishes sharply between the political and moral treatment appropriate for foreigners (*xenoi*) and for citizens (764b, 816e, 849ad, 853d–54d, 866bc), Magnesian citizenship is had by birth or initial immigration plus meeting a virtue-qualification, but Magnesia's initial immigrants come from all over Crete as well as from Sparta and Argos (708a), and the foreigners are simply later arrivals.
9. Which, even if they do not tell us just what Plato thought about the distinction, surely do tell us what attitudes were culturally available.
10. On Euripides' treatment of barbarians, see Helen Bacon (1961), ch. 3.
11. While it is a lie that citizens have these metals in their souls, the lie represents something of the truth in that they differ in virtue and therefore ought to occupy different civic roles.
12. Thus an unjust person is an anti-social hawk living in a human body; reincarnation gives him the body that fits his soul. Julia Annas (1982), pp. 125–7, has complained that the myth of the *Phaedo* is "confusing and confused" because it tries to fit the idea of reincarnation as punishment or reward into the *Gorgias* framework of a final judgment. But if we view the animal reincarnations of the *Phaedo* as representing who or what we really are (the *Gorgias* expresses this idea in terms of the soul being naked when it goes to receive judgment), there is no confusion. I am grateful to Omar Bozeman (unpublished mss.) for suggesting what different work stories of the afterlife might do apart from apportioning reward and punishment.
13. Thanks to Julie Ward for bringing this issue to my attention.
14. The distinction between nature and nurture is often drawn too sharply to be accurate, as if human and environmental effects are somehow outside of nature. For a critique of this distinction, see Richard Lewontin (1992), ch. 5.
15. Cf. Hippocrates (1986), 16, 23.
16. In Hippocrates (1986) the cause of national traits is climate rather than descent: Asians tend to be well built because of Asia's temperate and unvarying climate, for "everything [vegetable or human] grows much bigger and finer in Asia," but the same climate also makes them cowardly (this is aggravated by their monarchical constitutions [cf. 23]), and like one another (16). However, nurture and nature are not mutually exclusive, and environmental effects may become hereditary: the Macrocephali's long heads are due, initially, to their custom of manipulating the head to elongate it, but later because "nature collaborates with custom" so that offspring inherit their parents' long heads (14).
17. One may object that subscribing to the stereotypes in the first place is racist (this objection is due to Eric Brown). It is certainly true that we use the term "racist" to characterize stereotyping attitudes themselves. But even though subscribing to stereotypes may be prejudice, it is not strictly speaking racist if it does not explain the stereotypes by heredity – for a race is a group linked by heredity.
18. Cf. Edith Hall (1989), ch. 5.
19. Harry Bracken (1978), p. 250. In the same vein, Bracken writes elsewhere (1973), p. 83: "from Plato to Descartes racist doctrines have been more comfortably situated within the

Aristotelian tradition than among the dualists." But essential and accidental do not exhaust the possibilities.

20. Heredity is not a sufficient condition of virtue, of course, for in the absence of a good education, good men will have bad sons, as they do in Athens (*Meno*, 93c–94e); for without a good education even philosophic natures are perverted (*Republic* 497b). Thus the condition that is "according to nature," that good men have good sons, does not come about in the normal course of events but requires extensive social planning. Thanks to Steve Gerrard for bringing the *Meno* passage to my attention.

21. "Plato seems to be saying . . . that there is a fittingness of one kind of soul to one kind of body: the kind of soul you have shows in the kind of body you have, and can't be shown in another kind of body. Or perhaps he is saying that the kind of soul you have *ought* to show in the kind of body you have . . . and if there isn't a good fit in this life there will be in the next" (Elizabeth Spelman (1994), p. 100).

22. In the modern context, Peter Singer (1978), pp. 185–203, argues that what is wrong with racial discrimination is that it leads to bad consequences for individual and society, consequences that conflict with the deep moral principle of equal consideration of interests – not that race is irrelevant to work; Singer describes several cases in which race may be relevant, such as in considering only Black actors to play the role of a Black character.

23. Stephen Jay Gould (1981), p. 20.

24. Herrnstein and Murray (1994), ch. 13, esp. pp. 312–13.

25. Racism, like anti-Semitism on Sartre's brilliant analysis, gives people the sense that they possess something of value simply in virtue of their membership in a race, as a result of their birth and without their having to do anything to earn it; thus, it "is an attempt to give value to mediocrity as such, to create an elite of the ordinary" (Sartre (1948), p. 23).

26. There is a more egalitarian strand in Plato. In the *Phaedrus*, Socrates suggests that all human souls are equal in their capacity for virtue, since they have all seen the forms – which is necessary for a soul to be able to bring many perceptions together into a reasoned unity and thus to understand speech (249bc). But the equality of all human souls across reincarnations is compatible with extreme inequality among human lives, as one sees in the *Phaedrus* ranking of souls according to how much of the forms they have most recently seen: philosopher, lawful king or military commander, statesman, household manager or financier, trainer or doctor, prophet or priest, representational artist, manual laborer or farmer, sophist or demagogue, tyrant (248de).

27. Herrnstein and Murray (1994), ch. 22, esp. pp. 535–40, 547–8.

28. Gregory Vlastos (1978), p. 178, describes Plato's principle of distribution in the *Republic* as a principle of functional reciprocity: "all members have an equal right to those and only those benefits which are required for the optimal performance of their function in the polis." I am in agreement with Vlastos insofar as he denies that the distributive principle is meritocratic, and insofar as what one requires for one's work is *a* basis on which goods are distributed. However, I do not think it the exclusive basis for distribution, and I do not think it should be put in terms of citizens' *rights*. While it is indeed right that citizens should have what they need to do their work (because it maximizes the good), it is not clear that they have a right to it in the sense of being able to demand it and expect their demand to be upheld by the coercive forces of the state.

29. Many thanks to Katy Abramson, Chris Bobonich, Eric Brown, Noel Carroll, Steve Gerrard, Leon Kojen, Stephen Menn, Bojana Mladenovic, Yaseen Noorani, Julie Ward, and an APA audience in May 1999 for comments on previous versions of this paper. Work on this paper was supported by a Solmsen fellowship at the Institute for Research in the Humanities,

University of Wisconsin-Madison during 1998–9. And my deepest gratitude to Gurdip Kamtekar for the tireless newborn care which allowed me to complete the paper.

References

Annas, Julia 1982: Plato's Myths of Judgment. *Phronesis*, vol. 27, 119–43.

Bacon, Helen 1961: *Barbarians in Greek Tragedy*. New Haven: Yale University Press.

Banton, Michael 1987: *Racial Theories*. Cambridge: Cambridge University Press.

Bozeman, Omar (unpublished mss.): Heaven and Hell.

Bracken, Harry 1973: Essence, Accident, and Race. *Hermathena*, 116, 81–96.

Bracken, Harry 1978: Philosophy and Racism. *Philosophia*, vol. 8, no. 2, 241–60.

Davidson, Donald 1984: On the Very Idea of a Conceptual Scheme. In *Inquiries into Truth and Interpretation*, Oxford: Oxford University Press, 183–98.

Gould, Stephen Jay 1981: *The Mismeasure of Man*. New York: W. W. Norton & Co.

Hall, Edith 1989: *Inventing the Barbarian*. Oxford: Oxford University Press.

Herrnstein, Richard J. and Murray, Charles 1994: *The Bell Curve: Intelligence and Class Structure in American Life*. New York: Free Press.

Hippocrates 1986: Airs, Waters, Places. In G. E. R. Lloyd (ed.), *Hippocratic Writings*, Harmondsworth: Penguin, 148–69.

Kuhn, Thomas 1962: *The Structure of Scientific Revolutions*. Chicago: University of Chicago Press.

Lewontin, Richard 1992: *Biology as Ideology: The Doctrine of DNA*. New York: Harper Perennial.

Plato 1997: *Complete Works*. Ed. J. Cooper. Indianapolis: Hackett.

Popkin, Richard 1980: The Philosophical Bases of Modern Racism. In *The High Road to Pyrrhonism*. San Diego: Austin Hill Press, 79–102.

Quine, W. V. O. 1960: Translation and Meaning. In *Word and Object*, Cambridge, MA: Technology Press of the Massachusetts Institute of Technology, 26–79.

Sartre, Jean-Paul 1948: *Anti-Semite and Jew*. Tr. George J. Becker. New York: Schocken Books.

Shapere, Dudley 1981: Meaning and Scientific Change. In Ian Hacking (ed.), *Scientific Revolutions*, Oxford: Oxford University Press, 28–59.

Singer, Peter 1978: Racial Discrimination. *Philosophia*, vol. 8, no. 2, 185–203.

Spelman, Elizabeth 1994: Hairy Cobblers and Philosopher-Queens. In Nancy Tuana (ed.), *Feminist Interpretations of Plato*. University Park, Pa.: Pennsylvania State University Press.

Vlastos, Gregory 1978: The Rights of Persons in Plato's Conception of the Foundations of Justice. In H. Tristam Englehardt Jr. and Daniel Callahan (eds), *Morals, Science and Society*, Hastings-on-Hudson, NY: The Hastings Center, 172–201.

CHAPTER 2

Ethnos in the *Politics*: Aristotle and Race

JULIE K. WARD

Introduction

To ask whether Aristotle made use of the idea of racial differences in his political theory implies that he, perhaps along with other ancient Greeks, possessed an idea of *race*. This issue presents some initial difficulties as we might suppose that the question of *race* posed in relation to an ancient culture was anachronistic: insofar as the concept is of modern origin, the question of *race* would seem to be inapplicable to the ancient Greeks. Acknowledging the historical genesis of the concept, nevertheless we may find it necessary to examine whether the Greeks possessed a concept equivalent to a modern notion but using different terminology.[1] As a preliminary step, we need to specify some set of features, or a determinate concept, that we take the modern notion of *race* to signify so that we shall be able to determine whether the Greeks possessed an analogous or functionally equivalent concept. While both cultural and biological features figure in the notions of race currently being discussed,[2] I shall propose that we consider a biological notion of *race*, combining determinism and ranking such that biological variations in human populations, including superficial physical characteristics such as hair and skin color, are taken as determinatively fixed, and equated with an abstract hierarchy of intellectual and moral traits.[3] Some credence for supposing Aristotle subscribes to such a notion arises from an initial consideration of various aspects of his political thought, especially his theory of natural slavery. Therefore, the initial skepticism concerning the legitimacy of the issue of *race* to Aristotle's political theory may be thought to have been answered for an initial consideration of the topic.

There are, as I see it, three areas in Aristotle's political theorizing that suggest promising sources for racialist thinking. The first is the development among classical Greek intellectuals of a concept similar to *race* that appears to play an equivalent role

14

in their thinking, namely, that of being "barbarian." Aristotle employs this concept in his discussions throughout the *Politics*. Aristotle gives us two additional theories that provide suggestive bases for our investigation, first, a climate theory of national or racial differences, and second, a theory of natural slavery. In the following parts of this essay, the first section considers the evidence from literary and philosophical uses of color-terms: this evidence is inconclusive concerning terms such as "black" and "white," suggesting their lack of interest in a marker of skin color as indicative of moral or intellectual differences. Nonetheless, one does find an overriding concern by the Greeks to differentiate themselves culturally, and perhaps ethnically, from various non-Greek nations, especially the Persians after the Persian War. Thus, it may be suggested that the literary evidence of the classical period bears out a social or cultural concept of racial difference. The remaining sections of the paper consider the nature and role of the theories of climate and natural slavery in an attempt to decide whether Aristotle thinks that all or even some *barbarians* are slaves "by nature," and if so, whether their slavishness can be remedied by political institutions and education.

The Literary Background: "Barbarian" and "Pale Man"

It is undeniable that ancient Greek social and political institutions are non-egalitarian, based upon an acceptance of "natural" differences among humans, as is reflected in their thinking about slaves and women. Yet the presence of inequality in their institutions and practices does not appear to be linked one to one to their concern about racial differences. One obvious counter-example to the proposed correlation would be Greek citizen women: these women could be the same race as citizen men, but would be considered in Athens as elsewhere to be the social, political, and intellectual inferiors to men. Nonetheless, it might be supposed that Greek male citizens also found non-Greek men their inferiors for racial reasons. Admitting the hazard of generalizing about "ancient Greek thought," two kinds of evidence may be offered in the way of casting skepticism on the question of *race* for the Greeks. First, the ambiguous meanings connected to color-terms gives scant indication of a linkage between skin color or other morphological traits, and moral or intellectual differences. Greek writers and philosophers use the color-terms λευκός, *leukos* ("light", "pale") and μέλας, *melas* ("dark") to describe persons and things, but the meanings vary. For example, the term *leukos* shows a wide range of senses, some positive, others negative.[4] The term may be applied to persons to signify being "fair" and "beautiful," but significantly, when the term is applied specifically to human skin color, "white-skinned" (λευκόχρως, *leukochrōs*) is used to signify weakness in men, especially of moral character.[5] Plato employs *leukos* in the *Republic* in an ironic reference to those who, though praised by lovers, nonetheless are lacking in masculine qualities (*Republic*, 474e); thus, the terms "pale" and "pale-skinned" may signify weakness, perhaps "effeminacy" of character. In similar fashion, Aristotle employs terms for being pale-skinned or dark-skinned in reference to women in his biological works, claiming light-skinned women are typically feminine, and dark-skinned women, more masculine in nature (*On the Generation of Animals*, I. 20, 728a2–4).[6] Finally, in *Metaphysics*, VII. 4, Aristotle employs the term *leukos* in a discussion about essences and accidental compounds. Here the compound term ἄνθρωπον λεύκον, *anthropon leukon* ("pale man") is used to signify something that is not a real unity, but only accidentally one thing; what "pale man" signifies is not a genuine substance and so lacks an essence (1029b30–1030a15). We may thus infer that for Aristotle pallor in skin color fails to belong to the essence of what it is to be human.

The second kind of evidence emerges from consideration of the literary evidence concerning non-Greeks. In the archaic period, when Greeks write about non-Greeks, specifically about people from Africa, they reveal little or no inherited cultural or racial prejudice.[7] Even in the fifth century, the historian Herodotus reveals little, if any, bias against Africans, and demonstrates throughout his work great interest in the history of the Egyptians.[8] He also reports favorably on "Ethiopians," a term referring to those peoples from Libya and Egypt (*Histories*, 7. 69–70). He explicitly describes Libyan Ethiopians as a dark-skinned, curly-haired, long-lived people (*Histories*, 7. 70, 3. 17), and in addition to reporting on their weapons and clothing, he remarks that "the Ethiopians in question . . . are said to be the tallest and most attractive people in the world" (*Histories*, 3. 20). Herodotus seems to reflect the more complex, cosmopolitan attitude towards non-Greeks found elsewhere in archaic literature, as in Homer, who idealizes "Ethiopians" (*Odyssey*, I. 22–4, *Iliad*, I. 423).[9]

One should distinguish, however, between what Greek writers have to say about the Ethiopians or Egyptians from what they say about rival cultures from Asia Minor, especially the Persians, and to a lesser degree, the Medes. During and after the war with Persia (500–449 BCE), explicitly hostile, "racialist" categories appear in Athenian writing about non-Greeks, the most common of which is the dual category of *Greek–barbarian*.[10] Although the term "barbarian" (βάρβαρος, *barbaros*) originally meant any non-Greek-speaking people, in the fifth century the term is used to refer to members of specific ethnic groups, or nationalities, such as the Persians. As various scholars have recently shown,[11] the term is pressed into constant usage during the Greek conflict with the Persians, as Athenians deliberately reshape the Persians' identity as "barbarian" in order to polarize the conflict in cultural and ethnic terms, thereby strengthening Greek nationalism. By means of the *Greek–barbarian* opposition, Athenian writers constructed an image of the Persians as Asiatic "barbarians," placing them alongside Lydians and Medes in being characterized variously as intemperate, effeminate, or servile in nature. Xenophanes' criticism of his fellow Ionians is suggestive: ". . . they learned useless luxuries from the Lydians . . . they came to their meeting place in purple cloaks . . . flaunting their comely locks, and drenched in scented unguents" (Diels and Kranz, 1954, 21B3).[12] The excessive sensuality, and so "effeminacy," of the Lydians is represented in the details about their luxury: the purple garments, long hair, and use of perfume. The negative force of this representation becomes more evident when we compare it with the self-described Greek image as masculine, self-controlled, and democratic that emerged from the Greek literature of this period.

Greek tragedy, in particular, constitutes a fertile source of representation using the Greek conflict with barbarians. One such representation is to be found in Aeschylus' play, *The Persians*, produced in 472 BCE, during the Persian War. This work invokes the *Greek – barbarian* opposition throughout, creating the picture of the Greeks as self-controlled, manly, and egalitarian, in counterpoint to the Persians, who are depicted as possessing the opposite of these qualities.[13] General acceptance of Greek cultural supremacy seems to persist from the fifth through the fourth century, in spite of critical challenges posed by certain Greek enlightenment thinkers.[14] The logical extension of this attitude may be seen in the notion that non-Greeks are less worthy than Greeks, and so need to be ruled by Greeks, as is expressed in the line "it is fitting that Greeks rule barbarians" (βαρβάρων Ἕλληνας ἄρχειν εἰκός; Euripedes, *Iphigenia at Aulis*, 1400).[15]

Moving beyond drama, the idea of cultural and ethnic elitism is repeated in certain Platonic dialogues where, for example, Greeks and "barbarians" are said to be natural enemies, to belong to different kinds, or *gene*,[16] of peoples, and for Greeks of mixed ancestry to be "by nature barbarian" (*Republic*, 469b–71b; *Laws*, 692e–93e; *Menexenus*, 245d–e, respectively).[17] These statements appear to be straightforward expressions of the standard Greek elitism. Yet it should be noted that Plato's own views on the subject of "barbarians" are complex, not easily summarized, and this for two reasons. First, a consideration of his other dialogues indicates that Plato may employ the opposition of *Greek–barbarian* at times for dramatic, rather than scientific purposes.[18] Second, in the *Politicus*, Plato himself criticizes the opposition between Greek and "barbarian" that he elsewhere invokes, claiming that "barbarian" is not a real γένος (*genos*), or natural kind.[19] He finds that thinkers err when they divide the human race into two parts, taking Greeks as one homogeneous group, and taking "barbarians" as another, insofar as calling a group of individuals by one name does not make it an actual kind. For Plato, those who are commonly called "barbarians" do not form a natural kind because they lack shared characteristics required to make them unified: they constitute many groups and do not share a common language (*Politicus*, 262c10–d6).

If we consider the general picture relating to the opposition of Greeks and "barbarians" in Greek thought prior to Aristotle, two kinds of difference emerge.[20] One kind of distinction may be labeled cultural or behavioral, as for example, when Greeks think that Asian barbarians such as the Lydians or Medes dress opulently and behave immoderately – with their monarch acting as if there were no difference between humanity and divinity.[21] Another kind of distinction is clearly political, as when Greeks claim that barbarian peoples like the Lydians, Medes, or Persians are content living under tyrannies. In this regard, one may note Herodotus' view of the Medes: they choose rulership by a tyrant and so exhibit a trait of being both lawless and hubristic by requiring a rulership by a tyrant, rather than ruling themselves (*Histories*, I. 98–101).[22]

Aristotle and *Ethnos*

The above-mentioned distinctions emerging from the fifth- and fourth-century literature with regard to Greeks and "barbarians" remain relevant when one comes to consider Aristotle's discussion of "barbarians" in the *Politics*. In this political theory, Aristotle employs the traditional opposition of *Greek–barbarian*, but a survey of the contexts and the frequency of his usage shows that he does not make it fundamental to his theory. My examination of this work finds that he relies upon another pair of terms instead, shifting the weight from *Greek–barbarian* to a pair that emphasizes a political contrast. The term that he uses to signify the social or political aspect of a group of people is *ethnos*, usually translated as a "nation," "people," or "tribe."[23] He often uses the term ἔθνος (*ethnos*) in opposition to πόλις (*polis*) to signal the contrast between a group of people living together who possess laws and a common political end, and those who live in social arrangements without law and purpose.

For Aristotle, *ethnos* refers to a form of social organization that lacks political institutions, a society that we might consider to be "pre-political" in nature, whereas *polis* always refers to a society living under common laws for the sake of a common end, which he identifies as living the complete, excellent human life (1326b7–9). What Aristotle focuses on in distinguishing a *polis* is a shared conception of the good life: in III. 9, he claims "living well is the end of the city" (1280b39–40). So, he argues, an alliance of villages, even one that possessed agreements for commerce and defense, would not yet constitute a *polis* (1280b30–32). For a *polis* requires, first of all, shared agreements (e.g., on commerce), intermarriage among groups, common festivals and pastimes (1280b35–38), and also, common purpose: "for a city is the partnership of families and villages for a complete and self-sufficient life" (1280b40–1281a1).

What Aristotle perceives to be typical of *ethnē*, or pre-political societies, is a lack of organized institutions for a common purpose; he finds *ethnē* to be equivalent to mere alliances.[24] If we catalogue the frequency and use of the two terms in Aristotle's work, we find a shift in usage from the standard term, *barbaros* ("barbarian"), to the newer term, *ethnos*. The first observation to make is that the term *ethnos* appears about half again as many times as *barbaros* in the *Politics* as a whole. It is significant that the term *barbaros* appears in relatively few passages in the work and in only three of these passages does Aristotle employ "barbarian" with its paired opposite term, "Greek" (1252b8, 1285a20–21, 1295a11–13). So, although Aristotle employs the standard opposition of *Greek–barbarian* in his political treatise, it strikes this author as appearing to be an outmoded distinction for Aristotle. This usage may reflect the benefit of Plato's criticism in *Politicus*, 262d, concerning the notion that "barbarian" signifies merely an artificial, and not an actual, class of human beings.

Taken as a whole, the occurrences of both *barbaros* and *ethnos* in the *Politics* seem to show that Aristotle is concerned with drawing a political contrast between social groups, as well as a psychological contrast. Employing the distinction between *ethnos* and *polis*, Aristotle focuses upon the way in which a cultural group or "people" lacks the social and political institutions requisite to be considered a genuine city-state, or *polis* (1252b18–20, 1326b2–9). So, for example, a mere aggregate of people, even in large numbers, does not constitute a *polis*, though it may well count as an *ethnos*. Again, a community comprised of a number of small villages bound together by trade and mutual advantage may be self-sufficient for survival, but Aristotle considers such an aggregate to be merely an *ethnos*, and not a *polis*, since it lacks the common end of living the good life that distinguishes the *polis* (1326b1–5). For this reason, he deems the Arcadians, and other similar national groups, to be *ethnē*, not *poleis*, claiming that they are simply alliances of villages (1361a27–29).[25] In a similar vein, he thinks that large nations, like that of the Persians, are typically deficient in the right political institutions, and as such, he qualifies them as *ethnē*, and not as city-states. So, for example, he finds that *ethnē*, or "nations," which are capable of increasing their power tend to favor despotic rule, as he thinks Scythians, Persians, Thracians and Kelts do (1324b9–12). Since for Aristotle despotic rule is never just or "political" rule, his criticism of powerful "nations" is made evident (1324b26–27).

In all the above-mentioned uses of *ethnos*, Aristotle contrasts one form of Greek society and political culture, namely, the city-state, or *polis*, with that of many non-Greeks (e.g., Scythians, Persians, Thracians, or Kelts), who are characterized as living under a deficient mode of political government. But why might this deficiency occur? One suggestion as to why certain *ethnē* fail to develop politically is provided in Book VII, chapter 7, where he discusses the effects of climate on national character. Here the idea broached seems to be that various types of climate explain the specific deficiencies in a people's character, and this in turn accounts for why certain groups of people lack political governance (ἀπολίτευτα, *apoliteuta*, 1327b26). Yet since the question whether climate and physiological dispositions fully determine the ability to become political citizens is complex and difficult to assess briefly, it is deferred until the next section (below).

One distinctive use of *Greek–barbarian* in which Aristotle seems to equate being "barbarian" with being "slavish" in contrast to being a free citizen occurs in certain passages in Book I, chs. 1, 4, 5, 13. These passages appear to constitute the clearest examples of "racist" thinking in Aristotle's political writing insofar as he seems to be arguing that some people (*ethnē*) belong to the group termed "barbarians," and that these people are what he terms "slaves by nature." This interpretation is standardly found throughout the secondary literature, but is not without its difficulties, as I shall subsequently show. Finally, there are passages making use of the adjectival term βαρβαρικός, *barbarikos* ("barbaric") to describe what Aristotle takes to be archaic, or "primitive," practices or customs. This usage does not depend upon an explicit contrast with something Greek, but signifies something outmoded or unsophisticated. In *Politics*, I. 9, for example, Aristotle mentions a barter economy as distinct from a monetary economy and qualifies it as holding among many "barbarian peoples" (1257a25). Again, in II. 8, he refers to ancient laws concerning such things as carrying weapons and purchasing wives as "overly simple and barbaric" practices (1268b39–40).

In the passages discussed, we see that Aristotle employs the standard opposition between Greek and "barbarian" in his political work, but finds more use for a contrast I take to be of his own devising, that between *ethnos* and *polis*. Having noted this, a question might be raised whether Aristotle smuggles in racializing categories, nonetheless, by using this new contrast. For, it might be argued that Aristotle's classification of peoples into *ethnē* and *poleis* connotes a "racist" line of thought insofar as he prefers Greek, and specifically, Athenian culture to any other kind, and explicitly argues in VII. 7 that non-Greeks are prone to becoming enslaved under tyrannies. This objection leads us to consider further the relation of climatic to ethnic differences that arises in *Politics*, VII. 7.

Ethnos and Nature: the Climate Theory

One explanation Aristotle offers for what he sees as the pre-political level of development among many people, Greeks and non-Greeks alike, depends upon a theory involving climatic differences. The main passage relating the effect of climate upon human character occurs in *Politics*, VII. 7 where a question arises concerning what sort of natural character people in the ideal state or *polis* should possess (1327b18–20). The answer Aristotle gives identifies two main qualities of character that citizens ought to have: "spiritedness" (θυμοειδής, *thumoeides*) and "intelligence" (διανοητικός, *dianoētikos*, 1327b36–8). Following this claim, Aristotle offers a rudimentary form of the climate theory of *ethnos*, or national, differences. In outline, he maintains that peoples (*ethnē*) from colder parts of the world have too much spirit (θυμός, *thumos*), and not enough intelligence (διάνοια, *dianoia*) and as a consequence, lack political governance, whereas peoples from hotter parts of the world lack spirit and so, submit to tyranny and enslavement (1327b23–31).[26] He distinguishes the wild, ungovernable peoples from the cold climates as "Europeans," and those from the hotter climates as "Asians" (1327b24, 1327b27).[27] Finally, and predictably, we find that between the extreme regions of cold and heat lie the areas of the world inhabited by the Greeks, who alone possess the kind of disposition capable of governing themselves, because they possess both spiritedness and intelligence (1327b29–31).[28]

A preliminary question to be asked concerning Aristotle's climate theory concerns its origin: it does not arise with Aristotle but in fact bears close similarity to an earlier treatise in the medical tradition, as well as a brief reference associating climate to character in Plato's *Republic* IV (435e–36a). The fifth-century Hippocratic work, *Airs, Waters, Places*,[29] which appears to be Aristotle's model, gives a scientific, naturalistic account of the effect of climate and geography on human traits, including physical and moral features. Another original connection to Aristotle's account may be Sophistic sources, some of which are associated with the climate theory of national character as well.[30] For our purposes, we shall draw upon the Hippocratic treatise for its expression of the climate theory.

The general idea advanced in *Airs, Waters, Places* is that climates with marked seasonal changes cause variations in the semen which in turn gives rise to other effects, including bodily size, shape, and disposition of human character. In the opening section, the work sets out a contrast between Asia and Europe:

Asia differs very much from Europe as to the nature of all things, both with regard to the products of the earth and to the inhabitants . . . the country is milder and the dispositions of the inhabitants also are more gentle and less passionate.[31] The cause of this is the temperature of the seasons. (sec. 12)

It then proceeds to explain the cause of the dispositional differences:

the chief reason why Asiatics are less warlike and more gentle in character than Europeans is the uniformity of the seasons, which show no violent changes either towards heat or towards cold, but are equable. For there occur no mental shocks nor any violent physical changes which are more likely to steel temper and impart to it a fierce passion than is a monotonous sameness.[32] (sec. 16)

In contrast to the Asian temperament, Europeans are ungovernable: "the wild and unsociable, and the passionate occur in such a constitution, for frequent excitement of the mind induces wildness, and extinguishes sociability and mildness of disposition" (sec. 23). The author of the treatise then generalizes about the differing characters of the two, finding the Europeans more "courageous" from undergoing exertions and hardships, and the Asians less so due to a climate that "induces indolence" and for this reason, he finds European barbarians more warlike than Asians (sec. 23). In the Hippocratic work, variability of climate produces dispositional differences in people's character. On the one hand, the cold climate makes Europeans possess a kind of wild belligerence that leads to courageous disposition, while the mild climate of Asia makes Asians such as to be gentle and timid.[33]

An obvious parallel exists between the Hippocratic and Aristotelian accounts concerning the relation between climate and natural disposition. Yet the former also draws a correlative cause for character in the political regime:

> where men are governed by kings, they must be very cowardly; for their souls are enslaved, and they will not willingly undergo dangers in order to promote the power of another; those that are free undertake dangers on their own account, and not for the sake of others . . . for they themselves bear off the rewards of victory, and thus, their institutions contribute not a little to their courage. (sec. 23)

The question whether Aristotle, too, finds a connection between political regime and national character is complex, but will be touched upon in the conclusion, below.

Here in VII. 7, Aristotle suggests that political regime is the *result* and not the cause of natural disposition or character. For he notes a correlation between Asian nations and tyranny: "they lack spirit, which is why they continue to be ruled and enslaved" (ἄθυμα δέ, διόπερ ἀρχόμενα καί δονλεύοντα διατελεῖ, 1327b28–9). Yet he also claims in the same passage that Asians "have intelligent minds and are skilled in crafts" (1327b27–9), in sharp contrast to Europeans, "who are full of spirit but deficient in intelligence and skill" (τὰ περὶ τὴν Εὐρώπην θυμοῦ μέν ἐστι πλήρη, διανοίας δὲ ἐνδεέστερα καὶ τέχνης, 1327b24–25). As Aristotle sees it, European tribes are characterized by an excessively wild disposition such that although they remain free (ἐλεύθερα, *eleuthera*), they lack political organization and are incapable of ruling (1327b25–26). The passage in VII. 7 thus presents two views of "barbarians": Asians are said to be both "barbarian" and "slavish," while Europeans are indeed "barbarians," and yet not described as "slavish." Therefore, being a member of a "barbarian" tribe, or nation, is not enough to make someone have the character of a slave, or be a "slave by nature" in Aristotle's terms. Nonetheless, since Aristotle here states that some barbarians are "slavish," the question becomes whether Asian "barbarians" are those whom Aristotle singles out as "slaves by nature" in Book I, chs 4, 5, and 13. If so, then it may be argued that Asian "barbarians" are precisely those barbarians whose nature is such as to require their being ruled despotically. In a sense, the climate account in

VII. 7 seems to support this conclusion: the hot climate induces a kind of gentleness and timidity in the Asian disposition that supports becoming enslaved by Asian tyrants. It might be thought, therefore, that Aristotle thinks that Asians should be enslaved by Greeks to work in Greek cities. But although some scholars have maintained this interpretation,[34] it faces a number of problems.

Three difficulties, at least, arise from the argument of VII. 7 that undermine the conclusion that Asians must be natural slaves for Aristotle. In addition, other texts outside VII. 7 cast doubt on this equation, and these will be examined in subsequent sections of the paper. First, the actual argument in VII. 7 makes no reference to *natural* slaves, only to the Asian disposition to be "slavish" in the sense of being typically ruled by tyrants. But the inference from being "slavish" to being a *natural slave* is legitimate only if Aristotle has one meaning of the term *doulos* ("slave"), but this is not the case as Aristotle employs *doulos* to refer to many people who are clearly *not* natural slaves, such as the farming class described in his ideal regime (Books VII, VIII). Second, although Aristotle thinks that Asians lack spirit, he also claims that they also possess intelligence (*dianoia*), and are highly skilled in crafts (1327b27–9), which hardly squares with what he described as the deficient intelligence of the "natural" slave in Book I. Finally, Aristotle seriously compromises his claim about the natural differences among national groups in VII. 7 by noting that the same differences in temperament that exist among Europeans and Asians also exist among Greeks as a whole (1327b33–34). It follows that Greeks possess the same range of natural dispositions in their character – including a disposition to slavishness – that non-Greek "barbarians" do.

The greatest difficulty for the view that some, or all, Asian peoples are "natural slaves" concerns the issue whether it is reasonable to think that someone lacking a spirited disposition and possessing intelligence is a natural slave. Considering the passages in *Politics*, III. 14 and VII. 7, one might argue that it is not the presence of intelligence but the lack of spiritedness that makes Asians natural slaves.[35] This suggestion might seem plausible in making a psychological connection between a kind of natural timidity and slavishness, but the connection is negated by Book I, chs 5, and 13, where the natural slave is defined in terms of a rational or deliberative incapacity, not by a lack of spiritedness, and no such connection is suggested in the text. But perhaps one could focus on the other half of the equation and argue for a link between the intelligence ascribed to Asians and their *lack* of deliberative capacity. But the evidence for such a connection remains highly inconclusive, for even if the kind of intelligence being referred to here is merely of a technical sort – as has been suggested – nonetheless, it signifies a distinctively *mental* capacity that is ill-suited to the account in Book I of the natural slave.[36] Furthermore, Aristotle normally employs *dianoia* to refer to the mind or to the thinking faculty in general, and this usage constitutes a clear obstacle to the proposed reading. More specifically, Aristotle uses the term *dianoia* and its relatives (*dianoētikos*, *dianoeisthai*) in his psychology in either of two ways. In its general employment, *dianoia* refers to the faculty of thought as such, where the term is used to distinguish one of the human faculties such as nutrition, sense-perception, desire, local motion, or imagination (*De Anima*, 408b3, b9, 413b13, 414b17, 415a7–8, 433a18). For example, he claims: "the soul is the origin of the abovementioned functions . . . of nutrition, sensation, thought [*dianoia*], and motion" (413b13). In other occurrences, Aristotle relates *dianoia* to other capacities of thinking, sometimes pairing it with terms like λόγος, *logos*, λογισμός, *logismos*, νοῦς, *nous* ("reason," "rational," and "intellect"), as when he describes specifically human capacities of thinking (*De Anima*, 404a17, 414b18, 415a8, 421a15, 429a23, 433a2; *Metaphysics*, 1025b25, *Politics*, 1370b40). So, for example, he says "by intellect [*nous*] I mean that whereby the soul thinks [*dianoētai*] and reasons" (429a23). In all its uses in *De Anima*, the term *dianoia* signifies either the whole of the thinking faculty or an aspect of thinking that is typical of humans.

The fact that *dianoia* is not employed anywhere in *De Anima* to signify a kind of thinking consisting merely in a narrow technical knowledge or a craft knowledge leaves the claims made by these interpreters of the *Politics*, VII. 7 passage unsupported. They maintain that the line attributing "intelligent minds and skill in crafts" to Asians (1327b27–28) should be read pleonastically, with the two items signifying the same thing, a narrow technical intelligence and nothing else. By restricting the sense of the term for "intelligence" in this occurrence, they seek to connect this claim about Asians' lack of spiritedness with that of natural slavery in Book I. But their argument founders on a lack of textual support for reading *dianoia* in this narrow sense. On the contrary, the textual evidence in *De Anima* for interpreting the term *dianoia* as meaning "general intelligence" is clearly evident. Therefore, quite apart from clarifying the sense in which Asians may be said to be slaves, the attribution of "intelligence" to them only confounds the issue.[37] Since Asians possess intelligence (*dianoia*), and since this capacity is correlated with distinctively human rational thought, there is nothing here directly implying that Asians are the natural slaves described in *Politics*, Book I.[38] If one maintains, nonetheless, that Aristotle thinks that some Asians are to be identified as natural slaves, the basis for this claim must be found elsewhere. To this end, I examine Aristotle's account of what it is to be a slave by nature.

Slaves "by Nature"

While it is well known that ancient Greek political societies were slave societies with a very sizeable proportion of the resident population being comprised by slaves of one occupation or another,[39] it is hard to determine whether racial or ethnic differences as such contributed to the acceptance of slavery. A listing of ethnic groups from which Athenian slaves were drawn might suggest a connection between being barbarian and slave, and yet historically Athenians obtained chattel slaves through conquest from both Greek and non-Greek cities.[40] Greeks accepted chattel slavery as part of the social and political culture, apparently needing no reason to justify the practice on additional, racial grounds. Nor did chattel slavery exhaust the category as there existed as well other classes of persons "between slave and free" who provided the kind of manual labor needed by the typical Greek city-state.[41]

The identification between slaves and "barbarians" that emerges from Athenian literary sources of the classical period is, as noted, present in Aristotle's work. In *Politics*, I. 1, for example, Aristotle uses a contrast, *Greek–barbarian*, in order to show that barbarians have the sort of nature that makes them able to be enslaved by Greeks. This link between "barbarian" and "slave" may be thought of as supporting his discussion about "natural slaves" in I. 2 such that the two chapters then form a single argument. If so, this discussion would constitute a counter-example to the previous assertion that Aristotle offers no clear identification between "barbarians" and "natural slaves." To ascertain whether this reading is plausible, one needs to look more carefully at the argument in *Politics*, I. 1. This passage reveals that Aristotle's primary aim is to argue for a "natural" political ranking that he thinks "barbarians" ignore insofar as they identify women and slaves. For Aristotle, the proper ranking in descending order consists of free men, free women, children and slaves. The argument in I. 1 depends, first, upon a principle concerning nature having single ends (1252b1–4), and second, upon the claim that barbarians "lack a natural ruler" (τὸ φύσει ἄρχον οὐκ ἔχουσιν, 1252b4). Aristotle concludes that although barbarian men take women and slaves as equally inferior (1252b4), he suggests that all of them – men and women alike – are "slaves" because they lack a natural ruler.[42] He continues that *if* being barbarian and being slave were the same in nature (ὡς ταὐτὸ φύσει βάρβαρον καὶ δοῦλον ὄν, 1252b9), then it would seem that Greeks should rule barbarians (1252b6–7), his claim here being drawn from Euripedes' line, "Greeks should rule barbarians" (1252b7–8). But he does not go on to argue that the two have the same nature, and in fact his later references about barbarians demonstrate that he does not identify the two. In the subsequent chapter, I. 2, Aristotle nowhere mentions being barbarian in developing the arguments about being a natural slave, nor does he describe all those who are barbarian as slave-like in VII. 7.

In Aristotle's own account of what makes it just to be ruled despotically, his emphasis lies in the possession, or lack, of a capacity for deliberation, or βούλησις, *boulēsis*. Before we decide whether for Aristotle the capacity for deliberation is itself determined by an underlying racial or ethnic character, we need to consider his theory of natural slavery more closely. Aristotle draws his first definition of a natural slave in I. 4 on the basis of commonly held views about slaves: (1) a slave is a possession (κτῆμα, *ktēma*) of the animate sort (cf. 1253b30–2), (2) a slave is subordinate to the master in matters concerning action (πρᾶξις, *praxis*) as opposed to production (ποίησις, *poēsis*), (cf. 1254a5–9), (3) as a possession, the slave is like the part of a whole, belonging wholly to another (cf. 1254a9–13).[43] With regard to the first claim, the notion of being a possession is modified by τι, *ti* at 1253b32, so that we read "a slave is a sort of living possession" (ὁ δοῦλος κτῆμα τι ἔμψυχον).[44] In the second claim, Aristotle distinguishes the slave's proper function as the sphere of "acting" (*praxis*) and not that of "making" (*poēsis*), apparently restricting his discussion to personal or household slaves.[45] This is significant in that in fourth-century Athens, many slaves worked outside the household (e.g., banking, commerce,[46] and various skilled crafts[47]). The restriction of natural slavery to those whose function is acting and not producing suggests that the theory has no relevance to factory slaves (for example, those involved in mining), public slaves (who worked in the civic buildings and temples), tradesmen, or to skilled craftsmen.[48] With regard to the third claim, the asymmetrical relation of slave to master is compared to that of part to whole: just as a part is a part of something, a whole, so the slave belongs wholly to the master (1254a11–13). This analogy, however, is rather inadequate, first, because a whole also is a whole in relation to its parts, and second, because the argument shifts between structural and legal senses of belonging.[49] In order to see the foundation for the claim that the slave is someone who by nature does not belong to himself but to another (1254a14–15), we turn to *Politics*, I. 5.

The account of natural slavery in I. 5 proceeds by a series of analogies about ruling and being ruled that aim to focus the sense in which the slave is ruled: humans rule animals, soul rules body, intellect rules desire, male rules female. So, just as the soul differs from the body and by nature rules the body (1254a34–6), within the soul itself, reason (*nous*) differs from desire (ὄρεξις, *orexis*), and by nature rules the desiring part (1254b6–9). Aristotle here mentions two kinds of ruling: that of the soul over the body, and that of reason over emotion. These two are not the same, but distinguished as the rule of a master, and of a statesmen, respectively (ἀρχή δεσποτική, *arche despotiké*; ἀρχή πολιτικὴ, *arche politiké*, 1254b3–4). The difference for Aristotle lies in that the rule of a statesman, what he terms "political rule," aims at the good of the ruled (1255b20, 1277b7–9, 133a3–6), whereas the rule of the master, "despotic rule," aims at the benefit of the ruler (1278b32–37).

Aristotle's discussion then offers two characterizations of people whom he thinks should be ruled despotically, neither of which is without problems. His first description is physical: he claims that among humans some differ from others as much as soul from body or human from animal, and these are "those whose function is to use their bodies" (1254b17–18). Given that the best function that they can do is to perform manual labor, then such persons should be ruled in the way of despotic rule, and these would then be slaves "by nature" (1254b18–20). The problem with the characteristic of being fit to perform manual labor is that it reduces to having a certain kind of body, or having certain physical features, which Aristotle later casts doubt on as determinative markers. But the link between natural slaves and bodily traits is first stated: natural slaves are more like the body than the soul, more like the beast than the human, and this reflects their function to be working with their bodies. Aristotle even enlarges the connection between natural slaves and physicality by noting that nature's purpose makes the bodies of free and slave different, creating the body of the slave strong enough for manual labor and the free man useless for that kind of work (1254b27–30).

The first characterization of "natural" slaves, reminiscent of certain thinkers seeking to justify American slavery, promises to unravel in subsequent lines as he seems to realize that a bodily indication of a natural slave is inadequate: nature does not always exhibit itself in outward manifestations. As he notes, "some people have the body of a free man, others, the soul" (1254b32–34), acknowledging the possibility that a person's physical endowments need not be an indication of her internal character. If so, then having a powerful body implies nothing determinate about a slave designed for manual labor; it may equally well imply, for instance, fitness for athletic competition.[50]

Aristotle's subsequent description of the natural slave in I. 5 focuses on a psychological rather than a physical feature. Here Aristotle claims that one is a slave "by nature" if one belongs to another, and perceives reason, but does not possess reason (1254b21–23). Thus, the natural slave is defined in terms of a psychological deficiency, a characterization which introduces a number of further problems. First, while it relieves pressure on the physical or biological criterion, it does not go any way in specifying the nature of the psychological deficiency. A second problem is that since a natural slave does not, in fact, always have the kind of body fit for labor, it is unclear how one is to determine whose soul is in need of being ruled. As Aristotle notes, "the intention of nature is to make the bodies of free men and slaves different . . . though as a matter of fact often the opposite comes about, slaves have the bodies of free men and free men the souls only" (1254b27–34). In effect, then, trying to distinguish the natural slave using only a physical, bodily criterion is inadequate, and attempting to assess the capability of someone's soul even more so, since "it is not as easy to see the beauty of the soul as it is to see that of the body" (1254b39–1255a1).

The last critical issue concerns the coherence of his claim that slaves lack reason: since being human is an *infima species* with no further differentia, and since the final differentia of human essence is rational capacity, it would follow that anything human necessarily possesses reason. Aristotle cannot deny reason to natural slaves and maintain their humanity. While he does not deny reason as such to natural slaves, he attempts – unsuccessfully – to distinguish *levels* of capacity for rational thinking among humans, such that natural slaves possess the lowest level capacity. A hierarchy of capacities for reason is developed in I. 13, where Aristotle states that free men, free women and children, and slaves all possess the same parts of the soul (rational and irrational parts), but they do not possess them in the same way (1260a10–12).[51] So, although the slave has a reasoning part of the soul, he does not "have the deliberative part at all" (ὁ δοῦλος ὅλως οὐκ ἔχει τὸ βουλευτικόν, 1260a12). In contrast to the case of the slave, the female has the deliberative faculty, but it is "without authority" (ἄκυρον, *akuron*), and the [male] child has it but it is "incomplete" (ἀτελές, *ateles*), (1260a13–14).[52] Aristotle's denial of deliberative capacity to the slave by nature should be compared to his claim in I. 5 that the slave "participates in reason only to the extent of perceiving it, but does not possess it [fully]"[53] (1254b22–23). The last claim remains puzzling in that even if we take it to mean that the natural slave cannot "deliberate," it seems false. Surely, the slave has to deliberate in order to carry out the orders of the master: the slave has to understand the nature and manner in which a certain ordered action is to be done, and for such tasks, reasoning about ends seems inevitable. Furthermore, since Aristotle claims that the slave is sufficiently rational as to profit from "reasoned admonition" of the master (I. 13, 1260b5–7), he does not doubt a slave's capacity for understanding.

What Aristotle seems to have in mind in saying that the natural slave, like the free woman, lacks deliberative capacity is that the natural slave lacks one kind of practical reason. Thus, Aristotle finds differences among ways in which humans might be said to exercise rational deliberation (*boulēsis*). In a way, the slave does deliberate insofar as he or she understands and perceives the dictates of the master or mistress and may evaluate the relation of means to some specific end. But there seems to be another sense of deliberating and it is this sense of the capacity which Aristotle thinks that the natural slave, like the woman or the child, in unable to exercise. In the restricted sense, deliberation involves practical reasoning about actions in light of one's knowledge of the good, and not merely the capacity to reason out practical means to some end, as suggested by Aristotle's discussion of instrumental practical reason in *Nicomachean Ethics*, III. 3 (e.g., 1112b12–20). Considered in this narrow sense, deliberation, and especially excellence of deliberation (εὐβουλία, *euboulia*), is a state of character of the practically wise who possess a true conception of the human good (*Nic. Ethics* or *Nicomachean Ethics*, VI. 9, 1142b30–2).[54] Since Aristotle thinks that the natural slave, like women and children, cannot have a complete conception of the human good, he or she cannot "deliberate" in the restricted, normative sense of the term.[55]

However, if Aristotle is using a normative sense of deliberation in *Politics*, I. 13 when he denies that natural slaves possess a deliberative faculty, it appears that not only slaves but most people – including male and female citizens – must also be said to lack the capacity for rational deliberation. Since very few people can have a full conception of the human good for Aristotle, then very few people can be said to deliberate in the restricted sense of the term.[56] Furthermore, since most people, Greeks and non-Greeks alike, are unable to deliberate in the strict sense, it follows that the majority of people should be ruled by others.[57] This is a paradoxical result. And a further problem arises: if we assume that lacking deliberation in the strict sense implies being fit to be enslaved, we conflate various senses of what it is to be ruled. For, if we consider the cases of the free woman and the child that Aristotle raises in I. 5 and I. 13, we find that while women and children are similarly deficient in "deliberation," they are ruled as "free" persons by either *political* or *royal* rule, respectively, not by despotic rule (1259a40–b2). Therefore, lacking full deliberative capacity is not by itself sufficient for being a natural slave, i.e., the sort of person who should be ruled by a master. This result demonstrates a gap in Aristotle's reasoning: we cannot conclude fitness for despotic rule from the lack of ability to deliberate in the restricted sense alone.[58]

Returning to the passage in VII. 7 to apply the finding, we see that even if we grant that *dianoia*, the type of reason possessed by Asians, is insufficient to confer the ability to deliberate in the restricted sense, it does not follow that such persons should be ruled despotically, rather than royally or politically. Aristotle may, indeed, think that Asians lack knowledge of the good, and so, are unable to deliberate in the sense developed in *Nic. Ethics* VI, but according to such a standard not only Asians but most humans altogether – Greeks and non-Greeks alike – are unable to deliberate in the narrow sense. However, as was pointed out, Aristotle nowhere says that the majority of humans should be enslaved and ruled despotically; at most, his account implies that people lacking knowledge of the good should be ruled *in some fashion*, leaving it open whether they would be ruled as Greek citizen women or children are ruled – in a political or royal way – or in a despotic way (1259a40–b2). Consequently, from the interpretation of VII. 7 claiming that Asian "barbarians" lack deliberation, nothing follows about the way in which they should be ruled: it remains undetermined whether they should be ruled despotically, or politically or royally, as free women and children are ruled.

The question thus arises as to who, if anyone, is considered to be a natural slave if Asians are not being singled out by the text. A remaining possibility concerns whether Aristotle thinks that barbarians *in general* are natural slaves; a passage in III. 14 that connects "barbarians" with "slavishness" makes this a plausible suggestion. In III. 14, Aristotle is distinguishing various kinds of political regime, and he goes on to link despotism and barbarians in a suggestive way: "Barbarians are by nature more slavish (δουλικώτεροι, *doulikōteroi*) in character than Greeks, and those in Asia more so than those in Europe, that they endure despotic rule without distaste" (1285a20–22). But as the passage develops, he shows that it is not to the purpose of showing that barbarians *as such* are the natural slaves of Book I. Rather, Aristotle is here concerned to distinguish various types of kingships, desiring to single out a kind of kingship that is close to tyranny, but still based on law, and hereditary. He thinks that he finds it among the monarchies of barbarians (1285a16–22), perhaps having Persian kingships in mind. Therefore, the aim of this passage is to draw a political, not a racial, contrast between the *polis*-society of the Greeks with the undeveloped, despotic form of ruling that he associates with "barbarian" society.

Conclusion

Aristotle's *Politics* examines politically charged topics such as the roles of slaves and women in the state; the results he offers are more conventional than revisionary, finding some slavery justified, and allotting even free citizen women a non-participatory role in the *polis*. In light of the then-current criticism of these social roles provided by other philosophers such as Plato, Aristotle's views must be seen as conservative and retrogressive. In particular, the theory of natural slavery gives cause for concern in light of its historical application in the Americas against Native Americans and Africans, as argued by the Spanish philosopher, Sepúlveda, against Las Casas.[59] The connection between Western racist policies and Aristotle's theory of slavery in the modern period leads to the supposition that Aristotle himself forged a link between racial identity and slavery. The textual evidence in Aristotle's *Politics* is ambiguous for it supports conflicting conclusions on the connection, appearing to offer a connection between slavery and "barbarism" in some passages, but failing to bear it out in most. The difficulty of finding a consistent link between being barbarian and being slavish, taking all the passages together, leads me to conclude that there is no essential connection between being a barbarian and being a natural slave: since one can be a barbarian and not slavish (as VII. 7 shows), the former is not sufficient for the latter. Further, since no defended, concluding text states that being a natural slave entails being a barbarian, it appears that being barbarian is not a necessary condition for being a natural slave.

It seems to follow, then, that whoever is a natural slave may be either barbarian or Greek, with the decisive factor for Aristotle being an internal marker, having a deficiency in deliberative ability. Although one finds passages in Books I. 2, III. 14, and VII. 7 that state a loose connection between being barbarian and being "slavish" (e.g., 1252b9), these passages fail to establish a strict identification between being barbarian and a natural slave. A further difficulty linking the passages on barbarians with those on slavery is that the theory of natural slavery argued for in Book I, chs 4, 5, and 13 does not conceptually connect slavery and barbarians, nor does it relate being a member of one of the barbarian groups, say Scythian or Thracian, with being a slave "by nature." And although Aristotle specifies Asian barbarians as being "slavish" in

Politics, VII. 7, he also claims that European barbarians remain free and unenslaved. While he finds that European barbarians lack the ability to rule themselves politically, being deficient in intelligence and art, he does not argue that they should be enslaved (1327b23–7). Finally, the account of natural slavery in *Politics*, I. 4–5 does not characterize being a natural slave in terms of being a "barbarian" at all, but in terms of lacking a capacity for rational deliberation, on the parallel with free women and children. The problem found in placing weight on this marker is that one may lack deliberative capacity and remain unenslaved, not subject to despotic rule. Therefore, lack of deliberation cannot be the determining characteristic of being able to be enslaved. Nor can Aristotle's omission in naming a national group that he considers to be "natural slaves" be attributed to a lack of knowledge of various tribes and groups, as the text of the *Politics* demonstrates, mentioning a variety of ethnic groups, such as Thracians, Scythians, Kelts, Iberians, and yet nowhere identifying such peoples as those who ought to be slaves. So, being a slave by nature is not obviously associated with some ethnic or racial membership.

The references to the character of national or ethnic groups that he does draw, especially those in the passage in VII. 7 (1327b23–33), are better interpreted in light of their contrast to specific political regimes. A stronger reading of VII. 7 claiming that Asians must always be ruled despotically because of their lack of spirit must ignore lines in the same passage stating that the exact character differences found among the Asians and Europeans are also found among the Greeks: "the nations [τὰ ἔθνε] of the Greeks also display the same differences in relation to one another; some have a nature that is one-sided, while others are well-blended in relation to both of these capacities" (1327b33–34). If this is granted, then climate cannot be the only determinant of the natural dispositions of Asians and Europeans, since Greeks display the same range of dispositional differences as do barbarians. And so, if the effects of climate on character are not uniform across peoples, it would appear that climate itself is not the cause of bad character, nor, finally, can climate be blamed for what Aristotle considers deficient political regimes, like tyranny. It appears that Aristotle finds that political regimes themselves effect the character of the citizens. Textual evidence for this causal connection is found in V. 11 where Aristotle is discussing how tyrannies come to be preserved by the tyrant (1313a40ff). In general, tyrants aim at producing small-mindedness, indecision and incapacity for action among the citizens, so that they will not be overthrown. Various passages here suggest the connection between being ruled by tyranny and the mental states of being slavelike, unleisurely, and unable to act (1313b7–9, b20–21, b24–25, 1314a23–25). The climate account of character differences in VII. 7, then, has to be balanced with a more thorough account of the way in which Aristotle finds political institutions produce different character traits.[60]

Therefore, although one environmental factor, climate, may adversely affect the disposition of the Asian or European barbarian, it does not follow on Aristotle's theory that these groups must be ruled despotically because they are "by nature" unable to rule and be ruled politically. It seems, then, that the account of natural slavery in Book I should be read in contrast to those passages concerning climate and political training found in Book VII which suggest that one's natural disposition constituting *ethnos*

29

identity may be changed or modified by social and political institutions. In this regard, the similarity between Aristotle's account and the Hippocratic work, *Airs, Water, Places*, that linked climate with natural disposition of character, and character with political regime, may be more profound than it first appeared. The Hippocratic account links natural disposition not only to climatic differences, but importantly, to political regimes, and in this respect leaves open the possibility for the mutability of human character in the sense of modifying natural dispositions by changing political regimes. Aristotle's views in *Ethics* and *Politics* about human character in general and about barbarian *ethnē* in particular are consistent with such a conclusion. This is a surprising result in that one would expect him to identify the group, or groups, that he takes to be natural slaves since only this group is properly enslaved. His description of Asian barbarians as "slavish" and lacking in "spiritedness" in VII. 7 may be thought to provide the racial link, but, as I have argued, their "intelligence" and technical skill fail to match his psychological description of natural slaves in Book I.[61]

Historically, theories about human nature have been found to be replete with unexamined assumptions relating racial or ethnic identity with differences in moral and intellectual capacities. Although proponents of racist theories found support for their views in Aristotle's theory of natural slavery but, Aristotle's full account, as I see it, is undetermined with respect to racial or ethnic groups: he does not seem to know which national group, if any, should be put in the class that he terms "natural slaves." Furthermore, certain passages in *Politics* weaken the link between ethnicity and natural disposition by emphasizing the role of reason and social training over the importance of "innate," or biological, tendencies. Insofar as his political theory allows for social training, political institutions, and moral education to play substantive roles in forming the character of Greek citizens, the theory leaves open the possibility that members of "barbarian" groups, those belonging to *ethnē* and not *poleis*, would be able to be made into individuals capable of political participation, over some period of time. Admittedly, Aristotle does not raise such a possibility, one explanation being that Athenian elitism and nationalism acted as powerful conceptual deterrents to such a proposal. In comparison with other nations, or even other Greek cities, Aristotle thinks that Athens represents the highest level of political society, reflecting a familiar Athenian attitude as he writes about the national character of "barbarian" nations. In light of his position, Aristotle is far from supporting a cosmopolitan view – promoting an attitude of national equality and cultural pluralism in the *Politics*. But, like Plato, neither does he think that merely being Greek is sufficient for virtue of intellect or of character. For both thinkers, the human disposition to virtue is partly malleable, dependent upon various social and political institutions. Like Plato, Aristotle finds that the virtues are not inherited but acquired through difficult training, and although having a proper natural disposition for virtue provides a positive starting point, inherited ethnic identity does not determine success or failure of the process. Aristotle places greater emphases on cultural, political factors than on innate dispositions in his overall account of moral and political education. In this regard, his views on political capacity, virtue and *ethnos* – inegalitarian as they are – suggest that he is closer to holding what would be considered a cultural, social notion of race and ethnicity than a biologically determinist notion.[62]

Notes

1. The argument for the plausibility of the question with respect to the Greeks is clearly set forth in Rachana Kamtekar's essay on Plato (this volume).

2. For example, Gordon (1995), ch. 12, discusses aspects of both social and biological components in racism; Tommy L. Lott (1999) treats primarily the social and cultural aspects of racism.

3. Gould (1981), for example, considers the biological concept of race as correlating physical differences with intellectual capacities and ranking these capacities on a hierarchical scale. See also Popkin (1980) for the genesis of the modern biological conception of race in eighteenth-century thought.

4. For the positive sense, see Homer (*Iliad*, 2, 573; *Odyssey*, 23, 240); for the negative use, meaning "weakly," "womanish," Aristophanes (*Thesmophoriazusae*, 191, *Ecclesiazusae*, 428). In general, lexical entries show *leukos* ("light") means what is bright, gleaming, fair, clear in color, and by extension, clear in reason, also joyful, fortunate, or happy, and *melas* ("dark") means what is dark, black, or ink-colored, and by extension, what is obscure, enigmatic or malignant (Liddell and Scott, 1968).

5. For related uses of *leukos* meaning "cowardly," see Aristophanes, *Thesmophoriazusae*, 191, *Ecclesiazusae*, 428, and Euripedes, *Bacchae*, 457.

6. Similar senses are implied in the pseudo-Aristotelian work, *Physiognomics*, where "light-skinned" applied to men is thought to show excessive sensuality, emotionality, and in general, to denote "feminine" traits (808a34, 808b4).

7. Hall (1989), ch. 1, claims that a large point of difference consists in that in the archaic period one's identity is based upon family lineage, individual valor, and city-state membership, instead of having a collective ethnic identity like being "Greek."

8. Herodotus' *Histories*, I. 1 reflects a tone of cultural pluralism in its opening line: "The purpose is to prevent the traces of human events from being erased by time, and to preserve the fame of the important and remarkable achievements produced by both Greeks and non-Greeks." The entirety of Book II is devoted to accounts of Egyptian culture and history.

9. For full discussion of the "Ethiopian" in Greek literature, see Hall (1989), ch. 3, section 6, pp. 139–43 on "ethnography."

10. On *barbaros* and related Greek terms, see Liddell and Scott (1968).

11. See Edith Hall (1989), Georges (1994), Said (1978), and Juthner (1923).

12. See Georges (1994), ch. 2, p. 38ff on Xenophanes and the Asiatic barbarian.

13. On the opposition, see, e.g., Aeschylus, *The Persians*, 255; also Herodotus, *Histories*, I. 58; also Hall (1989), ch. 2, esp. pp. 69–81, discusses Aeschylus' play in the wider historical context.

14. Hall (1989), p. 57 finds that the Sophists gave impetus to the critical, philosophical examination of the opposition. Similarly, Steven Hirsch (1985), p. 146 and n. 22, maintains that the Sophists emphasized the priority of geographical and cultural factors in the development of what was taken to be national character, or race.

15. This line has been taken by Hall (1989), pp. 165, 197, to reflect the pairing-up of the category of "barbarian" with that of slave which, in Aristotle's repetition in *Politics*, I, 1252b7–9, which she thinks shows that he takes all barbarians to be naturally inferior to Greeks.

16. The term *genos* is a concept denoting lineage: it can signify "kind" as in a biological genus, or "stock," "kin," or "clan" in the sense of being in the line of direct descent or the offspring (Liddell and Scott, 1992).

17. See also Plato, *Laws*, 637d–e, where Plato specifically names Scythians, Persians, Carthaginians, Kelts, Iberians, and Thracians as groups who drink too much and are "belligerent races," as well as *Gorgias*, 524e–5a, on the Persian king's soul that is distorted from injustice, lying and insolence. For discussion of Plato on "barbarians," see Hirsch (1985), ch. 6, and Rachana Kamtekar (this volume).

18. As Rachana Kamtekar (this volume) has shown, in using the term "barbarian," Plato may be parodying and criticizing the very classification, especially since, as we have seen, when he is speaking from a genuinely philosophical standpoint, he has no use for the category.

19. We also find Plato in *Alcibiades*, I, pp. 120a–2a, giving a generally favorable account of Persian education: see Hirsch (1985), ch. 6, esp. pp. 142–5.

20. It should also be pointed out that all the Greek sources on "barbarians" are not univocal in their criticisms; so, Xenophon and Herodotus, for example, at times show respect and praise for certain Persian leaders like Cyrus. Hirsch (1985), p. 61, in particular, finds that much scholarship on Xenophon reveals the tendency to exaggerate the anti-Persian elements, even in the *Cyropaedia*.

21. For example, Edith Hall finds the three main features often emphasized in barbarian psychology to be "hierarchicalism, immoderate luxuriousness, and unrestrained emotionalism" (Hall, 1989, p. 80). Also, Georges (1994), pp. 176–86, discusses Herodotus' illustration of the barbarian's lack of restraint in Cyrus' decision to burn his enemy, Croesus, alive (though later he is moved by Croesus' words to spare him) (I. 86. 6).

22. For further discussion of Herodotus' account of Asiatic barbarism, see Georges (1994), esp. ch. 6.

23. The noun *ethnos* derives from the verb "to be accustomed," and the lexicon shows the core meaning to be "a number of people accustomed to live together" (Liddell and Scott, 1968), so that the concept of "nation" or "people" rendered for *ethnos* should be understood as having primarily the sense of a small social or cultural grouping.

24. It is possible to see an analogous distinction made by Enlightenment thinkers such as Locke and Hume in terms of African and Native American societies being "uncivilized" in contrast to that of Europeans; see Popkin (1980), Gates (1992), pp. 50–63.

25. The full meaning of the sentence is complex according to Carnes Lord (Aristotle, 1984, p. 249, n. 2) who takes the contrast to be between a string of autonomous villages, or an alliance of villages such as that had by Arcadians, and a city.

26. The modern version of the climate theory of race is developed by Montesquieu (1989), Books 14–17.

27. A question as to whether these place terms refer to the same geographical areas used in the modern period or not may be raised. In regard to Europe, it seems that Aristotle uses this term to refer both to the specific region between Thrace and the Peloponnesus, which would include the Thracians, Scythians, and Illyrians, and in a broader sense, as in Book VII. 10, where he refers to Italy as a promontory of Europe (1329b11). See Congreve (1874), nn. 184, 192. On the sense of "this promontory," see Herodotus, *Histories*, IV, 38.

28. It should be noted that the natural disposition of being both intelligent and spirited is not universal among all Greeks, however, as the same differences hold among various Greek peoples as between Europeans, Asians, and Greeks (*Politics*, 1327b33–36).

29. Translation by Francis Adams (1886), unless noted otherwise.

30. Hirsch (1985), p. 146 claims that the Sophists "had insisted on the predominance of geographic and cultural factors over racial traits in the formation of national character," though he does not mention the Hippocratic account. Oliver Reverdin (1961), pp. 85–107, claims that the view of a common human race, or common human nature, is reflected in various

Greek sources, including fragments of Sophocles' *Teresias* (Diels and Kranz, 1954, 532N, 528N2), Antiphon's claim that Greeks and barbarians are created similar by nature (ibid. B2), Thucydides' idea that ancient Greeks and present-day barbarians lived the same way (I. 6. 5), as well as in the cosmopolitanism of Hippias of Elis' pronouncement about being a citizen of the world, and Demokritos' "well-born soul has the world as one's country" (ibid., B247).

31. The term εὐοργητότερα (*euogetotera*) is translated "affectionate" by Francis Adams (Hippocrates, 1886) and "less passionate" by John Chadwick (Hippocrates, 1950).

32. The translation of these lines from sec. 16 cited in Garlan (1988), p. 121.

33. Kerferd (1984), p. 159 claims that the Hippocratic treatise, sec. 12, shows that climate is determinative of character in the sense that if Greeks emigrate to Asia Minor, they become like the Asiatic Lydians who are "effete and luxurious." It is unclear that Aristotle would follow this line of reasoning. Part of the difficulty resides in the differrent biological theories underlying the traditions: the Hippocratic tradition supports *pangenesis*, the view that seed is drawn from all parts of the body, whereas Aristotle rejects this tradition (see his discussion in *On the Generation of Animals*, I, 721b12ff).

34. For example, Kraut (forthcoming) maintains that Aristotle thinks that Asian barbarians are the "slaves by nature": I. 4–5, 13.

35. Depew (unpublished) and Garver (1994a) maintain that the lack of "spirit" attributed to Asian people leads to cognitive and moral deficiencies that preclude them from developing the full range of faculties that free Greeks have.

36. On this view, see Depew (unpublished), and Garver (1994a).

37. To this point, see Smith (1983a), reprinted in Keyt and Miller (1990), pp. 142–55.

38. Garver (1994a), pp. 173–95, holds that a lack in *thumos*, or spiritedness, conduces to a cognitive failure: thus, the link between the two accounts about slaves in Book I and Book VII.

39. Estimates of slave populations in the classical period vary from 20,000 to 400,000: see Finley (1960), pp. 58–9, (1986), pp. 100–103, Garlan (1988), pp. 59–60, Jones (1956), p. 187, and Randall (1953), pp. 199–200.

40. Bäbler (1998) gives a full discussion of the various ethnic groups in Athens that provided slaves, including Thracians, Phoenicians, Phrygians, and Paphlagonians, all of which were considered to belong to the barbarian slave class.

41. See Garlan (1988), p. 87.

42. The ambiguity of the phrase "a natural ruler" or "a natural ruling element" lends itself either to the idea that barbarians lack some part of reason, the "ruling" faculty, or that they lack a class of natural (i.e., virtuous) rulers. Carnes Lord (Aristotle, 1984) suggests the psychological reading, while Tricot (1962), and Susemihl and Hicks (1894) suggest the political reading.

43. The conclusion sums up these points: "So, it is clear from these things what the nature of the slave is, and what his capacity is. For one who does not belong to himself by nature but to another, though a human being, is a slave by nature; and a human being of another is one who is a possession in regard of being a human being; and a possession is an intrument of action [*organon praktikon*] and is separate [from the owner]" (1254a13–17).

44. It should be noted that *Nic Ethics*, V. 6 implies that other things that are "one's own" include possessions and one's children (1134b10ff), so ownership extends over a range of things.

45. Swanson (1992), pp. 32–3, also takes natural slaves to belong to the domestic sphere. Others make little of the distinction between acting and producing, e.g., Saunders (1995), p. 74,

argues that since production involves some activity, the distinction is "dubious." N. Smith (1983a), p. 110 notes that the distinction generates problems for the claim made in VII. 10 (1330a25–6) that farming in the polity, which involves production, should be done by slaves – suggesting, as I see it, that Books VII–VIII bear no relevance to the account of natural slaves in Book I.

46. See Cohen (1992), ch. 4, on the role of slaves in banking and commerce.

47. For example, we know from Xenophon (1968) that both free and unfree slaves worked alongside free men for the same wages on the temple of the Erechtheum on the Acropolis: of these 86 workmen, 24 were citizens, 42 were non-citizens, and 20 were slaves. See Randall (1953), pp. 199–210, and Finley (1986), pp. 100–103.

48. These last often lived where they liked and carried on their work activities much on their own decisions, paying a proportion of their wages back to their master. These people would be equivalent to the group he refers to as βάναυσοι, *banausoi* (or τεχνίτας, *technitas*), the common artisans whom he takes to be "under a delimited slavery" in contrast to the slave proper (1260a39–b2). This may be the group he hopes (ideally) will be farmers in the polity in VII. 10 (1330a25–6).

49. Saunders (1995), p. 74, notes that the way that the part belongs to the whole is structural, but the way the possession or slave belongs to the owner or master is legal.

50. I concur with Depew (unpublished) that the epistemological difficulty in identifying who is a natural slave does not lead Aristotle to claim, like Alcidamas and Philemon, that no one was born a slave, nonetheless, difficulties persist concerning who is to count as a slave by nature if there are no determinative physical features.

51. In I. 13, Aristotle holds that slaves are human beings and participate in reason (1259b27–8), and that they possess the same faculites of the soul as free men (1260a10–11), and have a share in moral virtue (1260a14–15).

52. Discussions about the "inability" of women's reason are varied and numerous; e.g., Cole (1994), Deslauriers (1998), Fortenbaugh (1977), Homiak (1996), Matthews (1986), Modrak (1994), Smith (1983b), Spelman (1983).

53. In I. 5, persons who are slaves by nature are those who share in reason to the extent that they perceive reason, but do not "possess" it (μὴ ἔχειν, *me echein*, 1254b22–3), an obscure distinction presumably filled out by that between levels of deliberative ability in what follows.

54. Here practical reason is defined as a true conviction of what is conducive to the end, and so, involves a true conception of the end; cf. VI. 12, 1144a8, where it involves means to the end.

55. In this respect, I agree with Kraut (forthcoming) concerning his distinction between a restricted, normative sense of deliberating, and a sense of deliberating about a certain end (cf. VI. 9, 1142b29).

56. This raises the issue whether practical reason (φρόνησις, *phronesis*) admits of a stronger and weaker sense so that those who are imperfectly virtuous can yet be said to possess it; on the difference, esp. between *Nic. Ethics* and *Politics*, see Wilcox (1995).

57. Thus, Smith (1983a), p. 116, makes the argument that because of psychic deficiencies, too many qualify as natural slaves; I find the psychic deficiency alone insufficient to justify slavery.

58. A related problem mentioned by Cole (1994), pp. 137–9, is that since Aristotle finds full deliberative capacity to arise from education and social training, he should favor educating "natural slaves" for full human virtue, rather than subjecting them to despotic rule.

59. On the debate in the New World between Las Casas and Sepúlveda over "natural slavery" with respect to the Native Americans, see Hanke (1959).

60. Additional evidence weakening a deterministic, biological connection between natural disposition and moral character emerges from VII. 13 where Aristotle claims that nature (φύσις, *physis*), habit (ἤθος, *ēthos*), and reason (*logos*) together constitute a basis for moral excellence (1332a38–b7).
61. The suggestion that because Asian barbarians lack spiritedness, they also lack other emotions that are necessary for proper intellectual and moral development stands as the only basis for a "racializing" reading of natural slavery (see Depew, unpublished, and Garver, 1994a).
62. I would like to express my thanks to: Elizabeth Asmis, Richard Kraut, and the members of the University of Chicago Classics Seminar for the opportunity to present an earlier version of this paper in 1998–9, and my co-editor, Tommy Lott, for providing the original invitation to an APA session on race for which this paper was written. I have also benefitted from the critical written comments made by David Depew on an earlier version of this essay.

References

Aeschylus 1972: *Fabulae*. Tr. Denis L. Page. Oxford: Clarendon Press.

Annas, Julia 1988: Naturalism in Greek Ethics: Aristotle and After. *Proceedings of the Boston Area Colloquium in Ancient Philosophy*, 4, 149–71.

Aristophanes 1973: *Ecclesiazusae*. Ed. R. G. Usher. Oxford: Clarendon Press.

Aristophanes 1994: *Thesmophoriazusae*. Ed. Alan Sommerstein. Warminster, England: Aris & Phillips.

Aristotle 1913: *Aristotelis Ethica Nicomachea*. Ed. Ingram Bywater. Oxford: Clarendon Press.

Aristotle 1943: *On the Generation of Animals*. English and Greek. Tr. A. L. Peck. Cambridge MA: Harvard University Press.

Aristotle 1957: *Aristotelis Metaphysica*. Ed. W. D. Ross. Oxford: Oxford University Press.

Aristotle 1984: *The Complete Works of Aristotle*, rev. edn. Ed. Jonathan Barnes. Princeton: Princeton University Press.

Aristotle 1984: *The Politics*. Tr. Carnes Lord. Chicago: University of Chicago Press.

Aristotle 1988: *Aristotelis Politica*. Ed. W. D. Ross. Oxford: Oxford University Press.

Bäbler, Balbina 1998: *Fleissige Thrakerinnen und wehrhafte Skythen: Nichtgriechen im klassischen Athen und ihre archäologische Hinterlassenschaft*. Stuttgart: B. G. Teubner.

Cohen, Edward E. 1992: *Athenian Economy and Society: A Banking Perspective*. Princeton: Princeton University Press.

Cole, Eve B. 1994: Women, Slaves, and Love of Toil in Aristotle's Moral Philosophy. In Bat-Ami Bar On (ed.), *Engendering Origins: Critical Feminist Readings in Plato and Aristotle*, 127–44. New York: State University of New York Press.

Congreve, Richard (tr.) 1874: *The Politics of Aristotle with English Notes*, 2nd edn. London: Longmans, Green, and Co.

Davis, Michael 1996: *The Politics of Philosophy: A Commentary on Aristotle's Politics*. Maryland: Rowman & Littlefield.

Depew, David (unpublished): Barbarians, Natural Rulers, and Natural Slaves: Aristotelian Ethnology Meets Aristotelian Psychology.

Depew, David 1995: Humans and Other Political Animals in Aristotle's *History of Animals*. *Phronesis*, XL, no. 2, 156–76.

Diels, H. and W. Kranz (eds) 1954: *Die Fragmente der Vorsocratiker*. Berlin: Weidmaunsche Buchhandlung.

Deslauriers, Marguerite 1998: Sex and Essence in Aristotle's Metaphysics and Biology. In Cynthia A. Freeland (ed.), *Feminist Interpretations of Aristotle*, University Park, Pennsylvania: Pennsylvania State University Press, 138–67.

Finley, M. I. 1986: *Ancient Slavery and Modern Ideology*. New York: Penguin.

Finley, M. I. (ed.) 1960: *Slavery in Classical Antiquity: Views and Controversies*. Cambridge: W. Heffer & Sons Ltd.

Fortenbaugh, W. W. 1977: Aristotle on Slaves and Women. In J. Barnes, M. Schofield, and R. Sorabji (eds), *Articles on Aristotle*, New York: St Martin's Press, v. II, 135–9.

Garlan, Yvon 1988: *Slavery in Ancient Greece*, rev. and expanded edn. Tr. Janet Lloyd. Ithaca: Cornell University Press.

Garver, Eugene 1994a: Aristotle's Natural Slaves. *Journal of the History of Philosophy*, 32, no. 2, 173–95.

Garver, Eugene 1994b: *Aristotle's Rhetoric: An Art of Character*. Chicago: University of Chicago Press.

Gates, Henry Louis 1992: *Loose Canons: Notes on the Culture Wars*. Oxford: Oxford University Press.

Gauthier, René Antoine (tr.) 1970: *Aristote L'éthique à Nicomaque*, 2nd edn, with a new Introduction. Paris: Béatrice-Nauwelaerts.

Georges, Perikles 1994: *Barbarian Asia and the Greek Experience: From the Archaic Period to the Age of Xenophon*. Baltimore: Johns Hopkins University Press.

Gordon, Lewis 1995: *Bad Faith and Anti-Black Racism*. Atlantic Highlands: Humanities Press.

Gould, Stephen Jay 1981: *The Mismeasure of Man*. New York: W. W. Norton & Co.

Grene, David and Lattimore, Richard (eds) 1954: *The Complete Greek Tragedies. Sophocles, v. I: Teresias*. Chicago: University of Chicago Press.

Grene, David and Lattimore, Richard (eds) 1958: *The Complete Greek Tragedies. Euripedes, v. IV: Iphigenia at Aulis*. Chicago: University of Chicago Press.

Hall, Edith 1989: *Inventing the Barbarian: Greek Self-Definition through Tragedy*. Oxford: Clarendon Press.

Hanke, Lewis 1959: *Aristotle and the American Indians: A Study in Race Prejudice in the Modern World*. Bloomington: Indiana University Press.

Herodotus 1982: *The Histories*. Tr. A. D. Godley. Cambridge: Cambridge University Press.

Hippocrates 1886: *The Genuine Works of Hippocrates*, vol. 1. Tr. Francis Adams. New York: William Wood.

Hippocrates 1950: *The Medical Works of Hippocrates*. Tr. John Chadwick and W. N. Mann. London: Blackwell.

Hirsch, Steven 1985: *The Friendship of the Barbarians: Xenophon and the Persian Empire*. Hanover: University Press of New England.

Homer 1961: *Iliad*. Tr. Richard Lattimore. Chicago: University of Chicago Press.

Homer 1975: *Odyssey*. Tr. Richard Lattimore. Chicago: University of Chicago Press.

Homiak, Marcia 1996: Feminism and Aristotle's Rational Ideal. In Julie K. Ward (ed.), *Feminism and Ancient Philosophy*, New York and London: Routledge, pp. 118–37.

Jones, A. H. M. 1956: Slavery in the Ancient World. *The Economic History Review*, 2nd series, no. 2: 185–99.

Juthner, Julius 1923: *Hellenen und Barbaren aus der Geschicte des Nationalbewusstseins*, series 2, viii. Leipzig.

Kerferd, G. B. 1984: *The Sophistic Movement*. Cambridge: Cambridge University Press.

Keyt, David and Miller, Fred (eds) 1990: *A Companion to Aristotle's Politics*. London: Blackwell.

Kraut, Richard (forthcoming): *Aristotle: Political Philosophy*. Oxford: Oxford University Press.

Kraut, Richard (tr.) 1997: *Politics. Books VII and VIII*. With a commentary. Oxford: Clarendon Press.

Liddell and Scott (eds) 1968: *English–Greek Lexicon*. Oxford: Clarendon Press.

Lindsay, Thomas 1994: Was Aristotle Racist, Sexist, and Anti-democratic? *Review of Politics*, 56, 127–51.

Lott, Tommy L. 1999: *The Invention of Race: Black Culture and the Politics of Representation*. Massachusetts: Blackwell.

Matthews, Gareth B. 1986: Gender and Essence in Aristotle. *Australian Journal of Philosophy*, supplement to v. 64, 16–25.

Mills, Charles W. 1998: *Blackness Visible: Essays on Philosophy and Race*. Ithaca: Cornell University Press.

Modrak, Deborah 1994: Aristotle: Women, Deliberation and Nature. In Bat-Ami Bar On (ed.), *Engendering Origins: Critical Feminist Readings in Plato and Aristotle*, New York: State University of New York Press, 207–23.

Montesquieu 1989: *The Spirit of the Laws*. Cambridge: Cambridge University Press.

Newman, W. L. (tr.) 1887–1902: *The Politics of Aristotle, II*. Oxford: Oxford University Press.

Outlaw, Lucius 1996: *On Race and Philosophy*. New York: Routledge.

Plato 1997: *Plato: Complete Works*. Ed. John Cooper. Indianapolis: Hackett.

Popkin, Richard 1980: The Philosophical Bases of Modern Racism. In *The High Road to Pyrrhonism*, San Diego: Austin Hill Press, 79–102.

Randall, R. H. 1953: The Erechtheum Workmen. *American Journal of Archeology*, 57, 199–210.

Reverdin, Olivier 1961: Crise spirituelle et evasion. In Hans Schwabl (ed.), *Grecs et Barbares: Entretiens sur l'antiquité classique*, vol. VIII. Geneva: Fondation Hardt, 85–107.

Said, Edward 1978: *Orientalism*. New York: Pantheon Books.

Saunders, Trevor J. (tr.) 1995: *Aristotle Politics Books I and II*. Oxford: Clarendon Press.

Simpson, Peter 1998: *Philosophical Commentary on the Politics of Aristotle*. Chapel Hill: North Carolina Press.

Smith, Nicholas 1983a: Aristotle's Theory of Natural Slavery. *Phoenix*, 37, no. 2, 109–22.

Smith, Nicholas 1983b: Plato and Aristotle on the Nature of Women. *Journal of the History of Philosophy*, 21, 467–8.

Spelman, Elizabeth V. 1983: Aristotle and the Politicization of the Soul. In S. Harding and M. Hintikaa (eds), *Discovering Reality: Feminist Perspectives on Epistemology, Metaphysics, Methodology, and Philosophy of Science*, Dordrecht: Reidel, 17–30.

Susemihl, Franz and Hicks, R. D. (trs) 1989 [1894]: *The Politics of Aristotle*. Revised text with Introduction, Analysis, and Commentary. London: Macmillan.

Swanson, Judith A. 1992: *Public and Private in Aristotle's Political Philosophy*. Ithaca: Cornell University Press.

Thucydides 1972: *The History of the Peloponnesian War*. Tr. Rex Warner. London: Penguin Books.

Tricot, J. (tr.) 1962: *Aristote: La Politique*. New translation with Introduction, Notes and Index. Paris: Vrin.

Wilcox, J. 1995: *Phronesis* in Aristotle's Political Theory. In K. I. Boudouris (ed.), *Aristotelian Political Philosophy*, vol. I, Athens: International Center for Greek Philosophy and Culture, 213–25.

Xenophon 1968: *Memorabilia*. Tr. O. J. Todd. Cambridge and London: Heinemann.

CHAPTER 3

Medieval Muslim Philosophers on Race

PAUL-A. HARDY

Introduction

The racialized discourse characteristic of our own era would have appeared strange to medieval Muslim philosophers. Stranger still would have been today's willingness to articulate human social identity almost entirely in racial terms. This is not surprising. Although Islamic society was multi-racial from the beginning, in none of the regions where Islam became dominant did the concept of race enter Muslim consciousness in any way similar to what we find in the United States and Europe today, for example. Social differentiation among Muslim peoples did not take on a predominantly racial character, at least, not in the classical age of Islamic philosophy (*c*.900 to *c*.1400). This should not suggest that we cannot find instances of discriminatory exclusion based upon a person's social standing during this period nor can we automatically rule out the possibility that race played some role in determining that standing.

But from where would racial exclusion have come? Clearly, it runs counter to the egalitarian spirit of Islam. Some argue that there is a quasi-logical connection between affirming the oneness of God and upholding the equality of human begins before Him.[1] But what a religion teaches and what people do on the basis of that teaching are two different things. Hence, it is useless to seek the answer to our question in Islam itself. Islam is a religion, not a culture, even if there exists a culture inspired by its revelation. Others argue that racial exclusion is all but inevitable in any human society, since the tendency to look down on people who belong to racial groups different from one's own is innate. Here I shall assume that racial discrimination is not inevitable and that it is, in fact, sociogenic. On this assumption, it is not unreasonable to canvas the institutions of Muslim society for the origin of racial exclusion. The institution of slavery seems an appropriate place to look.

38

Like the ancient Greek and Roman civilizations and their Byzantine successor, the Islamic world obtained most of its labor from slaves. Islamic culture accepted this as part of the existing social order, although, Islam's revealed book, the Qur'an, clearly commanded: "And contract [slaves] for freedom, if you think they are good" (24: 33). That is, it ordered Muslims to make a contract for slaves to purchase their freedom. The following conditional, "if you think they are good" is not a restriction upon freeing slaves. It means that if they cannot earn enough to purchase their freedom, then they cannot be expected to be independent so that, even when set free, their state of dependency would make them slaves all over again.[2] And what would have been the purpose of manumission if slavery was to continue under another form? Despite the steps that the Qur'an took to ensure slavery's eventual abolition, it persisted in Muslim societies for over a thousand years.

In time, slave labor was recruited from more or less predictable places: Africa, the Balkans, the Russian steppes. And the popular mind began to associate the servile state with the inhabitants of those regions. Of course, nothing in Islamic law, i.e., the *Sharīʿa*, restricts slavery to any single people. Slavery is the penalty for polytheism. Nevertheless, Muslims "recruited slave[s from the Slavic people] in glaring violation of the *Sharīʿa* because of the Islamization of the south Russian steppes of their neighborhood."[3] And around the years 1391–2 a letter arrives in Cairo from a ruler of Bornu in West Africa complaining that Arab tribes of the east were enslaving free Muslims. Complaints of this kind only increase, so that by the nineteenth century Muslim enslavement of other Muslims was commonplace. And slave recruitment acquired a distinctly racial coloration.[4]

But why should such a development concern philosophy? So often we hear modern Western philosophers say that race is irrelevant to philosophy. A similar sentiment is implicit in Muslim philosophy. After all, it's Aristotelian framework classifies everything in terms of core essential traits and accidental peripheral ones. Race and color is, then, accidental to human nature. From this premise, Muslim philosophers proceed to talk about what they deem to be most central to philosophical concerns, namely, building the human community. That community, they tell us, is constituted when people share things in common, a language, for example. The rational form of knowledge – the most universal kind there is – produces a common discourse whose interlocutors are co-terminous with humanity itself.

Still, people tend to recognize as human those with whom they can speak. Those whose tongue they cannot or will not learn are babblers, i.e., barbarians, and attempts at communication with them is envisioned as contamination of the pure signals transmitted in "articulate speech." Philosophers have proved themselves to be no exception to this tendency. Amongst the barbarians Aristotle placed natural slaves. To him a natural slave is one who can understand rational discourse but cannot initiate it. But who sets the standards for what is to count as rational discourse here? Besides, it is not at all obvious that races fitting Aristotle's conception exist. Obvious or not, Muslim philosophers like Abū Naṣr Alfārābī (d. 940) and Abū ʿAlī Ibn Sīnā (d. 1041), known as Avicenna, adopted Aristotle's theory. Hence, they affirmed the idea of a universal community of human discourse only to deny it by excluding human interlocutors of certain races. Blacks, Slavs and Turks, the races historically enslaved by Muslims, can hear the voices of philosophers; they have no capacity to engage in philosophical conversation. As a consequence, they do not control their fates in any ideal state conceived by Alfārābī or Ibn Sīnā.

A contemporary like Stanley Cavell, who defends the heritage of Austin and the later Wittgenstein, might attribute this to a conspiracy to silence the human voice, especially when that voice presents itself in a politically potent form. It seems a fact of the natural history of humans that their utterances make most sense when uttered by a particular members of their species, with particular voices. And we all know that human beings are called upon to give voice to their states, feelings and thoughts. In fact, the struggle to make sense, the struggle to speak intelligibly is plausibly regarded as instinctual. Yet philosophy more than once in its history has conspired against these facts of nature and resisted the human voice's instinct to make sense on its own terms. Philosophy, that is, has forsaken the democratic inclusiveness of ordinary speech in favor of pristine and "universal" language of logic and has posited the latter as the standard of intelligible communication. Does Muslim Peripateticism feature as a subplot in this all but perennial conspiracy?

Alfārābī's "virtuous city" or Ibn Sīnā's "just city" are constituted when people share a common language, when they make sense and can speak intelligibly, one to the other. At the same time, their overly intellectualized notion of what it means for the citizens of those cities to speak entailed that there was no linguistic framework for articulating the truths a large number of Muslims had to tell. I mean truths to which Muslim slaves of various non-dominant races could testify by virtue of the indignities they suffered, indignities brought about because their claim to be Muslim was not taken seriously by their co-religionists. This shortcoming helped motivate a deafness to any call to redress the wrongs generated by the society around them.

We will first attempt to grasp the moral significance of Muslims' treatment of other Muslims of a different race by examining the claim made by one scholar that the principles underlying contracts representative of the sphere of social exchange regulate access to that domain in terms of Aristotle's idea of proportional justice. Treating people justly, after all, would seem to involve treating them with seriousness, that is, taking seriously the concerns that they voice. How far, then, did the Muslim contracts of governing the relations between masters and slaves allow slaves to voice their concerns? From this we move to reflections on the conditions involved in redeeming the seriousness of human voices caught in the grip of a race-based slavery. The essay ends with the theme of Muslim philosophers' failure to accommodate the voices of Muslim slaves.

The Slave's Ambiguous Status in Islam

It is difficult to interpret Islamic law when it comes to the principles of justice it applied to the treatment of slaves. Problems appear at both the distributive and procedural levels. The ambiguous social status of slaves within Muslim society is partially to blame for this. Slaves in the eyes of the law were goods *in specie*. Slave traders were seen as dealing not so much with individual human beings as with generic kinds, things that do not admit of individuation except, perhaps, in certain circumstances where a defect is observed or the good manifests some unusual quality of excellence. Equal value, after all, is much easier to calculate when what is exchanged are items that are replaceable by others of the same kind: a horse for a horse, a camel for a camel or a slave for a slave. But then commercial exchange just *is* that realm where generality reigns, where like exchanges against like.[5] According to the eleventh-century Hanafī jurist Abū Bakr Muḥammad ibn Abī Sahl as-Sarakhsī, the Muslim and the non-Muslim under Muslim rule, the subject of a non-Muslim government, the free person and the slave who has been authorized to trade as well as the slave who has the permission to redeem his freedom, are equal in contracts of commercial exchange.[6]

In Islamic law the contract of sale, then, typifies transactions in the commercial sphere, the domain where things are equivalent and exchange on the basis of their mutual resemblance. In consequence, partners to the contract of sale enjoy equality all around with respect to the offer and acceptance of goods as well as the right of their appropriation and protection. Commercial exchange is thus open to everyone who has the capacity to reason and calculate profit and loss. This was true even for slaves, since slaves could enter into business relationships not only on behalf of their masters but also on their own behalf. So just as one could see slaves being exhibited for sale in the markets, one could see slaves actively engaged as traders equal to every other trader in the market insofar as both were partners to contracts of sale.

A slave, then, could act as the agent of his master in business, promoting his commercial interests as well as conducting business for himself, since "the slave may be legally competent in need and of sound judgement just like the free man."[7] The jurist al-ʿAynī continues: "Once the slave gains the permission of his master this situation is completely reversed" for "in sacred law the permission marks the dissolution of the legal restriction and the abrogation of the master's right because the slave would be capable of contracting and disposing even after enslavement were it not for the legal restriction placed upon him due to the right of the master." Therefore, "when the master grants him his permission, the master loses his right and the slave becomes competent to exercise his original capacity." According to Shaun Marmon, "What this meant for the slave was that he now had the right to retain his own earning, to contract and dispose in commercial matters and even to own slaves himself."[8]

While, on the one hand, slaves circulated as pure commodities, on the other, they enjoyed equal status to other Muslims when they traded on behalf of their masters. They could contract marriage as well and enjoy other rights which caused them to circulate in a realm of social exchange. And upon manumission the contract of clientage supposedly allowed them to circulate in society just as other free Muslims. Still, the slave as commodity was a phenomenon far more prevalent in classical Islam than the slave as agent of trade. This, of course, is what we find most troubling about the matter of slavery in general. Can a human being really be reduced to a commodity? Can human souls truly belong to a domain whose objects are characterized merely in terms of their equivalence to each other?

The Exchangist Model of Society

In Aristotle a society only comes about to the degree that things can exchange against one another: goods, services and even verbal communications. "For a community", he observes, "is not formed by two physicians but by a physician and a farmer, and, in general, by people who are different and unequal" so that "they must be equalized" and hence everything that enters into an exchange must somehow be comparable. So distributive justice is proportionate equality: "As a builder is to a shoemaker, so must the number of shoes be to a house."[9] A just polity in Aristotle's view equally distributes wealth according to such principles of proportion.

Muslim philosophers took over Aristotle's idea. We find it as late as the North African thinker Ibn Khaldūn (d. 1406 CE) who stressed that "the power of the individual human being is not sufficient for him to obtain [the food] he needs, and does not provide him with as much food as he requires to live."[10] Hence, there is need for both co-operation and an exchange of goods and services. But it goes back as early as Alfārābī's *al-Fuṣūl al-Madanī* where we read that the standard of justice is realized "first in the division of the good things shared by the people of the city among them all."[11] Each one is entitled to a share or a portion of these good things: security, wealth, dignity, etc. equal to his deserts. And in his *Principles of the Views of the Citizens of the Virtuous City* he pictures society as a system regulating the exchange of goods and services based on distributive justice:

> For the sake of self-preservation and to attain the highest perfection every human being is naturally in need of many things which no one can provide alone; each is in need of [other] people to supply some particular need. Everybody is in the same relation to everybody else in this respect. Therefore, humankind cannot attain the perfection, for the sake of which its inborn nature has been given to it, unless many [societies of] people who cooperate come together, each supplies everyone else with some particular need, so that as a result of the contribution of the whole community all things are brought together which everybody needs in order to preserve themselves and to attain perfection.[12]

Ibn Sīnā echoes Alfārābī:

> We now say: it is known that human beings differ from the other animals in that none of them can lead a proper life when isolated as a single individual, managing the affairs [of life] with no associates to help satisfy necessary needs. One human being must be complemented by another of his species, the other, in turn, by that one and his [or her] like. Thus, for example, one human being would provide another with vegetables; one man would sew for another, while the other would provide for that one needles. Associated in this way, they become self-sufficient. For this reason men have found it necessary to knit together cities and associations by means of contract [*ilā 'aqd al-mudun wa'l-ijtimā'at*]. So whoever does not encompass in the knitting together of the city by means of a contract based upon conditions proper to the city and he and his associates limit themselves to a grouping together [of individuals] perpetrates a device for a species remote from the likeness of humankind and lacking in the perfections proper to humankind.[13]

In Ibn Sīnā's view, the just city occurs among men who recognize an agreement in the sense of a contract, men who have the capacity to reckon equivalents in exchange through their ability to reason.

But in order to exchange goods and services humans must enter into an exchange of communication by words and signs. So Aristotle also maintained that a city cannot thrive without speech (*logos*). Accordingly, Ibn Sīnā in another place observes that:

> The human being has in his nature the capacity to inform the other who is his partner by means of an established sign (*'alāma waḍ'īya*) and he is specially adapted to what is suitable to that [sign] i.e., the *voice* (*aṣ-ṣawt*) . . . and after the voice the ostensive gesture (*ishāra*) . . . but the voice is more capable of signification than the gesture since the latter only guides to where [it wants] the glance of the eyes to fall.

So "what is proper to man is this necessity requiring him to inform and seek information due to an exigency for receiving and giving according to the measure of justice and other necessities."[14]

A text on legal theory echoes the same idea, namely:

> that one human being needs to inform and teach another what is in their souls, i.e., their minds with regard to the matter of their mutual subsistence in order to carry out transactions and associations; for the single human being is not independent with respect to his provision and livelihood due to his requiring food, clothing and a place for manufacture

and that

> the natural states of affairs are insufficient for them due to the softness of temperament . . . unlike the other animals [inasmuch] as the acquisition by manufacture only becomes complete through mutual cooperation between the sons of his species, sharing with them and having mutual transaction between them . . . in that this one gives to that one his own surplus and takes from him what he needs whenever [the other] acquires what adds to what suffices him in order that the matter of livelihood may be organized. [Therefore,] association and transaction requires that one person inform the other with respect to what is in their mind touching on life-needs and that mutual recognition involves an exchange of words.[15]

For legal theorists, this type of exchange is the leading motivation behind the theory of "*waḍ'u-l'lugha*" – "the establishment of language," the idea that "the language of the Arabs represents a fixed deposit of vocables and corresponding meanings which must not be altered or abandoned."[16] How this primordial assignment of meanings to vocables came about is a moot point among legal theorists. The majority hold that establishment took place by a primitive agreement between speakers of Arabic and thus represents a the idea that the mutual meaningfulness of the words of a language must rest upon some kind of compact among its users.

This sentiment stands behind Ibn Sīnā's view that: "One human being must be complemented by another of his species . . . to knit together cities and associations by means of contract" and suggest a quasi-political understanding of what it means for us to speak to one another, what it means to speak for oneself or have another speak in one's behalf. In other words, to recognize another human being is to begin with that person a kind of an exchange. This may be an exchange of goods in the commercial or an exchange of kinship in the commercial or social sphere. But for purposes of recognizing others an exchange of words is often more powerful. This is hardly surprising. Has Ibn Sīnā not said that "What is proper to man is this necessity requiring him to inform and seek information due to an exigency for receiving and giving according to the measure of justice and other necessities"? His appeal to the voice in people's mutual recognition is, of course, highly significant. It is a theme to which we will often return in the course of what follows.

Individuality

But let us begin with the idea that recognizing another is recognizing that person's significance in an economy of powers and productions. An Aristotelian community bases the worth of a producer, and thus of his goods or services, on his talent or expertise. And insofar as these, in their turn presuppose certain moral qualities, he bases the worth of a producer also upon his moral virtue.[17] But are all producers capable of moral virtue? Ibn Sīnā apparently thought not. He writes that "since the service of some people by others is inescapable, it is necessary that such people be compelled to serve the just city" inasmuch as "some people are naturally far from acquiring virtues; for they are slaves (ʿabīd) by nature like the Turks and the Negro (az-zanj).[18]

Influenced by Ibn Sīnā, the great Jewish philosopher Moses Maimonides speaks in the same way with regard to people's capacity for the true worship of God in his Arabic work, *Guide to the Perplexed*. He observes that:

> Among those who are incapable of approaching monotheistic belief are the Turks and the nomads in the North, the Blacks and the nomads in the South and those who resemble them in our own climates and their nature is like the nature of mute animals and, according to my opinion, they are not on the level of human beings, and their level among existing things is below that of man and above that of a monkey, because they have the image and the resemblance of a man more than a monkey does.[19]

Aristotle, of course, did not believe that all people who are held in slavery are natural slaves. He merely argued that there are some people somewhere whose natural capacities fitted them for slavery. Ibn Sīnā and Maimonides were more precise as to where this population could be found.

Yet Aristotle did see a direct link between the social relationships in which people stand and the virtues they practiced. And his idea on this score influenced philosophers writing in Arabic, although, with them, religion enters the picture as an expression of virtue. Aristotle argued that "there can be no friendship, nor justice, towards inanimate things, indeed not towards a horse or an ox, nor yet towards a slave as slave." Friendship and partnership involve relations of reciprocity and proportional justice which cannot exist between people related only by means and end. A slave is not an end, in other words, but a means to an end. He or she is, in fact, a living tool just as a tool is an inanimate slave.[20] As such, tools inhabit a domain of resemblance and equivalence. Like a tool, a slave is exchangeable. Although this suggests a certain kind of equality, the equality suggested implies a replaceability repugnant to our sense of each human individual's uniqueness.

True enough, Aristotle acknowledges that being regarded as a human being is tantamount to being seen as someone who could be someone's friend. But does not being a friend mean being irreplaceable in a way that nothing else is, in a way that nothing else can be? Friendship relies on a basic moral insight that human beings cannot be substituted for another. And this insight relates most profoundly to our ordinary sense of justice. Indeed, because our apprehension of a person's individual nature seems internal to our sense of what it is to wrong someone, no conception we have concerning human individuality can occur apart from this sense. Still, one could object and say that all people are, for some purposes treated as replaceable, just as all people are sometimes treated as means to other people's ends. Here we are inclined to follow the response of Raimund Gaita who argues that "just as no person is to be treated, on any occasion, only as a means to an end so no person is to be treated on any occasion, only as someone who is replaceable: they must be treated on every occasion in ways that reflect that their individuality conditions the way they limit our will."[21]

Did Muslim Peripateticism offer a conception of justice which could express our moral intuitions on this score? Muslim jurists of the Ottoman period apparently distinguished between "mute property" (*mal-i sāmit*) such as real estate and personal items and "property-with-voice" (*mal-i natik*) which included livestock.[22] Did philosophers like Alfārābī and Ibn Sīnā acknowledge such a distinction whereby the individual voices of slaves could, in principle, limit the wills manifest in their master's voices or were they like mute animals to be pushed aside as the master made his way? We will return to this question in due course.

Proportional Justice

Baber Johansen, examining the Muslim marriage contract, interprets the legal principles that regulate access to the realm of that social exchange in terms of Aristotle's proportional justice. "Under Muslim law," Johansen writes,

> 'the criteria for admission to social exchange, serve to underline a principle of proportional justice that would have satisfied Aristotle: social relations, i.e., relations concerning the association of new members with the household or the establishment of kinship relations through marriage are conditional on equal ranking of the exchange partners.'[23]

For according to the Stagirite "equals must exchange for equals" and "justice is equality . . . but not for all persons, only for those that are equal."[24] Jurists of the Hanafī legal school require that the prospective bridegroom of a free woman be equal to that woman's male relatives with respect to genealogy, religious probity and longevity in

45

Islam.[25] This is the well-known institution of *kafā'a*, peculiar to the Ḥanafī legal school which has the largest number of adherents.

However, not every familial affiliation in Muslim law comes about through marriage. The contract of *walā'*: *walā'u'l-mawālāt*, the contract of clientage or patronage, establishes a fictitious social bond of agnatic kinship whereby a free-born person or a freedman became incorporated into an Arab tribe. Islam, as Daniel Pipes has observed, strongly encouraged the type of patronage or *walā'* that followed upon manumission. Jurists, in fact, came to require that the contract of *walā'u'l-'itq* follow every manumission so that the manumitter will establish a relationship with his freed slaves and bring them into his family.[26] This was a way of introducing newly freed slaves into the society on the same footing as other of its members. Johansen dwells on the contract of marriage as representative of social exchange and as exemplifying Aristotelian proportional justice. But the two contracts of *walā'*: the contract of clientage (*walā'u'l-mawālāt*) and that attending manumission (*walā'u'l-'itq*), by his criteria, qualify as representatives of the sphere of social exchange as well. Let us consider for a moment their similarities.

According to Johansen, marriage contracts should not be viewed as contracts of sale where a commodity exchanges against a non-commodity. That is why they are representative of the sphere of social exchange and not commercial exchange.[27] But in contracts of clientage a commodity is exchanged against a non-commodity as well, since clientage cannot become an object of commercial exchange according to the Prophet's saying: "Clientage is a relationship like the relationship of kinship, it cannot be sold or given away."[28] Johansen also notes that admission to contracts representative of social exchange is exclusive. Marriage, for example, excludes a number of categories of individuals. *Kafā'a* implies a social hierarchy.[29] The highest-ranking group are the Prophet's tribe and family, the Quraysh, then Arabs ranked according to nobility of tribe. Below the latter two categories are non-Arabs and amongst these latter were salves.[30] But the contract of clientage is also exclusive. It excludes all those who lack the "favor" (*ni'ma*) of freedom and/or patronage to bestow. "Clientage," the Prophet had said, "belongs to the one who frees."[31]

Given that the contract of marriage, when *kafā'a* is operative, excludes persons who are lower partners in contracts of manumission and clientage from marriage with those who are higher, the two types of contracts complement one another with respect to exclusivity. Such exclusivity, by the way, did not mean that being a freedman constituted an insuperable barrier to social ascent in Muslim society. It did mean, however, that slave ancestry could be a heavy social burden, as John Hunwick observes, "simply on account of colour or because of the indisputable evidence such colour normally provided of slave origin."[32] And Albertine Jwaideh and J. W. Cox, summing up how freedmen were looked upon in later Islamic society, write: "The distinction between *ḥurr* [i.e. free] and *'abd* [i.e. slave] was binding and unalterable. It was a case of once an *'abd* always an *'abd*, whether manumitted or not. And while not all *'abīd* [i.e. slaves] were black, the terms for Negro and slave were used interchangeably."[33]

Yet marriage, at least in modern times, has been described as "a meet and happy conversation."[34] And the covenant one enters upon in marriage has been viewed as emblematic of that type of convenant that constitutes society at large, the covenant to which Ibn Sīnā alludes when he says that human beings are knit together in cities and associations "by means of contract." Threading through his thought on these matters is the idea that justice is something prepared for in the fact that human beings must by nature "inform and seek information [from each other] due to an exigency for receiving and giving according to the measure of justice" that is proper to them. That is, propadeutic to justice is an aspect of negotiation proper to human association (*almushāraka*) where one speaks to another and have others speak in one's behalf. Yet what is obvious is that this exchange can only occur amongst equals. Had not Aristotle said: "Justice is equality . . . but not for all persons, only for those that are equal." In this light, we should place Ibn Sīnā's view that divorce should not be initiated by women since "women are quick to follow passion and not very rational."[35] Women can enter into that "meet and happy conversation" called marriage but cannot terminate it. But then do women have the power to initiate it? Yet his view on this score is backed up by Islamic law. How helpful, then, is it to claim, as Johansen has, that "the criteria for admission to social exchange, serve to underline a principle of proportional justice that would have satisfied Aristotle"?

But we can put the same question to contracts of manumission and clientage. Are their terms ones for which slaves would have negotiated had they been free and equal? In exchange for manumission the master acquires title to his former slave's estate. Entitlement here is clearly unilateral, since the freedman acquires no title to his former master's estate nor does he qualify for membership in the manumitter's blood-money group. By effect of the contract of clientage the patron likewise acquires a title to the client's estate. Again, succession as well as the payment of blood money is unilateral.[36] Nevertheless, Johansen maintains that as a result of the contract of manumission the slave enters the field of social exchange and "circulates according to the rules of proportional justice."[37]

From the standpoint of Aristotelian proportional justice, relationships are to be equalized by distributing benefits in proportion to the deserts of their partners. In business relationships, for example, this equalizing process is facilitated by employing units of money. Money allows different species of goods to be compared numerically.[38] What seems to distinguish contracts representative of the social sphere as described by Johansen is that money cannot bridge the gap of inequality. And this accords with Aristotle's view that there are cases where associations are so unequal that all the money, honor, and affection one party has at his or her disposal cannot equalize it, such that the recipient of a favor is condemned to be a debtor always.[39] The master/slave relation is one of these. In such cases, norms of proportional justice do not and cannot apply.

If the evocation of principles of proportional justice is to prove illuminating to the character of justice involved in Muslim contractual relations, should they not apply across the board and take in all contracts representative of the social sphere of exchange? Muslim contracts of manumission and clientage seem to exemplify the failure of proportional justice and back up Aristotle's view of the unequal status between master and slave. They back up the views of Muslim philosophers on the status of slaves as well. But how does all this square with those ordinary intuitions of justice mentioned earlier? Johansen rightly observes that contracts representative of social exchange "follow the principle of a strict formalism which leaves very little place for intention, purpose and knowledge of the parties concerned."[40] In the realm of social exchange room for maneuvering is restricted to the utmost. If a social norm is to be considered just, should it not be possible for anyone whom it affects to have an effective voice in its consideration and be able to agree to it without coercion? Our problem is that for Muslim Peripatetics it is a given of nature that slaves could have no voice in such matters.

Natural Slavery

Alfārābī writes: "The parts of the city are thus ranked down to those who perform their tasks only according to the designs of others; they are those who serve and are not served, the lowest of the ranks and the most base."[41] These are people whose natural function it is to be slaves inasmuch as they are disposed by nature to perform only certain lines of work.[42] There are, of course, peoples who were unwilling to be ruled by someone more capable or who failed to perceive that being ruled by their superiors would constitute the realization their own perfection or good. Alfārābī, following Aristotle, justifies war against these peoples, "those who do not submit to the servile state and slavery, of those for whom it is best and most fortunate that their station in the world should be that of the slave."[43]

Ibn Sīnā, as we have seen, also believed that some races are slavish by nature. Behind Ibn Sīnā's view, as well as that of Maimonides cited earlier, is the ancient idea that climate is responsible for differences among peoples, particular air temperature and exposure to the sun, "like the Turks and the Negro (*az-zanj*) and those who generally speaking have not grown up in noble climates where conditions are for the most part such that the peoples growing up in them are balanced of temperament and sound of disposition and intellect."[44] The temperamental dispositions of human substances arise from the interaction of climate and the bodily humors, namely, blood, bile, phlegm and choler. The interaction of these factors results in certain actions, mental states and external behavior.

Still, one may question Ibn Sīnā's consistency on this point. Although he posits a hierarchy of races, he at the same time, asserts that: "Human souls are the same in species (*mutafiqun fī'n-naw'*)"[45] and "There exists in man a faculty by which he is differentiated from the rest of animals . . . called the rational soul . . . found in all men without exception but not in all its particulars, since its powers vary among men."[46] That is, all human beings are born with the capacity to engage in intellectual thinking, even if this capacity is manifested in different degrees among different peoples. The human soul is distinguished by being an intelligible substance; except that the accidents caused by varying climactic conditions modify it to greater and lesser degrees.

Ibn Sīnā, then, is not being inconsistent. He sees the relation between a people and their environment in causal terms. That is, the relation between the human essence and the things outside it is a causal one so that people living in different environments may not possess the property of being rational to the same degree. For an essence tends to cause things to have certain properties, but only if the conditions are right. Hence, temperate zones provide the right conditions for producing people that are normal with respect to rational capacity. Inhabitants of intemperate zones, then, are not normal. So what is essential to all human souls is not the presence of actual rationality; what is present is the potential for rationality. For the human essence need not be completely actualized. Physical or chemical injuries may leave their victim defective in one or another way. But the case of the enslaveable races is different. They are not simply classes of individual contingently unable to rise to the requirements of the human standard. They are in a real sense essentially incapable of being "sound of disposition and intellect."

Abū'l-Barakāt al-Baghdādī (d. 1164) dissented from Ibn Sīnā's view that all human souls are one in species.[47] Although Abū'l-Barakāt was Jewish, we may count him among the Muslim philosophers, since he seems to have converted to Islam in the very last year of his life. In any case, Abū'l-Barakāt argues that a soul powerful enough to turn water into fire and sticks into snakes as did the prophet Moses is capable of this power not merely because of the mixture of his humours in some accidental fashion. Such a soul differs from other human souls in its very substance.[48] Abū'l-Barakāt found no logical defence for his position except the example of natural slavery. "[Aristotle] had said that freedom is a capacity of the soul which is present in it substantially and not as the result of art or skill." Thus, given that we know that free human beings exist, "If the substances and natures of [individual] souls were one and the same, it would follow that all men are free."[49]

The views of Muslim philosophers on race reached beyond their immediate circles. An example of this is Ibn Khaldūn's espousal of the hum oral/climatic theory of racial difference. "We have seen" he writes, "that Blacks are in general characterized by levity, excitability and great emotionality. They are eager to dance whenever they hear a melody. They are everywhere described as stupid." He goes on to assert that: "The real reason for these (opinions) is that joy and gladness are to due to expansion of the animal soul as philosophers have shown in the proper places." To support his stand that is due to climate he repeats the view of Ibn Sīnā whose *Urjūza fī't-tibb* he quotes:

> Where the Zanj live is a heat that changes their bodies
> Until their skins are covered all over with Black.
> The Slavs Acquire whiteness
> Until their Skins turn soft.[50]

When he speaks of the characteristics of Blacks, Ibn Khaldūn is clearly complaining about the historian al-Masʿūdī's view about "the reason for the levity, excitability and emotionalism in Negroes."

According to Ibn Khaldūn "[Masʿūdī] did no more than to [repeat] what was reported [to him] on the authority of [the Greek physician] Galen and [the Arab philosopher] Abū Yūsuf Yaʿqūb ibn Isḥāq al-Kindī[51] that the reason is a weakness in their brains which, in turn, results in a weakness of their intellect." For Ibn Khaldūn: "This is an inconclusive and unproved statement."[52] Although the facts remain that Blacks are "in general characterized by levity, excitability and great emotionalism . . . eager to dance whenever they hear a melody"[53] he adds that "The same applies to the

Slavs." But in both cases "the reason for this is their remoteness from being in temperate zones produces in them a disposition and character similar to those of dumb animals."[54] He says that "the qualities of character [of the peoples of these regions] are close to dumb animals."[55] But as one begins to approach temperate zones the mental dispositions and physical character of people change, even if their skin color is black. He gives the example of "the Abyssinians who are neighbors of the Yemeni Arabs and have been Christians from pre-Islamic times . . . and the Mālī, the Gawgaw and the Takrūr."[56]

But this was not the only explanation Muslim thinkers offered for racial differences. Ibn Khaldūn observes that:

> It is mentioned in the Torah that Noah cursed his son Ham. No reference is made there to blackness. The curse included no more than that Ham's descendants should be the slaves of his brother's descendants. To attribute the blackness of the Negroes to Ham, reveals disregard of the true nature of heat and cold and of the influence they exercise upon the air (climate) and upon the creatures that come to be in it. The black color common to the inhabitants [of these zones] . . . is the result of the composition of the air in which they live and which comes about under the influence of the greatly increased heat in the south.[57]

Ibn Khaldūn thus refutes the claim that skin color is the result of descent in favor of the ancient theory of the effect of climate on skin color temperament and mental ability.

Although Ibn Khaldūn rejected the idea that the cause of skin color was the fact that blacks had a common ancestor in Ham, he did accept that slavery was inflicted upon Ham's descendants. In discussing the reasons why nations which are defeated and fall under alien rulers soon perish, he returns again to the subject of blacks. Disintegration of a people occurs when they "lose control of their own affairs and become the instrument of someone else;" for this reason, the black nations are as a rule submissive to slavery, because they have little that is essentially human and have attributes that are quite similar to dumb animals, as I have stated."[58]

It troubles us to read these opinions. Philosophers claim that humanity is one and the same. And this seems to include all of us. But they couch this sameness in such terms that certain races are excluded, since they hold forth people living in temperate zones as a human paradigm. The implication is that all human beings are admitted to the conversation of justice, indeed, to the conversation of philosophy itself but only if they conform to this paradigm. What deviates from it is merely the accidental other and has nothing to do with what is truly essential to the human nature.

So what really bothers us is Muslim philosophers' doctrine of essentialism and its picture of reality as consisting of a number of mutually independent substances, each having certain essential properties that ensure that they remain the same. Yet judgments of sameness carried an air of paradox even for Aristotle. "Sameness is a kind of oneness," he noted, "either of being more than one thing or when a thing is treated as more than one (as for instance when someone says that a thing is the same as itself which is to treat it as two things)."[59] So we find ourselves affirming that many items are one and the same, when in fact they are different. For example, "Bill Clinton is what Tony Blair is – a populist politician." For each thing has both similarities and differences with other things and are neither completely identical or absolutely other. Thus, the effort to bring about sameness invariably entails expulsion of difference. Here Karl Popper's observation is apposite: "Objects can be classified and can become similar or dissimilar only in this way – by being related to the needs of the classifier."

Still, one may ask whether the needs of the natural slaves were ever considered in this connection? Exactly who is the classifier in this instance? It is, in fact, difficult to tell. Classifiers have a way of disappearing from the frameworks that they create. This fact even Ibn Khaldūn noted:

> The inhabitants of the North are not called by their color, because the people who established the conventional meaning of words were themselves white. For this reason, whiteness was something usual and common and they did not see anything sufficiently remarkable in being white to cause then to use "white" as a special term.[60]

On these words one may take Tracy Fessenden's observation as a contemporary gloss: "Generally, black is clearly marked out as a category, whereas white, because it seems to be nothing in particular, manages also to be 'everything', coterminous with the entirety of human diversity."[61]

Is it not possible that those living in temperate zone might have dismissed certain human characteristics as inessential to the human species which those living in intemperate zones would have deemed essential? But how could underlings ever have dreamed of formulating a better statement of what their masters said about them? They would have found it difficult to even voice a clear alternative to the way they had been classified; for the very language in which they would have formulated such restatements was governed by a logic which assumed the stance of being universal. In a universal language the point of view of any one speaker is always absent, because it claims to speak for no one in particular. It, in fact, claims to speak for everyone, at least, for everyone who matters. Muslim philosophers' role in the framing of such a speakerless language can hardly be overlooked.

Appealing to the Voice

Before proceeding further, however, we should note that in Muslim law which races are enslaveable is not something fixed by nature. Slavery arises out of set of historical circumstances. Thus, the jurist Sarakhsī states: "The slave and the free are one genus . . . Slavery supervenes as an accident" and "emancipation annihilates this accidental slavery."[62] So it is clearly not the case that Muslims of the Middle Ages and later periods denied that slaves are human beings. Still, by the very practice of slavery they acted counter to the moral intuition that human beings are not intersubstitutable, that they "must be treated on every occasion in ways that reflect that their individuality conditions the way they limit our will." This brings us back to the question posed earlier:

51

Did Muslim philosophers like Alfārābī and Ibn Sīnā acknowledge that the individual voices of slaves could, in principle, limit the wills manifest in their master's voices or were they like mute animals to be pushed aside as the master made his way?

Simone Weil noted in this connection that when a person blocks our path and turns our steps away from the path on which we had been walking we know that he or she does not turn our steps away in the same manner as a street sign. To Weil this knowledge means that:

> The human beings around us exert just by their presence a power which belongs uniquely to themselves to stop, to diminish or modify each movement which our bodies design . . . no one stands up or moves about, or sits down again in quite the same fashion when he is alone in a room as when he has a visitor.[63]

One does not look into the eyes of another with the focus of jeweller examining a gem or the eye of a surgeon examining a patient. One's look softens before the eyes of another. Mobility is disarmed and a look of vulnerability is mirrored in one's glance. The face of another, then, is a surface on which one senses forces that issue directives that orders our behavior. Our response to these forces arises out of a willingness to take other people seriously as human beings. It informs our sense of justice in dealing with them.

Peter Winch believed that "treating a person justly involves treating with seriousness his own conception of himself, his own commitments and cares, his own understanding of his situation and of what the situation demands of him."[64] Raimund Gaita, commenting on Winch's remark, explains that taking someone seriously "is to see him as a potential partner in that conversational space in which we are answerable to the demand or to the plea that we try to invest our thoughts and our words with the authority of an individually achieved lucidity." For him "lucidity is what we refer to when we speak of people finding their own voice, of 'having something to say.'" He concludes: "Failing all that, we can have, at best, only an attenuated sense of what it is seriously to wrong them."[65]

The appeal to voice, then, appears to hold the key to conceiving the individuality characterizing human beings, the individuality that makes each of us irreplaceable. The appeal to the voice, for this reason, is also an appeal to the morality of speech, since the human voice reveals to us that sense of irreplaceable individuality that has been acknowledged as being internal to our sense of what it is to wrong someone. It is the voice, after all, that harbors our most idiosyncratic characteristics. Indeed, it shares this feature with our faces. The voice, then, holds the key to our sense of that human singularity, the reason why we believe that human souls cannot belong to the domain of resemblance or equivalence and why, from the moral standpoint, human souls cannot circulate in the sphere of commercial exchange as objects of the contract of sale. In fact, the human voice has historically been used to symbolize what is unique about each of us just as the inability and refusal to heed people's voices is used to symbolize the denial of their need for that recognition.

I approached this point earlier when I quoted Ibn Sīnā's view on the role of the voice in human affairs:

Man has in his nature the capacity to inform the other who is his partner by means of an established sign and he is specially adapted to what is suitable to that [sign] i.e., the *voice* . . . and after the voice the ostensive gesture . . . but the voice is more capable of signification than the gesture since the latter only guides to where [it wants] the glance of the eyes to fall.

It seems right, then, for him to emphasize the powers of the human voice over even the force of human gestures. The latter are only significant if we can translate them somehow into words. When I look out from my window, what proves to me that the figures that I see in the street are not hats and coats covering robots is that I can take the sounds they make as words that are intended to communicate. We recognize as human someone with whom we can speak. This, of course, seems precisely what the Moroccan Muslims, of whom the late nineteenth-historian an-Nāṣirī speaks, were unable to do. Chastising them for enslaving their co-religionists for no other apparent reason than their color, an-Nāṣirī writes: "How can a man who has scruples about his religion permit himself . . . to take their women as concubines, considering that this involves entering upon a sexual liaison of doubtful legality."[66]

It is useful to pause here in order for the reader to reflect on the profound indignity suffered by these slaves when measured by the standards of Muslim law. For the *Sharīʿa* demarcates the Muslim body into gender specific zones of shame (*ʿawra*). These zones of shame must be hidden from the sight of strangers. Access to such zones, visual or tactile, is licit for strangers only through the contract of marriage. Bodies of free persons thus circulate in a state of "sacred inviolability" (*ḥurma*). But when a female body becomes an object of the contract of sale public access to the zones of shame becomes licit. Indeed, the principle effect of the contract of sale is that this *ḥurma* utterly vanishes.[67] Therefore, jurists, particularly from the majority Ḥanafī school, took it for granted that "a man who buys a female slave is entitled to look at her, to uncover her legs, her arms, her breast and to touch her carefully 'to examine the softness of her skin.'"[68] So we must envision female slaves displayed in the markets of the Middle East naked or half-naked for potential buyers to examine for possible bodily defects.[69] This immediately shows us the disparity of treatment between slaves and those women Muslims would never have thought of enslaving.

Given the Islamization of West Africa, an-Nāṣirī argued, his contemporaries should have acted upon the assumption that its inhabitants were Muslim and not enslave them. Instead, he reports that since ancient times they have indulged in "the indiscriminate enslaving of the people of the Sūdān [i.e. West Africa]," importing "droves of them every year to be sold in the market places . . . where men trade in them as one would trade in beasts – nay worse than that"[70] He adds that: "people have become so inured . . . generation after generation, that many common folk believe that the reason for being enslaved according to Holy Law is merely that a man should be black in color and come from those regions."

Returning to our original point, what is important in all this for us is that these Moroccans could not acknowledge the full humanity of their slaves because they seemed unable to adequately interpret the intentions conveyed in their voices. At least, this seems to be the significance of an-Nāṣirī's warning to his contemporaries not to take

West African's denial of their Islam seriously. "No reliance," he says, "should be placed upon the protestations of a slave man or slave woman, as the jurists have ruled, since motives and circumstances differ in this regard." He warns:

> A seller may do them so much ill that they would not admit to anything which would affect their sale. Or a slave may have the objective of getting out of the hands of his master by any means, thus finding it easy to admit to slave status so that the sale may be promptly effected. Other motives may also exist.[71]

Yet when Muslim slave buyers looked into the Black faces of their co-religionists they failed to sense any force that would direct or order their behavior. They could not read off the imperative to which an-Nāṣirī exhorted them, the imperatives which Muslim religious scholars, in any case, had urged them for centuries to heed.

How could it have been otherwise? The majority of Muslim legal scholars had taught the principle of *tabādur*, the idea that speakers possess an innate disposition to make their intention manifest (*bayān al-mutakallim*). They backed this up with a corollary to the effect that the most apparent interpretation (*al-ẓāhir*) of the speaker's words is the intended one. No doubt it became a commonplace that taking a speaker's intention seriously is a matter of understanding the meaning of the speaker's words that comes most immediately to mind (*tabādur*) and was installed within the culture, even though it was a hermeneutic principle specifically formulated for the interpretation of sacred scripture. Speakers' meaning, therefore, was associated with the idea that the language of the Arabs represents a fixed deposit of vocables and corresponding meanings primordially established by an ideal community of Arabic-speakers. These idealized meanings must be mirrored in the intentions of any interlocutor. This is the theory of "*waḍʿu-l'lugha*" mentioned earlier. According to it, effective communication presupposes identical pronunciations, shared lexicons and grammatical norms. What is crucial in the reciprocity involved in verbal exchange, therefore, is identity of the participating elements of communication. However, such identity is best achieved when the elements can be idealized and wrenched from their ordinary contexts of utterance.

In fact, the jurist Ibn Qayyim al-Jawzīya (d. 1350) criticized legal theorists for doing just this. Here, Ibn Qayyim sees them as following the path of the philosophers "in abstracting meaning and assuming it absolutely free from all [contextual] stipulation."[72] And so the community of Arabic-speakers they looked to as establishing the language is formed on the exchange abstract entities, idealized signs of idealized referents so that they, for example, "affirm a human being that is neither tall nor short; neither white nor black; neither in time nor in space; neither motionless nor moving; neither in the world nor outside it; with no flesh, no bone, no nerve, no nail; possessed of no stature nor shadow; [such a human being is] uncharacterizable and undelimited" and "remain in a state of confusion whether to deny their existence in the external world and invalidate the essences they consider to merely absolute."[73] Ibn Qayyim is comparing the meaning contents they posit to Ibn Sīnā's common nature or natural universal. The latter neither exists nor fails to exist and is neither universal nor particular, neither in the mind nor outside it.[74]

No doubt the theory of *"waḍʿu-l'lugha"* is in the background, when the legal theorist Abū'l-Ḥusayn al-Baṣrī (d. 1044) reasons that:

> If it were possible for a speaker not to intend his speech to be understood, then it would be possible for a Black person to address an Arab in his language (*bi-zinjīya*), even though the Arab did not speak his language inasmuch as it is unnecessary to make the addressee understand; for the Arab has no apparent meaning (*ẓāhir*) [to attach to] the language of Blacks.[75]

That is, the language of Blacks is assumed to be opaque to Arabs and not immediately translatable. Is Abū'l-Ḥusayn's assumption valid? Certainly, it appears to be so, especially if we, like him, accept the principle of *tabādur*, which demands an identity in verbal productions and interpretations. Yet such a principle appears obvious only because a certain linguistic idiom employed by members of the dominant verbal community had in Abū'l-Ḥusayn's time become standardized.

But would not other idioms have also emerged from the repeated transactions occurring between slave traders, masters and Black slaves whose native language was other than Arabic? "Pidgin" or "contact languages" provide a vivid example of how linguistic norms can develop through *ad hoc* coping strategies among interlocutors who are otherwise different, unequal or even antagonistic. Effective communication then does not, in principle, presuppose identical pronunciation, shared lexicons, etc, any more than effective intellectual exchange presupposes shared cognitions or orientations. The non-identity of our verbal productions and interpretations does not automatically lead to verbal chaos.[76]

Still, a cultural dichotomy like *"ʿarabīya"* (i.e., Arabic) versus the language of the *"ʿajam"* (non-Arab) may cause one to think otherwise. The expression *"ʿajam"* in its etymology and semantic evolution reflects exactly the Greek term, *"barbaros"* and refers to people characterized by an obscure way of speaking. *ʿAjam* always bore in its connotation a contempt for non-Arabic-speakers. Certainly, this dichotomy lurks in the principle of *tabādur* and the associated theory of *"waḍʿu-l'lugha."* With the latter prevailing among the most educated speakers of Arabic, how was it possible to take any "pidgin" language seriously? Why would an-Nāṣirī's Moroccans be motivated to look further than the slave's patent denial that they were Muslims?

But one suspects that the problem goes deeper. It is not that the Moroccan slave buyers failed to look behind the slaves' denial of their Islam. The real problem is their failure to look behind the appearance of Blacks themselves. Why was this the case? The daily fact of societal description, what scholars like Masʿūdī reported about West Africans was already in place. Had not Ibn Khaldūn already told them what the people of the Sudan were like? So the latter were already chatted about even before they appeared in slave markets. Potential slave buyers would have only seen these reports materialize before their eyes prior to hearing any word they spoke. To a degree, perhaps, this is understandable. When we recognize even a loved one's face in a caricature, after all, our recognition is motivated by nothing anatomical. We see something we regard as essential to the personality of that person. This is why we cannot escape the language of caricaturist's art. Our perception tries to look behind the mask he draws only to find another one and the image he makes keeps doubling back on us *ad infinitum*. Who, then, amongst an-Nāṣirī's Moroccans could take seriously the Islam of a "people who are in general characterized by levity, excitability and great emotionality . . . eager to dance whenever they hear a melody [and] everywhere described as stupid"?

Just as their faces would have been veiled in a host of legends like Noah's cursing of Ham, the voices of West African Muslims would have been muffled by reports of philosophers, lawyers and historians, reports structured in time-honored oppositions like that of *'Arab* versus *'Ajam*. As far as legal theory and philosophy is concerned, then, the community of human speech is formed as an alliance *against* the stammerings, mispronunciations and regional accents as well as malapropisms "pidginisms," and other non-standard usages. Indeed, any community that forms itself on the exchange of idealized signs of idealized referents seems to be an alliance formed against what philosophy deems to be the opacity of the human voice, the voice of what Ibn Sīnā calls "external discourse" (*nuṭq khāriji*) as opposed to "internal discourse" (*nuṭq dākhilī*).[77] "Internal discourse" refers to "meanings" (*ma'ānī*) that fix the reference of terms and determine the truth-values of propositions. These meanings signify the common natures or natural universals criticized by Ibn Qayyim. In Ibn Sīnā's reasoning and that of other Peripatetics like Alfārābī "internal discourse" is "the same for all communities" because it is "given by nature" and differs from what is conventionally adopted.[78]

Recalling Karl Popper's advice cited above, we feel constrained to ask: for which communities are these meanings the same? Certainly, this sameness has not been posited in response to the needs of the natural slaves, not sub-Saharan Africans nor the inhabitants of the Russian steppes on Islam's borders whom, though already confessing Islam, their Muslim neighbors forcibly enslaved. We have already seen why this is the case. Our own conclusion, then, must be that in the view of Alfārābī and Ibn Sīnā, the community that is constituted when people share something in common, the community, that is, which is established on the human capacity to reason and to speak, does so only by excluding the barbarians – it excludes their utterances. But in excluding what they have to say it excludes their bodies as well. For Muslim Peripateticism loves to ignore what, in any case, philosophers have always tended to ignore: the fact that human speech is constrained to the life of the body.[79] This tendency manifests itself in Ibn Sīnā's statement that: "If it were possible for the interlocutor to become informed of his mental content (*mā fī nafsihi*) by some other device, then there would be no need for any verbal utterance (*lafẓ*) at all." That is, if it were possible, the voice could do without physical speech altogether just as, the human intellect, in his opinion, can do without the body. That the fulfilment of this aspiration is unfeasible Ibn Sīnā readily acknowledges, since "it is impossible for internal reflection to put meanings into any order without imagining expressions for them" and the imagination depends upon the bodily faculties of perception.[80]

Still, it is hard to see how Ibn Sīnā would even wish to separate words and voice from the body from which they issue, the body in which they resonate and thus "exert just by their presence a power which belongs uniquely to themselves to stop, to diminish or modify each movement which our bodies design." The words of our interlocutors do not acquire their power to limit our wills simply in the grammar of indicative or informative speech-acts. Such words are like bodily gestures and are just as physical as facial features. There are, it is true, those non-physical logical properties which Ibn Sīnā privileges as internal to language, meanings that fix reference and determine truth-values.

But more deeply inherent to language are aspects which do not refer and which yet themselves act. Austin called attention to this deeper aspect in his distinction between illocutionary as opposed to locutionary speech-acts or acts of uttering or inscribing. Illocutionary speech-acts are performed by way of locutionary acts so that "to perform a locutionary act is . . . is eo ipso to perform an illocutionary act."[81] Once such a distinction is in place, it immediately occurs to one that, while speech-acts like asserting, commanding, promising, etc. can be performed by uttering sentences, they can be performed in other ways as well. "One may say something," as Nicholas Wolterstorff has argued, "by producing a blaze, or smoke, or a sequence of light-flashes."[82] On this conception, language use involves more than words and sentences. It includes the entire context of utterance. The illocutionary force of utterances is easily detectable by a listener. Indeed, illocutionary uptake is a necessary condition of understanding any utterance. Without such uptake we cannot effectively hear the voices of others nor can they hear us. Speaking in your own voice and learning to listen to different voices, then, is a matter of deploying and interpreting illocutionary force.

But is not what Ibn Sīnā banishes in his logical reform of "external discourse" precisely this illocutionary force, a precise understanding of how words are to be taken? Like the artificial Latin of Western scholasticism, the Arabic he promotes is a language reformed according to the rules governing "internal discourse," a language that marks a half-way house on the road to the formalism of today's predicate calculus.[83] Ibn Sīnā's disembodied voice of "internal reflection" (*rawīya bāṭina*) or "internal discourse", in fact, corresponds to what Stanley Cavell and others have called the "metaphysical voice."

Cavell discovers in this "metaphysical voice" an ever-recurring prop in philosophy's perennial conspiracy to silence the human voice, at least, in its most politically potent form. "It is evident," he writes, "that the reign of repressive philosophical systematizing – sometimes called metaphysics, sometimes called logical analysis – has depended upon the suppression of the human voice"[84] and it is "as if what philosophy meant by logic, demanded in the name of rationality, the repression of voice."[85] Muslim Peripateticism emerges, therefore, as a subplot to that conspiracy uncovered by Cavell.

For the "metaphysical voice," the voice of Avicennan "internal discourse," automatically sabotages any attempt at that lucidity of which Raimund Gaita, for example, speaks. It offers no mode of access to that conversational space in which both master and slave can become answerable to any imperative commanding them to invest their words with an individually achieved lucidity. By lucidity, one means, the kind to which we refer when we speak of people finding their own voice and of having something to say, especially in the face of institutionally defined truths that have come to operate as modes of oppression. That is, lucidity is achieved when one maintains one's own voice in situations where the only statements that can be true and meaningful are those determined by ideal cities maximally purged of the noise of stammerings, mispronunciations and regional accents as well as malapropisms and other non-standard usages, cities, that is, which are purged of the voices of the oppressed.[86]

Conclusion

Muslims like an-Nāṣirī's contemporaries could have only behaved differently if they had possessed the moral ability to act in the appropriate way, an ability obviously not easily achieved given the constraints under which they exchanged information. Ibn Khaldūn's description of Blacks as a "people who are in general characterized by levity, excitability and great emotionality . . . eager to dance whenever they hear a melody [and] everywhere described as stupid", for us, is a caricature, to be sure. Yet it reveals how many of the Arabs of his time, both before and after, saw people from sub-Saharan Africa. Blacks did not appear to them as only accidentally incapable of anything as deep as Islam. They believed that they were that way not on the basis of any empirical generalization. Empirical generalizations are, at least, susceptible to disconfirming counter-examples. They believed that Blacks were that way essentially.[87] But through this denigration of spiritual lives of Black people also runs a denigration of the possibility of them thinking and reflecting as we have seen in Ibn Sīnā and Maimonides. Whatever signs they displayed of Islamization could only have appeared superficial to their North African neighbors. These neighbours thought, that is they were. And that they were like that is why they found it inconceivable that they should have been treated the same as other fellow Muslims.

How could it have become otherwise? Certainly, not through an education in philosophy. If building the community was more central to the concerns of Muslim philosophers than race, race, nevertheless, was a consideration. This became apparent in their adoption of the idea that the mutual meaningfulness of the words of a language must rest upon some kind of compact among its users, suggesting a quasi-political understanding of what it means for us to speak to one another, what it means to speak for oneself. Race became apparent when it is revealed to whom philosophers considered worth listening as well as whom they allowed to speak.

So while it is true that Alfārābī's virtuous city or Ibn Sīnā's just city are founded on the idea of communication as a mutual exchange of expressions. The value of those expressions reduce to a uniform value, an exchange value which excludes the noise of voices deemed too barbarous to participate in philosophy's perennial conversation. In fact, being a participant in the community of which Alfārābī and Ibn Sīnā' speak means surrendering the individuality of one's voice and assimilating it to voiceless and abstract variables and constants of formal logic. No doubt, logical constants and variables in their interchangeablity enjoy a certain kind of equality. Yet the equality suggested implies a replaceability repugnant to each human individual's uniqueness, the uniqueness conveyed by human voices, voices which harbor the idiosyncratic characteristics that make each of us irreplaceable. The human voice symbolizes what is unique about each of us. The inability and refusal to heed people's voices symbolizes the denial of that recognition.

But entering into conversation also means becoming "other" also for the "other." A true community forms when one exposes oneself to the "other," to the forces of those vocal powers that limit our wills. Yet above all this involves listening to the voice of the other, not affirming oneself and one's powers but becoming vulnerable to the unexpected, to contestation, to inculpation. Muslim Peripateticism's failure to deal with these moves in the morality and politics of speech means that it could not have taught Muslims to truly hear the voices of others. And because it could not have taught them this it could not have taught them to see the dignity of those naked West African Muslim women standing on blocks in the market waiting to be sold. Such women knew that their testimony to Muslim faith was true. They found verification for it not through Ibn Sīnā's "internal discourse" nor in the Arabic of an ideal community of speakers. They found verification in the feelings of shame and humiliation experienced in their own bodies.

But wherever the command posts of Alfārābī's virtuous city or Ibn Sīnā's just city are founded their citizens must obey its institutional imperative on pain of not being heard. This is the condition for the exchange of words whereby mutual recognition results, the condition for having one's voice taken seriously. Whoever speaks must employ a discourse manifesting the truths of the "just" and "virtuous" city, even if the "truths" dictated by that city are not one's own, even if they are, in fact, the instruments of one's own oppression. The corpus of truths established by Muslim philosophers thus shut out the articulation of any verities alien to its own. The only response it could have made to black Muslim slaves' testimony of their bodily humiliation is "You are incapable of truth."

Notes

1. See Louise Marlow, *Hierarchy and Egalitarianism in Islamic Thought* (Cambridge: Cambridge University Press, 1997), p. 2.
2. See Fazlur Rahman, *Islamic Methodology in History* (Islamabad, Pakistan: Islamic Research Institute, 1965), pp. 186–7.
3. David Ayalon, "The Mamluk Novice: On his Youthfulness and on his Original Religion," *Revue des Etudes Islamiques*, 56, 6. Reprinted in D. Ayalon, *Islam and the Abode of War* (London: Variorum Reprint, 1994), pp. 1–8.
4. John Hunwick, "Islamic Law and Polemics on Race and Slavery in North and West Africa (16th–18th Century)," in *Slavery in the Islamic Middle East*, ed. Shaun Marmon (Princeton: Markus Wiener Publishers, 1999), p. 43.
5. Gilles Deleuze, *Difference and Repetition* (London: Athlone, 1994), p. 1.
6. Abū Bakr Muḥammad ibn Abī Sahl as-Sarakhsī, *al-Mabsūṭ*, XV, p. 134, quoted in Baber Johansen, "The Valorisation of the Human Body in Muslim Sunni Law," in *Law and Society in Islam*, ed. Devin Stewart, Baber Johansen and Amy Singer (Princeton: Marcus Wiener, 1996), pp. 72, 100 n.4.
7. al-ʿAynī, *Sharh al-Kanz*, II, p. 182, quoted in Shaun E. Marmon, "Domestic Slavery in the Mamluk Empire," in *Slavery in the Islamic Middle East*, p. 7.
8. Ibid.

9. *Nicomachean Ethics*, ed. I. Bywater (Oxford: Clarendon Press, 1890), 1133a10–11; Tr. *The Complete Works of Aristotle*, ed. Jonathan Barnes (Princeton: Princeton University Press, 1984), vol. II, 1788.

10. A. Muḥammad, *Muqaddima Ibn Khaldūn* (Cairo: n.d.), p. 35ff. Tr. Franz Rosenthal, *The Muqaddimah: An Introduction to History* (New York: Bollingen Foundation, n.d.) vol. I, p. 89ff.

11. Alfārābī, *al-Fuṣūl al-Madanī*, ed. and tr. D. M. Dunlop (Cambridge: Cambridge University Press, 1961) pp. 53–4.

12. Abū Naṣr al-Fārābī, *Mabādiʾ ārā ahl al-madīna al-fāḍila*, ed. and tr. R. Walzer (Oxford: Oxford University Press, 1985), pp. 228–9.

13. Abū ʿAlī Ibn Sīnā, *ash-Shifāʾ: Ilāhīyāt*, ed. G. Anawati and S. Zayed (Cairo: al-Hayʾa al-ʿĀmma li-Shuʾūn al-Maṭābiʿ al-Amīrīya, 1960.) (1380), p. 441. Tr. in R. Lerner and M. Mahdi (eds), *Medieval Political Philosophy: A Sourcebook* (Ithaca, NY: Cornell University Press, 1963), p. 99.

14. *Avicenna's De Anima*, ed. Fazlur Rahman (London: Oxford University Press, 1959), pp. 203–4.

15. ʿAḍūḍuʾl-Milla waʾd-Dīn, *Sharḥ Mukhaṣar al-Muntahā li Uṣūlī li-Ibnuʾl-Ḥājib*, 2nd edn. (Beirut: Dārul-Kutubiʾl-ʿImmīya, 1983), p. 115. Cf. Aristotle, *Politics*, 1. 2.

16. Bernard Weiss, "ʿIlm al-Waḍʾ: An Introductory Account of a Later Muslim Philological Science," *Arabica*, 34 (1987), p. 343.

17. *Nicomachean Ethics*, 1131a24–9. English tr. vol. II, 1786.

18. *Kitāb ash-Shifāʾ: al-Ilāhīyāt* (2), 453, pp. 6–9.

19. Mūsā Ibn Maimūn, *Dilālat al-ḥāʾirīn*, ed. Husayn Atay (Ankara: 1972), iii, ch. 51.

20. *Nicomachean Ethics*, 1161b1. English tr. vol. II, 1835. Aristotle adds that though "there can be on friendship with a slave as slave, there can be [insofar as] as he is a human being."

21. Raimund Gaita, *Good and Evil: An Absolute Conception* (London: Macmillan, 1991), p. 154.

22. See Yvonne Seng, "A Liminal State: Slavery in Sixteenth Century Istanbul," in *Slavery in the Islamic Middle East*, p. 25.

23. Baber Johansen, "The Valorisation of the Human Body in Muslim Sunni Law," pp. 72–3.

24. *Politics*, 1282b14.

25. On this institution see Farhat Ziadeh, "Equality (*kafāʾa*) in the Muslim Law of Marriage," *American Journal of Comparative Law*, 6 (1957). Sunni Islamic law is interpreted according to four major legal schools.

26. See Danel Pipes, "Mawlas: Freed Slaves and Converts in Early Islam," in J. R. Willis (ed.), *Slaves and Slavery in Muslim Africa* (London, Frank Cass, 1985), p. 208.

27. Cf. J. R. Willis, "Islam and the Ideology of Enslavement," in J. R. Willis (ed.), *Slaves and Slavery in Muslim Africa*. Willis's source for the analogy he draws between marriage and slavery is F. H. Ruxton, *Maliki Law* (London: 1916), chs V and XI. However, Muslim jurists declare that "the female sex is no object of trade" See Abū Bakr, b. Masʿūd al-Kasānī, *Kitāb Badāʾi aṣ-ṣanāʾiʿ fī tartīb ash-sharāʾiʿ* (Cairo: 1910) tr. and cited in Johansen, "The Valorisation of the Human Body in Muslim Sunni Law," p. 77.

28. See Patricia Crone, *Roman, Provincial and Islamic Law: The Origins of the Islamic Patronate* (Cambridge: Cambridge University Press, 1987), pp. 80–1, who notes exceptions to this rule in the Umayyad period.

29. See Joseph Schacht, *An Introduction to Islamic Law* (Oxford: Oxford University Press, 1964), pp. 162–3.

30. Cf. Bernard Lewis, *Race and Slavery in the Middle East* (Oxford: Oxford University Press, 1990), ch. 12.

31. According to the fourteenth-century jurist Maḥmūd ibn Aḥmad al-ʿAynī. See his *an-Niyāba fī sharḥ al hidāya*, 2nd edn (Beirut: Dār al-Fikr, 1411 AH/1990 CE), vol. II, p. 178.

32. John Hunwick, "Black Africans in the Islamic World: An Understudied Dimension of the Black Diaspora," *Taʾrikh*, vol. V, no. 1 (1975), p. 35.

33. Albertine Jwaideh and J. W. Cox, "The Black Slaves of Turkish Arabia During the 19th Century," *Slavery and Abolition*, 9:3 (1988), pp. 45–59.

34. See Stanley Cavell quoting John Milton in *Conditions Handsome and Unhandsome* (Chicago: University of Chicago Press, 1990), p. 104.

35. *Kitāb ash-Shifāʾ: al-Ilāhīyāt* (2), p. 450.

36. At least, this is the case unless previously stipulated in a prior agreement by the partners to the contract that the exchange should be bilateral. Cf. Crone, *Roman, Provincial and Islamic Law*, ch. 3.

37. Baber Johansen, "The Valorisation of the Human Body in Muslim Sunni Law," p. 98.

38. See *Nichomachean Ethics*, 1133b6–28. English tr. vol. II, 1789.

39. Ibid.

40. Baber Johansen, "The Valorisation of the Human Body in Muslim Sunni Law," p. 74.

41. Ibid., p. 233.

42. Abū Nasr al-Fārābī, *al-Siyāsa al-madanīya* (Beirut: 1964), p. 77.

43. *The Fusul al Madani of al-Farabi* (Aphorisms of the Statesman), ed. D. M. Dunlop (Cambridge: Cambridge University Press, 1961), p. 57. Cf. Aristotle, *Politics*, 1256b24–5.

44. *Kitāb ash-Shifāʾ: al-Ilāhīyāt* (2), 453, pp. 6–9.

45. *Kitāb ash-Shifāʾ: fiʾn-Nafs*, p. 223.

46. *Ithbātuʾn-nabuwa*, ed. Michael Marmura (Beirut: Dār an-Nahar, 1968), p. 43. Tr. Michael Marmura, "On the Proof of Prophecies and the Interpretation of Symbols and Metaphors," in R. Lerner and M. Mahdi (eds), *Medieval Political Philosophy: A Source Book*, p. 113.

47. See Hossein Ziaʾi, *Knowledge and Illumination* (Atlanta, GA: Scholars Press, 1990), pp. 19–20.

48. *Kitāb al-Muʿtabar*, ed. Şerefettin Yaltkaya (Haydarabad: 1938) (1357), ii, 303, pp. 18–22; 440, pp. 1–2.

49. Ibid., ii, 387, pp. 4–6.

50. *Muqaddima*, Arabic, p. 74; English, vol. II, p. 171. For the poem's reference see Rosenthal's footnote.

51. This is the ninth-century thinker called the "Father of Arab philosophy. See M. Abū Rīda, *Rasāʾil al-Kindī al-falsalfīya* (Cairo: Dār al-Fikriʾl-ʿArabī, 1950–3).

52. *Muqaddima*, Arabic, pp. 73–4; English, vol. I, pp. 169–70.

53. Ibid., English, vol. I, p. 174.

54. Ibid., Arabic, p. 72; English, vol. I, p. 169.

55. Ibid., Arabic, p. 72; English, vol. I, p. 168.

56. Ibid., Arabic, p. 74; English, vol. I, p. 174.

57. Ibid., Arabic, p. 74; English, vol. I, p. 174.

58. Ibid., Arabic, p. 129; English, p. 301.

59. *Metaphysics, Books Γ, Δ, E*, tr. C. Kirwan (Oxford: Clarendon Press, 1971), 1018a7–9.

60. *Muqaddima*, Arabic, pp. 73–4; English, vol. I, pp. 169–70.

61. Tracy Fessenden, "The Soul of America," in *Perspectives on Embodiment*, ed. Gail Weiss and Honi Fern Haber (Routledge: New York/London, 1999), p. 23.

62. as-Sarakhsī, *al-Mabsūt*, XII, pp. 83–4, quoted in Johansen, "The Valorisation of the Human Body," p. 82, with a slightly different translation.

63. Simone Weil, "The Iliad: A Poem of Might' in *Intimations of Christianity Amongst the Ancient Greeks* (London: Routledge & Kegan Paul, 1957) 28.

64. Quoted by Raimund Gaita in *A Common Humanity* (London: Routledge, 2000), p. 59.

65. Ibid.

66. Quoted in John Hunwick "Islamic Law and Polemics or Race and Slavery in North and West Africa (16th–18th Century)", 61.

67. Ibid., pp. 75–6.

68. Baber Johansen, "The Valorisation of the Human Body," p. 80.

69. See Yusif Rāgib, "Les Marchés aux Esclaves en Terre d'Islam," in *Mercatie Mercanti nell'Alto Medioevo L'Area Euroasiatica c L'Area Mediterranea* (Spoleto: Presso La Sede del Centro, 1993).

70. Quoted in John Hunwick, "Islamic Law and Polemics," p. 60.

71. Ibid., p. 61.

72. Muhammad al-Mawṣilī, *Mukhtaṣar al-Ṣawāʿiq al-Mursala ʿalāʾl-Jahmīya waʾl-Muʿaṭṭila lʾIbni Qayyim al-Jawzīya* (Beirut: Dāruʾl-Kutub al-ʿIlmīya, 1985) (1405), p. 265.

73. Ibid.

74. *al-Shifāʾ: al-Manṭiq: al-Madkhal*, ed. A. Anawati. M. Khodayri and F. Ahwani (Cairo: General Egyptian Book Organisation, 1953), p. 15. Cf. *ash-Shifāʾ: Ilāhīyāt* (1), pp. 195–7.

75. Abūʾi-Husayn al. Baṣrī. *al-Muʿtamad fī Uṣūliʾl-Fiqh*, ed. K. al-Mays (Beirut: DāruʾKutubiʾl-ʿIlmīya, 1983), I. 316.

76. Cf. Donald Davidson, "A Nice Derangement of Epitaphs," in *Truth and Interpretation: Perspectives on the Philosophy of Donald Davidson*, ed. Ernest LePore (Oxford: Basil Blackwell, 1986), pp. 443–6.

77. *Kitāb ash-Shifāʾ: al-Manṭiq: al-Madkhal*, p. 22.

78. See *Alfarabi's Commentary and Short Treatise on Aristotle's "De Interpretatione,"* ed. and tr. F. Zimmerman (Oxford: Oxford University Press, 1987), pp. 12–13.

79. Cf. Stanley Cavell, *Philosophical Passages: Wingenstein, Emerson, Austia, Derrida* (Oxford: Blackwell, 1995), p. 53.

80. *Kitāb ash-Shifāʾ: al-Manṭiq: al-Madkhal*, p. 21.

81. J. L. Austin, *How to Do Things with Words*, ed. J. O. Urmson (London: Oxford University Press, 1962), p. 98.

82. Nicholas Wolterstorff, *Divine Discourse* (Cambridge: Cambridge University Press, 1995), p. 13.

83. Ordinary Arabic, e.g., lacks a copula "Yet this is something," Alfārābī observes, "that is needed in the theoretical sciences and in the discipline of logic." Hence, logicians resort to the artificial expedient of utilizing the third person masculine. "*huwa*" (he) in place of the Greek copula "*esti*" to fulfill the syntactical requirements of Aristotelian formal logic. This is one way the words of external discourse must be restricted and refined for the proper conduct of science.

84. Stanley Cavell, "The Politics of Interpretation," in *Themes Out of School* (San Francisco: North Point Press, 1984), p. 48.

85. Stanley Cavell, *A Pitch of Philosophy* (Cambridge, MA: Harvard University Press, 1996), p. 69.

86. Cf. Alphonso Lingus, *The Community of Those Who Have Nothing in Common* (Bloomington, IN: University of Indiana Press, 1994), pp. 69–106.

87. For this formulation see Raimund Gaita in *A Common Humanity*.

CHAPTER 4

Patriarchy and Slavery in Hobbes's Political Philosophy

TOMMY L. LOTT

Recently Hobbes has been criticized for maintaining a biased view of gender and race. Given the central place in his political theory occupied by his justification of colonial conquest, this criticism appears not difficult to sustain. Yet, some of the criticism is based on a misrepresentation of his doctrine. His view of gender and race demands a more nuanced interpretation in the light of his remarks regarding human equality. One major source of confusion has been his realist revision of the notion of equality to mean only that humans have an equal ability to kill each other. I address the question of whether his notion of equality is consistent with his endorsement of patriarchy by taking into account important passages in his major political works in which he not only acknowledges that a patriarchal commonwealth is an *artificial* social arrangement, but also presents matriarchy as an alternative. After a brief consideration of some of the recent criticism, I discuss Hobbes's neglected remarks that suggest a different line of thought regarding the role of gender and race in his political philosophy. I want to draw attention to the manner in which the idea of a social contract as an artificial bond allows Hobbes to represent other forms of subordination based on race and class as manifestations of patriarchy.

In his account of sovereignty by acquisition, Hobbes characterizes the transition from the state of nature to civil society in terms of a social evolution from paternal to despotic dominion. His assimilation of the sovereign of a commonwealth to the master of a household is explained by reference to a political-economic model of the household involving the subordination of women and children along with servants and slaves. One important implication of his account of dominion is that the subordination of a slave in a household is also a manifestation of patriarchy. My reflections on Hobbes's account of authority in the household and in civil society highlight his view of gender and race. Although Hobbes was directly involved in the affairs of the

Virginia Company, he does not discuss the Atlantic slave trade. I extend his view to slavery based on race.[1] For my limited purpose, it is needless to deny that Hobbes operated with many European male biases. These biases notwithstanding, he deserves credit for having challenged some of the fallacious reasoning used to support the prevailing idea that patriarchy is natural. Indeed, as I will argue, he is constrained by his political theory to acknowledge the artificial nature of male authority in the household and the state.[2]

Hobbes conceived the commonwealth in terms of a series of negotiated agreements within, and among, households. There are passages in his major political works that indicate he understood gender and race to be social categories largely created for political-cal economic purposes. He recognizes a fundamental role that violence plays in the early formation of the family and commonwealth. This realist aspect of his doctrine is a key to understanding several features of his political theory that provide a rationale for a racialized patriarchy. Although Hobbes's conception of monarchy supports the perpetuation of patriarchy through kinship, he does not rely on gender, or race per se, as criteria on which to ground the authority of a head of household, or sovereign, for in some of his remarks he makes clear that these positions need not always be filled by white men.

Paternal Dominion and Political Obligation

Hobbes employs his social contract theory to account for the origin of the household, but his account of the household also figures into his account of the origin of the state.[3] Commentators have drawn in question Hobbes's reasoning regarding the contract that originally establishes authority in the household. Some are puzzled as to how such an agreement, which precedes the social contract establishing civil society, could ever transpire if women are assumed to be rational and equal in the state of nature.[4] Susan Moller Okin has questioned the coherence of Hobbes's account of paternal dominion. She asks, "if women are the original sovereigns over their children how did men become patriarchs, while still in the state of nature?"[5] She takes Hobbes's remark in the *Dialogue* that "the Father of the Family by the Law of nature was absolute Lord of his Wife and Children" to reveal his inconsistency.[6] Citing his statement in *Leviathan* that "for the most part Commonwealths have been erected by the Fathers, not by the Mothers of families", she concludes that he was "not prepared" to decide the issue of gender equality one way or the other and only pays "lip service" to the idea of a female sovereign (*Leviathan*, 20, 4, p. 129). According to Okin, "Given his initial premises of human equality and egoism, there was no way that Hobbes could logically arrive at the institution of the patriarchal family, on which his political structure is based, for this institution depends on the assumption of the radical inequality of women."[7] Underlying the concern Okin raises is the question of whether Hobbes's view of gender is consistent with his view of equality.

Okin's puzzle rests on the idea that sovereignty by institution is the best model of Hobbes's political theory. But his natural rights argument to show the legitimacy of sovereignty by acquisition provides his justification of patriarchy. In chapter 20 of

Leviathan, the idea of conquest frames his discussion of the generation of a commonwealth. He speaks of the growth and expansion of nuclear families in the state of nature as a social formation created through conquest. A "patrimonial kingdom" is the outcome of the merging of small families to become larger, an endeavor that occurs either voluntarily or by force.[8] An overriding concern with security in a state of nature provides sufficient motivation for each member's decision to enter into a household arrangement that establishes "paternal" dominion (ibid., 20, 4, p. 128). Hobbes's description of life in a state of nature in chapter 13 as a "solitary" existence is misleading, for this image is entirely superseded in chapter 20 by the idea of a family household providing security. The fact that, in chapter 13, Hobbes mentions as a source of diffidence the threat of being dispossessed, not only of one's person, but also of "wives, children, and cattle" cautions against adhering too strictly to his individualiztic rhetoric regarding survival. Even more telling in this regard is his reply to the fool in chapter 15 of *Leviathan*. There he makes explicit his presupposition that groups are involved in war, wherein every man to every man . . . is an enemy." He claims that, by selectively breaking disadvantageous agreements in the state of nature, the fool risks losing confederates that are necessary for defense.[9]

In *Leviathan*, chapter 13, Hobbes explains the cause of conflict in the state of nature in terms of three factors: competition, diffidence and glory. The insecurity fostered by the few who are motivated by glory to seek domination over others in turn produces diffidence in everyone else, who in anticipation of being dispossessed of their "wives, children, and cattle" adopt a first-strike defense strategy (ibid., 13, 7, p. 76). Hobbes argues that invasion of a neighbor is a recourse everyone must consider as a rational means of self-preservation under such conditions.

> Also, because there be some that taking pleasure in contemplating their own power in the acts of conquest, which they pursue farther than their security requires, if others (that otherwise would be glad to be at ease within modest bounds) should not by invasion increase their power, they would not be able, long time, by standing only on their defence, to subsist. And by consequence, such augmentation of dominion over men being necessary to a man's conservation, it ought to be allowed him. (Ibid., 13, 4, p. 75)

The state of nature is an extremely dangerous situation, not so much because of competition for resources, but due to the fear and insecurity that renders invasion and conquest a rational means of self-defense for modest people. In this situation the primary function of a head of household is to provide protection. For this reason, Hobbes maintains that authority and obligation within the household rests on the same ground as authority and obligation in the state. Members of a household, and subjects in a commonwealth, are obligated by an agreement to exchange obedience for protection. Obligation ceases when that condition is not met.

Although Hobbes does not spell this out in each of his major works, the process by which the state evolves from the merging of several households is inextricable from the process by which the household unit is initially formed. It is worth noting the variation in language Hobbes uses to define the family. An important shift in his view of gender relations in the family is reflected in the fact that he includes women in his definition only in *Elements of Law*. He states, "And the whole consisting of the father or mother or both, and of the children, and of the servants, is called a FAMILY; wherein the father or master of the family is sovereign of the same; and the rest (both children and servants equally) subjects."[10] His explicit reference to women is changed in *De Cive* to a statement that mentions only fathers, sons, and servants. "A *Father*, with, his *sonnes* and *servants* growne into a civill Person by vertue of his paternall jurisdiction, is called a FAMILY."[11] Again women are not mentioned in *Leviathan*. Instead he stipulates that a family can consist of "a man and his children, or of a man and his servants, or of a man and his children and servants together" (*Leviathan*, 20, 15, p. 132). With Okin's question regarding Hobbes's account of the origin of the patriarchal household in mind I want to consider whether these alterations in his definition of the family reflect an important shift in his view of the role of women in the family. In particular, I want to address her worry that, on Hobbes's account, the mother has no good reason to relinquish sovereignty over herself and her children in a state of nature. The key phrase I would like to emphasize in the passage she quotes (above) from the *Dialogue* is Hobbes's qualifying remark "for the most part" with reference to the prevalence of male-headed households. Before I turn to consider the implications of this remark for Okin's interpretation I would like to add another charge to the criticism of Hobbes's view of gender.

The Transfer of Mother-right

Christine Di Stefano has criticized Hobbes for conceiving the state of nature in masculine terms that deny maternity.[12] She takes Hobbes's view of the state of nature to be entirely hypothetical. It is "an imaginary zone which represents an intermediary state of reconstruction from the building blocks of human nature, the passions, to the completed architecture of civil society."[13] Citing his use of the metaphor about mushrooms in *De Cive*, she claims, "As a latent image in *Leviathan*, it provides an indispensable means of access to the gender-specific symbolic and emotional substructure of his state of nature."[14] She points out that the ideological function of this metaphor is to advance the idea "that men are not born of, much less nutured by, women, or anyone else for that matter."[15] She concludes that "Maternal authority embodies a view of authority to which Hobbes's scheme is thoroughly opposed."[16] Di Stefano goes on to take Hobbes to task on a number of related points, but I want to focus on her criticism of the biased view of gender Hobbes presents in his account of the state of nature.

One quite obvious shortcoming of Di Stefano's interpretation of Hobbes's view of the state of nature is the absence of *any* reference to his remarks regarding women sovereigns and mother-right in her discussion of his view.[17] For Hobbes, the formation of household relations in the state of nature involves a transition similar to the transition from the state of nature to civil society. In either case, questions of dominion and authority are decided on the basis of contracts or agreements. Mother-right arises not from having borne the infant, but from having nurtured and protected it. In turn, having received the benefit of preservation, the infant is tacitly obligated to obey the mother. Mother-right is grounded on the infant's exchange of obedience for preservation. What is important to note here is that Hobbes appeals to consent, even in the case of a newborn child, as a criterion to determine the title of dominion.[18]

The fact that Hobbes's statements regarding mother-right, along with his general discussion of the formation of the household in a state of nature, occur in the context of his account of conquest and sovereignty by acquisition indicates a realist perspective that recognizes the historical importance of violence and extortion in establishing political obligation. In *Elements of Law*, Hobbes's earliest political work, he maintains that the mother has the initial right and what needs to be explained is "how the father, or any other man, pretendeth by the mother" (*Elements*, 4, 1, p. 132). He raises two concerns that have a direct bearing on his contractarian view. After pointing out that father-right can only be established after birth, and that mother-right begins with a pregnant woman's propriety to her own body "of whose body it is part, till the time of separation," he tells us,

> [T]hey show not, neither can I find out by what coherence, either generation inferreth dominion, or advantage of so much strength, which, for the most part, a man hath more than a woman, should generally and universally entitle the father to a propriety in the child, and take it away from the mother. (Ibid., 4, 2, p. 132)

With regard to the contractarian ground for the transfer of dominion from mother to father, he cites two ways for "the pretences which a man may have to dominion over a child by the right of the mother" (ibid., 4, 4, p. 133). This dominion is justified as a product of conquest whereby the mother is coerced into servitude: "And thus the children of the servant are the goods of the master in *perpetuum*" (ibid., 4, 4, p. 133). There is no reason, however, to assume that women will always enter into such an arrangement. Hobbes refers to the case of the Amazons to illustrate how paternal dominion can be grounded on a covenant of cohabitation, or copulation, only that amounts "not to subjection between a man and woman" (ibid., 4, 5, p. 133). What must also be noted here is that Hobbes adds an appeal to empirical evidence of women surviving in the state of nature as equal to his logical refutation of the idea that the father, and not the mother, becomes Lord "by reason of the preeminence of sexe" (*De Cive*, 9, p. 122). He was prepared to defend a view of gender equality on anthropological grounds.

With the argument that the mother's will determines dominion, Hobbes aimed to demonstrate that mother-right is not grounded simply on having given birth to the child. But again there is an important shift in his account of what constitutes the mother's will. Although he maintains in all three major works that, as primary caretaker, the mother has the option to refuse to nourish her newborn, hence, her will is expressed in choosing to preserve her infant, in *De Cive* he adds the statement that since in the state of nature the father cannot be known but by the testimony of the mother, the "birth followes the belley" (ibid., 9, 3, p. 123). Aside from this remark, he does not mention in *De Cive* or *Leviathan* the earlier claim that the mother has propriety in her own body, of which the unborn is a part. There is even greater emphasis in *Leviathan* on the contractarian ground of the transfer of mother-right to the father.

Consistent with his earlier view, Hobbes can admit that the infant is first in the power of the mother, for he focuses on her decision to either nourish or expose the infant as a sign of her will to enter into a contractual relation that establishes her title of dominion. If she chooses to expose the infant, Hobbes points out that "the dominion is in him that nourisheth it. For it ought to obey him by whom it is preserved" (*Leviathan*, 70, 5, p. 130). The implied transfer of mother-right occurs when, having renounced it by her act of exposing the infant, the father's act of nourishing satisfies the conditions of a tacit agreement. In accordance with the demands of his political theory, Hobbes wanted a gender-neutral concept of maternity.

The best way to meet Di Stefano's objection to Hobbes's use of the metaphor about mushrooms is to accept it. I believe, however, a more adequate understanding of Hobbes's doctrine can be gained from considering how this metaphor is supposed to indicate the contractarian ground of dominion. Hobbes's remarks can be placed in relief by considering the passage containing the metaphor from *De Cive* in relation to parallel passages in his other works. He states,

> Let us return again to the state of nature, and consider men as if but even now sprung out of the earth, and suddainly (*like* Mushromes) come to full maturity without all kind of engagement to each other. There are but three wayes only whereby one can have the *Dominion* over the *Person* of another. (*De Cive*, 8, 1, p. 117)

Hobbes aims to set up his discussion of the three ways of establishing dominion in the state of nature. In his earlier work, *Elements of Law*, he makes essentially the same statement without the use of the metaphor. He tells us,

> Considering men therefore again in the state of nature, without covenants or subjection one to another, as if they were but even now all at once created male and female there be three titles only, by which one man may have right and dominion over another; whereof two may take place presently, and those are: voluntary offer of subjection, and yielding by compulsion; the third is to take place, upon the supposition of children begotten amongst them. (*Elements*, 3, 2, p. 127)

Notice that Hobbes explicitly refers to women and men. Ironically, the asexual meaning of the metaphor suggests a denial of maternity, as Di Stefano claims, yet, rather than deny maternity, Hobbes presupposes it in order to privilege the mother's act of nurturing, over her act of merely giving birth, as a sign of her will to enter into a contractual arrangement with her infant. In *Leviathan* he states,

> But the question lieth now in the state of mere nature, where there are supposed no laws of matrimony, no laws for the education of children, but the law of nature, and the natural inclination of the sexes, one to another, and to their children. In this condition of mere nature either the parents between themselves dispose of the dominion over the child by contract or do not dispose thereof at all. If they dispose thereof, the right passeth according to the contract. (*Leviathan*, 20, 4, p. 129)

There is a very important reason for Hobbes's greater emphasis on the mother's act of nurturing rather than on her giving birth to explain her authority over her infant and the latter's obligation to the mother. He wanted to ground mother-right on a tacit contract, and, equally important, he wanted to establish a contractarian ground for the transfer of mother-right to the father. If the ground of mother-right is a woman's propriety in her own body, then Hobbes has no contractarian ground on which to account for the transfer to father-right.[19]

The basic scheme of presenting his account of "voluntary" subjection before he discusses "forced" subjection remains the same in *Elements of Law*, *De Cive*, and *Leviathan*. Although he consistently couches the explanation of the contractarian grounds of dominion in terms of his justification of conquest, it is worth noting that in *Leviathan* he breaks with his earlier practice of including sovereignty by institution under the heading of dominion. With no reference to the metaphor about mushrooms, he introduces his account of the right of dominion by first stating the conditions under which extorted agreements from the vanquished justify sovereignty by acquisition, and points out that such agreements are no less binding than those incurred voluntarily. He then turns to discuss obligations arising from reproduction and conquest. In no uncertain terms he tells us that "Dominion is acquired two ways: By generation and by conquest" (ibid., 20, 4, p. 128). As I have already noted, the fact that Hobbes's discussion of obligation in the household occurs in the context of his account of conquest raises a fundamental question regarding the application of his theory of obligation to explain social relations. Here I want to draw attention to his reliance on extorted promises as a consensual ground of social and political obligation. When he presents his view of the state of nature as a hypothetical construct – i.e., as an inference from the passions – he is at liberty to describe the transition to civil society in any order. One purpose of the metaphor about mushrooms is to facilitate Hobbes's abstraction of the contractarian principles he needs for the theory of obligation he advances on the basis of reason in his political treatises from the underlying anthropological view he maintains on empirical ground. This latter view is displayed in historical works such as *Behemoth* and the *Dialogue*.[20] The argument for political obligation in all of his political works is tantamount to an argument for the validity of extorted agreements, an idea he wanted to maintain on the basis of reason and experience.

I have suggested that Hobbes presents his theory of political obligation in reverse order because the argument in his political treatises is based on reason. Given that his strategy was to persuade on logical grounds, that argument need only be consistent with experience. In his political treatises he begins with a discussion of sovereignty by institution, followed by a discussion of sovereignty by acquisition, under the rubric of which he includes a discussion of authority in the household. His debate with Brahmall, Hobbes indicates his awareness that the idea of a social contract that authorizes an absolute sovereign is better received when grounded on a voluntary act of consent, and becomes less favorable when grounded on coerced agreements.

Amazons and Savages in Hobbes's Anthropological View

For this reason, sovereignty by institution gets center stage as the model of the social contract in his political treatises. When he relies on history to support his theory, however, he chooses to highlight a conquest model. In the *Dialogue*, for instance, he not only gives up the state of nature construct – as an inference from the passions – but appeals to a straightforward history of the Norman conquest of England to illustrate his political theory.[21] To the extent that Hobbes intended *Behemoth* to be an application of his political theory to the English Civil War, and, similarly, the *Dialogue* to be an application of his political theory to English law, it seems an understatement to say that in neither case is there a need to speak of a state of nature in hypothetical terms.[22] With only elliptical references to the conditions that obtain in the state of nature, he relies instead on a discussion of various aspects of international relations and civil war – examples used to illustrate his concept of the state of nature in chapter 13 of *Leviathan*. The realist dimensions of Hobbes's political theory reflect his desire to have his political philosophy confirmed by experience. One reason Hobbes's view of gender appears inconsistent is that in the *Dialogue* he limits the exchanges to a description of the world as it is, but in his political treatises he challenges certain views, such as Aristotle's, that had become orthodox.[23]

Hobbes's reference to the Amazons as a historical illustration of an alternative to patriarchy is designed to show several things. The main purpose is to provide a counterexample to the claim that men are naturally superior to women. He takes this case to constitute empirical evidence that there is not always a difference of strength or prudence between men and women sufficient to determine paternal right without war. Secondly, he wanted to show that paternal right is grounded on contracts that, even in violent, life-threatening circumstances, sometimes require men to acknowledge women as equals. He tells us,

> [T]he inequality of their naturall forces is not so great, that the *man* could get the Dominion over the women without warre. And custome also contradicts not; for *women*, namely Amazons, have in former times waged war against their adversaries, and disposed of their children at their own wils, and at this day in divers places, women are invested with the *principall authority*. Neither doe their husbands dispose of their *children*, but *themselves*; which in truth they do *by the right of nature*. (*De Cive*, 9, 3, p. 122)

When Hobbes introduces the Amazon example in *Leviathan* he uses the phrase "We find in history" (*Leviathan*, 20, 4, p. 129). By this he meant to characterize his statement as evidence. The anthropological view of gender he invokes in *Behemoth* and the *Dialogue*, however, makes no reference to Amazons. Perhaps he wanted this example to serve a theoretical purpose, namely, to support his argument regarding gender equality that was based on reason. But what about his view of women based on experience? Immediately after he presents the Amazon case in the above quote from *De Cive*, he speaks of other societies in which women retain mother-right. I want to consider the question of whether Hobbes believed there were alternatives to patriarchy in relation to his view of nonEuropean societies. In particular, I want to consider whether "savages" have a function similar to "Amazons" in Hobbes's account of the state of nature.[24] What, then, was Hobbes's anthropological view and how was it tailored to fit his political theory?

Charles Mills maintains that Hobbes, along with Locke and other Enlightenment philosophers, engaged in conceptual partitioning of people by means of a restricted use of "all men."[24] Although the term has a generic meaning, they use it to refer to *white* men.[25] As evidence of this practice, Mills cites Hobbes's use of terms such as "barbarian" and "savage." White men from civilized societies encounter nonwhite "savages" who inhabit the state of nature – characterized as a wilderness, jungle, or wasteland. Whites bring nonwhites partially into society as subordinate citizens, or exclude (and isolate) them on reservations, or deny their existence, or exterminate them. According to Mills, not only was the social contract idea consistent with European racism towards nonEuropeans, Hobbes employed it to reconcile a contradiction between Enlightenment notions of equal rights, autonomy, and freedom and the practice of massacre, expropriation, and enslavement by European colonizers. He accomplished this reconciliation by denying personhood to nonwhites.

Although Mills wants to draw in question the anthropological view of nonEuropeans Hobbes relies on to speak of "savages" who inhabit a region outside of civil society, his criticism aims to accommodate the hypothetical, as well as the anthropological, aspects of Hobbes's account of the state of nature. He attributes to Hobbes a worldview of civilized Europeans and uncivilized nonEuropeans, a worldview with empirical and conceptual dimensions that operate in concert to support his political theory. Mills's interpretation raises an important question regarding the relation between Hobbes's view of the state of nature and his view of nonEuropeans. Given his use of the term "savages" to refer to Native Americans, did he, for instance, view them as inferior to Europeans?

Hobbes's view of the "savage people in many places of America" mentioned in *Leviathan* was based on the ethnographic accounts available to him.[26] But his use of terms such as "barbarian" and "savage" was influenced more by his study of the classics. The account of the state of nature in *Leviathan* is dominated by an image of civil war – a paradigm he studied when translating Thucydides' *Peleponnesian Wars*.[27] But the savagery of civil war is not the only image Hobbes employs in *Leviathan*, 13. His reference to Native Americans as "savages" suggests a presocial paradigm of rugged individuals living outside of civil association. He sometimes employed the term "savage" to indicate a relationship between social dissolution and the presocial condition, specifically that the social dissolution of a civil war is a return to the presocial condition. That this "natural condition" lurks beneath the artificial bond of political obligation supplies the major thrust of his argument for absolute sovereignty.[28]

Rousseau criticized Hobbes's conception of the state of nature as an inaccurate representation of people living in a "natural" condition prior to civil society. According to Rousseau, the people in Hobbes's state of nature are civilized, not natural.[29] This does not seem to be a criticism Hobbes has to reject, for he clearly understood his idea of social dissolution, which permeates his discussion in chapter 13, to presuppose a civil society. Nonetheless, Rousseau's point that Hobbes may have read too much of the "civilized" person into his characterization of the natural condition must be well taken. For theoretical purposes Hobbes needed an image of "savages" living under survival conditions to contrast with people living in "civil" association. Such an image appears rather starkly in his commentary on Gondibert. "[W]hatsoever distinguisheth the civility of Europe, from the barbarity of the American savages, is the workmanship of fancy, but guided by the precepts of true philosophy."[30] While, in this instance,

Hobbes's remarks seem to lend credence to Mills's charge of racial bias, the elaboration of this theme in other places mitigates against such a strong reading.

To understand Hobbes's account of the state of nature to be strictly anthropological is no less misleading than to suppose that he viewed the state of nature as *only* a theoretical construct. While acknowledging both aspects of Hobbes's view, Mills over-invests in the former, giving in to a tendency to place a racialized construction on some of Hobbes's remarks. But it is remarkable that even when he speaks from an ethnographic standpoint, Hobbes does not use racial concepts, or terms such as "Negro" and "African," in a negative fashion to imply inferiority, a common practice among European intellectuals of the period.[31] Hobbes's desire for his political theory to be consistent with the facts contributes to an important ambiguity in his view of race. In keeping with his theory of social evolution, he uses the term "savage" generally to refer to groups of people that have not developed a civil society. When he refers to Native Americans in this regard, sometimes he includes the ancient Germans and the early inhabitants of other "civil countries" in the same statement (*Elements*, 14, 12, p. 73). The best reason for believing that the dichotomy of "savage" and "civil" with which Hobbes operated was not racialized is his appeal to these historical and contemporary examples to provide corroborating evidence of his view of human nature – a view he applies universally. Mills's criticism, however, is directed toward the specific application of this dichotomy to Native Americans to support a justification of their colonization by Europeans.

With regard to Native Americans, rather than assert the superiority of Europeans, in his remarks regarding differences in social evolution, Hobbes insists that no such conclusion can be drawn. Instead he draws in question whether European accomplishment in the arts and sciences indicates superiority by comparison with the accomplishment of nonEuropeans. First he tells us,

> For those men who have taken in hand to consider nothing else but the comparison of magnitudes, numbers, times and motions, and their proportions one to another . . . wherein we differ from such savage people as are now the inhabitants of divers places in America; and as have been the inhabitants heretofore of those countries where at this day arts and sciences do most flourish. . . . [W]hatsoever either elegant or defensible in building: all which supposed away, what do we differ from the wildest of the Indians?[32]

There is an important reason Hobbes explains this difference in terms of social development and environmental influences rather than in terms of greater intelligence. According to Hobbes, although Native Americans are not philosophers, they have a basic capacity to reason. He believed the use of reason to develop the concepts of math and science requires leisure. "*Leisure* is the mother of *philosophy*; and *Commonwealth*, the mother of *peace* and *leisure*."[33] He lists India, Persia, and the Priests of Chaldea and Egypt as "the most ancient philosophers; and those countries were the most ancient of kingdoms." There is certainly no suggestion of European superiority in his statement that "*Philosophy* was not risen to the Grecians, and other people of the west, whose *commonwealths* (no greater perhaps than Lucca or Geneva) had never *peace* . . . nor the *leisure* to observe any thing but one another" (*Leviathan*, 46, 6, p. 455). He appeals to history to show that only those groups free from the necessities of survival will undergo the process of social evolution to make the transition to civil society, an appeal that resonates with the "commodious life" he posits at the end of *Leviathan*, chapter 13 as a motive to seek peace. Civil society is a condition for cultural advancement in the sense that the latter is made possible by having greater leisure time.[34]

Although Hobbes includes many non-Western societies under the heading of "civil society" is there any reason to suppose he thought there were any non-Western societies that were not patriarchal? This question reflects an important asymmetry in his treatment of race and gender. He is silent on the question of the European enslavement of Africans, whereas his resolution of the question of paternal dominion is a cornerstone (albeit buried) of his political theory. One explanation of his silence on the Atlantic slave trade is that, in his political treatises, with the Greek and Roman paradigm of the war-captive in mind, he argues in favor of the slave's right of resistance.[35] Because the question of paternal dominion is crucial to his account of sovereignty by acquisition, he resolves it in favor of the father, but on grounds that recognized other possibilities. If the bearer of a womb can defend herself and her infant by her own means, and does not need a husband, or family, she has, on Hobbes's view, a natural right to pursue this course of action. He employs the Amazon case to make this idea plausible. To what extent, however, is the argument Hobbes presents in his political treatises on the basis of reason confirmed by observation of custom?

Heirs and Hierarchy: Sovereignty by Succession

In his political treatises Hobbes allows for societies in which authority does not reside in the father, a view that is largely absent from the *Dialogue*. The universal view he presents in his earlier works is replaced with an account of authority in the household and state focused almost entirely on the history of England. When the question of what were the ancient laws and customs is raised in the exchange the reply is that "The *Saxons*, as also the rest of *Germany* not Conquer'd by the *Roman* Emperors, not compelled to use the imperial Laws, were a Savage and Heathen People living only by War and Rapine" (*Dialogue*, p. 198). He had in mind the fact that their rule over family, servants and subjects was absolute. This feature of his anthropological view is also a feature of his political theory. Here I want to return to Okin's charge that Hobbes only paid lip service to female sovereigns. His allowance for female-headed households and women sovereigns in his political theory does not seem to square with his claim that it is by the law of nature that fathers have absolute authority in households. Although his account of the ancient customs on which much of English law is based is largely consistent with the theory of obligation he presents in his political works, this discrepancy indicates that there may be important differences.

The account of the social formation of the household that Hobbes presents in the *Dialogue* is meant to be empirical. He appears to be making a historical claim when he states that "the beginning of all Dominion amongst Men was in Families" (ibid., p. 191). He goes on to claim that fathers have absolute authority by the law of nature. In a later passage where he is discussing the right of succession he adds qualifying phrases to this earlier statement, suggesting a more tentative view: "[It] *was held for the Law of nature*, not only amongst the Germans, but also *in most Nations* before they had written law" (ibid., p. 199). His remark that the right of succession from father to son was "held" for natural law suggests that this is a view he is willing to question – a skepticism further displayed in his claim that it is a custom "most" nations held to be so. He had two reasons for this reservation. First, right of succession is not a problem for forms of government other than monarchy. Secondly, the transfer of political authority in the commonwealth from father to son is asserted by a sovereign as a right of nature.[36] The law of nature supports this extension of father-right only insofar as male-headed households are the best means of providing security from death, pain, or injury. Hobbes claims that,

> Generally men are endued with greater parts of wisdom and courage, by which all monar-chies are kept from dissolution, than women are; it is to be presumed, where no express will is extant to the contrary, he preferreth his male children before the female. Not but that women may govern, and have in divers ages and places governed wisely, but are not so apt thereto in general as men. (*Elements*, 4, 14, p. 136)

While Hobbes is clearly biased in favor of men, he is not opposed to women sover-eigns. If prudence dictates that a female child be given preference, it would not be against the law of nature for a sovereign, by express will, to grant the right of succes-sion to his eldest daughter.

In several exchanges regarding justice and propriety in the *Dialogue* Hobbes pre-sents a political economic justification of authority in the household. In accordance with his earlier teachings regarding natural right he stipulates that "Without Law every thing is in such sort every Mans, as he may take, possess, and enjoy without wrong to any Man, every thing, Lands, Beasts, Fruits, and even the bodies of other Men, if his Reason tell him he cannot otherwise live securely" (*Dialogue*, p. 10). With explicit ref-erence to Aristotle's notion of justice as "giving to everyman his own" he equates pro-priety with self-preservation. The purpose of statute laws is to protect property rights and, in this sense, they are necessary "for preservation of all Mankind" (ibid., p. 10). He reasserts this view with the claim that "[W]hen our laws were silenced by Civil War, there was not a Man, that of any Goods could say assuredly they were his own" (ibid., p. 36). What remains consistent in the *Dialogue* and Hobbes's political treatises is his view that the first stage of the transition from the state of nature to civil society is the transfer of mother-right to father-right. Hobbes resolves the issue of dominion over children on the side of the father because this transition involves, along with the right of succession, a transfer of property to male heirs.

Colonialism, Slavery and Patriarchy

European colonial expansion was a major source of land acquisition in the seventeenth century. I want to consider an important relationship between Hobbes's justification of conquest within the household and his justification of colonial conquest.[37] When he insists that "a just pretense of invading those whom they have just cause to fear" is a natural right, he does not consider the extension of this justification to British slaveholding colonies in America (*Elements*, p. 192). The plausibility of his appeal to self-preservation and natural right to justify colonial conquest is facilitated by a conflation of security and self-interest. He does this by categorizing both under "the necessity of subsisting."[38] His stipulation that the acquisition of land "is manifest in all Conquests" is supported with a list of illustrations of this practice. Along with the Hebrew, Greek, and Roman examples from antiquity, he refers to a contemporary example with the question, "Is there at this day among the *Turks* any inheritor of Land, besides the *Sultan?*" (ibid., p. 193). Here he completely evades any reference to the appropriation of Native-American land by British colonizers in the New World, but in *Leviathan* he recommends a more moderate view of the appropriation of land by conquest.

> The multitude of poor . . . are to be transplanted into countries not sufficiently inhabited, where, nevertheless, they are not to exterminate those they find there, but constrain them to inhabit closer together, and not range a great deal of ground to snatch what they find . . . And when all the world is overcharged with inhabitants, then the last remedy of all is war, which provideth for every man, by victory or death. (*Leviathan*, 30, 19, pp. 228–9)

The Norman conquest of England is the most important case Hobbes employs in the *Dialogue* to show that the land of the vanquished belongs to the conqueror. In the exchange between philosopher and student the question is raised, "And was not all the Land in *England* once in the hands of *William* the Conqueror?" (*Dialogue*, p. 194). This occurs in the context of a historical narrative regarding the social formation of English civil society. In *Behemoth* Hobbes reveals some of the anthropological underpinnings of his theory of obligation. "The Normans also, that descended from the Germans, as we did, had the same customs in this particular; and by this means, this privilege of the lords to be of the King's great council, and when they were assembled, to be the highest of the King's courts of justice, continued still after the Conquest to this day" (*Behemoth*, 2, p. 77). Notice that he appeals to common descent to explain the origin of certain customs still in practice. I want to consider the implications of these customs with regard to race. In particular, does the appropriation of Native American land by European lords who perpetuate their wealth and power through kinship constitute a form of racially structured subordination?[39]

The role of conquest in land acquisition is an important issue Hobbes discusses in all of his political writings. His account of the growth of families by conquest in his political treatises is consistent with his account in the *Dialogue*. Likewise, his justification of the appropriation of land by a conqueror is consistent with his justification of paternal dominion. Subjects seeking protection can demand only security, not property. Moreover, they are obligated to contribute their "whole strength and fortunes" for defense (*Dialogue*, p. 160). When Hobbes discusses the growth of monarchies, he claims that they have developed from small families by war "wherein the Victor not only enlarged his Territory, but also the number and riches of his

Subjects" (ibid., p. 196). While this claim certainly justifies the appropriation of Native American land by European colonizers, Hobbes instead points to a quite different implication. He tells us, "After the first manner which is by War, grew up all the greatest Kingdoms in the World, *viz.* the *Egyptian, Assyrian, Persian* and the *Macedonian Monarchy*; and so did the great Kingdoms of *England, France,* and *Spain*" (ibid., p. 196). His identification of the political economic interest of the commonwealth with invasion and conquest indicates the extent to which he embraced a view of "great Kingdoms" founded on violence and oppression. Nevertheless, the colonial domination he championed, under this banner of "greatness," included nonEuropean kingdoms.

When Hobbes discusses the growth and development of monarchies in the *Dialogue*, he presents three different options gleaned from history. He reverses the order of sovereignty by acquisition and by institution and the option of reproduction is replaced by rebellion. If we take the aim of Hobbes's political treatise to be a justification of sovereignty by conquest, which he acknowledges to be the most common method of expansion, we can better understand his tendency to treat the agreements made in each case as equally binding. According to Hobbes, "The cause in general which moveth a man to become subject to another, is . . . the fear of not otherwise preserving himself. And a man may subject himself to him that invadeth, or may invade him, for fear of him" (*Elements*, 19, 11, p. 105). What is most significant about his talk of the "voluntary conjunction" of many lords of families into one great aristocracy is that he suggests that this form of monarchy is less stable than that which is established by conquest.[40] He also suggests that by "voluntary subjection" in the case of sovereignty by institution, rather than savages who live outside of a civil society, he had in mind a select group of lords who have already established, by conquest, their political authority in households. On this reading, his theory of political obligation *presupposes* that conquest in the household has already taken place. He upholds the validity of coerced agreements in his political theory because the realism he aimed to capture with the idea of the state of nature required a thoroughgoing commitment to the use of force by a sovereign to maintain security from rebellion and to maintain peace with rivals in international affairs.

The household unit is the most important feature of Hobbes's political theory, for without the formation of the household as a political economic unit, neither civil society, nor the colonial expansion required to maintain it, is possible. The process by which the commonwealth is created through the union of households is in many ways similar to the process by which the commonwealth grows through colonial expansion. Hobbes's appeal to the right of nature to justify invading a neighbor in the *Dialogue* is consistent with the first-strike policy he advocates in *Leviathan*. Speaking from the standpoint of the vanquished, he asks, "How shall I be defended from the domineering of Proud and Insolent Strangers that speak another Language, that scorn us, and seek to make us Slaves?" (*Dialogue*, p. 15). The primary political function of the incorporation of households into a commonwealth is to maintain peace and security. To what extent, however, does gender, race, and class figure into Hobbes's view of relations within the household?

Hobbes stipulates that a female heir to the throne retains mother-right over her children and authority over her husband. Despite his preference for male sovereigns, he speaks of a female monarch entering into an agreement, as an equal, with another male monarch regarding the paternal dominion of their offspring. The criterion of paternal authority in such cases is residential, or geographic. Paternal dominion is an extremely important issue to resolve because the outcome may determine the right of succession. Unlike sovereignty by institution and by acquisition, sovereignty gained through succession is passed on by birth – a custom that facilitates the transfer of authority once conquest has occurred. By invoking blood and kinship as a ground for succession Hobbes adds a noncontractarian justification of political authority.

This stipulation regarding the right of succession accords with Hobbes's belief that there would be few women heirs. But what about the racial implications of kinship, especially with regard to the inheritance of property? In the British colonies in the New World the proprietary aspects of reproducing white male heirs was a basis for the social privilege denied to servants and slaves.[41] On Hobbes's account an important racial distinction between the subordination of European women (wives) and the subordination of servants and slaves is maintained, for the conquest of a neighboring household may result in some of its members becoming servants and others slaves. What distinguishes servants and slaves in this instance is a contract establishing obligation. According to Hobbes, unlike servants who are not in bondage, the subordination of a slave involves a denial of corporal liberty. A slave has no obligation to a master and has a natural right to kill him, or to escape. When Hobbes's reasoning regarding natural right is applied to the situation of American slaves, his doctrine gives rise to a conflict involving race and gender. His notion of natural right permits him to remain committed to a justification of colonialism, as well as to a justification of resistance to colonialism by slaves.

Slavery is a key concept in Hobbes's account of political economic relations not only within the household, but also between households; hence, it is an important feature of domestic and international relations. Subordination based on gender and class is justified by virtue of coerced agreements, whereas, for Hobbes, slavery is at par with death, pain and injury and, for that reason, it is never justified. In the context of American slavery kinship is an important racial factor that distinguishes the subordination of wives and children from the subordination of servants and slaves. Hobbes employs classical sources to construct a definition of slavery that matches his contractarian view of servitude. With the subjection of women in place, servants and slaves are acquired through a process of invading neighbors. Subordination within the household functions in tandem with the invasion and conquest of neighboring households. When race is an added factor, there arises a conflict with gender and class. Hobbes's view fully accords with the fact that British lords reaped economic benefit from the conquest of the New World and the enslavement of Africans. On Hobbes's account of patriarchy important distinctions between the position of women, servants and slaves are recognized in terms of obligation and natural right. Nonetheless, we can glean from his account the suggestion that subordination based on gender and race is, like class, a manifestation of economic interests.

Notes

1. See Malcolm Noel, "Hobbes, Sandys, and the Virginia Company," *The Historical Journal*, 24, 2 (1981), pp. 297–321.

2. According to Christine Di Stefano, Hobbes was committed to masculinity "constituted in terms of gendered experiences and interests" and his thought adhered to a deep ideological structure that "embodies a gender-based logic, epistemology, ontology and intellectual style" ("Masculinity as Ideology in Political Theory: Hobbesian Man Considered," *Women's Studies International Forum*, 6, 6, 1983, p. 634). Carole Pateman claims, "In the natural state all women become servants, and all women are excluded from the original pact. That is to say, all women are also excluded from becoming civil individuals" (*The Sexual Contract*, Stanford, CA: Stanford University Press, 1988, p. 50).

3. Lawrence Krader has pointed out that Hobbes's conception of the household as a group of close kin and servants is the Roman model of the patriarchate ("The Anthropology of Thomas Hobbes: Violence as a Primitive Human Condition," unpublished, p. 13).

4. See Diane Coole, "Re-reading Political Theory from a Woman's Perspective," *Political Studies*, 34 (1986), pp. 129–48.

5. Susan Moller Okin, *Women in Western Political Thought* (London: Virago, 1980), p. 198.

6. *Dialogue*, p. 191. References to Hobbes's works are made to the following editions: *A Dialogue between a Philosopher and a Student of the Common Laws of England*, ed. Joseph Cropsey (Chicago: University of Chicago Press, 1971); *De Cive*, ed. Howard Warrender (Oxford: Clarendon Press, 1983); *The Elements of Law*, ed. Ferdinand Tönnies (New York: Barnes and Noble, 1969); *Leviathan*, ed. Edwin Curley (Indianapolis: Hackett, 1994). Subsequent references to Hobbes's works will be given in parentheses in the text as follows (when appropriate): title, paragraph, chapter number, section number and page number.

7. Okin, *Women in Western Political Thought*, p. 199.

8. *Leviathan*, 10, 4, p. 128; *Elements*, 4, 10, p. 135.

9. Cf. Gregory S. Kavka, *Hobbesian Moral and Political Theory* (Princeton: Princeton University Press, 1986), ch. 4.

10. *Elements*, 4, 10, p. 135.

11. *De Cive*, 9, 10, p. 128.

12. Di Stefano, "Masculinity as Ideology," p. 637.

13. Ibid., p. 636.

14. Ibid., p. 638.

15. Ibid., p. 638.

16. Ibid., p. 639.

17. See Diane Coole's criticism of Di Stefano's view: Coole, "Re-reading Political Theory," p. 142ff.

18. The hypothetical nature of this contract still satisfies Hobbes's behavioral criterion of consent. The infant's acceptance of the mother's nurturing constitutes a sign of the will – a voluntary act that amounts to consent, in the sense that the infant receives a benefit of the agreement.

19. Hobbes claims that both parents have equal claim to the child at birth, but this is a problematic assertion given his stipulation that only the mother has knowledge of the father. Given his commitment to a labor theory of property (*Dialogue*, p. 191), there is some reason to suppose that the mother's propriety in her infant can also be established in accordance with a principle of entitlement. See Anita Allen, "Slavery and Surrogacy," in *Subjugation*

and Bondage: Critical Essays on Slavery and Social Philosophy, ed. Tommy L. Lott (Lanham: Rowman & Littlefield, 1999), pp. 229–54.

20. Thomas Hobbes, *Behemoth*, ed. Ferdinand Tönnies (London: Frank Cass & Co., 1969).

21. See *Dialogue*, pp. 30 and 194. Hobbes also discusses the Norman conquest in *Behemoth*, pp. 76–7. According to M. M. Goldsmith, "*Behemoth* is an illustration of Hobbes's system. It is that system applied to explain the historical events of 1640–1660" in Thomas Hobbes, *Behemoth*, ed. Ferdinand Tönnies, p. x. See also Royce MacGillivray, "Thomas Hobbes's History of the English Civil War: A Study of Behemoth," *Journal of the History of Ideas*, 31 (1970), pp. 179–98.

22. But see Hobbes's remarks at *Dialogue*, pp. 10, 37 and 196. Joseph Cropsey seems puzzled by the fact that Hobbes does not refer by name to the state of nature. He complains that "nothing that Hobbes could ever do by way of silence alone could withdraw that powerful conception from the crannies of the world into which it had long since penetrated." Introduction, Thomas Hobbes, *Dialogue*, p. 14.

23. In *Leviathan* Hobbes challenges Sir Edward Coke's views on English law with his own command theory. He again asserts his positivist view in the *Dialogue*, but the remarks in the exchanges regarding Coke's doctrine are not always critical. See James Stoner, Jr, *Common Law and Liberal Theory: Coke, Hobbes, and the Origins of American Constitutionalism* (Lawrence, Kansas: University of Kansas Press, 1992), ch. 7. For the best discussion of the relation between Hobbes's political treatises and the *Dialogue* see Larry May, "Law, Contract and Civil Morality," Ph.D. dissertation, New School for Social Research, 1977.

24. See Alison Taufer, "The Only Good Amazon is a Converted Amazon: The Woman Warrior and Christianity in the Amadis Cycle," in *Playing with Gender: A Renaissance Pursuit*, ed. Jean R. Brink, Maryanne C. Horowitz, and Allison P. Coudert (University of Illinois Press, 1991), pp. 35–51, and Robert P. Kraynak, *History and Modernity in the Thought of Thomas Hobbes* (Ithaca: Cornell University Press, 1990), ch. 2.

25. Charles Mills, *The Racial Contract* (Ithaca: Cornell University Press, 1997).

26. Lawrence Krader claims that Hobbes was aware from the literature then in circulation that Native Americans included not only "savages" but also patrimonial kingdoms. Krader, "The Anthropology of Thomas Hobbes," p. 28.

27. Clifford Orwin, "Stasis and Plague: Thucydides on the Dissolution of Society," *Journal of Politics*, 50 (1988), pp. 833–46.

28. In *Leviathan*, chapter 13, Hobbes makes this point facetiously in an aside to the reader who doubts "that nature should thus dissociate." With regard to monarchy, when there is no successor, he refers to the conditions that obtain in the state of nature to indicate the conditions under which obligation ceases. "And by these three ways, all subjects are restored from their civil subjection to that liberty which all men have to all things; to wit, natural and savage (for the natural state hath the same proportion to the civil (I mean, liberty to subjection), which passion hath to reason, or a beast to a man)" (*De Cive*, 7, 18, p. 116).

29. Jean-Jacques Rousseau, *Discourse on the Origin of Inequality*, Part 1 (London: J. M. Dent & Sons, 1975).

30. Thomas Hobbes, "The Answer to Davenant's Prefact Before Gondibert," in *The English Works of Thomas Hobbes*, vol. 4, ed. William Molesworth (London: John Bohn, 1841), p. 449.

31. See *De Cive*, Dedicatory, p. 23; *The Questions concerning Liberty, Necessity, and Chance*, in *The English Works of Thomas Hobbes*, vol. 5, ed. William Molesworth (London: John Bohn, 1841), p. 302.

32. *Elements*, 13, 3, pp. 65–6. See also *Leviathan*, 46, 6, pp. 454–5 and 30, 5, p. 220.

33. *Leviathan*, 46, 6, p. 455.

34. *Elements*, 14, 12, p. 73; *The Questions concerning Liberty, Necessity, and Chance*, p. 303.
35. Hobbes discusses the slave's right of resistance at *Elements*, 3, 3, p. 128; *De Cive*, 8, 4, p. 118; *Leviathan*, 20, 10, pp. 130–1. See my "Early Enlightenment Conceptions of the Rights of Slaves," in Lott, *Subjugation and Bondage*, pp. 103–8.
36. Hobbes discusses the problem of a king in possession who refuses to disinherit a diseased heir. See his lost fragment in Arnold A. Rogow, *Thomas Hobbes: Radical in the Service of Reaction* (New York: Norton, 1986), appendix II, p. 254.
37. See Hobbes's remarks at *Elements*, 3, 3, p. 128.
38. I discuss Hobbes's conflation of self-defense and self-interest in my "Hobbes's Right of Nature," *History of Philosophy Quarterly*, 9, 2 (April, 1992), pp. 159–80.
39. Some of what Hobbes says is in keeping with Mills's notion of a Racial Contract underwriting the social contract. Mills defines the Racial Contract as a set of formal or informal agreements or meta-agreements between whites and from which all whites benefit. *The Racial Contract*, p. 11.
40. *Dialogue*, p. 11.
41. Indeed, colonial laws were changed to render the offspring of masters and slaves the property of the master. Frederick Douglass and Harriet Jacobs insisted that the purpose of this legal change was to deprive the master's children begotten by slaves their right to freedom and property. Frederick Douglass, *Narrative of the Life of Frederick Douglass, an American Slave* and Harriet Jacobs, *Incidents in the Life of a Slave Girl*, in *Early African American Classics*, ed. Anthony Appiah (New York: Bantam, 1990).

CHAPTER 5

"An Inconsistency not to be Excused": On Locke and Racism

WILLIAM UZGALIS

"To contend for liberty, and to deny that blessing to others involves an inconsistency not to be excused."

John Jay

Given the appeals to freedom, equality and inalienable rights by American revolutionaries, Thomas Jefferson and Patrick Henry to name but two, there is a good deal of force to Jay's remark. The American revolutionaries were caught up in this inconsistency not to be excused. It was clear to many slaves that the doctrine of their masters argued powerfully for their own freedom. Similar remarks apply to the relation between American colonists and Native Americans. While Patriots denounced English efforts to tax them without consent, they were a people in the process of dispossessing native peoples of the lands and possessions of their ancestors.

If we trace one strand of the revolutionary doctrine held by these American Patriots to its intellectual origins, we find ourselves looking at the political philosophy of John Locke. Scholars have, in effect, raised the question of whether Jay's remark applies to Locke as well as it does to Jefferson, or Patrick Henry. Locke was a philosopher who strongly objected to oppression and persecution. Like Jay and Jefferson, he was the spokesperson of a revolutionary movement. There is thus no surprise that Locke's political philosophy would appeal to American revolutionaries in the next century.[1] Behind the Jeffersonian writing about liberty and equality lies not only Locke's discussion of these same concepts but his explicit rejection of the principle that might makes right. Locke recognizes that robbers and pirates live according to this principle, for they violate the rights of others. Locke claims that robbers, be they kings or highwaymen, destroy their own humanity by their actions and reduce themselves to the level of beasts of prey. So, if Locke were shown to be a racist who legitimizes and justifies the robbery and enslavement of peoples of color, the contradiction would be quite as striking as that of men who could say: "All men are created equal with certain inalienable rights . . ." or "Give me liberty or give me death" and at the same time own slaves.

Did Locke wish to deny the blessings of liberty and property to others? Locke lived a century before the American Revolution, and he was involved in an earlier stage of the same economic and political system which embroiled the American revolutionaries in that inconsistency not to be excused. The English slave trade that was at its zenith when the American Revolution began was in its infant stages in Locke's lifetime. The colonies that revolted in 1776 were being founded during Locke's lifetime. Locke's work for his patron Lord Ashley, later the First Earl of Shaftsbury, involved him with colonies and trade and slavery in a variety of ways. As the secretary to the Lords Proprietors of the Carolinas (1668–71), he wrote out the fundamental constitution of the Carolinas, in which is included the provision that every freeman shall have absolute power over his Negro slaves. Although Locke did not own slaves, he did buy (and sell at a profit) shares in the Royal Africa Company and the Bahamas Adventurers – both of which were slave-trading companies. Locke had a friend, business partner, and correspondent, Peter Colleton, who owned slaves. Locke was deeply involved in the details of colonial government including colonial policy towards the Native Americans. Some find these facts sufficiently compelling to conclude, on this basis alone, that Locke was a racist.[2] Some historians of these matters, on the other hand, hold that the modern concept of race had not yet been invented in Locke's time. So the question becomes what one might mean in claiming that Locke was a racist.

Richard Popkin has suggested that modern racism begins in Spain in 1492, and that the characteristic feature of modern racism is that it seeks to show that one group of people is rendered permanently inferior to some other group by factors such as biology and climate (Popkin, 1980, p. 85). Popkin's modern racism requires a reason, or an account, or a theory, which explains the permanent inferiority of one group to another. James Farr makes a distinction between *weak* and *strong* racism. *Strong racism* provides an empirical account or a theory to explain the inferiority of one group to another and a moral theory to justify enslavement or other ill treatment of that inferior group (Farr, 1986, p. 278). *Weak racism* on Farr's account involves disliking people in a group (or groups) other than one's own (and perhaps even thinking them inferior), but without any reason to justify this claim. It is worth noting that the evidence of Locke's various connections with the slave trade would not qualify him as a racist in Popkin's sense at all, and would only provide evidence that he was a racist in Farr's weak sense. For this evidence gives no empirical theory of the inferiority of one group to another nor a moral theory to justify ill treatment. Some scholars take claims to cultural superiority as a form of racism. This is sometimes referred to as *soft* or *liberal* racism, as it is not permanent in the way biological differences are permanent. I will treat it as another form of strong racism. So, strong racism will be either biological or cultural. Given these distinctions, it is clear that to convict Locke of racism in the *strong* sense we need to examine his writing, both philosophical and otherwise, to see if it contains the kind of theory which Popkin and Farr tell us we must have.

In this paper I show that a number of the claims that Locke is a racist in the strong sense are quite unconvincing. I will consider efforts to attribute to Locke both theories of biological and cultural inferiority of Blacks and Native Americans. At the same time I will show that Locke has a non-racist account of differences between peoples. In fact, we can find in Locke at least the foundational principle for a liberal theory of the multi-cultural state.

"Essence, Accident and Race"

Harry Bracken, in an article titled "Essence, Accident and Race," claims that seventeenth-century rationalism tends towards being a non-racist philosophy, while empiricism tends towards racism. Cartesian dualism is what Bracken has in mind by seventeenth-century rationalism. Bracken claims that: "For the Cartesian, a person's color, language, his biology, even his sex – are in the strictest sense accidental . . . The empiricists on the other hand do take color, language, biology and sex to be essential. Locke seems to have been the decisive influence here" (Bracken, 1973, p. 82). It is true that Brachen claims that there is only a weak historical connection between empiricism and racism. But for this weak historical connection to hold there must be some content to empiricist doctrines which encourage racist thinking.

If color or language were an essential property, this would mean that a person would be human if they had the proper color or spoke the right language or group of languages. A person not having the proper skin tone or language group would not be human.[3] This is a much stronger claim than many racists would be willing to make. Not even the Aristotelian theory of natural slavery which Spanish apologists invoked to justify the conquest and enslavement of the Native Americans of the New World goes this far. In the seventeenth and eighteenth centuries claims that other races were not human would have been widely regarded as implausible and likely heretical. So, Bracken is invoking a philosophical basis for racism that is too strong to fit with Popkin's claim that Locke is one of the originators of the degeneracy theory.[4] Let us turn from Bracken's general claims about empiricism and racism to his critique of Locke.

One of Bracken's contentions is that Locke's anti-essentialism leaves us in such great ignorance of the essences of things that there is no way to evaluate, argue about, or criticize wildly different, competing proposals about the essence of any substance. Bracken remarks on Locke's willingness to allow that, for all we know, matter fitly disposed might think. So, Bracken claims, Locke has no way to avoid saying that one of the essential properties of gold might be pain. Bracken is correct in believing that Locke holds that we have almost no knowledge of the necessary connection between the properties of substances. This makes it very hard for us to specify the essences of substances. We have a considerable amount of knowledge of the necessary connection between the properties of mathematical objects. But we do not have that same kind of knowledge in regard to the essential properties of substances. Part of the reason for this is that the atomic constitutions of things are inaccessible to us. Mainly what we encounter are the secondary qualities of objects, e.g. color, smell, taste and sound, which depend on those atomic constitutions in ways of which we are completely ignorant. If our ignorance of substances is as vast as Locke supposes, and the boundaries between species are indeterminate in the way which he suggests, it would seem that no argument would be available to "correct" or "refute" any proposal for what might constitute the essence of a species. So, anyone who claimed that black color should not be included in the idea of man, would get no argument from Locke, for he would be unable to contest such a claim on his principles. These are clearly the concerns that Bracken has about Locke's anti-essentialism (Bracken, 1973, pp. 83–4).

Brachen has been answered by a number of fine scholars.[5] Kathy Squadrito in particular takes up the job of answering his concerns about the connection between Locke's general anti-essentialist philosophy and racism. She remarks that Bracken focuses on a few passages dealing with real essences, and fails to consider Locke's account of nominal essences. Real essences are the atomic constitutions of things; nominal essences are collections of apparent qualities, which we use to sort individuals into different kinds. So had Bracken focused on nominal essences, he would have discovered that Locke's philosophy has the resources to critique and reject racist theories. But what about color? Isn't it possible that the particular bodily form that makes a man includes some restriction on color? Perhaps, on Locke's view, only a being of the proper shape and color, namely white, is a man? This is surely what Bracken thinks. There is a passage in the chapter on Maxims in Book 4 of *An Essay Concerning Human Understanding* that has been taken to show that this is what Locke thinks.[6] Even Professor Squadrito holds that this passage might have a suggestion of racism in it (Squadrito, 1975, p. 46). In examining this passage, however, it becomes apparent that this is not so. To the contrary, Locke holds it is both childish and dangerous to claim that a Negro is not a man. It also turns out that Locke thinks that on a more sophisticated view of man, soul would play an important part.

In considering the passage from the chapter "Of Maxims" from Book 4 (sections 16–20) we should remember that Locke is not fond of maxims. Maxims are axioms or self-evident truths. Locke is engaged in this chapter in refuting those who take maxims to be of great importance in acquiring knowledge. At the beginning of section 16 he says: "For instance: let *Man* be that, concerning which you would by these first Principles demonstrate anything, and we shall see, that so far as demonstration is by these principles, it is only verbal, and gives us no certain, universal, true Proposition, or knowledge, of any Being existing without us" (Essay, 4, 7, 16; all subsequent references to the *Essay* and *Second Treatise* give Book, chapter and section numbers).

Locke's first example in this passage is a child who can demonstrate that a Negro is not a man. This is because the child's idea of man contains only visible appearances, and lacking experience of other races, he includes the idea of "white" or "flesh-color in England" in his idea of man. Since this idea includes "white" in it, it is clear how the child will demonstrate that a Negro is not a man. Locke makes it clear that he views the child's idea of man as superficial. He says: "it is probable that his idea is just like that picture which the painter makes of the visible appearances joined together" He goes on to note that: "the foundation of his certainty being not that universal Proposition, which perhaps he never heard nor thought of, but the clear, distinct Perception he hath of his own simple *Ideas* of Black and White, which he cannot be persuaded to take, nor can ever mistake one for another, whether he knows that Maxim or no." The point is that it is the intuitive knowledge that white is not black, together with an inadequate idea of man (inadequate because of childish lack of experience) which is doing all the damage here, and that the maxim contributes nothing. Locke continues: "And to this child, or any one who hath such an *Idea*, which he calls *Man*, Can you never demonstrate that a *Man* hath a Soul, because his *Idea* of Man includes no such Notion or *Idea* in it" (Essay, 4, 7, 16). This remark is a criticism. It should be emphasized that Locke is indicating (by its placement in the series of examples) that this is the most superficial and dangerous of the views of "man" which he considers. In sections 17 and 18 Locke goes on to examine two more cases, each inadequate in its own way. In 17 "laughter" and "rational discourse" are added to outward shape (color has significantly dropped out) but this is still not an adequate idea of man, because it means that imbeciles and children would not count as human. In section 18 Locke rejects dropping out shape altogether, for this too has unacceptable consequences.

Locke thinks that on a more sophisticated view of man than the child has, soul would play an important part. Many empiricists in the seventeenth and eighteenth centuries were dualists, or immaterialists like Berkeley, and thus had just as much of a race- and gender-neutral view of the essence of humans as Descartes or other rationalists. Did Brachen forget this? Perhaps he did. In this passage on maxims Locke is doing everything which Professor Brachen claims Locke would not and cannot do. Locke is criticizing as inadequate a series of ideas of man. Brachen holds that Locke's justification for African American slavery is that Blacks are not men[7] (Brachen, 1973, pp. 84–5). Yet in this passage Locke rejects this view as dangerous and absurd.

Native Americans as Animals, Children, or Idiots

Let us turn to Native Americans. In a paper titled "Locke and the Dispossession of the American Indian" Kathy Squadrito notes that Locke gives "somewhat conflicting descriptions" of Native Americans – there is the gentle and moral native on the one hand and the immoral and sinful native on the other (Squadrito, 1996, p. 148; this volume p. 102). In describing Locke's negative image of native people, Squadrito notes that Locke groups Native Americans along with children, idiots, and illiterates. She cites a passage in which Locke says that Native Americans "being of all others the least corrupted by customs, or borrowed opinions, learning and education . . ." show no evidence of having any innate ideas. She continues:

> The mind of the indigenous person is thus considered one of the closest to his *tabula rasa* as possible. Since abstract ideas are considered that which puts a perfect distinction between man and beast, the reader is led to regard American Indians, who are confined to simple ideas or a few abstract ideas, as akin to animals. (Squadrito, 1996, p. 149; this volume p. 103; the reference is to Locke, *Essay*, 2, 11, 10)

This seems pretty damning. Still, there is something quite wrong about this. Locke distinguishes between *innate* ideas and *abstract* ideas. He spends all of Book 1 of the

Essay arguing that there are no innate ideas or principles. He believes abstract ideas exist, explains how we make them and thinks they are enormously important to genuine knowledge. But Squadrito is claiming that because Locke says Native Americans do not have *innate* ideas they do not have *abstract* ideas. I suppose that she might claim that since Locke holds that there are no innate ideas, the ideas of sciences which he is looking for and not finding in Native Americans (since these ideas actually exist) must be abstract. Let it be so. Locke's point then becomes that certain abstract ideas which ought to be universal if they were innate do not show up in other cultures as they should. In *Essay*, 2, 11, 10, we are told that the distinction between human beings and animals is the use of abstract ideas. In that passage, there is not a single mention of Native Americans. So, this is an inference that Squadrito thinks Locke's reader will make. She puts this distinction between man and animals together with Locke's treatment of Native Americans when he is talking about innate ideas in Book 1, to conclude that Native Americans are akin to animals in not actually having any abstract ideas. But the claim that Native Americans do not have these abstract ideas of the sciences does not prevent them having such abstract ideas as "berries," "deer," "river," and all of the variety of abstract ideas connected with their particular culture and environment. Squadrito's claim that Native Americans are thus "the closest to [Locke's] *tabula rasa* as possible" simply shows that she does not grasp the difference between a very restricted subset of abstract ideas (those that are claimed to be innate though they are not) and the larger set of abstract ideas. Her claim that Native Americans are like animals in not actually having any abstract ideas rests on this mistaken conflation.

In the passage Squadrito cites in which Locke mentions Native Americans along with children, idiots and illiterates, it is worth noting that all of these are classed together just insofar as they show no signs of having innate ideas. There is no implication that Native Americans are like idiots or children in failing to be reasonable. But this is just what Squadrito thinks these passages do imply. Squadrito's claims thus raise an important issue. What relationship do Native Americans and other peoples of color have to reason? Animals, because of their make, are incapable of reason. Children lack it until they grow into adults, and so require parental guidance. Idiots, because of defects, lack it throughout their life and so must be cared for by those who possess it. A number of scholars have claimed that on Locke's account Native Americans lack reason.

Barbara Arneil, for example, sees Locke's account of reason as implying an acceptance of the existence of the Christian God. She writes: "The means by which Locke and later liberal thinkers marry the ethical rights of the English farmer and European thinker, and exclude others from civil society, is reason – reason perceived as a unitary, singular entity which leads us to one truth, and indeed one god" (Arneil, 1996, p. 210). Earlier she writes:

> For Locke, the Amerindian, like the English child, has the potential for reason or rationality. Unlike the English, however, rationality and understanding will only be achieved by the Amerindian when he goes beyond the "Ways, Modes and Notions" of his own people to adopt the knowledge of another "more improved" People – namely the English. (Ibid., p. 149)

She goes on to quote (in part) the following passage from Locke's *Essay*:

> Had you or I been born in the Bay of *Soldemia*, possibly our Thoughts and Notions had not exceeded those brutish ones of the *Hottentots* that inhabit there: And had the *Virginia* king *Apochancana*, been educated in *England*, he had perhaps, been as knowing a Divine, and as good a Mathematician as any in it. The difference between him and a more improved *English-man* lying barely in this, That the exercise of his faculties was bounded within the Ways, Modes and Notions of his own Country. (*Essay*, 1, 4, 12)

Before continuing to consider Locke's views about reason and culture, it is worth noting that this remarkable passage provides compelling evidence that Locke is not a racist in Farr's strong sense interpreted biologically either in regard to Native Americans or Black Africans. Locke is saying that all people are essentially the same biologically, and that the significant differences between Englishmen and those in other lands is purely cultural. If we had been born in their culture, we would very likely think like them, and if they had been born in our culture, they might well be as good as the best of us at mathematics and theology. For those skeptical of my claims that the passage on maxims shows that Locke does not view Black Africans as less than human, this passage should be decisive.

This passage also makes it plain that Native Americans (and Hottentots) are as capable of reason as the best of Englishmen. So Native Americans are not animals, because animals do not have the capacity to reason. Still, if not animals, Native Americans (and Hottentots) might be worse than children in being adults who have not actualized their potential to reason, thus justifying the charges that they are lazy, sinful and immoral. Arneil continues:

> It is through the application of rational thought that one develops arts and sciences, and comes to recognize the first principle, "the Notion of God". The relation between the cultivation of land, the secondary principle of the arts and sciences, and the first principle of God's existence is for Locke a very close one; the failure of the Amerindians to adopt any of them is due to their failure to apply reason beyond "the opinions of their own people". (Arneil, 1996, p. 149)

Arneil, Squadrito and others are claiming that Locke's view is that the failure of Native Americans to be actually reasonable in not recognizing the Christian God provides Europeans with a justification for taking their lands and destroying their culture (Squadrito, 1996, pp. 150, 170, 171–2; this volume p. 117).

Locke, however, explicitly, emphatically and eloquently rejects this claim. In a passage from Popple's translation of Locke's first *Letter Concerning Toleration* we find this:

> No man whatsoever ought, therefore, to be deprived of his terrestrial enjoyments upon account of his religion. Not even Americans, subjected unto a Christian prince, are to be punished either in body or goods for not embracing our faith and worship. If they are persuaded that they please God in observing the rites of their own country and that they shall obtain happiness by that means, they are to be left unto God and themselves. Let us trace this matter to the bottom. Thus it is: An inconsiderable and weak number of

Christians, destitute of everything, arrive in a Pagan country; these foreigners beseech the inhabitants, by the bowels of humanity, that they would succour them with the necessaries of life; those necessaries are given them, habitations are granted, and they all join together, and grow up into one body of people. The Christian religion by this means takes root in that country and spreads itself, but does not suddenly grow the strongest. While things are in this condition peace, friendship, faith, and equal justice are preserved amongst them. At length the magistrate becomes a Christian, and by that means their party becomes the most powerful. Then immediately all compacts are to be broken, all civil rights to be violated, that idolatry may be extirpated; and unless these innocent Pagans, strict observers of the rules of equity and the law of Nature and no ways offending against the laws of the society, I say, unless they will forsake their ancient religion and embrace a new and strange one, they are to be turned out of the lands and possessions of their forefathers and perhaps deprived of life itself. Then, at last, it appears what zeal for the Church, joined with the desire of dominion, is capable to produce, and how easily the pretence of religion, and of the care of souls, serves for a cloak to covetousness, rapine, and ambition. (Locke, 1991, p. 38)

It is quite plain that the Pagans Locke has in mind here are Native Americans. Presumably in the story he is telling, we recognize the colonists of Jamestown and the Pilgrims of Plymouth as those destitute of everything who beseech the native to succour them with the necessities of life. This passage makes it quite clear that Native Americans' observance of the laws of nature and equity is enough to prevent their property (and note that this property includes " the lands . . . of their forefathers") being taken from them on account of differences in religion. Nor should we underestimate the importance of this passage. It is not only a powerful condemnation of the religious justification for robbery from native peoples, it is also part of a theory of toleration. In that context, since this passage applies Locke's principles of religious toleration to a hypothetical state with different cultures in it, it provides what amounts to the fundamental principle for a liberal theory of the muli-cultural state: "Thou shalt not rip thy neighbor off on the basis of even the deepest cultural differences, e.g. religious differences."[8] This should, I contend, make us skeptical of claims that Locke would countenance robbery or other ill treatment of peoples of color on the basis of any cultural difference.

Locke rejects dispossession of Native American lands on account of religion. So, we need a different account of reason, one that does not lead to the conclusion that Native Americans should be dispossessed of their land because they do not believe in the Christian God. I would suggest that Locke's account of the kind of reason required to exercise rights to life, liberty, health and property is much less Eurocentric than Arneil and Squadrito claim.[9] Locke defines "person" in the chapter "Of Identity and Diversity" as: "a thinking intelligent Being that has reason and reflection, and can consider itself as itself, the same thinking thing in different times and places . . ." (Essay, 2, 27, 9). It turns out that being a person in this sense is crucial for living according to the law. If I know that I am about to break the law and I consider that in the future it is I who will be punished, I may be deterred from my lawbreaking. On the other hand, if I am being sentenced for having committed a breach of the law, it is crucial to Locke that I remember having committed the crime, so that I know what I am being punished for.[10]

In Locke's account of the state of nature, there is a law of nature, "and reason is that law." The law of nature is the Golden Rule interpreted in terms of natural rights. Just as I want to live with my rights to life, liberty, health, and property unviolated, so I will treat others – I will not violate their rights (*Second Treatise*, 2, 5–7). To fail to live so, to violate others' rights, is to reduce oneself to the level of the beasts. This is so because one now lives by the principle of the beasts – that might makes right. In *The Second Treatise of Government* Locke talks about Native Americans in a state of nature. The implications of Locke's inclusion of Native Americans in the state of nature are that they are not just human, they are both reasonable and people in the full sense of that term. Native Americans who have the rights to the berries and deer they collect and who hunt and do not violate the rights of others are living according to the law of nature – the Golden Rule. This makes them morally superior to King Charles II and his brother James – or any other European who does not live by the law of nature.

Native Americans, Agriculture and Just Wars

Even if we grant that Locke regards Native Americans as reasonable people, it may still be objected that Locke does not regard Native American cultures as equal to European cultures. Locke has a developmental account of the state of nature and civil society. This developmental scheme plays a role in his explanation of the origin and nature of legitimate civil government. It begins with hunting and gathering cultures in which relatively few people occupy more land than they need with a barter economy to deal with surplus. Then comes the development of agriculture and ownership of land. Then comes the stage in which money is introduced. This allows for commerce and vast inequalities of wealth. Population increases at each stage of development. Along with increasing population comes a reduction in available resources and increasing conflicts over property. These conflicts eventually require the institution of civil government and the fixing of property in land. Locke places the Native Americans in the various stages of the state of nature while European nations are in the "advanced" state of civil society. The role of Native Americans in this section of the *Second Treatise* is open to alternative interpretations with significantly differing consequences.

One way to interpret the *Second Treatise* is to hold that Locke is using the contrast between America and Native American cultures on the one hand and Europe on the other to try to make it clear that civil society has benefits that make it preferable to the state of nature. I will call this the *Contrast Interpretation*. This interpretation starts with the view that Locke's chief concern in the *Second Treatise* is making plain the evils of absolute monarchy and the nature and benefits of legitimate civil government as Locke conceives it. The differences between the state of nature and civil government shows both why government is necessary when population increases and resources become scarce, and why the economic system in the state of civil society is preferable to that of the state of nature. The contrast between Native Americans and European cultures illustrates these differences. If this interpretation is correct, Locke is not trying to justify European settlement in America much less the seizure of Native American lands and genocidal attacks on those who resist such seizure. I am going to argue that this interpretation is to be preferred to the one considered next.

A second interpretation suggests that the point of the contrast between America and Europe is that it is legitimate for Europeans to settle in America and to dispossess Native Americans of their land. I will call this the *Dispossession Interpretation*. From Popkin and Brachen, to James Tully's influential article "Rediscovering America: Aboriginal Rights and the Two Treatises" and beyond, a constant charge against Locke is that in the chapter on property in the *Second Treatise* he is making an effort to justify European (and in particular English) appropriation of Native American lands on the grounds that the natives fail to engage in agriculture in the way in which Europeans do.[11] Thus, while allowing that Native Americans are people, and have rights, this argument focuses on a single right, that to property, and not all property, but land as property, and holds that Native Americans may be dispossessed of their lands. The issue of racism comes up in this context because Popkin, for example, holds that Locke is one of the originators of the degeneracy theory, holding that Native Americans may be dispossessed of their land because of their own personal failings in not being like Europeans. These Europeans farm and enclose lands and produce more than they themselves need and use money to trade (Popkin, 1980, p. 84). There are two distinct variants of the Dispossession Interpretation.[12] The first holds that resistance to dispossession legitimizes conquest and slavery for those who resist. Popkin and Tully subscribe to this variant. The second is a peaceful assimilation model. Squadrito and Arneil are adherents of this view.

The Contrast and Dispossession Interpretations share a certain amount in common. The claim that Locke's experience as a colonial administrator and trade expert inform the relevant paragraphs in chapter 5 of the *Second Treatise* is compatible with both interpretations, as is the observation that the language in these sections bears striking similarity to the language of works by colonial writers (whose books were in Locke's library) justifying the dispossession of Native Americans of their lands. That Locke might use European settlement in America to illustrate legitimate acquisition of land is quite compatible with the Contrast Interpretation. Where the two interpretations differ is in what to make out of all this.

James Tully is the foremost exponent of the Dispossession Interpretation. Tully makes a number of points. First, he claims that, in treating America as a state of nature, Locke fails to recognize the sovereignty of Native American governments. The British government, by contrast, routinely made treaties with tribes, thereby recognizing their sovereignty. On the Dispossession Interpretation, Locke's failure to recognize native sovereignty removes from native peoples their best line of defense against the taking of their lands. If there is going to be a discussion about land in America, it is going to be on the basis of individual land holding. If, however, Locke is not trying to justify European seizure of Native American lands, his failure to recognize Native American sovereignty takes on a less sinister meaning. On the Contrast Interpretation, Locke is using the contrast between Native Americans and Europeans to explain the difference between the various stages of the state of nature and civil society. Locke clearly recognizes that some native American societies have civil governments, but he is not focusing on these. In doing this he is distorting, very likely badly distorting, the facts, but his aim is not robbery and pillage. Let us turn to the issue of land.

The crucial issue here is the term "wasteland." What exactly does the term "wasteland" mean and how does it relate to Native American land? "Wasteland," Locke says, is "land which is wholly left to nature, that hath no improvement, of pasturage, tilling or planting" (*Second Treatise*, 2, 5, 42). Was there any such land in America? Locke, along with his colonial sources, claimed there was. Samuel Purchas, for example, remarks that the English "seek habitation there in vacant places" (quoted in Arneil, 1996, p. 109). Locke writes: "let him plant in some in-land vacant places in America." Englishmen and other Europeans had a right to settle that land in America, which was not being used by its inhabitants, and to do so without their consent. I will call this the "unused land" interpretation of "wasteland."

Locke clearly recognizes Native Americans as hunting and gathering people. Locke grants that Native Americans have the right to the berries they gather, and the deer they kill. Native Americans hunted over considerable areas. But Locke seems clearly to hold that while the animals hunted might be made private property by the labor of hunting, the land over which they hunted was still common and so open for settlement. The analogy here seems to be that the wilderness is like the sea, which Locke calls the last great commons. Hunting, then, is like fishing (*Second Treatise*, 2, 5, 30). Locke makes the criterion for property in land tilling, planting, improving, and cultivating as much as one can use the product. Native Americans also farmed. Locke does not explicitly use Native Americans as examples in talking about farming, as he had done in giving examples of hunting and gathering.[13] Still, it would seem that where Native Americans did farm, they would have a right to their lands. It might seem that the upshot would be this. Europeans could settle in the wilderness in which Native Americans hunted, as long as they left as much and as good for the natives. They certainly could not appropriate Native American agricultural land. This is the account of "wasteland" which seems correct to me. D. Bishop gives a similar list of conditions for legitimate settlement (Bishop, 1997, p. 317).

According to some scholars, however, Locke seeks to undercut Native American ownership not only of their traditional hunting grounds but of their agricultural lands as well. There are two or perhaps three arguments that are deployed to suggest this. First, property in land might mean not only land that is farmed by private individuals, but that such land must be enclosed by fences to constitute legitimate property. Arneil and Bishop hold that Locke, along with various colonial writers, thinks that enclosure means putting up fences, and without this there is no property (Arneil, 1996, pp. 140–1; Bishop, 1997, p. 313). Since Native Americans did not put up fences, they did not enclose. Since they did not enclose, the land they labored on was not theirs. I don't think this is what Locke meant by enclosing. When he introduces the concept of enclosure, Locke writes: "He by his labour does, *as it were*, inclose it from the common" (italics added). The "as it were" means that labor and not fences is the defining characteristic of enclosure for Locke. Fences make no sense until property becomes a contentious issue and needs to be specified precisely – in a state of civil society (*Second*

Treatise, 2, 5, 38). Thus, Native American agricultural land that was tilled and culti-vated, though not fenced, should count as property for Locke.

The second argument has to do with productive use of land. Locke does claim that European use of land makes it more productive than Native American use of similar land in America. In large part, however, this is because the European economic system as a whole is more productive than the American economic system as a whole. Locke makes the claim of greater productivity repeatedly and in stronger and stronger terms. As Locke says, "A king of a large and fruitful territory there feeds, lodges, and is clad worse than a day labourer in England" (ibid., 2, 5, 41). Drawing the contrast between European and American use of land, Locke goes from asserting that 90 percent of the value of a product is produced by labor (compared to 10 percent from the land itself) in section 40 to 99.9 percent in section 43. What is the point of this emphatic con-trast? Both Squadrito and Arneil cite Locke's remark that: "God gave the world . . . to the use of the industrious and rational (and labour was to be his title to it; not to the fancy of the covetousness of the quarrelsome and contentious" (ibid., 2, 5, 34). They claim that by "the rational and the industrious" Locke means Europeans but not Native Americans (Arneil, 1996, pp. 148–9; Squadrito, 1996, p. 158).

Though one sense in which Native Americans might not be rational (that they have not discovered the Christian God) has been considered and rejected above, there is yet another. Reason is the law of nature. The law of nature tells us we are obliged to help in the preservation of all mankind (Squadrito, 1996, p. 154). The vast differ-ence between the productivity of the Devonshire farmer and the Native Americans on equally fertile land thus becomes the proof that natives do not obey the law of nature while Englishmen do (Arneil, 1996, p. 149). Since Native Americans do not recog-nize the obligation of the law of nature, e.g. the duty to preserve all mankind by labor and accumulation of private property, they are not fully rational. Thus, those who do recognize this obligation could take their lands from them. So, a right to land can be trumped by more productive use of the land, at least in the state of nature. But is this so? In section 6 of the chapter "Of the State of Nature," the only passage where this issue is discussed, Locke says:

> Everyone, as he is *bound to preserve himself*, and not to quit his station willfully, so by the like reason, when his own preservation comes not into competition, ought he, as much as he can, *to preserve the rest of mankind*, and may not, unless it be to do justice on an offender, take away or impair, the life, or what tends to the preservation of the life, liberty, health, limb or goods of another. (*Second Treatise*, 2, 2, 6)

This passage makes the preservation of the individual fundamental. It is only after this condition has been fulfilled ("when his own preservation does not come into competi-tion") that the preservation of mankind becomes an obligation and then it only requires that the individual do "as much as he can." So, how could one square this passage with the Dispossession Interpretation? According to the advocates of the Dispossession Interpretation, Native Americans, because they have a subsistence economy, cannot help in the preservation of the rest of mankind. This is their offense. But it is plain that on Locke's account, if one can only manage to achieve one's own subsistence, and can do no more, because of the "as much as he can" clause, one has no natural law obligation to help the preservation of the rest of mankind. Clearly there can be no violation of an obligation which one does not have. So, *ex hypothesi*, Native Americans cannot be violating the law of nature. Thus Locke is not claiming that Native Americans are less rational than Europeans because they are less productive, and he would surely reject the dispossession of Native American lands on this basis. It is also worth pointing out that in that remarkable passage from the *Letter Concerning Toleration* quoted above, Locke gives the Native Americans credit for preserving English colonists upon their arrival in America. So it is clear that Locke knows that the Native Americans did fulfill this clause in respect to his own countryman.

The third argument also makes claims about relative productivity, but adds the claim that Native American agricultural land is wasteland. Note that the "unused land" interpretation of the Contrast Hypothesis would not allow that Indian agricultural land could be wasteland. The basis of the claim that Locke regards Indian agricultural land as wasteland is the spoilage provision. This provision is one of the limitations that Locke places on the acquisition of property in the state of nature. One can legitimately take from what is held in common by mankind what one needs and can use for subsistence and barter. But as soon as one lets something spoil, one becomes a robber. The same qualification applies to the use of land. In section 38 Locke writes: "But if either the grass of his inclosure rotted on the ground or the fruits of his planting perished without gathering, and laying up, this part of the earth, notwithstanding his inclosure, was still to be looked on as waste, and might be the possession of any other" (ibid., 2, 5, 38). So what follows from this? The argument is that since European methods of agriculture are vastly more productive than the Native Americans' land use, it follows that the Native Americans are wasting the land, and it can be legitimately taken from them (Squadrito, 1996, pp. 156–7, 170). I claim that a careful consideration of each of the passages where Locke talks about wasteland shows that it is defined as being left to nature and unused as opposed to being tilled, planted, etc. It is never defined in terms of relative productivity such that land in less productive agricultural use would count as wasteland compared to land subject to more productive use. If the spoilage provision were to apply to Native American agricultural land, it would be because the Native Americans stopped using it. Still, if Locke is not trying to show that Native Americans are irrational and thus can be dispossessed of their lands, why does he insist so emphatically on the difference in productivity between the European and Native Americans economic systems? What other purpose could that contrast serve?

We might begin to answer this question by noting that Locke's analysis of the state of nature and civil society has several interrelated dimensions. There is the political dimension. Here the contrast is between no government, minimal government or bad government in the state of nature on one side and civil government on the other side. The state of nature is marked by the absence of real and genuine political power, while in civil society there is genuine political power. Then there is the economic dimension that complements and interrelates with the political dimension. The point of the contrast between the productivity of European agricultural methods and that of Native Americans is that in civil society, human beings are vastly more productive than they are in the state of nature. Indeed, they are so much more productive that they can fulfill the secondary provision of natural law to help preserve the rest of mankind far better than those in a state of nature. Thus there is an economic justification based on the law of nature for civil government, and not simply the justification that it is the remedy for the inconveniences of the state of nature. This is what I take to be the meaning of this contrast.

The final step on the Dispossession Interpretation is that, should the Native Americans resist the taking of their lands, they would be engaged in an unjust war, and could be justly slaughtered and enslaved by their European conquerors. And should they seek to retake their lands, they would be unjustly injuring those who took them (Arneil, 1996, p. 151). Thus Tully writes:

> The argument for dispossession by agricultural improvement was often supplemented by the natural law for just conquest if the native peoples resisted. But in Locke's theory of conquest (written for another purpose) the conqueror has not title to the property of the vanquished (180, 184). Therefore, if the Amerindians had property in their traditional land, conquest would not confer title over it. However, as Locke repeats twice in this section, in the case of conquest over a people in the state of nature, "where there is more land than the inhabitants possess, and make use of," the conqueror, "like any one[,] has liberty to make use of the waste." thereby bringing his theories of conquest and appropriation into harmony. (Tully, 1993, pp. 154–5)

Tully remarks that scholars have regularly interpreted Locke's account of slavery as applying to African slavery. He suggests that it may have been intended to apply to Native Americans.

Let us move backwards, starting with conquest and enslavement. First, against the scholars whom Tully cites, I have argued that Locke's theory of slavery would condemn the institutions and practices of Afro-American slavery. (Uzgalis, 1998) There is even less reason to think that it applies to Native Americans. As a colonial administrator, Locke, and the proprietors for whom he worked, were in regular conflict with the Carolina colonists over the issue of trade with the Native Americans and Indian slavery. The proprietors wanted the colonists to engage in agriculture, but the money was in the Indian trade that included the trade in Indian slaves. (Sirmans, 1996, p. 33) Why then would Locke, who struggled with colonists to prevent them from engaging in the Indian slave trade, suddenly turn around and in a few paragraphs of the chapter on property in the *Second Treatise* justify such activities?

Barbara Arneil in her book *John Locke and America* argues for a different variant of the Dispossession Interpretation. She holds that Locke is writing a defense of England's claims to land in America against aboriginal rights, but that "Locke argues forcefully against the right of property by virtue of conquest. This argument is a direct attack on the views of Hugo Grotius and, more particularly, the Spanish who justified appropriation of land by right of force" (Arneil, 1996, p. 19). Both Arneil and Squadrito present powerful evidence against Tully's claim that Locke's argument is aimed to justify the conquest of Indian agricultural lands (ibid., pp. 163–5; Squadrito, 1996, pp. 157, 159–63, this volume pp. 110–11).

Arneil and Squadrito agree with every step in Tully's argument except the last. I have already suggested that one can reject the argument at an earlier point. I think there are excellent reasons not to attribute the dispossession argument from agricultural productivity to Locke. In fact, I think there are good reasons to completely reject the idea that Locke wrote this section of the chapter "Of Property" in order to justify English settlement in the Americas. First, Locke does not explicitly announce this as his project, and it is open to an alternative interpretation that is better supported by the text. Second, he fails to mention a single specific colony or to consider any of the other grounds for justifying settlement. Where he does mention acquiring land in America, it is always those "inland vacant places." This seems to imply that the entire seaboard of America is not open for settlement, yet he never discusses who owns various portions of it or what their title is to it. This is a remarkably short and vague performance for someone weighing in on what Tully calls the most contentious issue in the seventeenth and eighteenth centuries (Cf. Squadrito, 1996, p. 158). On the other side, if the Contrast Interpretation is correct, these passages are doing their job adequately, for they have much less weight to bear than the Dispossession Interpretation would put on them.

On my interpretation of this section of the Chapter "Of Property" in the *Second Treatise*, Locke's view is that there is enough room in America for both colonists and Native Americans, and that the colonists should leave the Native Americans as much and as good as they found there, and that they certainly have no rights to Native American agricultural land. Locke was wrong, indeed disastrously wrong, in assuming that there was enough and as good to satisfy both cultures. Still, the point of the comparison between Europe and America is not to provide a justification for European settlement, much less to justify the dispossession of Indian lands. Rather, it is to show the vast difference between the stages of the state of nature and a state of civil society, and in particular to show the vast superiority of the latter over the former in economic terms, something which would not otherwise be obvious.

Locke and Cultural Development: Degeneracy

Richard Popkin claims that Locke is the originator of the degeneracy theory. He claims that Locke believes that Native Americans have forfeited their right to property because of "personal failings" in not using their labor to develop the land in the ways that Europeans have. "Personal failings" is a rather vague term. It is possible that Popkin had in mind the argument from reason, natural law and productivity refuted in the last section of this paper. But he may have meant that, while reasonable, Native Americans are lazy and sinful, and thus fail to engage in agriculture in the way in which Europeans do. Arneil and Squadrito say similar things.

In trying to determine whether Locke is a degeneracy theorist in Popkin's sense, it will be useful to compare his account of the Native Americans with that of Jared Diamond. Diamond's recent book, *Guns, Germs and Steel*, is a study of the ultimate causes of the Spanish (and hence European) conquest of the New World. Diamond claims to be designing a nonracist explanation of the European conquest of most of the world in the centuries following the voyages of Vasco de Gama and Columbus (Diamond, 1997, pp. 18–24). Diamond claims that the proximate causes of the Spanish conquest are that one side, the Spaniards, had guns, germs and steel as weapons, while the other side, the Aztecs, the Incas and the tribes who unsuccessfully opposed the conquest, had none of these things (ibid., ch. 3). Diamond proposes an explanation of the ultimate causes that produced these proximate causes (ibid., chs 4–10).

Diamond takes geographical variation of domesticated species of plants and animals as the ultimate causes that explain the split between hunting/gathering and agricultural societies, and the differences in speed of development of these cultures. In brief, agricultural cultures tend to acquire guns, germs and steel (and much else that is connected with these things), while hunting and gathering cultures do not. I am not concerned here with the details of Diamond's theory or even if it is plausible. I am interested in why it is non-racist. What makes his theory non-racist is that he postulates uniform human abilities, creativity and intelligence in dealing with the varying conditions provided by geography and chance. So, it is not differences in the abilities or intelligence of people which explains why Spain invaded the Americas and conquered the Aztecs and the Incas and not vice versa. Rather, it is the cumulative effect of differences in the biogeography of the planet, which produced these differences. This is why the theory is claimed to be a non-racist explanation.

There are a number of fascinating parallels between Locke's account of development and Diamond's. But what is of more importance, for present purposes, is that Locke, like Diamond, argues that it is the particular conditions that a culture is faced with that determines the forms of property which that culture will develop and not the abilities or failings of particular individuals. Thus, in section 48 Locke imagines an island separate from all possible commerce with the rest of the world in which there are a mere hundred families. In this island there are sheep, horses, cows, and other useful animals, and land enough for corn "for a hundred thousand times as many." But in this island there is nothing to serve in the place of money. Under these conditions Locke asks: "what reason could anyone have to enlarge his possessions beyond the use of his family, and a plentiful supply to its *consumption*, either in what their own industry produced, or they could barter for like, useful commodities with others?" He replies: "Where there is not some thing, both lasting and scarce, and so valuable to be hoarded up, there men will not be apt to enlarge their possessions of land, were it never so rich, never so free for them to take . . ." He then goes on to apply this model explicitly to conditions in America. He writes:

> for I ask, what would a man value ten thousand, or an hundred thousand acres of excellent *land*, ready cultivated, and well stocked too with cattle, in the middle of the inland parts of *America*, where he had no hopes of commerce with other parts of the world, to draw *money to* him by the sale of product? It would not be worth the inclosing, and we should see him give up again to the wild common of nature, whatsoever would be more than would supply the conveniences of life to be there for him and his family. (*Second Treatise*, 2, 5, 48)

On Locke's account, this is what one of those rational and industrious Europeans would do under these conditions. These are precisely the conditions in which the Native

Americans lived. So, there is no personal failing on the part of the Native Americans in not cultivating the land in that way that Europeans do. Nor are they failing to be reasonable.

One might, however, push the question back a level. Why is it that at Locke's period Native Americans have not discovered money and commerce? The answer is that such discoveries depend on the vagaries of fortune, and in particular on the unpredictable advent of cultural heroes who make such discoveries (Essay, 4, 12, 11). In this sense, Locke's account is neither as explanatory nor interesting as that of Jared Diamond. But insofar as it insists that the conditions under which people operate determine the kind of property system which they have, and not their personal achievements or failings, it is a non-racist account for precisely the same reason as that which Diamond gives. So Popkin is wrong, and Locke is not the originator of the degeneracy theory.

Conclusion

The European colonial system in operation in Locke's lifetime, and thereafter, perpetrated injustices on a colossal scale against peoples of color. Some ten million Black Africans were transported across the Atlantic into American slavery in the three and a half centuries of the slave trade. Over two centuries, aboriginal peoples in the Americas saw their number disastrously diminished and saw their lands and cultures dominated by European invaders. At the same time, European philosophers were fashioning political philosophies of equality and natural rights and creating a democratic ideal. Locke is particularly remarkable in this regard because of his rejection of the principle that might makes right. Locke's philosophy, if applied in a straightforward way, condemns the economic and political practices of many Europeans and American colonists. How are we to explain this inconsistency?

Scholars have attempted to reduce the inconsistency by arguing that Locke is a racist who never intended his doctrines of natural rights and liberty to apply to people of color. The conclusions which I have reached in the course of this paper is that this way of resolving the problem is quite unlikely to provide the explanation we want. In particular, strong racism, and we might take this as ranging over both biological and cultural varieties of racism, requires an empirical account or a theory to explain the inferiority of one group to another and a moral theory to justify enslavement or other ill treatment. What Locke says in the course of his philosophical works provides no such empirical account of the inferiority of one group over another or a moral theory which would justify the enslavement or other ill treatment of any particular group. Indeed, quite the contrary; Locke's philosophy provides much good material for an anti-racist philosophy.

Was Locke then simply oblivious of the developing processes of domination and the injustices they were spawning in the colonial system of which he was one of the architects? The passage from the *Letter Concerning Toleration* quoted earlier is an instance where Locke shows a clear awareness of the low motives and high-sounding justifications for robbery of some of his own countrymen. He condemns them in emphatic terms. In this case, the public condemnation of the religious justification for robbery is perfectly in accord with the emphasis on justice in Locke's political philosophy in the *Second Treatise*. He also extends his principles of religious toleration to natives and so, in effect, proposes the basic principle of a liberal theory of the multi-cultural state. My own view is that Locke had no real conception of what the system he was building would become. He saw problems, but thought they could be controlled and resolved. Still, in using his considerable powers to nurture a colonial system some of whose participants committed serious crimes and immoralities, while at the same time writing a philosophy which clearly condemned those evils and proposed an alternate way for different cultures to relate, John Locke surely was involved, in a truly remarkable way, in that inconsistency not to be excused.

Notes

1. There is a debate among historians about how much influence Locke's philosophy actually had on the American revolutionaries. However this debate plays out, the point here is about the conceptual similarities between the ideology of the American revolutionaries and Locke's political philosophy. Locke's philosophy could serve to inform and explain the ideology of the American revolutionaries, even if it did not influence their thinking. I am inclined toward the view that in important cases, such as Jefferson, it not only could explain, it in fact did have an important influence.

2. I regard almost all of this evidence as quite inconclusive. Regarding Locke's involvement in the writing of the Fundamental Constitution of the Carolinas, and in particular the passage about freedman having power over their Negro slaves – the notion that this is an expression of personal racism on Locke's part seems to me rather improbable. A much more plausible explanation of its presence in the Fundamental Constitution is that Sir John Colleton (the real founder of the Carolina enterprise) was a Barbados planter. Part of the plan for the Carolinas was that people were going to emigrate from Barbados with their slaves to the Carolinas. They would naturally worry about whether this move might endanger the power they held over their slaves. It would be natural for Colleton to propose such a clause to allay their fears. Thus the inclusion of this clause may well say little or nothing about Locke's views. Similarly, while Peter Colleton (Sir John Colleton's son) may have been Locke's friend and correspondent because of Locke's involvement with the Carolina enterprise, Locke had another friend, Benjamin Furley, who was so seriously opposed to slavery that he published a plan for abolition. Finally, slavery was not as exclusively connected with Negro slavery, and thus involvement with the slave trade was not as much an indicator of racial prejudice, as it became in the eighteenth and nineteenth centuries. In the *Second Treatise* Locke makes no reference to African-American slavery. The slave master he gives as an example is a galley captain. Some of the soldiers from Monmouth's rebellion (in which Locke was deeply involved) were sent into slavery as punishment for their part in that effort in the mid-1680s – some years after Locke wrote the *Two Treatises of Government*. As for Locke's views about Native Americans as a colonial administrator, I take this topic up later in this paper.

3. One might think that the proper interpretation of this claim would be using language of any kind as opposed to not being a language-user. But this, while vastly more plausible, would get one very close to the Cartesian view which Brachen sees as non-racist. For this reason, I think the interpretation in the text must be the correct one.

4. Popkin (1980) distinguishes the degeneracy theories from the polygenetic and when he

discusses Locke cites Brachen (1973) for support. Evidently he failed to notice that the kind of racism implied by Brachen's claims is different from the kind which he attributes to Locke.

5. Two such are Kathy Squadrito (1975) and Bernard R. Boxill (1998).

6. For a discussion of these claims see Uzgalis (1998), pp. 73–4, note 19. Wayne Glausser thinks this passage (along with others he cites) suggests "a prejudice well rooted in English society." I conceded this point, simply noting that Locke does not endorse that prejudice. Upon consideration, however, I think this passage goes against the suggestion that there was a well-rooted prejudice in English society. Locke thinks the conclusion that a Negro is not a man is absurd. If he expected that his readers would not find it absurd, it would not have served his purposes in showing how useless and dangerous maxims could be. So, I would suggest this passage provides some evidence that at the time Locke wrote this passage, the claim that "a Negro is not a man" would have been regarded as absurd in the circles in British society for whom the *Essay* was written.

7. Brachen also claims that Locke does not regard Catholics as persons and thus disenfranchises them. In fact, Locke does not disenfranchise Catholics because they are not persons, but because they are, he holds, agents of a foreign power – the Pope. Thus Locke regards Catholics much in the same way some conservative and patriotic Americans regarded members of the Communist Party in the United States during the 1950s.

8. In Squadrito (1996), p. 173 (this volume p. 118) she notes that Locke's position in *The Fundamental Constitution of the Carolinas* is one of toleration. She continues: "Natives are to be left alone to practice their own customs and religion. Again, this position was developed for a particular context and may not express Locke's more general view." I believe the quotation from the *Letter Concerning Toleration* makes it quite plain that this was a consistent application of principle and does represent Locke's general view.

9. I disagree with them even about the degree to which the sense of reason they identify is "Eurocentric." In her (1996), p. 150, Squadrito rejects James Farr's claim that Locke approves of the "rustic reason" of the Native Americans in *Essay*, 4, 20. She indignantly remarks that Locke is certainly not saying that Native Americans are more reasonable than scholastic philosophers. I would suggest that this is just what he is saying.

10. One might reasonably complain that Locke's account of person in *Essay*, 2, 27, 9 was written in 1694, well after the *Second Treatise* was published. I would argue, however, that the *Second Treatise* shows clear signs that Locke already saw this connection between personhood, reason and the law. See, for example, 2, 6, 57 through 2, 5, 63, which begins: "That *freedom* then of man and liberty of acting according to his own will, is grounded on his having *reason*, which is able to instruct him in that law he is to govern himself by . . ." etc.

11. For a partial list of authors who subscribe to this view, see Squadrito (1996), p. 155. This would have to be updated to include Arneil's (1996) and also Bishop's (1997). Bishop, while he claims to accept Tully's view, makes a number of points which suggest that the Dispossession Interpretation is false.

12. There is yet another pair of variants: some advocates of the Dispossession interpretation who hold that the *Second Treatise* is only appropriate to the American context (Lebovics, 1986, and perhaps Arneil, 1996), and, on the other hand, those who hold that it serves both Locke's purposes in struggling against English absolutism and in justifying American settlement (Tully, 1993, and Squadrito, 1996).

13. There is disagreement among scholars as to whether Locke was aware of native agriculture in North America. Squadrito (1996) claims he was aware, Bishop (1997) suggests that he was not. Given that Locke seems to see Native American cultures as ranging through all of the stages of the state of nature, this would suggest that he knew that some native

cultures engaged in agriculture. Whether this was true about North America may not be important. It also seems to me that the passage I quoted earlier from Locke (1991) at least suggests that he did know.

References

Arneil, Barbara 1996: *John Locke and America*. Oxford: Clarendon Press.
Berlin, Ira 1998: *Many Thousands Gone: The First Two Centuries in North America*. Cambridge MA: the Belknap Press of Harvard University. Section III: "The Revolutionary Generations."
Bracken, Harry 1973: Essence, Accident and Race. *Hermathena*, CXVI, Winter 1973, 81–96.
Bishop, John Douglas 1997: Locke's Theory of Original Appropriation and the Right of Settlement in Iroquois Territory. *Canadian Journal of Philosophy*, vol. 27, no. 3, September 1997, 311–37.
Boxill, Bernard R. 1998: Radical Implications of Locke's Moral Views: The Views of Fredrick Douglas. In Tommy Lott (ed.), *Subjugation and Bondage: Critical Essays on Slavery and Social Philosophy*, Oxford: Rowmann and Littlefield Publishers, 29–49.
Diamond, Jared 1997: *Guns, Germs and Steel: The Fates of Human Societies*. New York: W. W. Norton & Co.
Farr, James 1986: So Vile and Miserable an Estate: The Problem of Slavery in Locke's Political Thought. *Political Theory*, no. 13, 263–89.
Lebovics, Herman 1986: The Uses of America in Locke's *Second Treatise of Government. Journal of the history of Ideas*, vol. 47, no. 4, 567–82.
Locke, John 1975: *An Essay Concerning Human Understanding*. Ed. P. Nidditch. Oxford: Clarendon Press.
Locke, John 1980: *The Second Treatise of Civil Government*. Ed. C. B. Macpherson. Indianapolis: Hackett Publishing Co.
Locke, John 1991: *A Letter Concerning Toleration in Focus*. Ed. John Horton and Susan Mendus. London: Routledge.
Popkin, Richard 1980: The Philosophical Basis of Modern Racism. In Richard A. Watson and James E. Force (eds), *The High Road to Pyrrhonism*, San Diego, Calif.: Austin Hill Press.
Squadrito, Kathy 1975: Locke's View of Essence and Its Relation to Racism: A Reply to Professor Bracken. *The Locke Newsletter*, no. 6, Summer 1975, 41–54.
Squadrito, Kathy 1996: Locke and the Dispossesion of the American Indian. *American Indian and Research Journal*, vol. 20, no. 4, Fall, 145–81.
Sirmans, M. Eugene 1966: *Colonial South Carolina: A Political History 1663–1763*. Chappell Hill: University of North Carolina Press.
Tully, James 1993: Rediscovering America: The Two Treatises and Aboriginal Rights. In James Tully, *An Approach to Political Philosophy: Locke in Context*, Cambridge: Cambridge University Press.
Uzgalis, William 1988: The Anti-Essential Locke and Natural Kinds. *The Philosophical Quarterly*, vol. 38, no. 152, July, 330–9.
Uzgalis, William 1998: The Same Tyrannical Principle: Locke's Legacy on Slavery. In Tommy Lott (ed.), *Subjugation and Bondage: Critical Essays on Slavery and Social Philosophy*, Oxford: Rowmann and Littlefield Publishers, 49–79.

CHAPTER 6

Locke and the Dispossession of the American Indian*

KATHY SQUADRITO

In the *Second Treatise of Civil Government* Locke remarks that "in the beginning all the world was America," viz., "uncivilized."[1] Roy Harvey Pearce contends that during centuries of native dispossession "virtually all Americans were, in the most general sense, Lockeans," Lockeans primarily in their attitudes toward land and private property.[2] James Tully argues that Euroamericans are at present Lockeans in the sense that Locke provides "a set of concepts we standardly use to represent and reflect on contemporary politics."[3] Tully, Michael K. Green, and an increasing number of historians accord Locke's *Second Treatise* a prominent role in American Indian dispossession.[4] Richard Drinnon, Francis Jennings, Russell Thornton and David E. Stannard do not assign the *Second Treatise* as influential a role as Tully, but place it in a context, unlike Tully, of historical genocide, of an American Holocaust.[5]

In this paper I address two different interpretations of Locke's social and political work. First, the generous interpretation that Locke did not have disparaging things to say with regard to American Indians and that his works do not exhibit ethnocentric arguments. Second, the interpretation popularized by James Tully that Locke's agricultural argument was developed with the intention of taking American Indian land without consent, that Locke's work is in large part responsible for the dispossession of the American Indian. I argue that a generous reading of Locke does not adequately portray his attitude toward American Indians. At the same time, interpretations placing Locke's political arguments as *central* to the history of dispossession are not entirely warranted. Most commentators focus exclusively on Locke's *Two Treatises of Government*. I present a more comprehensive analysis and argue that considering the religious and political aspect of Locke's theory of knowledge, it is the *Essay Concerning Human Understanding* which has had a more lasting influence for American Indians.

Descriptions of American Indians in the *Essay*

In general, the European attitude toward native people of America was negative, characterized by the stereotypes of "savage," "ignorant," "lazy," and "wild beasts." Was this negative opinion one that Locke held? According to Neal Wood, Locke's "view of natives and tribesmen was not marked by the negative attitude and anti-primitivism to be found in much contemporary and later literature on the subject."[6] James Farr contends that Locke did not hold an "empirical theory of racial inferiority," that "even 'savages' are born free and equal, with a full complement of natural rights." It is interesting, he says, "that Locke had generous or nondisparaging things to say about other peoples of color, especially American Indians;" further, Locke "was intrigued by their customs and their medical practices . . . convinced of their 'native rustic reason,' and praising of their forms of government."[7] According to Thomas L. Pangle, Locke's view of American Indians is an aspect of his overall political theory, a theory which exhibits a sincere commitment to the natural needs of all humanity.[8]

Locke's knowledge of colonial affairs was extensive. An avid reader of navigation and travel literature, Locke also served as commissioner of the Board of Trade. Richard Hakluyt's *The Principle Navigations, Voyages, Traffiques, and Discoveries of the English Nation* provided Locke with some fairly accurate descriptive information with regard to native dress, customs, government, and religion. However, stereotypes of the ignorant, wild and immoral natives were also prevalent throughout the work. Robert Berkhofer, Jr, argues that how the English moved from "supposedly factual descriptions of Native Americans to the symbolism of the Indian can be traced from Richard Hakluyt to Thomas Hobbes and John Locke."[9] Hakluyt's compendia contains conflicting descriptions of native people. They were described as handsome, good, civil, generous, loving, gentle, faithful, industrious in labor and quick of apprehension; on the other hand, as deceitful, ignorant, sinful, having no government or religion, as thieves and barbarians. For example, one finds:

> They are of much simplicity and great cowards, void of all valor, and are great witches. They use diverse times to talk with the Devil, to whom they do certain sacrifices.

> We found the people most gentle, loving, and faithful, void of all guile and treason, and such as live after the manner of the golden age.[10]

Given the wealth of information at his disposal, which images of native people did Locke employ? It would appear that he uses somewhat conflicting descriptions to suit his ideological needs. In contradistinction to Hobbes's notion of pre-political society as one of constant war, Locke needs to use the image of a relatively gentle and moral native to support his own political views. This notwithstanding, the more consistent image is of the immoral, sinful native.

Locke frequently uses examples of native people to support his epistemological theories concerning the origin of knowledge. In his polemic against innate ideas he uses natives to confirm that all ideas originate from experience, *viz.*, sensation and reflection. The ignorance of native people is a constant theme. Locke classifies American

Indians into a group along with children, idiots, the illiterate, and other savages.[11] In spite of his knowledge of American Indian cultural diversity (languages, art forms, land use, and government), he chooses to ignore varied achievements and stress that which he assumes to be deficiency. Locke says:

> Amongst *children*, *idiots*, *savages*, and the grossly illiterate, what general maxims are to be found? What universal principles of knowledge? Their notions are few and narrow, borrowed only from those objects, they have had to do with, and which have made upon their senses the frequentest and strongest impressions. A child knows his nurse, and his cradle, and by degrees the play thins of little more advanced age. And a young savage has perhaps, his head filled with love and hunting, according to the fashion of his tribe. But he that from a child untaught, or a wild inhabitant of the woods, will expect these abstract maxims and reputed principles of sciences, will I fear, find himself mistaken. Such kind of general propositions, are seldom mentioned in the huts of *Indians*.[12]

Locke's point could have been expressed in an entirely different way. Contrasting scientifically literate Europeans with Europeans lacking such knowledge would have been sufficient. Here native tribes are compared to European nations, the former considered unlearned *in general*. American Indians could also make the same point with regard to innate ideas by stressing supposed deficiencies in European thought and learning, e.g., inability to see spiritual value in land, inability to comprehend the advantages of communal living, lack of generosity, etc. Locke's example perpetuates the stereotype of native people as lacking diversity, as immoral, ignorant, wild, nomadic hunters. Savages, he says, "being of all others the least corrupted by customs, or borrowed opinions; learning, and education, having not cast their Native thoughts into new molds" still do not show innate ideas (*Essay*, 1, 2, 27). The mind of the indigenous person is thus considered one of the closest to his *tabula rasa* as possible. Since abstract ideas are considered that which puts a perfect distinction between man and beast, the reader is led to regard American Indians, who are confined to simple ideas or a few abstract ideas, as akin to animals (ibid., 2, 11, 10).

Locke further deprecates indigenous people of the world by considering their religions to be nothing but superstition or atheism. American Indians, like the children and young people Locke compares them to, may employ the name of God, yet says Locke, "the notions they apply this name to, are so odd, low, and pitiful, that no body can imagine, they were taught by a rational man" (ibid., 1, 4, 16). He classifies native religions as ideas developed by "the lazy and inconsiderate part of men" who simply receive such notions by chance from common tradition and "vulgar conceptions, without much beating their heads about them." True notions of God are acquired, he says, only by "a right and careful employment" of thought and reason (ibid., 1, 4, 15).

Locke does not appear to consider the possibility that American Indians *enjoyed* living as they did. He speaks of the "Ancient savage Americans" as *lacking* and *wanting* the conveniences of life (ibid., 4, 12, 11). Locke's choice of examples obviously reflects the ethnocentric attitude of his time. Since American Indians would hardly consider such remarks generous or nondisparaging, Farr's analysis *appears* to make sense only because he places Locke in a non-Aristotelian context. Unlike Aristotle, Locke does not consider any human to be innately inferior to other humans. In the *Second Treatise*, he asserts that all men are created free and equal with similar *capacities* for rational thought and knowledge (*Second Treatise*, 4). Differences are explained by environment and education. Locke does not confine derisive language to American Indians; he speaks of criminals, the unemployed, lazy, and poor of England in the same way. In fact, it is often difficult to determine which group he is speaking about. References to "wild savage beasts," e.g., in chapter II of the *Second Treatise*, are often about criminals of the world. However, the view that all men are created equal does nothing to eliminate ethnocentrism and its unfortunate consequences for indigenous people. Historically, *forced* assimilation has followed the claim of original equality.

Descriptions of American Indians in the *Two Treatises* of Government

The images of American Indians found in the *Two Treatises* are consistent with those of the *Essay*. The natives in the wild woods of America are categorized as "needy and wretched," as "poor in the comforts of life" (ibid., 37, 41). Locke's comparisons between Europeans, American Indians, and various ancient people reflect his belief in stages of human development from savagery to civilization: "Thus in the beginning all the world was American, and more so than now; for no such thing as money was any where known" (ibid., 49). Ronald Meek has traced the essential component of developmental theories to modes of subsistence, the "normal" progression defined as hunting, pasturage, agriculture, and commerce: "To each of these modes of subsistence . . . there corresponded different sets of ideas and institutions relating to law, property, and government, and also different sets of customs, manners, and morals."[13] Meek considers Locke's contribution to the development of this theory significant. Locke contends that the difference between a native and "a more improved English-man" lies in the exercise of faculties bound within customs of their respective country (*Essay*, 1, 4, 12).

Locke was aware of narratives which attested to the sophistication of native government and agriculture. In his accounts of Virginia (1607–9), John Smith wrote that the natives participated in "such government as that their magistrates for good commanding, and their people for due obedience and obeying, excel many places that would be accounted very civil."[14] The first illustrations of Virginia depict natives living in settled villages with agricultural plots. Smith points out that natives lived with the understanding of precise boundaries demarcating the land of each tribe. Early English accounts indicate a wide variety of crops planted on a single field. Neal Salisbury notes: "as the descriptions imply, agriculture had replaced hunting as the principal source of food for Indians in southern New England by the seventeenth century." Locke nonetheless presents the reader with the historically inaccurate generalization of American Indians as hunters roaming over, and never cultivating, the land. Anthony Wallace surmises that such a disregard for fact "may in part have been caused by a kind of gender bias." For many Europeans, "What constituted a people's character, their economic system, their political structure, was what *men* did."[15] Since American Indian men were often described as wandering over their tribal hunting grounds, Locke categorizes their culture as pre-political or uncivilized. He chooses to present the image of American

Indians discussed by Joseph Acosta: "and if Josephes Acosta's word may be taken, he tells us, that in many parts of America there was no government at all" (*Second Treatise*, 102).[16]

Locke equates American Indian society with the first stages of life in Asia and Europe; "the Kings of the Indians in America" are merely generals of their armies and have little authority and dominion in times of peace (*Second Treatise*, 108). As William G. Batz suggests, given Locke's respect for Acosta's work on the West Indies, it may be more than coincidental "that Acosta's history of the Aztec civilization corresponds quite closely with Locke's developmental hypothesis."[17] In his history of Central America, Acosta describes the first inhabitants of the Indies as "barbarous . . . without law, without king, and without any certain place of abode, but [they] go in troupes like savage beasts."[18] Since there are few inhabitants and no such thing as money, people are not inclined to enlarge their possessions, especially in land.

What Locke does not mention is just as significant as what he does. Acosta's praise of American Indians does not fit into the ideological context of "primitive man." In this context it is more important for Locke to pick negative images from Acosta's work. Acosta often vacillates between describing American Indians as a mixture of man and beast and as rational and civil men.

Locke uses the American Indian as an example to explain the *origin* of political power. He makes it clear that the purpose of the *Two Treatises* is to justify the glorious and bloodless revolution of 1688, to restore power in the consent of the people. Consent theory was defended by a sustained attack on the doctrine of absolute monarchy or the divine right of kings to arbitrary power. Filmer's popular defense of this doctrine, *Patriarcha*, was Locke's primary focus throughout the *Treatises*. With regard to the origin of government, Filmer argues that people are not free but born in subjection to their parents. This royal or fatherly authority was first vested in Adam and by right subsequently belongs to all princes. Locke contends that people are born free and have a natural right to life, liberty, and private property. Monarchy can be justified only by the indirect consent of the people through parliament. He explains that "to understand political power right, and derive it from its original, we must consider what state all men are naturally in" (ibid., 4).

Locke needs to present an image of the peaceful, friendly American Indian to represent the primitive condition of humans and explain the origin of private property and government. Contrary to Hobbes's notion of life in a state of nature being nasty, brutish, and short, a war of all against all, Locke argues that this pre-political society is a state of peace, good will, mutual assistance, and preservation. This is a state of liberty, but not license, for people do not have the right to destroy themselves or others. The state of nature, says Locke, "has a law of nature to govern it, which obliges every one: and reason, which is that law, teaches all mankind who will but consult it, that being all equal and independent, no one ought to harm another in his life, health, liberty, or possessions" (ibid., 6). Moral rules are given by God and form the law of nature, natural law or law of reason; this law is "set as a curb and restraint" to exorbitant desires (*Essay*, 1, 3, 13). Locke maintains that contracts are morally binding in a state of nature. "The promises and bargains for truck, etc., between . . . a Swiss and an Indian, in the woods of America, are binding to them, though they are perfectly in a state of nature in reference to one another. For truth and keeping of faith belongs to men as men, and not as members of society" (*Second Treatise*, 14).

Locke paints such an attractive picture of this stage that one wonders why people would consent to leave it for membership in a political society. Locke's answer involves recasting the American Indian (as he described all pre-political people) as somewhat less than peaceful and good-willed. The state of nature itself involves stages of progress, from peaceful co-existence with few possessions to conflict when possessions are enlarged, to a possible state of war when money is introduced. He contends that even though the law of nature is intelligible to all rational people, bias, self-interest, and ignorance of the law makes its adoption impractical. Further, since "everyone in that state being both judge and executioner of the law of nature, men being partial to themselves, passion and revenge is very apt to carry them too far" (ibid., 125). since there is a need for an established, settled, known law people "are quickly driven into society" (ibid., 127).

Property Rights

Locke points out that when harmony in a state of nature is disturbed by war, people have need for civil authority to settle disputes. The consent that establishes government entails sacrificing individual liberty to majority rule for the safety and good of the whole. The "great and chief end" of government, says Locke, is the preservation of property, property defined as life, liberty, and estate (ibid., 124). Locke's concern is with private property and its justification. In addition to Acosta, Locke was influenced by the early developmental views of Grotius, Hobbes, and Pufendorf. Like Pufendorf, Locke contends that in the first stage of society all things lay open to all men:

> God, who has given the world to men in common, has also given them reason to make use of it to the best advantage of life and convenience. The earth and all that is therein is given to men for the support and comfort of their being . . . all the fruits it naturally produces and beasts it feeds belong to mankind in common, as they are produced by the spontaneous hand of nature; and nobody has originally a private dominion, exclusive of the rest of mankind in any of them as they are thus in their natural state. (Ibid., 26)

Given the assumption of an original commons Locke attempts to justify private property "and that without any express compact of all the commoners" (ibid., 25). Unlike Grotius and Pufendorf, Locke insists that private ownership of land does not rest on the consent of anyone who may occupy such land.

Locke's view of property has been read as a justification for the displacement of American Indians. According to Lebovics, the arguments as set forth in the *Second Treatise* are logically inadequate and irrelevant "to English society both at the moment of the composition . . . and that of its publication." Locke's intention, he argues, is to justify "land for the taking in the New World."[19] In an unpublished apaper, Michael K. Green contends that Locke's whole account of property can be read as a justification for the displacement of the Native Americans. Arneil claims that "aware that

106

Indians in the New World could claim property through the right of occupancy, Locke developed a theory of agrarian labour which would . . . specifically exclude the American Indian from claiming land."[20] Tully construes the central concepts of the *Second Treatise* as an argument intended to justify "European settlement in America without the consent of the native people."[21] Although these claims go beyond the evidence provided in the *Essay* and *Second Treatise*, they may not be entirely lacking in credibility.

Locke contends that since God gave the world to men for the greatest conveniences of life, "it cannot be supposed he meant it should always remain common and uncultivated." He gave it to "the use of the industrious and rational (and labour was to be his title to it)" (ibid., 39). The "law of self preservation" dictates taking without consent, for "this law of reason makes the deer that Indians who hath killed it; 'tis allowed to be his goods who hath bestowed his labour upon it, though before, it was the common right of every one" (ibid., 30). The American Indian can claim property in the fruit or venison and other goods which nourish him as well as shells and other items removed from the common for the support of his life. The amount to be justly appropriated is limited to "as much as any one can make use of to any advantage of life before it spoils" (ibid., 31). Locke's major claim is that the chief matter of property is the earth itself. Yet American Indian dispossession is theoretically possible because land, says Locke, "is acquired as the former. As much land as a man tills, plants, improves, cultivates, and can use the product of, so much is his property. He by his labour does, as it were, inclose it from the common" (ibid., 32).

The waste limitation holds for land as well as perishable goods, for Europeans as well as American Indians. An individual may appropriate as much land as he can use and cultivate. Any property which spoils or lies in waste is not appropriated and may be taken by others. Waste is defined as "land that is left wholly to nature, that hath no improvement of pasturage, tillage, or planting" (ibid., 42). Once money is introduced into the state of nature the spoilage limitation is lifted; a person may thus "fairly possess more land than he himself can use the product of, by receiving in exchange for the overplus, gold and silver, which may be hoarded up without injury to anyone, these metals not spoiling" (ibid., 50).

Locke's agricultural argument was certainly not new. In the 1630s, John Winthrop, the first governor of the Massachusetts Bay Colony, argued that "that which lies in common, and hath never been replenished or subdued is free to any that possesse and improve it." Further, that "if we leave them sufficient for their use, we may lawfully take the rest, there being more than enough for them and us."[22] Similar views were expressed by Luther, Calvin, Purchase, Sir Thomas More and other well-known figures. Locke's arguments are essentially Puritan. Colonists were both morally and legally justified in taking native wasteland and subduing it, because God intended that land be cultivated.[23]

The image of the "wild Indian who knows no inclosure" (ibid., 26) is typical of the sixteenth and seventeenth centuries; roaming over land did not constitute labor or rational use of land. Locke's view of waste is not confined to hunting or roaming tribes. That many tribes did labor (plant, cultivate, and improve land) was obviously known to Locke. Enclosure and planting, however, are not sufficient to establish property rights. Locke argues: "But if either the grass of his inclosure rotted on the ground, or

107

the fruit of his planting perished without gathering, and laying up, this part of the earth, notwithstanding his inclosure, was still to be looked on as waste, and might be the possession of any other" (ibid., 38). This dictate occurs in the context of a discussion of biblical ages.

There is nothing in the above arguments that would indicate that Locke believes American Indians can be exterminated for land. Locke does not say that Europeans are justified in violent invasions of non-sedentary agricultural lands or that American Indians can be taken as slaves. He does not say *how* wasteland is to be taken by others. His account is descriptive, at times normative, and usually predictive. He explains that in the beginning:

> Cain might take as much ground as he could till, and make it his own land, and yet leave enough to Abel's sheep to feed on; a few acres would serve for both their possessions. But as families increased, and industry inlarged their stocks, their possessions inlarged with the need of them; but yet it was commonly without any fixed property in the ground, they made use of, till they incorporated, settled themselves together, and built cities, and then by consent, they come in time, to set out the bounds of their distinct territories, and by laws within themselves settled the *properties* of those of the same society. (Ibid., 38)

Locke may have made the same prediction concerning all inhabitants of America. He often compares the first peopling of the world by the children of Adam or Noah to European relationships with American Indians. The analogy demonstrates smallness of possessions, but does not account for cultural variance in America. Most often his primary concern is not with American Indians. Paragraph 39 clearly shows his focus: "And thus without supposing any private dominion, and property in Adam, over all the world, exclusive of all other men . . . we see how labour cold make men distinct titles to several parcels of it, for their private uses; wherein there could be no doubt of right, no room for quarrel." His concern is absolute monarchy. Contrary to Lebovics's claim, Locke's arguments were relevant to a host of problems facing English society; as Locke points out, it was important to argue for the preservation of natural rights "to save the nation when it was on the brink of slavery and ruine" (ibid., Preface). It was not sufficient for Locke to refute Filmer without providing an alternative consent theory which justifies private property.

Locke was undoubtedly interested in various justifications for colonizing America. He was familiar with the theories of Vitoria, Las Casas, Sepúlveda, Grotius, Pufendorf, and many others. As Arneil points out, the "question of property and the right of England to appropriate land already claimed by native Americans or other European nations is central to the colonial debates" of Locke's era.[24] It is possible that he intended to refute Filmer, provide an alternative theory, and at the same time justify taking Indian land. However, Locke's arguments when applied to American Indians are confused and incomplete. He is certainly not as explicit as his predecessors or contemporaries concerning the problem of developing occupied wasteland. Locke does not have a sustained theory or argument concerning cultural conflict and its consequences. He seems to assume that American Indians share at least some European values.

The desire to accumulate property beyond immediate or short-term need is regarded as universal. Locke was familiar with the sophisticated and often lucrative systems of trade that American Indians developed with Europeans. Since natives participated in the trade of perishable goods for shells, metal, and other durable goods, Locke concludes that they "have agreed to disproportionate and unequal possession of the earth" (ibid., 47–50). This "tacit and voluntary consent" to enlarge possessions by the use of money is justified prior to the establishment of government (ibid., 47). C. B. Macpherson notes that Locke sees land itself as just a form of capital, money to be distributed in trading stock or materials and wages, land to be used to produce commodities for trade.[25] When it comes to land, Locke does not consider American Indians "industrious and rational." Since they do not participate in commercial cultivation, they cannot complain when land is cultivated by Europeans. Of course, American Indians did not consent to private and disproportionate ownership of land. They did complain and did resist.

Conquest and Resistance

Locke's exact position on just war and native resistance is not clear. Glausser notes that "Locke nowhere says that those who would develop a wasteland may justly kill or enslave those who resist."[26] Nonetheless, recent interpretations place Locke in the historical context of More, Purchase, and Sepúlveda, or conquest and genocide rather than peaceful negotiation, treaties, or agreements. Green, for example, argues that Locke characterizes resistance as a war between the rational-industrious and the covetous-lazy: "These latter are unable or unwilling to labor . . . according to the law of war, it is legitimate for the victor to reduce the unjust aggressors in a war to slaves and to exercise despotic power over them."[27]

Tully construes several passages of the *Second Treatise* as evidence that Locke supported dispossession by force. The sections of concern, 8–11 and 17–19, are intentionally taken out of context and applied to American Indians. Tully states:

> When either slavery failed or all other means of dealing with the Amerindians proved ineffective, the practice in the colonies was to make war against the local tribes in a piece-meal fashion. . . . The usual justification for wars of this type was that the indians had resisted the settlers in some way or stolen something, and so violated natural law, activating the settlers' right to defend themselves and avail themselves of the rights of war. Locke underscores in no uncertain terms the natural law right to punish theft and violence with death and he construes this as a state of war.[28]

He goes on to point out that offenders are characterized by Locke as "Wild Savage Beasts" who "may be destroyed as a Lyon or a Tyger" (ibid., 11, 16). Tully points to section 10, in which Locke argues that the governments of England, France and Holland have a right to put to death an Indian who violates natural law. Similar interpretations are offered by M. Seliger, W. Glausser, H. M. Bracken and Richard H. Popkin.

109

Bracken and Popkin base their interpretation on a connection between Locke's empiricism and racism. If Locke does not openly support slavery and waging war against natives, this position can be deduced from his theory of wasteland, his financial involvement in the slave trade, and his position that humans are to be judged by observable characteristics only. According to Bracken, Locke assumed that "Africa and the Americas were waste land. If their residents resisted the take over of these waste lands, they could properly be taken as captives in a just war and made perpetual slaves."[29] Seliger contends that whether natives consent to the use of money or not, the "unavoidable implication of the whole inane argument is that the natives resistance to the conquest of their waste land turns them into aggressors and the Europeans, who appropriate the 'waste,' into the party which wards aggression off."[30]

Although there may be some grounds for this type of interpretation, Locke says a good deal to make one remain skeptical about his position. In paragraph 180, he indicates that his view of conquest is historically different from traditional doctrines. He explains that a conqueror "has not thereby a right and title to the possessions of those conquered." Conquest does not give a nation the right to rule or the right to the land of the vanquished. This, he says, "I doubt not, but at first sight will seem a strange doctrine, it being so quite contrary to the practice of the world." The common practice gave nations the right to territory and spoils; the conquered could be banished or forced into slavery. Perpetual slavery is not a view that fits into Locke's theory of just war. The children of slaves, not having committed an act of violence that deserves death, could not become slaves.[31] A just war is a defensive war to protect life and property, slavery justified only if aggressors are captives taken in such a war: "Indeed having, by his fault, forfeited his own life, by some act that deserves death; he, to whom he has forfeited it, may (when he has him in his power) delay to take it, and make use of him to his own service" (ibid., 23). With regard to conquest, Locke states:

> But granting that the conqueror in a just war has a right to the estates, as well as power over the persons of the conquered; which, 'tis plain, he hath not: Nothing of absolute power will follow from hence, in the continuance of the government. Because the descendants of these being all free-men, if he grants them estates and possessions to inhabit his country . . . they have, so far as it is granted, property in. The nature whereof is, that without a man's own consent it cannot be taken from him. (Ibid., 193)

Locke's views can be applied to American Indians only with some difficulty. The passages referred to by Green and Tully are not intended to be descriptive of natives. Locke is discussing resistance in civil society, the right of the people of England to resist arbitrary power and abuses of government. The noxious, wild and savage beasts of prey who may be destroyed as a lion or tiger is a reference to despots; as Laslett points out, the subject "is clearly the established government of a country, Locke's country, and these are the words applied to it when it claims the right to 'Absolute, Arbitrary Power' ('Having quitted Reason' to do so)." Charles and James Stuart "fit easily enough into the role of those 'wild Savage Beasts.'"[32] Tully nonetheless believes that these passages *fit* the punishment of American Indians for resisting commercial cultivation of land. "I am quite aware," he says, that these passages in chapters 2 and 3 are standardly interpreted as references to the right to punish Charles II in an armed revolt. Be this as it may, the very terms Locke uses to describe the offenders who may be 'destroyed' are the terms used to describe, and so dehumanize, Amerindians in the books in Locke's library.[33]

This may not be sheer speculation on the part of Tully or Green, but grounded on a reasonable suspicion that Locke's unstated view may conflict with the liberal or egalitarian philosophy for which he is known. However, given the books in Locke's library, it is just as possible to argue a more generous interpretation.

Locke was an enthusiastic reader of literature and debates concerning the character of American Indians, slavery and conquest. Felix Cohen dates the antecedents of Indian legal history to Vitoria's 1532 work concerning the right of Spain to title in the New World. Vitoria was addressing the question of whether conquest and enslavement were necessary to convert natives to Christianity, whether the *encomienda* system with its attendant brutality was inconsistent with the Catholic religion.[34] The system enslaved, tortured and decimated native populations. The consequences of Spanish conquest were so appalling that in 1550 the King convened a council to decide future policy. The issues concerning the justice of the methods used to extend the Spanish empire were debated at Valladolid by Las Casas and Sepúlveda. Locke was thoroughly familiar with these debates.

According to Tully, Locke follows Vitoria's justification of conquest and supports the right of Spaniards to use force against natives who violate natural law.[35] Unfortunately, this interpretation just begs the question. Use of force in self-defense was not at issue. Vitoria's work does not cohere with the interpretation of Locke presented by Tully. Vitoria's analysis would make Europeans the usual aggressors in war, not American Indians. Natives, he claims, are the true owners of land and consequently cannot be conquered by force of arms and enslaved. Land could be purchased or taken only with the express consent of the natives. This influential view provided the basis for European relations with American Indians; Vine Deloria, Jr and Clifford Lytle point out that "the impact of Vitoria's view on European–Indian relations for the next two hundred years was very important because it encouraged respect for the tribes as societies of people. Treaty-making became the basis for defining both the legal and political relationships between the Indians and the European colonists."[36]

Sepúlveda argues that war against natives is justified if not waged cruelly and not waged for riches alone. It is justified to spread the Christian faith, to convert natives to the use of reason and to teach proper morals. Natives are regarded as natural slaves and war against such infidels is justified for their own good. Sepúlveda regards force as a necessary prelude to Christianizing; since natives do not entirely lack reason they can be educated in Spanish law and ethics. If natives refuse to assimilate, a just war may be waged and their goods confiscated as property of the conquering prince. The conqueror in such a just war may kill or enslave his enemy. Sepúlveda concludes with a utilitarian justification; the bringing of iron, wheat, barley, horses, goats, the Christian religion, etc., to the natives justifies conquest. The *encomienda* system is regarded as just retribution for those who wage war against the Spanish.

Las Casas contends that the souls of all men are created equal, the law of nations and natural law apply to Christian and gentile alike. Rejecting the Aristotelian notion of natural inferiority and slavery, he argues that American Indians possess the same positive characteristics as other men. Not only are they devout workers, but appear to be more religious than the Greeks and Romans. American Indians are not beasts or semi-animals, but just as rational as Europeans. Las Casas stresses the great diversity among tribes, the beauty of their art, efficiency of their government, and their peaceful nature. Conquest is considered to be cruel and unjust war and contrary to the Christian religion. Natives are not to be dispossessed of their property and should not be enslaved for any reason. The conversion of American Indians to Christianity should be conducted by peaceful persuasion. Although the judges as Valladolid did not reach a decision on the dispute, the views of Las Casas were those which influenced future legal theory; the Council of the Indies, says Acosta, prescribed very different methods for new expeditions.[37] Locke's work exhibits a curious blend of these theories. His descriptions of American Indians are similar to those of Sepúlveda; natives are thought to be inferior in morals, have no religion, do not work, and live by passions rather than reason. He also employs a utilitarian argument that conversion benefits natives in obtaining the comforts of life. Yet like Vitoria and Las Casas, Locke does not believe in innate inferiority and rejects natural slavery as well as conquest as a means to take property. Shaftsbury and Locke favored peaceful relations with the natives of Carolina.

Wasteland, Genocide, and Treaties

In the *Fundamental Constitutions of Carolina*, Locke states:

> But since the natives of that place, who will be concerned in our plantation, are utterly strangers to Christianity, whose idolatry, ignorance, or mistake, gives us no right to expel, or use them ill; and those who remove from other parts to plant there, will unavoidably be of different opinions concerning matters of religion, the liberty whereof they will expect to have allowed them, and it will not be reasonable for us on this account to keep them out; that civil peace may be maintained amidst the diversity of opinions, and our agreement and compact with all men may be duly and faithfully observed; the violation whereof, upon what pretence soever cannot be without great offence to Almighty God, and great scandal to the true religion, which we profess.[38]

Farr points out that the temporary laws Locke had a part in drafting might give one a different impression of his view than that of the *Second Treatise*. As Farr notes, Locke instructs, for example, that "no Indian upon any occasion" is to be "made a slave; or without his own consent be carried out of our country." There is also a suggestion that he may not have been interested in the development of all wasteland. Another temporary law would require that territory occupied by American Indians be respected and that land near such settlements "be left untaken up and unplanted on for the use of the Indians."[39]

Given such proclamations, Arneil is led to speculate that Locke's theory of conquest is completely consistent with the case made by the defenders of the English plantation; "agricultural settlement rather than conquest, considered to be the Spanish technique, is the better method of colonization." For she points to Locke's instruction to the colonists of Carolina: "Neither doe we thinke it advantageous for our people to live by rapin and plunder which we doe not nor will not allow. Planting and trade is both our designe and your interest and . . . shall lay a way open to gett all the Spaniards riches."[40] Locke's position in the *Constitutions* is decidedly practical, a position consistent with lucrative trade and with the concern of France gaining title to native lands. It does not, however, represent a general theory. Nothing Locke says explains *how* wasteland is to be appropriated when occupied by natives who resist such expropriation. Here he appears to suggest that a just war may not be waged against American Indians. The *Second Treatise* does not *directly* speak to the issue, but *appears* to support the views of Sepúlveda, Purchase, Winthrop and others who argue that just war may be waged if natives resist expansion.

Tully claims that Locke's view is consistent throughout, that neither the *Constitutions* nor the *Second Treatise* gives natives a natural right to own vacant land. He argues that Locke's proposal to grant natives individual tracts of land in Carolina is predicated on native consent to European values, viz., "aboriginal peoples consented to" the use of money and "to the system of commercial agriculture, and so their natural right to the means of preservation must be realized in this system."[41] This certainly does not comport with Locke's description of the natives given use of this land. They may have consented to trade, but there is no evidence that they consented to a market economy or commercial agriculture. There is definitely a tension between the *Constitutions* and the *Second Treatise*.

Locke may have attempted to deflate such concerns by speaking of America as such a vast wilderness that conflict need not occur. He says, for example, that appropriation and improvement of any parcel of land does not prejudice any other man, for "there was still enough, and as good left; and more than the yet unprovided could use. So that in effect, there was never the less left for others because of his inclosure for himself. For he that leaves as much as another can make use of, does as good as take nothing at all" (*Second Treatise*, 33). However, at some point in the state of nature conflict is inevitable. Reservations were created on Long Island in 1666; Locke may have had this type of arrangement in mind. This obviously does not solve the problem of resistance or the justice of forced removal. Locke's statement in the *First Treatise* (130) that a planter in the West Indies "might, if he pleased," muster an army against Indians "to seek reparation upon any injury received from them," does not show, as Glausser suggests, that "he takes it for granted the justice of a developer's 'resistance' to such 'aggression.' "[42] The claim is simply too ambiguous; Locke does not provide a context nor state the type of injury. Further, the "army" in this passage is a patriarch's family.

Locke clearly does not recommend, nor would he approve of, genocide.[43] If by "genocide" one means the intentional attempt to eliminate all members of a culture, natural law and charity would explicitly rule this out. American Indians have a natural right to self-preservation, for no one should "be left to starve and perish" (*Second Treatise*, 184), and therefore, "no man could ever have a just power over the life of another, by right of property in land, or possessions; since 'twoud always be a sin in any man of estate, to let his brother perish for want of affording him relief out of his plenty" (*First*

Treatise, 42). Further, given the importance he attaches to treaties and promises, it is unlikely that he would have approved of the egregious treaty violations of eighteenth and nineteenth century Euroamericans. Promises and treaties are binding in a state of nature, "for truth and keeping of faith belongs to men, as men, and not as members of society" (*Second Treatise*, 14). In the *Essay* he points out: "that men should keep their compacts, is certainly a great and undeniable rule in morality" (*Essay*, 1, 3, 5).

Overall, Locke's claims suggest that he was confident that American Indians would eventually enter civil society and assimilate through education. That commercial agriculture was superior to native agriculture and use of land was something he thought obvious:

> There cannot be a clearer demonstration of any thing, than several Nations of the Americans are of this, who are rich in land, and poor in all the comforts of life; whom nature having furnished as liberally as any other people, with the materials of plenty, i.e. a fruitful soil, apt to produce in abundance, what might serve for food, rayment, and delight; yet for want of improving it by labour, have not one hundreth part of the conveniencies we enjoy: And a King of a large and fruitful territory there feeds, lodges, and is clad worse than a day labourer in England. (*Second Treatise*, 41)

Like Sepúlveda, Locke offers what might be taken as a well-intentioned justification for taking land, viz., economic gain, greater conveniences for American Indians and true religion. Since the American Indian often became an obstacle to English wealth, paternalistic arguments of this sort were not uncommon. Because he was not always forthright with the facts as he knew them, Locke's intentions are not beyond question.

European and American Indian value systems differ so significantly it is highly doubtful that Locke really understood native culture. The spiritual value of land is an important aspect of land use for American Indians, a concept Locke did not comprehend. The so-called conveniences produced by a market economy were not considered as such by native people. Yet, as Salisbury points out, cultural differences are not the only major variable in dispossession: "when land-hungry settlers did not immediately follow the explorers and traders, Indians survived and interacted with Europeans over long periods with varying degrees of advantage." Salisbury points to the "unprecedented economic and social revolution that had begun to transform parts of Europe, particularly England," and spreading to North America.[44] Locke's interest in America is primarily economic.

Assessing Locke's responsibility in American Indian dispossession is difficult, if not impossible. Portions of the *Second Treatise* have been used by those seeking a justification for taking native land as well as by those seeking a justification for native rights to their land and culture. Since Locke falls short of committing himself on central issues, his work lends itself to conflicting interpretations. As Tully points out, Locke's view of property was not significantly different from that of his predecessors. Locke popularized the agricultural argument and distanced himself from the views of Grotius and Pufendorf with the claim that land can be taken *without consent*. One can nonetheless remain skeptical about claims that this theory, as Tully contends, was central to native dispossession and to United States policy toward American Indians. The Crown's proclamation of 1763 favored peaceful purchase of American Indian land. American radicals did not simply appeal to Locke's argument for appropriating wasteland, but quoted any source that would support the right to appropriate and govern their own affairs, including Grotius, Pufendorf, and classical sources. As John Dunn correctly notes, the only *sustained* application of Locke's theory of property to American circumstances came from John Buckley.[45]

Locke's arguments were interpreted in a more favorable light by those using his natural law view of self-preservation to argue for native title to territory occupied. Robert W. Venables, for example, argues that Locke's native is the "noble savage," that natural law and compacts preserve American Indian title.[46]

Locke's argument that land can be taken without consent was not influential and was not appealed to by policy-makers in England or the United States. Land was purchased and treaties continued to be signed well into the nineteenth century.[47] Whether natives were thought to have sovereignty or not, British and US policy generally dictated that force of arms was not a legitimate way to obtain land, that land could not be taken without the voluntary consent of the natives who occupied and used the land. Policy and theory often conflicted with the realities of colonial life and frontier expansion. When American Indians could not be convinced to sell their land, could not be bribed or tricked, theory was often dismissed in favor of arms. John Chester Miller contends that the function of government was not to eradicate American Indians, but to eradicate the superstitions, customs, and attitudes which impeded their transition from the state of nature to civilized society.[48] In this regard, Locke's *Essay* had more of an impact on native culture than the *Second Treatise* theory of property.

Impact of the Essay: Assimilation

In the *Essay*, Locke contends that all ideas are derived from experience. He argues that because humans are not born with innate ideas or knowledge, the type and degree of knowledge exhibited by any human being is a function of environment and culture. Locke's contention that all men are created with equal capacities influenced Thomas Jefferson's view of American Indians as people who were simply backward and capable of entering civilization with proper education. Insofar as they gave up tribal organization and communal ownership of land, adopted European religion, farming and education, they would possess the same rights to life, liberty and property as Euroamericans. Short of assimilation, they were to be granted property on reservations. The *Essay*'s environmentalism led Jefferson to the position that the transition from savagery to civilization was to be gradual. As Bernard W. Sheehan explains, the land would be surrendered at a rate corresponding to the alteration in the native's way of life: "the Indian would never be asked to give up more than the circumstances of their gradual transformation required; the white man would never request more land than the orderly advance of civilized life across the continent demanded."[49] Like Locke, Jefferson was not exactly consistent in theory and practice. Not only did he seek passage of a constitutional amendment to transport Eastern natives beyond the Mississippi, he also attempted to run them into debt with the hope of payment by cession of lands. Sheehan correctly places Locke's *Essay* as more crucial to native dispossession than the *Second Treatise*. If the mind is a blank tablet, American Indians would only need to receive new and correct ideas about God and man's relationship to the land to be spared. Since man does not have a real essence, he can be transformed by changing the environment. The roots of nineteenth-century allotment acts date back to the colonial period, Locke's epistemology providing the seeds of removal and cultural extinction. With the hope of transforming natives to an appreciation of private property and farming, the 1887 Dawes Allotment Act authorized the president to allot reservation land in small parcels to individual American Indians. Surplus land was purchased and made available to white settlers.

The fact that Locke may not hold an empirical *theory* of racial inferiority, as Farr contends, does not necessarily place his philosophy in a positive light as far as American Indians are concerned. Assimilation policies were often based on racism as well as religion. Bracken argues that Locke's empiricism lends itself to "soft racism," namely, the position that people of color are inferior, but that this inferiority is remedial. It is remedial for Locke by stripping natives of their entire culture, by replacing spiritual relationships with economic relationships. Locke's "Indian" is an inferior, ignorant, uncivilized human, a being capable of rising to a state of civil society by the use of reason; although not biologically inferior, inferior nonetheless, and more akin to animals than rational humans. For most American Indians, reservations and assimilation meant death, both physical and spiritual. The Kiowa chief Satanta proclaimed: "I have heard that you intend to settle us on a reservation near the mountains. I don't want to settle. I love to roam over the prairies. There I feel free and happy, but when we settle down we grow pale and die."[50] Assimilation policy fostered dependency on whites. For Locke, abstract reasoning, religion, morality, and property are intimately connected. That land can be taken without consent even when enclosed is a view that he can justify only by appealing to God. In 1676, a Pequot complained: "How they could go to work to enslave a free people, and call it religion is beyond the power of my imagination."[51]

Tully is perplexed that scholars of European history have passed over Locke's argument of appropriation without consent in silence. This argument, he contends, justifies "the most contentious and important events of the seventeenth century and one of the formative events of the modern world." On the other hand, he says, "among scholars who specialize in the European dispossession of Amerindians reference to Locke's argument is commonplace."[52] I do not find this surprising. First, Tully may exaggerate the historical importance of this argument; second, the references which are commonplace are mere citations; in general, European specialists of dispossession do not discuss Locke at great length, James Axtell not at all. American Indian scholars rarely discuss Locke's appropriation arguments or his political works. A few revisionist historians, e.g., Drinnon and Stannard, are the exception to the rule. In all cases, the agricultural argument is usually analyzed in detail, but this argument was not peculiar to Locke and he is often not mentioned. Granting that Locke's argument was somewhat influential, it is usually passed over or simply mentioned as part of a larger more influential argument, *viz.*, the argument from God's will. While there seems to be no general agreement about Locke's influence and responsibility, there is little question concerning the role of Christianity in dispossession. American Indian scholars consider Locke just one of many European philosophers who used Christianity as an ideological weapon. His views are given no more importance than those of Augustine, Descartes, More, Jefferson and others. The common thread of European thought is the emphasis placed on reason, logic and religion.

The *Essay* and Religion

The ultimate justification for appropriation without consent, that which legitimizes chapter 5 of the *Second Treatise*, is both economic – the utilitarian notion of greater conveniences – and religious – God's command. "So that God," says Locke, "by commanding to subdue, gave authority so far to appropriate" (*Second Treatise*, 35). In a great wilderness people do not need the consent of fellow commoners – they have the consent of God. God, "when he gave the world in common to all mankind, commanded man also to labour, and the penury of his condition required it of him. God and his reason commanded him to subdue the earth, i.e. improve it for the benefit of life. . . . He that in obedience to this command of God, subdued, tiled and sowed any part of it, thereby annexed to it something that was his *property*, which another had no title to" (ibid., 32). The law of reason, God's law, demands hard labor. The inhabitants of the "wild woods" and "uncultivated waste" of America are "needy and wretched" *because* they lack sufficient reason to obey the laws of God (ibid., 37, 41). Thus, any land granted to lazy and ignorant natives is by charity only. To own property is to be civilized and to be civilized is to follow Christian morality. Locke does not discuss the attempts by Europeans to educate American Indians in schools and praying towns. Since he is pessimistic about most humans overcoming their "passionate nature" or "brute appetites" for a life of reason, he may have regarded the outcome of assimilation attempts with some skepticism. Since American Indians were considered to be like children or the idle poor of England, it might be reasonable to assume that Locke would approve of the use of force to instruct them in morality; once laboring, without the leisure to cultivate reason, they would live by faith.

Richard Ashcraft argues that the *Essay* must be understood in the context of religion. Since "Locke believes the principles of morality capable of being *known* with certainty, while the truth conveyed through revelation must be *believed* by men, demarcating the boundaries between faith and knowledge becomes the paramount issue of the *Essay*."[53] Locke explains that "morality and divinity" are "those parts of knowledge, that men are most concern'd to be clear in" (*Essay*, Epistle to the Reader, p. 11) . Roland Hall speculates that "the rationality of true religion could be the point of the *Essay* . . . so that in effect 'religion which should most distinguish us from beasts, and ought most peculiarly to elevate us, as rational creatures, above brutes, is that wherein men often appear most irrational'' (*Essay*, 4, 18, 11). Thus, Locke equates "the possession of religion with that of reason."[54] The political impact of this equation is considerable. For American Indians who do not accept Christianity it entails a place in a moral hierarchy which is close to beasts. Bracken complains that Locke's account of concept-acquisition and learning has proved to be readily compatible with social conditioning and political control. The *Essay* appears to support a performance model of man in which certain political rights must be earned, the right to freedom as well as property, predicated on the correct use of reason.

Peter Laslett points out that Locke did not argue "that the basis of political life is the rule of the rational man over his irrational fellows."[55] Nonetheless, critics simply point to the compatibility of his views with this practice. Bracken contends that the blank tablet model has not been on the side of egalitarianism precisely "because the model carries with it the need for a group which will be charged with 'writing' on the blank tablets. The model has helped justify the creation and growth of an elite class of experts who handle human programming."[56] The program which would civilize American Indians and make them full members of a moral community involves conformity to the Christian mandate of labor and profitable use of land.

Revolutionaries utilized Locke's *Essay* as well as the *Two Treatises*. Gordon S. Wood notes that Lockean sensationalism "told the revolutionaries that human personalities were unformed, impressionable things that could be molded and manipulated by controlling people's sensations." The mind, said John Adams, could "be cultivated like a garden, with barbarous weeds eliminated and enlightened fruits raised, 'the savages destroyed . . . the civil people increased.' "[57] The premises of the *Essay* gave way to a renewed preoccupation with education. Anthropologists, psychologists, philosophers and social scientists became the "experts" on stereotyping American Indians and attempting to convert them. Deloria complains: "The fundamental thesis of the anthropologist is that people are objects for observation, people are then considered objects for experimentation, for manipulation, and for eventual extinction." The total impact of the scholarly community on Amerindians "has become one of simple authority."[58] Ironically, Locke criticized Descartes' doctrine of innate ideas for its potential abuse at the hands of "experts" and politicians.

Whether it is innate ideas of God and morality or Christians writing on blank tablets, American Indians have suffered under the weight of assimilation policies. Robert Burnette protests that the current goal of the school system fostered by the Bureau of Indian Affairs is not education but acculturation: "Never have I known one teacher in an Indian school or one BIA employee who troubled himself to learn the Sioux language or to acquaint himself with the cultural background of his student."[59] American Indian scholars can find fault with Descartes as well as Locke. The European insistence on scientific method, Christianity and reason puts all indigenous people at risk. Deloria recounts the 1954 congressional hearings on the termination of federal supervision of Amerindians: "Unbelieveably, it recommended using the philosophy of René Descartes . . . as a method of research." Descartes' *Discourse on Method*, emphasizing clear and distinct ideas, progression from simple ideas to the more complex, was utilized to justify termination of federal services to all natives.[60]

Locke's position in the *Constitutions* is one of toleration; natives are to be left alone to practice their own customs and religion. Again, this position was one developed for a particular context and may not express Locke's more general view. The Puritans considered American Indians to be morally bankrupt and in league with the devil. Locke likewise concludes that they have no religion (morals) at all. Although he argues for religious toleration, atheists, lacking a moral code, are considered dangerous and not to be tolerated. That Locke was a sincere Christian does not entail that his beliefs were beneficial to all humans. He has little to say about the education or assimilation of American Indians, remains silent concerning how wasteland is to be taken if natives resist, and does not find the African slave trade inconsistent with Christianity. Seliger argues that Locke's failure to answer such questions reflects his "reluctance frankly to admit that in its entirety natural law is not equally applicable to the whole species of men."[61] Locke, of course, argues that it is, and thus conquest and genocide are theoretically wrong; further, American Indians cannot be denied the means of self-preservation. This view of natural law is consistent with the practice of removal, reservations, assimilation, namely, with cultural genocide. Steven Katz defines "cultural genocide" as the "actualization of the intent, however carried out, to destroy the national, ethnic, religious, political, social or class *identity* of a group as these groups are defined by the perpetrators."[62] Locke does not express this intent, but does in a sense predict its actualization; natives would assimilate as they naturally progressed to the stage of civilization.

Locke might be read as one of the many early assimilationists, as Alvin M. Josephy, Jr explains, who "considered themselves well intentioned with the best interests of the Indians at heart."[63] Locke, Jefferson and others were fundamentally wrong, most American Indians having no desire to convert to European ways of life. Forced assimilation therefore became prevalent in the nineteenth century. Massive removal and relocation of American Indian tribes to reservations, followed by laws denying natives the right to speak their own language, to keep their own names, to express their religion, to dance and dress as they wished, became the rule. This was supposedly done with the best of intentions, to save the American Indian from extinction — to exterminate the culture or tribe and preserve the individual.

As Josephy points out, in most cases conversion to Christianity proved of little help to natives. Many of the Christianized natives during Locke's lifetime were murdered and sold into slavery. John Eliot's converts, isolated in "praying towns," were exterminated by settlers during King Philip's war. In the nineteenth century the "civilized" tribes fared no better; assimilation was not sufficient to keep the Eastern Cherokee from being imprisoned in stockades and later removed from their homes and land. Drinnon argues that white racism has made it impossible for all but a handful of American Indians to achieve full church membership and full citizenship.[64] The origins of assimilation policy have been traced to ethnocentric ideology, racism, and economic greed. Deloria contends: "There was never a time when the white man said he was trying to help the Indian get into the mainstream of American life that he did not also demand that the Indian give up land, water, minerals, timber, and other resources which would enrich the white man."[65] Hill also notes that the only consistent policy of the United States has been to maintain control over economic development within American Indian territory.[66]

Locke's disdain of American Indian culture may indicate either a conscious or unconscious belief in white superiority. The *Essay* may not be a work of politics, but it has nonetheless had a lasting influence on how Americans relate to one another in the political sphere; people of color are still generally thought deficient to whites, the remedy, now disputed in America's culture wars, European education and assimilation.

119

American Indian land is still subject to the *Second Treatise* dictate of profitable use and treaty rights are still violated in the name of economic and cultural progress. The Christian perspective of land as a commodity to be exploited for profit is the dominant paradigm of American government. The land, says an American Indian, "has been eroded, plundered, misused and spoiled. It is the Indian's only real possession. Its destruction assures the destruction of the Indian."[67]

The *practice* of colonists, settlers and government was often to take native land by any means necessary, with or without consent. The fact that millions of people had to die to fulfill the Christian mandate to subdue the land is appalling; to much of this horror Locke might have objected. Locke can be read in many contexts. As Glausser notes, he "has built too many confusions of theory and practice, too many defenses against either being caught in the act or missing the boat." One must recognize "within Locke's work a destabilizing competition of values."[68]

For Tully and others a solution to the injustice suffered by American Indian people might come from Locke himself. For example, Ashcraft argues that Locke's "broad definitions of property and property rights and his definition of a 'freeman' in terms of equality, age, and reason – rather than the ownership of property – supplied the basis for a democratic distribution of political power." Locke's defense of elected legislative assembly and his commitment to popular sovereignty, "and to the right of popular resistance, as well as his defense of religious freedom, the right to free speech, free assembly, and free press," constitute the core values of liberal democratic theory.[69]

To many Americans, this aspect of Locke's work has not, and cannot, constitute a solution to native problems. Deloria notes that the world of the American Indian is non-Western in conceptualization and philosophy, that: "Liberalism took the ideals and dreams of Western European civilization and dangled them in front of the blacks and young while attempting to force them on the Mexicans and Indians. Then liberalism couldn't produce." Recognition of the spiritual value of humans and the environment may not be possible in a nation dominated by corporate greed. Deloria goes on to note: "The ideals of the Constitution proved unable to hurdle such roadblocks as Congressional seniority, vested economic interests, the impotent morality of a Christian religion that was 'of the world but not in it.' Liberalism pushed the ideology of Western man to its logical extremes and it was found to be unsuitable for racial minorities."[70] If one seeks a solution from Locke, it would entail admitting that most wars with American Indians were unjust wars and that, as Locke says, "the aggressor, who puts himself into the state of war with another, and unjustly invades another man's right, can . . . thereby have no title to the subjection and obedience of the conquered" (*Essay*, 176).

Conclusion

Locke can certainly be faulted for being ethnocentric, for not clarifying his positions, for presenting arguments that neglect to mention sophisticated American Indian cultures in favor of arguments that include disparaging images of American Indians. However, the claim that Locke is primarily responsible for American Indian dispossession is not warranted. It is obvious that arguments in the *Second Treatise* were often taken out of context and occasionally used by policy makers to support their goal of taking native resources; Locke is not responsible for such use. His agricultural argument simply did not play the vital role in dispossession that some scholars have assigned to it. Locke's *Essay* and theory of knowledge has had a more lasting influence on American Indian culture than anything to be found in the *Two Treatises*. His theory has been used historically to bolster the position of *forced* assimilation, a position that cannot be found in Locke's work.

Notes

* This paper is a revised version of "Locke and the Dispossession of the American Indian," *American Indian Culture and Research Journal*, vol. 20, 4, 1996, pp. 145–81.

1. John Locke, *Two Treatises of Government*, ed. Peter Laslett (New York: New American Library, 1965), par. 49. Subsequent references in text to *Second Treatise* are by paragraph number. I have followed the current practice of decapitalization and deitalicization of this work.
2. Roy Harvey Pearce, *The Savages of America: A Study of the Indian and the Idea of Civilization* (Baltimore, Johns Hopkins University Press, 1965), p. 68.
3. James Tully, *An Approach to Political Philosophy: Locke in Contexts* (Cambridge: Cambridge University Press, 1993), p. 137.
4. Herman Lebovics, "The Uses of America In Locke's *Second Treatise*," *Journal of the History of Ideas*, vol. 47, 1986, pp. 567–581. Barbara Arneil, "John Locke, Natural Law and Colonialism," *History of Political Thought*, vol. 13, 1992, pp. 587–603. Wayne Glausser, "Three Approaches to Locke and the Slave Trade." *Journal of the History of Ideas*, vol. 51, 1990, pp. 199–216. Michael K. Green, "John Locke, Native Americans, and The State of Nature," unpublished paper presented to the American Philosophical Association, Eastern Division, December, 1993.
5. Richard Drinnon, *Facing West: The Metaphysics of Indian-Hating and Empire Building* (New York: Shocken Books, 1990). David E. Stannard, *American Holocaust: Columbus and the Conquest of the New World* (New York: Oxford University Press, 1992). Francis Jennings, *The Invasion of America: Indians, Colonialism and the Cant of Conquest* (Chapel Hill: University of North Carolina Press, 1975). Russell Thornton, *American Indian Holocaust and Survival: A Population History since 1492* (Norman: University of Oklahoma Press, 1987).
6. Neal Wood, *The Politics of Locke's Philosophy* (Berkeley: University of California Press, 1983), pp. 81–2.
7. James Farr, "So Vile and Miserable An Estate: The Problem of Slavery in Locke's Political Thought," *Political Theory*, vol. 13, 1986, pp. 263–89, pp. 278–9.
8. Thomas L. Pangle, *The Spirit of Modern Republicanism* (Chicago: University of Chicago Press, 1988), p. 12.
9. Robert Berkhofer, Jr, *The White Man's Indian* (New York: Vintage Books, 1979), p. 16.
10. Richard Hakluyt, *Hakluyt's Voyages to the New World: A Selection* (New York: Bobbs-Merrill, 1972), pp. 151–2, 86, 160.
11. The term "savage" variously used to mean backward or illiterate, as well as to signify men of the forest or woods. Savages could be noble or brutal.
12. John Locke, *An Essay Concerning Human Understanding*, ed. Peter H. Nidditch (Oxford: Clarendon Press, 1975), Book 1, ch. 2, par. 27. I have followed the current practice of

decapitalization and deitalicization of the *Essay*. Subsequent references to *Essay* in text are by book, chapter and paragraph numbers.

13. Ronald Meek, *Social Science and the Ignoble Savage* (New York: Cambridge University Press, 1976), p. 2.

14. Quoted by Robert Williams, Jr, *The American Indian In Western Legal Thought* (New York: Oxford University Press, 1990), p. 208.

15. Neal Salisbury, *Manitou and Providence: Indians, Europeans, and the Making of New England, 1500–1643* (New York: Oxford University Press, 1982), p. 31. Anthony F. C. Wallace, *The Long Bitter Trail* (New York: Hill and Wang, 1993), p. 48.

16. Joseph Acosta, *Natural and Moral History of the Indies*, 1589 (Grimston English translation, 1604).

17. William G. Batz, "The Historical Anthropology of John Locke," *Journal of the History of Ideas*, vol. 35, no. 4, 1974, pp. 663–70, p. 669.

18. Quoted by Batz, "Historical Anthropology," p. 670.

19. Lebovics, "Uses of America," p. 568.

20. Green, "State of Nature," p. 1; Arneil, "Natural Law and Colonialism," p. 603.

21. Tully, *Political Philosophy*, p. 146.

22. *Winthrop Papers* (Boston: Massachusetts Historical Society , 1931), vol. 2, p. 141.

23. Locke may have been influenced by More's *Utopia*, a work in which Utopians pressed for land are said to be justified in colonizing an area where the natives have a good amount of it left unoccupied and uncultivated. Sir Thomas More, *Utopia* (1516).

24. Arneil, "Natural Coward Colonialism," p. 601.

25. C. B. Macpherson, *The Political Theory of Possessive Individualism: Hobbes to Locke* (New York: Oxford University Press, 1962), pp. 205–6.

26. Glausser, "Three Approaches," p. 208.

27. Green, "State of Nature," p. 7.

28. Tully, *Political Philosophy*, p. 144.

29. Harry M. Bracken, "Essence, Accident and Race," *Hermathena*, no. 116, Winter 1973, pp. 81–96, p. 85. See Richard H. Popkin, "The Philosophical Bases of Modern Racism," in *Philosophy and the Civilizing Arts*, ed. Craig Walton and John P. Anton (Athens, Ohio: 1974).

30. M. Seliger, "Locke, Liberalism and Nationalism," in *John Locke: Problems and Perspectives*, ed. John W. Yolton (Cambridge: Cambridge University Press, 1969), pp. 19–33, p. 28. Also, see Seliger, *The Liberal Politics of John Locke* (London: Allen and Unwin, 1968).

31. Locke was obviously aware of the fact that the practice of taking slaves from Africa could not be justified by just war theory. He nonetheless presents the African slave trade as justified by this theory.

32. Laslett, Introduction to the *Two Treatises*, p. 96.

33. Tully, *Political Philosophy*, p. 144.

34. Felix Cohen, *Handbook of Federal Indian Law* (Charlottesville, VA: Miche/Bobbs-Merrill, 1982). The *encomienda* system, established in 1512, regarded native people as part of large land grants given to settlers. Natives were enslaved and required to work for the landowner.

35. Tully, *Political Philosophy*, p. 143.

36. Vine Deloria, Jr and Clifford M. Lytle, *American Indians, American Justice* (Austin: University of Texas Press, 1983), p. 3.

37. An excellent review of this debate is contained in Lewis Hanke's *Aristotle and the American Indian: A Study in Race Prejudice in the Modern World* (Bloomington: Indian University Press, 1959), p. 90. Information on the Valladolid dispute was available in English as early as 1603. It was discussed in Purchase, *Hakluytus Post Humus*, a text in Locke's library.

38. *Fundamental Constitutions of Carolina, The Works of John Locke* (Germany: 1963 edition), p. 194, article XCVII.

39. Farr, "Vile and Miserable," p. 285. These laws were never implemented. The trade in slaves was common in the Carolinas. As Tully notes, by 1680 the fur trade and the sale of native slaves to the West Indies were the staples of Carolina's economy.

40. Quoted by Arneil, "Natural Law and Colonialism," p. 603. Letter written in Locke's hand.

41. Tully, *Political Philosophy*, p. 170.

42. Glausser, "Three Approaches," p. 209.

43. A more liberal definition of "genocide" specified by the United Nations and legislated in 1988 *may* place Locke in this context; here "genocide" is defined as the intent to destroy in whole or *in part* a national, ethical, racial or religious group. It is, however, not certain that Locke ever harbored such an intent. For a discussion of genocide and its various definitions see Steven T. Katz, *The Holocaust in Historical Context* (New York: Oxford University Press, 1994).

44. Salisbury, *Manitou and Providence*, p. 12.

45. John Dunn, "The politics of Locke in England and America in the eighteenth century," in Yolton, *Problems and Perspectives*, pp. 45–78, p. 71. John Buckley, "An inquiry into the right of the aboriginal natives to the land in America," in *Poetical Meditations*, ed. Roger Wolcott (London: 1726), pp. 12–16. Buckley's treatise is a refutation of Mohegan claims to sovereignty and property.

46. Robert W. Venables, "The Founding Fathers: Choosing to be Romans," in *Indian Roots of American Democracy*, ed. Jose Barreiro (New York: Akwe-Kon Press, 1992), pp. 96–7. For an excellent *revisionist account* of Locke on land and land use see Kristin Shrader-Frechette, "Locke and Limits on Land Ownership," *Journal of the History Ideas*, 54, 1993, pp. 201–19.

47. In 1871 Congress declared that American Indian tribes were not foreign nations. Treaties were therefore discontinued, although past treaties were not invalidated.

48. John Chester Miller, *The Wolf by the Ears: Thomas Jefferson and Slavery* (New York: Meridian, 1977), p. 72.

49. Bernard W. Sheehan, *Seeds of Extinction: Jeffersonian Philanthropy and the American Indian* (New York: W. W. Norton & Co., 1973), p. 169.

50. Quoted in *Native American Testimony*, ed. Peter Nabokov (New York: Viking Press, 1991).

51. Quoted in *From the Heart: Voices of the American Indian* (New York: Alfred A. Knopf, 1995), p. 76.

52. Tully, *Political Philosophy*, p. 146.

53. Richard Ashcraft, "Faith and knowledge in Locke's philosophy," in Yolton, *Problems and Perspectives*, p. 197.

54. Roland Hall, "The Place of Reason in Locke's *Essay*," *The Locke Newsletter*, no. 23, 1992, pp. 11–23, p. 15.

55. Laslett, *Two Treatises*, p. 97.

56. Harry M. Bracken, *Mind and Language: Essays on Descartes and Chomsky* (Holland/USA: Foris Publications, 1984), pp. 57–8.

57. Gordon S. Wood, *The Radicalism of the American Revolution* (New York: Alfred A. Knopf, 1992), p. 190.

58. Vine Deloria, Jr, *Custer Died for Your Sins* (New York: Avon, 1969), pp. 86–7.

59. Robert Burnette, *The Tortured American* (New Jersey: Prentice-Hall, 1971), p. 24.

60. Deloria, *Custer*, p. 65.

61. Seliger "Locke, Liberalism and Nationalism," p. 29.

62. Katz, *Holocaust*, p. 137.

63. Alvin M. Josephy, Jr, *Now That the Buffalo's Gone* (Norman and London: University of Oklahoma Press, 1989), p. 78.
64. Drinnon, *Facing West*, p. 94. The Cherokee met all of Locke's criteria for ownership of land.
65. Deloria, *Custer*, p. 174.
66. Gregory L. Hill, "Attempts at Genocide," *Turtle Quarterly*, vol. 6, no. 1, 1994, pp. 24–9, p. 26.
67. Quoted in Edgar S. Cahn (ed.), *Our Brother's Keeper* (New York: New Community Press, 1970), p. 69.
68. Glausser, "Three Approaches," pp. 215–16.
69. Richard Ashcraft, "Exclusive and Inclusive Theories of Property Rights: A Rejoiner to Horne," *Critical Review*, vol. 8, no. 3, Summer 1994, pp. 435–40. p. 439.
70. Vine Deloria, Jr, *We Talk, You Listen* (New York: Dell Publishing Co., 1970), pp. 83–4.

CHAPTER 7

Between Primates and Primitives: Natural Man as the Missing Link in Rousseau's *Second Discourse*

FRANCIS MORAN III

In his letter to Christophe de Beaumont (1762) Rousseau informs the Archbishop that the "fundamental principle of all morality . . . is this: That man is a naturally good being, who loves justice and order; that there is no original perversity in the human heart and that the first movements of nature are always right."[1] This would seem to make the *Discourse on Inequality* (the *Second Discourse* [1755]) and its discussion of the natural condition of the human species the cornerstone of Rousseau's ethical and political philosophy. If this is indeed the case, then it is essential that we understand his conception of natural man as accurately as possible. Recent studies of the *Second Discourse* have increasingly portrayed this creature as some type of protohuman or "primate with unused potentialities," rather than as a fully human being.[2] The more ambitious of these studies have suggested that Rousseau was not only intimating human descent from simian ancestors[3] but also anticipating modern developments in anthropology,[4] sociobiology,[5] and primatology.[6]

Of course Rousseau's discussion of *orang outangs* and natural human beings initially appears to encourage evolutionist speculation. After all, in Note X of the *Discourse* Rousseau quotes the abbé Prévost describing *orang outangs* as a "sort of middle point between the human species and the baboons,"[7] and in Part II he places his own natural human beings "at equal distances from the stupidity of brutes and the fatal enlightenment of civil man."[8] By describing natural man in terms similar to those used to describe *orang outangs*, Rousseau seems to be suggesting a close relationship between the two species. In the following discussion, however, I aim to temper some of the enthusiasm for this evolutionist reading by demonstrating that the natural man of the *Second Discourse* is in fact a true human being modeled after eighteenth-century conceptions of the "missing link" connecting human beings and animals in the "chain of being" – at that time the dominant European theory of natural history.[9]

I. Primates, Missing Links, and the Chain of Being

By referring to natural man as a mid-point between animals and human beings, Rousseau is providing his audience with a recognizable framework for understanding the kind of creature he will be describing.[10] In the context of mainstream eighteenth-century thought, this reference would probably have been read as an allusion to the chain of being rather than as an indication of human descent, for unlike the later evolutionists, eighteenth-century naturalists who suggested a possible relationship between primates and human beings were generally uninterested in tracing the genealogy of these populations. Instead, their claims were meant to establish the relative position of each in the chain of being.

Because there was some concern that the human species represented a possible break in the natural hierarchy of the chain of being, those naturalists interested in preserving the chain began to search for possible "missing links" which would reunite human beings with other animals. This search focused primarily on the (alleged) anatomical, morphological, and behavioral similarities of the populations presumed to be closest to the break – i.e., primates (as the highest animal) and the native populations of Africa, the South Pacific, and the Americas (as the lowest human beings).

As we can see in the passage from Prévost cited above, the single most important primate species featured in the accounts were the so-called "*orang outangs.*" We should be careful, however, not to confuse these animals with modern orangutans since naturalists at this time had not yet begun to distinguish among the different species of higher primates. In general "*orang outang*" is roughly synonymous with our "great ape." We should also bear in mind Victor Gourevitch's (1988) point that very few Europeans in the mid-eighteenth-century (including Rousseau) had actually seen a living *orang outang.*[11] When reading the following descriptions of these animals it is best to try to erase any preconceptions one might have about the kind of animal being discussed and imagine that one has never seen a chimpanzee, orangutan, or gorilla.

Perhaps the most striking aspect of seventeenth-century and eighteenth-century descriptions of *orang outangs* is their emphasis on the *orang*'s human physical appearance. For example, the primate receiving the fullest attention in Rousseau's Note X – the "pongo" – is said to have a "human face" and to "resemble man exactly."[12] Likewise, Edward Tyson (1699) described a primate he called a "pygmie" that had a "human face" and ears which "differe nothing from the human form";[13] and William Smith (1744) described an animal called a "boggoe" or "mandrill" that bore a "near resemblance of a human creature, though nothing at all like an Ape."[14]

When naturalists sought more specific references for their comparisons, they generally turned to the native populations of Africa, especially the Hottentots. Thus, Francois Leguat (1708) compared an ape directly to a Hottentot and claimed that "[i]ts Face had no other Hair upon it than the Eye-brows, and in general it much resembled one of those *Grotesque* Faces which the Female *Hottentots* have at the Cape";[15] and Daniel Beeckman (1718) opined that his *orang* was "handsomer I am sure than some Hottentots that I have seen."[16] Beeckman included an illustration of this animal (figure 7.1) and one cannot help being struck by its human appearance.

Figure 7.1: Reprint of "Oran-ootan" described by Beeckman (1718).

Another common feature of these accounts was the claim that *orang outangs* could walk like human beings. Samuel Purchas (1625), Tyson, Leguat, Beeckman, Smith, Benoît de Maillet (1748), and Buffon (1766), for instance, all describe some primate in this fashion.[17] Tyson's study is particularly instructive on this point in that Tyson studied a live specimen shortly before its death and observed that while it occasionally walked upright, it regularly walked on its knuckles. When he eventually dissected the animal, he concluded that nothing anatomical prevented it from walking like a normal human being and attributed its inability to walk upright to its weakened condition. Accordingly, his illustrations of the pygmie show it standing on two legs but supporting itself either by leaning on a cane (figure 7.2) or by clinging to a rope (figure 7.3). This practice becomes fairly common in later drawings of these creatures. Prévost, for example, includes an engraving of a "chimpaneze" supporting itself with a cane (figure 7.4), and Buffon includes an illustration of a "jocko" standing with a walking stick (figure 7.5).

Perhaps at this point we ought to pause and examine the way in which this type of illustration can influence our understanding of these animals.[18] For by presenting a

Figure 7.2: Front view of pygmie in Tyson. Taken from reprint in Gould (1985).

Figure 7.3: Rear view of "pygmie" described by Tyson (1699).

picture of a creature bearing such a close physical resemblance to human beings standing in a human pose and using human tools, these drawings leave the impression that the apparent gap between human beings and animals may not be as large as originally suspected. This would be especially true for an audience that has had little direct contact with the animals themselves. These drawings help us to appreciate Rousseau's uncertainty over whether such creatures were animals or primitive human beings who had been misidentified by careless observers. Recall that in Note X Rousseau wonders whether "various animals similar to men [i.e., *orang outangs*], which travelers have without much observation taken for Beasts . . . might not indeed be genuine Savage men whose race . . . had not acquired any degree of perfection, and was still in the primitive state of nature."[19] Indeed, this speculation becomes all the more plausible when we take into account European descriptions of primate ethology.

Seventeenth- and eighteenth-century European reports of primate behavior provide some of the clearest examples of the way in which the demands of the chain of being could influence scientific observation. Naturalists, in their zeal to make these animals appear as human as possible, were willing not only to describe *orang outang* behavior in anthropomorphic language but to compare that behavior favorably to contemporary European standards. Thus Purchas hints that pongos may have a nascent religious understanding,[20] and Lord Monboddo (1773) presents evidence that *orang outangs* have

Figure 7.4: Reprint of "Chimpaneze" from Prévost (1747).

Figure 7.5: Reprint of "Jocko" from Buffon (1766).

a fairly well developed sense of justice.[21] European naturalists also overcame one of the more obvious difficulties of finding a missing link between human beings and animals by speculating that some primates might be capable of speech.[22]

Orang outang behavior could also be used to sanction more mundane aspects of European social mores. Prévost and Tyson, for example, report on the elegant table manners of primates introduced to European dining.[23] Tyson also claims that his pygmie naturally adopted a conservative attitude towards alcohol consumption and nudity;[24] and Tulp (1641), Jacobus Bontius (1658), Leguat, Buffon, and Monboddo all discuss the superior sexual morals – particularly the modesty – of the females of some primate species.[25]

This last behavior was effectively captured in visual representations of the animal, as we can see in an illustration of a female *orang* taken from Prévost's *Histoire générale* who is shown covering her genitals and directing her eyes away from the viewer (figure 7.6).[26] Notice that in presenting the *orang* in this manner, the artist is able to convey the idea that the creature understood both what she would have been revealing and the impropriety of the revelation.

Further confirmation that these creatures were the potential missing link between human beings and animals can be seen in Tyson's claim that when given a choice of associating with either human beings or monkeys, they markedly prefer the company of the former. He suggests, in other words, that the *orang outangs* themselves recognized their proximity to human beings.[27] As de Maillet notes in summarizing his account of *orangs*, "if we could not say that these living creatures were men, at least they resembled them so much that it would have been unfair to consider them only as animals."[28]

Figure 7.6: Reprint of female "Orang outang" from Prévost (1747).

Figure 7.7: Reprint of female "Orang outang" from Tulp (1641).

The preceding discussion provides some valuable context for Rousseau's discussion of pongos and the other anthropomorphic primates mentioned in Note X. Given the close physical and behavioral similarity between *orang outangs* and human beings, his suggestion that *orangs* might be primitive human beings does not appear as revolutionary as some recent studies have suggested nor as farfetched as some of his contemporary critics supposed.[29] Rousseau's response to Charles Bonnet's objections to this characterization seems perfectly adequate: "[t]hat the monkey is a Beast, I believe it, and I have stated my reason for believing it; you are good enough to inform me that the Orang-outang also is one, but I must admit that given the facts I cited, that seemed to me a difficult fact to prove."[30] Throughout Note X Rousseau is simply questioning how we define a human being. His concerns on this score come into sharper focus once we begin to examine the treatment of so-called "primitive" human populations in the travel literature of the day.

II. "Primitives," Missing Links and the Chain of Being

The discovery of anthropomorphic primates was but one part of eighteenth-century attempts to link human beings and animals in the chain of being. European naturalists also tried to narrow this gap by drawing attention to the purportedly simian attributes (both physical and behavioral) of some human populations – usually African and specifically Hottentot. Sir John Ovington (1696), for example, described the Hottentots as "the very Reverse of Human kind . . . so that if there's any medium between a Rational Animal and a Beast, the *Hotantot* lays the fairest claim to that Species."[31] Similarly, Beeckman claimed that Hottentots "are not really unlike Monkeys or Baboons in their Gestures and Postures, especially when they sit Sunning themselves."[32]

Beeckman goes on to relate that Hottentot men have "broad flat Noses, blubber Lips, great Heads, disagreeable Features, short trifled Hair" and that "nothing can be more ugly."[33] Hottentot women fared little better in Beeckman's eyes, as he adds that they were "as ugly in the kind as the Men, having long flabby Breasts, odiously dangling down to the Waste; which they can toss over their Shoulders for the Children to suck. . . ."[34] This confirms an earlier claim made by English explorer Sir Thomas Herbert (see figure 7.8) concerning these same women.[35] Oliver Goldsmith (1774) later extended this attribute to include all African women, noting that once these women begin childbearing, their breasts "hang down to the navel; and it is customary with them, to suckle the child at their backs, by throwing the breast over the shoulder."[36]

Given that Europeans were willing to describe the physical attributes of black Africans in such terms, it should not be too surprising to find them using similar language in their accounts of African behavior and intellectual development.[37] Indeed, European naturalists saw a direct correlation between the physical and intellectual inferiority of black Africans. As Goldsmith notes in describing Africans, "[a]s their persons are thus naturally deformed, at least to our imaginations, their minds are equally incapable of strong exertions."[38]

For many eighteenth-century naturalists the mind of a black African was incapable not only of strong exertions but of most feats associated with human intelligence. Buffon, for example, claims that the Africans of Guiney "appear to be perfectly stupid, not being able to count beyond the number three, that they never think spontaneously; that they have no memory, the past and the future being equally unknown to them,"[39] and Beeckman refers to Hottentots as "filthy Animals," who "hardly deserve the name of Rational Creatures."[40] And where some naturalists speculated that some primates might be capable of speech, others compared the Hottentot language to animal vocalizations. Beeckman, for instance, heard it as the cackle of hens or turkeys;[41] and Herbert described it as "apishly sounded (with whom tis thought they mixe unnaturally)" and "very hard to be counterfeited" since it was voiced "like the Irish."[42]

Herbert's description of Hottentot speech provides another striking example of the way in which African behavior was cast in animal terms; namely, European descriptions of African sexual practices. Whereas female *orang outangs* were credited with a fairly high degree of sexual modesty, African women were depicted as having a rather liberal attitude towards sex. Thus, Herbert claimed that Hottentot women expressed gratitude by displaying their genitalia and noted that these people live communally, "coupling without distinction, the name of wife or brother unknowne among these incestuous Troglodites."[43] Similarly, Prévost mentions that marriage was unknown among the Africans who inhabited the Islands of Bomma,[44] and John Green (1745)

131

Figure 7.8: Reprint of male and female Hottentot from Herbert (1638).

describes the Africans of Teneriffe as a "rude uncivilized People" living in a society where "everyone took as many women as he pleased. . . ."[45]

Several European explorers suggested that male primates exploited this difference in the behavior of human and simian females and actively pursued African women as their sexual partners. It is not particularly uncommon to find European naturalists suggesting that *orang outangs* may be the offspring of successful human/simian copulation. Olfert Dapper (1688), for example, claimed that the *orang outangs* of the Congo were so numerous and so nearly human in appearance that "it has entered the minds of some travelers that they may be the offspring of a woman and a monkey."[46] Similarly, Leguat noted that

> Nature, who does not oppose the Copulation of Horses with Asses, may well admit that of an Ape with a Female-Animal that resembles him, especially where the latter is not restrain'd by any Principle. An Ape and a Negro slave born and brought up out of the knowledge of God, have not less similitude between them than an Ass and a Mare.[47]

One final aspect of these accounts that I want to mention concerns their description of the relations between different African peoples and between African peoples and primates. The European slave trade was rationalized at least in part by the claim that primitive black tribes subjugated more primitive tribes and that some primates subjugated at least some black tribes. Indeed, the ability for human beings to subjugate both other people and other animals was so important for eighteenth-century naturalists that so respected a figure as Buffon could use this trait to distinguish human beings from all other creatures.

In his discussion of human nature, Buffon points out that while there is no shortage of powerful animal species capable of destroying the members of other species, none of these species are capable of making slaves of inferior species. He notes that human beings alone have been able to tame other species and that animals do not recognize any sense of subordination vis-a-vis other animal species. This enables him to conclude that human nature is different in kind from that of other animal species.[48]

Monboddo will later draw on Buffon's authority and use reports of primates making slaves of some local African population to indicate that these creatures should be included in the human species: "the great Orang Outang carries off boys and girls to make slaves of them, which not only shews him, in my apprehension to be a man, but proves that he lives in society, and must have made some progress in the arts of civil life; for we hear of no nations altogether barbarous who use slaves."[49]

We should now be better able to appreciate the structure of the argument in the *Second Discourse*. Contemporary descriptions of both primates and primitive human populations were meant to demonstrate continuity in God's creation and the viability of the chain of being. This implied that if the chain of being was an accurate account of natural history, then inequality was a necessary feature of human society: "ORDER is heav'ns first law; and this confessed,/Some are, and must be, greater than the rest. . . ."[50] Natural history becomes relevant to Rousseau because it was the basis for an important counterargument to his egalitarianism; that is, according to the chain of being, inequality was both natural and just.[51] Rousseau must therefore demonstrate that the natural condition of the human species is much like the condition Buffon sees in other animal species. He must show that human beings are by nature equal.

III. Natural Man as a Physical Being

Rousseau approaches his discussion of natural human beings by arguing that the only sure means we have of knowing human nature is to separate what is natural from what is artificial in the human species, where artifice is understood to mean socially produced effects on human nature. In drawing this distinction he appears to pattern his account after a similar discussion in Buffon's essay on domestic animals.

Buffon argues that it is difficult to discover the true nature of domestic animals because of the changes wrought by their excessive contact with human beings.[52] Yet he also claims that it is incumbent upon the naturalist to try to separate what God created from what human beings have produced: "it is the duty of the naturalist . . . to distinguish those facts which depend solely on instinct, from those that originate from education; to ascertain what is proper to them from what is borrowed; to separate artifice from nature; and never to confound the animal with the slave, the beast of burden with the creature of God."[53]

We should note that Buffon is advocating a radically new understanding of nature, one which releases the concept from its Aristotelian moorings. For Buffon the natural condition of an animal is no longer its highest manifestation but rather the one most removed from human interference. Rousseau will push this idea much further and apply it to his examination of the human species. Thus, he starts with the assumption that natural man can only be discovered by stripping from him anything that can be ascribed to life in a particular society.

Rousseau begins his discussion of natural man with a brief account of human morphology. In the opening paragraph of Part I and again in Note III he argues that the physical appearance of human beings has generally remained constant; that, for example, human beings have always been bipeds. This is not to say that he denies variation in the physical attributes of the human species. In Note X, for instance, he draws attention to the diversity in such attributes as skin color, body size, and hair texture, as well as to reports of some human populations with tails.[54]

Rousseau's willingness to entertain this last possibility and his reluctance to specify any further details of human morphology in the state of nature is significant given that at this time naturalists were certain that Europeans were the prototypical human being. Other human forms were simply progressive degenerations of this superior European stock.[55] Rousseau's failure to specify the morphology of natural human beings in any great detail leaves open the possibility that Europeans were not the original human beings. It also signals the kind of criteria he will be using throughout his description of natural man – that is, he will define natural man in terms of the minimal traits necessary to classify a being as human.

Rousseau's account of human ethology in the pure state of nature describes a being that is healthy, vegetarian, physically strong, well coordinated, stupid, and solitary; and each of these characteristic behaviors can be supported by the relevant literature. In terms of health Prévost provides an account describing the Africans in the Kongo as quite healthy despite having neither doctors nor a rudimentary medical establishment.[56] Buffon claimed that the inhabitants of the Marianna Islands were stronger and more robust than Europeans, were free of disease, and had a life expectancy of one hundred years;[57] and Lionel Wafer (1699) noted that the Indians of South America are generally free of deformities and cripples.[58] The strength of natural man could be deduced from the superior strength of Hottentots and pongos (related in Rousseau's Notes VI and X respectively); and the suggestion that natural man may have been vegetarian (a speculation developed most fully in Rousseau's Notes V and VIII), can be supported by the vegetarianism of pongos[59] and the human population of Teneriffe.[60]

The final two claims (those dealing with natural man's intellectual development and social arrangements) are slightly more problematic in that they seem to raise doubts about whether a creature so situated can be considered a fully human being and not simply an animal with an anthropomorphic body. Rousseau's summary of natural man does little to allay such concerns; as early in Part II of the *Discourse* he notes that "Savage man, by nature committed to instinct alone, or rather compensated for the instinct he perhaps lacks by faculties capable of substituting for it at first, and then of raising him far above nature, will therefore begin with purely animal functions."[61] Specifically, Rousseau points out that natural man's desires do not exceed the physically necessary[62] and that his mind is consumed by its present existence.[63] Although it might seem difficult to accept the fact that a creature with no sense of self extending through time could be a human being, we should recall that European explorers had described several contemporary human populations in these terms. We have already seen, for example, Buffon's report that the Africans of Guiney have neither memory nor foresight, and we also have Herbert's testimony that Hottentots are "an accursed Progeny of Chan, who differ in nothing from bruit beasts save forme."[64] Rousseau thus had concrete examples of presently existing human populations with the intellectual capacity of animals.

Many of the byproducts of this low intellectual development could also be supported with contemporary ethnographic information. For example, when Rousseau acknowledges that he is at a loss to explain how a human being with this level of intelligence would have been able to discover and use fire, we need to recognize that he had access to accounts of presently existing human populations – the African natives of Teneriffe and the Marianna islanders – who were ignorant of the use of fire prior to their contact with Europeans.[65] Likewise, his speculation that natural man was without possessions and a settled home can be supported by Buffon's reports that the natives of New Holland "have no houses, and . . . sleep on the ground without any covering,"[66] and that black Africans in general share their few possessions freely among the needy "without any other motive than that of pure compassion for the indigent."[67]

Rousseau's speculation that natural man was a solitary creature, however, was already controversial when the *Discourse* was first published and was rejected by a number of his contemporary critics.[68] Perhaps the most telling objection to Rousseau's view was the claim that the family was the minimal social arrangement which would ensure the perpetuation of the species. As Buffon argued,

> Even supposing the constitution of the human body to be very different from what we see it, and that its growth were more rapid [Rousseau speculates in Note XII that human children in the pure state of nature may have developed faster than present day children], it is impossible to maintain that man ever existed without forming families; because, if not cherished and attended for several years, the whole children must have inevitably perished.[69]

This is a fairly powerful objection to Rousseau's conception of natural man, if not the general argument of the *Second Discourse* itself. For if his natural human beings could not have survived as a biological species, it is difficult to see how they could be used to support his normative claims.

In order to defend himself from this type of counterargument, Rousseau needs to demonstrate that the human species could have survived without any settled social arrangements; that human fathers, human mothers, and their children would have had little need for prolonged social arrangements. I believe that he does offer such an argument. He demonstrates that fathers have no physical reason (after successful copulation) to care for either mother or child, and that mothers can care for their children absent the father's assistance.

The first claim appears fairly easy to defend once we accept that natural human beings have neither memory nor foresight. Rousseau correctly points out (see Note XII) that natural man would lack the requisite intellectual acumen to remain with a woman after conception and through a pregnancy. As he argues, fathers may have a moral obligation to care for mother and child, but they certainly have no physical reason to do so, and "moral proofs do not have great force in matters of physics."[70] The second claim, however, is probably both more important and more difficult to defend.

Rousseau begins this argument by pointing out that while human children appear to develop slower than those of other species, a human mother has an advantage over her counterparts in most other species in that she can use her arms both to defend herself and to carry her children when fleeing an attacker. Thus, unlike other mothers, a human mother need not abandon her young when retreating nor endanger herself by slowing her retreat to her children's pace:

> If they [i.e., human beings in the state of nature] have only two feet to run with, they have two arms to provide for their defense and their needs. Perhaps their children walk late and with difficulty, but mothers carry them with ease: an advantage lacking in other species in which the mother, being pursued, finds herself forced to abandon her young or to regulate her speed by theirs.[71]

Some critics have seen a potential difficulty for this argument. Roger Masters, for example, argues that if we accept Rousseau's earlier claim that natural human beings were vegetarians who used their hands and arms when gathering food and if, as Rousseau concedes (see Note XVI), vegetarians need to spend a great deal of time collecting food, then human infants would be vulnerable if the mother was attacked while foraging. Masters points out that a mother would be forced to separate from her children during the time she was foraging since she could not simultaneously carry her children, defend herself, and gather food.[72]

But in raising this objection Masters is assuming that the mother must use her arms to hold her infant. Yet this need not be the case since Rousseau does not specify how mothers carried their children, only that they do so with ease, and we have several examples of viable alternatives. Andrew Battel, for example, observed that in the pongos (who like Rousseau's natural human beings are vegetarian) the infant clings to its mother's body.[73] We also have seen that the Hottentot infant in Figure 8 is able not only to cling to its mother's back but to be suckled in this position. The ability to transport and nurse a baby in this fashion would seem to be a considerable advantage for natural woman since it would allow her to retain relative freedom of movement of both her arms and her legs. Because Rousseau has not specified the morphology of natural woman, it is at least theoretically possible that human females in the pure state of nature could have been similarly endowed.

Since human mothers in the state of nature may have been able to transport and nurse their children while they foraged, fought, or fled, they would not have been too inconvenienced by the requirements of tending for their children; and the prospects for the children would not necessarily have been as dire as Buffon suggests. Therefore, notwithstanding Buffon's objections to the contrary, Rousseau's suggestion that natural human beings were solitary creatures could be sustained by the relevant literature.

IV. Natural Man as a Moral Being

Now that we have examined the biology of natural human beings, we can turn our attention to what Rousseau refers to as their "metaphysical" or "moral" dimension. These two sides – physical and metaphysical – of natural man are intimately connected, in that the physical being establishes the parameters for the moral being. Perhaps the most important factor in natural man's moral self is Rousseau's assessment of his intellectual development. According to Rousseau, the key elements in the moral relations of human beings in the state of nature are peace, freedom, equality, and compassion or pity; and as was the case with natural man's physical attributes, each of these could be corroborated by actually existing primitive populations.

Green reports that the inhabitants of Teneriffe, for example, "dislike Blood-shedding of any kind . . .";[74] and he draws heavily on Kolben's generally sympathetic portrait of the Hottentots to assert that these people appear to be "some of the most humane and virtuous (abating for a few Prejudices of Education) to be found among the Races of Mankind."[75] Buffon also refers to the love of liberty among the Hottentots, characterizing them as "a wandering, independent people, frightfully nasty, and extremely jealous of their liberty." Moreover, we have already seen Buffon's testimony that Africans in general share their possessions with the needy.[76]

The common trait underlying each of the features Rousseau is willing to credit to natural man is the limited intelligence of human beings in the state of nature, since stupidity prevents the development of jealousy, vanity, exploitation and slavery. Rousseau's claim that inequality is "almost null" in nature is based on his insight that inequality demands a certain level of intelligence in order to judge and compare the merits of different attributes.[77] Nonrational animals, to say nothing of plants and rocks, are incapable of making these kinds of judgments and are therefore unable to construct inter- and intraspecific hierarchies. One might object that the low intelligence of natural human beings also poses a major difficulty in Rousseau's conception of their moral relations, since it appears to undermine the possibility that pity was one of natural man's basic sentiments.

Although Rousseau claims that pity operates prior to reason, some critics (e.g., Plamenatz, Masters, and Charvet) have argued that that is impossible because pity demands a higher degree of intellectual development that Rousseau was willing to credit to natural man.[78] Charvet, for example, argues that in order to experience pity an individual must be able to imagine himself in the position of the thing experiencing the suffering.[79] And as we have seen, Rousseau's natural man does not appear to possess the requisite intelligence to accomplish this mental shift.

This is a potentially devastating critique; for inasmuch as pity is the source of such emotions as generosity, clemency, humanity, friendship, and benevolence, it is also

Rousseau's solution to the social problem.[80] As Charvet points out, pity (in some form or another) becomes the primary means for uniting previously solitary individuals into a social unit.[81] Thus, if Charvet is correct and pity is impossible in a being with the mental development Rousseau credits to natural man, the argument in the *Second Discourse* fails.

This type of criticism, however, is misplaced for two interrelated reasons. First, while Charvet may have accurately described the mental process involved when an individual experiences pity for the suffering of another (a process which Rousseau discusses in similar language in his *Essay on the Origin of Languages*),[82] this does not necessarily mean that the pitying individual consciously calculates the process. It is possible that natural man simply feels the pain of the sufferer without understanding why. As Rousseau notes, pity is "obscure and strong in savage man, developed but weak in civilized man."[83] This claim becomes more plausible once we examine how this sentiment was treated in the context of eighteenth-century physiology.

Naturalists at this time did not discuss pity in terms of its intellectual components. Buffon, for example, begins his discussion of pity by drawing a distinction between sensation and sentiment and claiming that the former is rooted in the brain and refers to the mental capacity necessary for a creature to be receptive to external stimuli, while the latter is the internal process responsible for transforming sensation into such emotional responses as pleasure, pain, anxiety, and sickness. He then argues that the brain is not involved in experiencing sentiment, so that "in man, the sentiment of pity belongs more to the body than to the mind" and that "horror and pity are not so much passions of the mind, as natural affections depending on the sensibility of the body, and similarity of structure."[84]

Buffon attributed this to the fact that in human beings and other similar species, the diaphram is the center of sentiment and thus it is in the diaphram "that all the movements of the sensible system are exerted. . . ."[85] Thus, far from representing a contradiction in his conception of natural man, Rousseau's discussion of pity was fully in accord with mainstream natural science. Natural man did not need to understand the complexities of how pity was experienced; he simply felt it.

V. The Politics of Natural Man

Rousseau's description of natural man deftly turns the chain of being against itself. Where naturalists using the chain of being subdivided and ranked groups within the human species according to the purportedly highest attributes of the species (e.g., intelligence, civilization, and culture), Rousseau sought the baseline attributes shared by all members of the species. That is, he searched for those attributes a being needed to possess in order to be classified as human. This baseline conception of human nature was necessarily determined by the descriptions available in the literature; and as we have seen, increased European contact with the native populations of Africa and Americas extended the possibilities of human culture dramatically. Moreover, because these accounts sought to minimize the gap between human beings and apes, the line between these populations was not drawn very sharply. Rousseau's baseline, then, is correspondingly low and seems to equate natural man with an animal because Europeans had discovered human beings that looked and acted like animals and animals that looked and acted like human beings.

The decision to apply Buffon's distinction between natural and artificial to his own account of the human species provided Rousseau with an alternative set of criteria for defining the natural condition of the human species, and these new criteria supported his egalitarianism. In Rousseau's hands equality, freedom, health, and happiness replace developments in the arts and sciences as the truly relevant indications of what is human. Rousseau prefaces his account of the human history outlined in Part II of the *Discourse* by conceding that

> as the events I have to describe could have happened in several ways, I can make a choice only by conjectures. But besides the fact that these conjectures become reasons when they are the most probable that one can draw from the nature of things, and the sole means that one can have to discover the truth, the conclusion I want to deduce from mine will not thereby be conjectural, since, on the principles I have established, one could not conceive of any other system that would not provide me with the same results, and from which I could not draw the same conclusions.[86]

The "principles" he claims to have established are based on his conception of natural man. This human being is not some chimpanzee, gorilla, or orangutan but a composite of actually existing human populations representing an alternative to European culture. Rousseau presents us with two facts given as real (to paraphrase from the last paragraph of Part I): the inequality, misery, and slavery of modern Europe, and the equality, freedom, and happiness of various "primitive" populations.

In order for his argument to succeed, Rousseau did not need to provide an accurate account of human history since the actual direction of that history is largely irrelevant. Whether human history moves as he will suggest it does, beginning with "primitive" human beings and ending with Europeans, or as Buffon suggests,[87] beginning with Europeans and ending with "primitives," the validity of his egalitarian claims will be unaffected.

In the *Second Discourse* Rousseau accepts the assumption that nature is a viable normative standard and then demonstrates that regardless of the actual direction of human history, European society should no longer serve as the standard for what is natural. If he is correct in his assumption concerning the trajectory of human history, then primitive populations are the original human beings and the true representatives of what God intended for the species. If Buffon is correct, then primitive peoples represent a part of the species who, for whatever combination of circumstances, have degenerated so far from the European norm that they have been able to produce social arrangements which are both closer to nature and which provide for greater health, happiness, equality, and freedom.

These developments evidently came with the price of sacrificing the arts, sciences, and other corollaries of "higher" intelligence. The key question thus becomes: which set of standards is more worthwhile? Those who see Rousseau as a pessimist[88] are tacitly acknowledging that they accept his criteria as the true measure of humanity.

VI. Conclusion

Rousseau's understanding of human nature and the natural condition of the human species deftly turns the chain of being against itself. His natural human beings are modeled on European conceptions of the missing link between human beings and animals in the natural chain and indicate that the true measure of man was not in the parlors of Europe but in the jungles of Africa. We should recall that the epigraph for the title page of the Discourse reads "Not in corrupt things, but in those which are well ordered in accordance with nature, should one consider that which is natural."[89] For Rousseau Europe offers a corrupt form of the species and the inequality inherent in its societies should not be taken as the standard for assessing either other cultures or other species.

Notes

1. Jean-Jacques Rousseau, "Letter to Christophe de Beaumont" (1762), *The Indispensable Rousseau*, ed. John Hope Mason (New York: 1979), p. 232.
2. Lester G. Crocker, *Jean-Jacques Rousseau* (2 vols; New York: 1979), I, p. 232. Also see Aryeh Botwinick, *Rousseau's Critique of Liberal Democracy* (Bristol, Ind.: 1983), p. 15.
3. See, for example, Maurice Cranston, "Introduction," *Jean-Jacques Rousseau: A Discourse on Inequality*, ed. Maurice Cranston (New York: 1984), pp. 28–30; Lester Crocker, "Diderot and Eighteenth-Century French Transformism," *Forerunners of Darwin: 1745–1859*, eds Bentley Glass, Oswei Temkin, and William L. Straus (Baltimore: 1959), pp. 133–4; A. O. Lovejoy, "The Supposed Primitivism of Rousseau's Discourse on Inequality," *Modern Philology*, 21 (1923), pp. 165–86; Roger D. Masters, "The Structure of Rousseau's Political Thought," *Hobbes and Rousseau*, eds Maurice Cranston and Richard S. Peters (Garden City, N.Y.: 1972), pp. 403–4; Masters, "Jean-Jacques is Alive and Well: Rousseau and Contemporary Sociobiology," *Daedalus*, 107 (1978), pp. 93–105; Masters, "Nothing Fails Like Success: Development and History in Rousseau's Political Philosophy," *Trent Rousseau Papers*, eds Jim MacAdam, Michael Neuman, and Guy LaFrance (Ottawa: 1980), pp. 99–118; René Pomeau, "Voyage et lumières dans la littérature française du XVIIIe siècle," *Studies on Voltaire and the Eighteenth Century*, 57 (1967), pp. 1269–89; Robert Wokler, "Perfectible Apes in Decadent Cultures: Rousseau's Anthropology Revisited," *Daedalus*, 107 (1978), pp. 107–34; and Robert Wokler, "The Ape Debates in Enlightenment Anthropology," *Studies on Voltaire and the Eighteenth Century*, 192 (1980), pp. 1164–75.
4. See Christopher Frayling and Robert Wokler, "From the Orang-utan to the Vampire: Towards an Anthropology of Rousseau," *Rousseau After 200 Years*, ed. R. A. Leigh (New York: 1982), pp. 109–24; Asher Horowitz, *Rousseau, Nature and History* (Buffalo: 1987); and Horowitz "Laws and Customs Thrust Us Back to Infancy: Rousseau's Historical Anthropology," *Review of Politics*, 52 (1990), pp. 215–42.
5. See especially Masters, "Jean-Jacques is Alive and Well."
6. See especially Frayling and Wokler, "From the Orang-utan to the Vampire," and Wokler, "The Ape Debates."
7. "Discourse on the Origin and Foundations of Inequality Among Men (1755)," in *Jean-Jacques Rousseau: The First and Second Discourses*, ed. Roger D. Masters (New York: 1964), p. 150; hereafter *SD* followed by the page number in the Masters edition.

8. *SD*, p. 204.

9. For an historical overview of the idea and its importance in eighteenth-century thought, see A. O. Lovejoy, *The Great Chain of Being* (Cambridge, Mass.: 1936), pp. 183–287; John C. Greene, *The Death of Adam* (Ames, Ia.: 1959), pp. 132–52; William F. Bynum, "The Great Chain of Being After Forty Years: A Reappraisal," *History of Science*, 13 (1975), pp. 1–28; and Norman Hampson, *A Cultural History of the Enlightenment* (New York: 1968), pp. 63–95.

10. For the most part I have confined my remarks to those sources that either were cited directly by Rousseau or were cited in works he cites. Although some of the anthologies I cite (in particular, those by Lord Monboddo and Oliver Goldsmith) were published after the *Second Discourse*, many of the episodes they relate are taken from sources originally published before the *Second Discourse*. For a thorough discussion of Rousseau's sources for the *Second Discourse* see Jean Morel, "Recherches sur les sources du discours de l'inégalité," *Annales de la Société Jean-Jacques Rousseau*, V (1909), pp. 119–98. Also useful on this score are Jean Starobinski, "Notes et Variantes," *J.-J. Rousseau: Oeuvres complètes*, eds Bernard Gagnebin and Marcel Raymond, (4 vols; Paris: 1959–69), III, pp. 1285–1379; Roger D. Masters, "Editor's Notes," *Jean-Jacques Rousseau: The First and Second Discourses*, ed. Roger D. Masters (New York: 1964), pp. 229–48; and Victor Gourevitch, "Editor's Notes," *Jean-Jacques Rousseau: The First and Second Discourses and Essay on the Origin of Languages*, ed. Victor Gourevitch (New York: 1986), pp. 328–58. For a discussion of Rousseau and the travel literature of the period, see George Pire, "Jean Jacques Rousseau et les relations de voyages," *Revue d'histoire littéraire de la France*, 56 (1956), pp. 355–78. For an overall introduction to the relevant travel literature see Gilbert Chinard, *L'Amérique et le rêve exotique dans la littérature française au XVIIe et au XVIIIe siècles* (Paris: 1913); Geoffrey Atkinson, *The Extraordinary Voyage in French Litterature: 1700–1720* (Paris: 1922); and R. W. Frantz, "Swift's Yahoos and the Voyagers," *Modern Philology*, 29 (1931), pp. 48–57.

11. Victor Gourevitch, "Rousseau's Pure State of Nature," *Interpretation*, 16 (1988), pp. 43–5. I have used the spelling *orang outang* whenever I refer to eighteenth-century descriptions of these animals.

12. *SD*, p. 204.

13. Edward Tyson, *Orang-Outang or the Anatomy of a Pygmie Compared with that of a Monkey, an Ape, and a Man* (1699), cited in Ashley Montagu, "Edward Tyson, M.D., F.D.S. 1650–1708," *Memoirs of the American Philosophical Society*, 20 (1943), p. 244; hereafter *Orang-Outang*.

14. Cited in John Green, *A New General Collection of Voyages and Travels* (4 vols; London, 1745–47), II, p. 718; hereafter *NGCVT*. This anthology was the basis for the first seven volumes of Prévost's *Histoire générale des voyages*, thus, a similar summary of Smith's account may also be found in Prévost, *HGV*, IV, p. 240. These animals were also mentioned in Rousseau's Note X, see *SD*, p. 207.

15. Francois Leguat, *The Voyage of Francois Leguat* (1708), ed. Pasfield Oliver (2 vols; London: 1891), II, p. 234; hereafter *Voyage*.

16. Daniel Beeckman, *A Voyage to and from the Island of Borneo*, (London: 1718), p. 37; hereafter *Borneo*.

17. Purchas, *Hakluytus Posthumus*, VI, p. 398; Tyson, *orang outang*, p. 261; Leguat, *Voyage*, II, p. 234; Beeckman, *Borneo*, p. 37; William Smith, *A New Voyage to Guinea* (1744), in *HGV*, IV, p. 240; Benoît de Maillet, *Telliamed* (1748), tr. Albert O. Carozzi (Chicago: 1968), p. 201; and Buffon, "Natural History of the Orang-Outangs, or the Pongo and Jocko" (1766), *Natural History: General and Particular*, ed. William Smellie (8 vols; London: 1781), VIII, p. 86; hereafter *NH*.

18. Stephen Jay Gould, *The Flamingo's Smile* (New York: 1985), p. 272.
19. *SD*, p. 204.
20. Purchas, *Hakluytus Posthumus*, VI, p. 399.
21. James Burnett, Lord Monboddo, *Of the Origin and Progress of Language* (6 vols; Edinburgh, 1773–92), I, pp. 87–8; hereafter *Origin and Progress*.
22. According to Prévost "guinous" are suspected of feigning muteness in order to escape being used as slaves; see Prévost, *HGV*, III, p. 293. Green offers similar speculations on two other types of primates: "magots" and the quojas-morrow"; see Green, *NGCVT*, II, pp. 349–50.
23. See Tyson, *Orang-Outang*, p. 241; Prévost, *HGV*, V, p. 89. Rousseau included the passage from Prévost in Note X, see *SD*, p. 206.
24. Tyson, *Orang-Outang*, pp. 257, 280.
25. Tyson, *Orang-Outang*, p. 280; Leguat, *Voyage*, II, p. 234; Buffon, "Natural History of the Orang-Outangs, or the Pongo and Jocko," p. 56; and Monboddo, *Origin and Progress*, I, p. 270. For a summary of Tulp and Bontius, see T. H. Huxley, *Man's Place in Nature* (1863), ed. Ashley Montagu (Ann Arbor: 1959), p. 17.
26. This drawing appears to have been based on an earlier illustration (see Figure 7.7) of the same animal that was published in Tulp's *Observationum Medicarum*; see Nicolas Tulp, *Observationum Medicarum* (Amsterdam, 1641). We should note two subtle differences between the two illustrations: 1) the artist of the Prévost drawing augments the orang's mammaries so that they resemble more closely those of a human female; and 2) modifies the jaw to create a more human facial structure.
27. Tyson, *Orang-Outang*, p. 257.
28. De Maillet, *Telliamed*, p. 201.
29. The purportedly evolutionist implications of the *Second Discourse* have been drawing increased attention of late. See, for example, Cranston, "Introduction," pp. 29–30; Bertrand de Jouvenal, "Rousseau the Pessimistic Evolutionist," *Yale French Studies*, 28 (1961), pp. 83–96; Frayling and Wokler, "From the Orang-utan to the Vampire"; Roger D. Masters, *The Political Philosophy of Rousseau* (Princeton: 1968); Masters, "The Structure of Rousseau's Political Thought"; Masters "Jean-Jacques is Alive and Well"; Masters "Introduction," *Jean-Jacques Rousseau: On the Social Contract*, ed. Roger D. Masters (New York: 1978), p. 13; Masters, "Nothing Fails Like Success," pp. 99–102; Marc Plattner, *Rousseau's State of Nature* (DeKalb, Ill.: 1979), pp. 36–40; Wokler, "The Ape Debates," p. 1171; and Wokler, "Perfectible Apes in Decadent Cultures." The earliest example of this type of reading that I could locate is C. E. Vaughan's introductory essay in his edition of Rousseau's political writings; see C. E. Vaughan, *The Political Writings of Jean Jacques Rousseau* (1915) (2 vols; New York: 1971), pp. 120–3. Also see Charles Bonnet, "Lettre de M. Philopolis" (1755) *Jean-Jacques Rousseau: Oeuvres complètes*, III, p. 1384.
30. Rousseau, "Letter to Philopolis" (1755), *The First and Second Discourse*, ed. Victor Gourevitch, p. 235.
31. Cited in Frantz, "Swift's Yahoos and the Voyagers," p. 55.
32. Beeckman, *Borneo*, p. 187.
33. Ibid., p. 184.
34. Ibid., pp. 184–5.
35. Thomas Herbert, *Some Yeares Travels into Divers Parts of Asia and Afrique* (London: 1638; 2nd edn), p. 17; hereafter *Some Yeares Travels*.
36. Oliver Goldsmith, *An History of the Earth and Animated Nature* (8 vols; London: 1774), II, p. 228; hereafter *HEAN*. Buffon reported the same characteristic in Eskimo women, see Buffon, "Of the Varieties of the Human Species," (1753), *NH*, III, p. 59.

37. For more on the problem of racism in eighteenth-century natural history see Phillip R. Sloan, "The Idea of Racial Degeneracy in Buffon's Histoire Naturelle," *Studies in Eighteenth Century Culture*, III (1973), pp. 293–321; Richard Popkin, "The Philosophical Basis of Eighteenth-Century Racism," *Studies in Eighteenth Century Culture*, III (1973), pp. 245–62; and Henry Vyverberg, *Human Nature, Cultural Diversity, and the French Enlightenment* (New York: 1989).

38. Goldsmith, *HEAN*, II, p. 228.

39. Buffon, "Of the Varieties of the Human Species," p. 151.

40. Beeckman, *Borneo*, p. 186.

41. Ibid., p. 188.

42. Herbert, *Some Yeares Travels*, p. 18.

43. Ibid., pp. 16–17.

44. Prévost, *HGV*, IV, p. 614.

45. Green, *NGCVT*, I, p. 534; also see Prévost, *HGV*, II, p. 229.

46. Cited in Prévost, *HGV*, V, p. 88; also reported by Rousseau at *SD*, p. 206.

47. Leguat, *Voyage*, II, p. 235.

48. Buffon, "Of the Nature of Man" (1749), *NH*, II, p. 362. Although Buffon criticizes slavery elsewhere (e.g., "Of the Varieties of the Human Species," pp. 152–3), the general tenor of his theory could be used to support this institution. See Sloan, "The Idea of Racial Degeneracy in Buffon's Histoire Naturelle."

49. Monboddo, *Origin and Progress*, I, p. 344.

50. Alexander Pope, *An Essay on Man* (1734), ed. Frank Brady (New York: 1965), Epistle IV, lines 49–50; hereafter *Essay*.

51. The chain of being was frequently deployed by conservatives to provide a form of what Basil Willey has called "cosmic toryism;" see Basil Willey, *The Eighteenth Century Background: Studies on the Idea of Nature in the Thought of the Period* (New York: 1940), pp. 43–56. Some examples of this use of the theory may be found in G. W. Leibniz, *Theodicy* (1710), tr. E. M. Huggard (LaSalle, Ill.: 1985) sec. 241–6; Pope, *Essay*, IV; Buffon, "Of the Varieties of the Human Species," pp. 57–207; Bonnet, "Lettre de M. Philopolis," pp. 1383–6; Edmund Burke, *Reflections on the Revolution in France* (1790), ed. Thomas H. D. Mahoney (Indianapolis: 1955), pp. 110–11; Soame Jenyns, "A Free Inquiry into the Nature and Origin of Evil" (1757), and "Disquisition on Government and Civil Liberty" (1782), *Works of Soame Jenyns*, ed. Charles Nalson Cole (4 vols; London: 1793), III, pp. 43–52 and III, pp. 258–75; and Joseph Marie, comte de Maistre, "Study on Sovereignty" (1793), *The Works of Joseph de Maistre*, ed. Jack Lively (New York: 1965), pp. 95–6.

52. Buffon, "Of Domestic Animals," *NH*, III, p. 301.

53. Ibid., pp. 301–2.

54. Buffon, for example, mentions several accounts describing the people of the Philippines as having four- or five-inch tails, as well as one uncorroborated account (which he questions as exaggerated) of the people of Formosa having foot-long tails; see Buffon, "Of the Varieties of the Human Species," p. 87. Also see de Maillet, *Telliamed*, pp. 202–6.

55. See Buffon, "Of the Varieties of the Human Species"; Buffon, "Of the Degeneration of Animals" (1756), *NH*, VII, pp. 392–452; and Goldsmith, *HEAN*, I, p. 239.

56. Prévost, *HGV*, IV, p. 643.

57. Buffon, "Of the Varieties of the Human Species," p. 91.

58. Lionel Wafer, *A New Voyage and Description of the Isthmus of America* (1699), ed. L. E. Elliot Joyce (London: 1934), pp. 78–9. Also see George Pire, "Jean-Jacques Rousseau et les relations de voyages," p. 368.

59. Purchas, *Hakluytus Posthumus*, VI, p. 398; and Prévost *HGV*, V, p. 87.

60. Ibid., II, p. 229.

61. *SD*, p. 115.

62. Ibid., p. 116.

63. Ibid., p. 117.

64. Herbert, *Some Yeares Travels*, p. 16.

65. Prévost, *HGV*, II, p. 229; Buffon, "Of the Varieties of the Human Species," p. 91.

66. Ibid., p. 95.

67. Ibid., p. 152.

68. See, for example, Buffon, "A Dissertation on Carnivorous Animals" (1758), *NH*, IV, pp. 183–93; and George Havens, *Voltaire's Marginalia on the Pages of Rousseau* (Columbus, Ohio: 1933).

69. Buffon, "A Dissertation on Carnivorous Animals," p. 186.

70. *SD*, p. 215.

71. Ibid., p. 112.

72. Masters, *Political Philosophy of Rousseau*, p. 124.

73. Purchas, *Hakluytus Posthumus*, VI, p. 399; and Prévost, *HGV*, V, p. 88.

74. Green, *NGCVT*, I, p. 534; also Prévost, *HGV*, II, p. 229.

75. Green, *NGCVT*, III, p. vi.

76. Buffon, "On the Varieties of the Human Species," p. 154.

77. *SD*, p. 180.

78. John Charvet, *The Social Problem in the Philosophy of Rousseau* (London: 1974), pp. 18–19, hereafter *Social Problem*; Masters, *Political Philosophy of Rousseau*, pp. 138–40; John Plamenatz, *Man and Society*, 2 vols (New York: 1963), I, p. 375.

79. Charvet, *Social Problem*, p. 18–19.

80. *SD*, pp. 131–2.

81. Charvet, *Social Problem*, p. 19.

82. Rousseau, "Essay on the Origin of Languages" (1755), *The First and Second Discourses*, ed. Victor Gourevitch, p. 261.

83. *SD*, p. 132.

84. Buffon, "A Dissertation on Carnivorous Animals," pp. 167–8.

85. Ibid., pp. 169–70.

86. *SD*, pp. 140–1.

87. See Buffon, "Of the Degeneration of Animals," *NH*, VII, pp. 392–4. For further discussion of Buffon's theory of racial degeneracy see Sloan, "The Idea of Racial Degeneracy in Buffon's Histoire Naturelle," pp. 307–8.

88. See, for example, deJouvenal, "Rousseau the Pessimistic Evolutionist"; Masters, "Nothing Fails Like Success," p. 102; William Pickles, "The Notion of Time in Rousseau's Political Thought," *Hobbes and Rousseau*, p. 380; and Jean Starobinski, "Discours sur l'origine et les fondements de l'inégalité," *J. J. Rousseau: Oeuvres Complètes*, III, pp. xlii–lxx.

89. Rousseau's original is in Latin. I follow Masters's translation. My thanks to Larry Arnhart, Donald Tannenbaum, Donald R. Kelley, and the anonymous reviewers for their comments on earlier versions of this paper.

CHAPTER 8

Kant as an Unfamiliar Source of Racism

ROBERT BERNASCONI

1

In 1972 Isaiah Berlin gave a lecture on "Kant as an Unfamiliar Source of Nationalism", which has recently been published in *The Sense of Reality*.[1] The lecture began:

> At first sight nothing would seem more disparate than the idea of nationality and the sane, rational, liberal internationalism of the great Königsberg philosopher. Of all the influential thinkers of his day, Kant seems the most remote from the rise of nationalism. (*SR*, p. 232)

Just as Berlin shows a connection between Kant and nationalism, I propose to do the same for Kant and racism. However, the form of Berlin's argument is somewhat different from mine. Berlin does not question the legitimacy of the image of Kant's philosophy as "deeply rational and cosmopolitan" (*SR*, p. 244). Berlin's interest is, rather, to show how "ideas turn into their opposites" (*SR*, p. 248). He has in mind what became of Kant's ideas in Herder and Fichte. My thesis, by contrast, is that, in spite of Kant's avowed cosmopolitanism that is evident in such essays as his "Idea for a Universal History with a Cosmopolitan Purpose," one also finds within his philosophy expressions of a virulent and theoretically based racism, at a time when scientific racism was still in its infancy. Although the blatant and unremitting racist declarations of Europeans at this time, like Edward Long's *History of Jamaica* of 1776, are shocking and deplorable and call for further intellectual inquiry, some authors present a further puzzle that has a particular interest for philosophers and historians of ideas. This is because they join their racism to the new universalism or cosmopolitanism, which is supposed to be one of the great achievements of the Enlightenment and an antidote to

145

racism. That is to say, the puzzle lies in the fact that some of Europe's greatest minds appear to have held beliefs that strike us as contradictory. The most famous and most debated example is provided by Jefferson,[2] but the more puzzling case is Kant, because, unlike Jefferson, he was neither under political pressure on this particular issue nor compromised by the self-interest of being a slave owner.

It remains something of a mystery how an articulate racism can within a given society co-exist with ideas of "human brotherhood," as happened during the Enlightenment to an unprecedented degree.[3] The same question must, of course, also be asked of sexism as well, but because, at least to late twentieth-century ears, the very term "human brotherhood" indicates sexism, the puzzle is in that case highlighted, although no closer to being resolved. It is not a case of ideas turning into their opposites during the course of their development. Nor does it seem to be a case of timelag as a society struggles to catch up with a transformation in its morality. If one takes up Horkheimer's and Adorno's suggestion in *The Dialectic of the Enlightenment* that humanism, egalitarianism, and cosmopolitanism do not so much contradict racism as lend themselves to racism, affirming it as they seek to deny it, this raises more questions than it resolves and so can only be taken as a starting-point.[4] Why were so many Enlightenment thinkers apparently unable to articulate the new sense of humanity without at the same time drawing the boundaries within humanity more rigidly and explicitly than before? Does not the historical record show that cosmopolitanism not only was not introduced to combat racism, but also readily accommodated racism? Does this not suggest that the ease with which scholars today define the two terms as contraries and then read these definitions back into history distorts the historical relation of the two ideas? Did the advocacy of cosmopolitanism also give to its supporters a sense of superiority over all those whom they perceived as tied to their particularisms? Even if universalism does not necessarily take the form of a demand that others assimilate to those standards that the dominant group holds to be universal, thereby establishing a universalism for everyone else, while the dominant group retains its particularism, is it not a constant threat? Perhaps if we had better answers to these questions, we would be better equipped to understand the persistence of racism within our own society and the disguises behind which it conceals itself. But the problem of making sense of this conflict within a particular society's values is not as difficult as making sense of this same conflict within a single individual, particularly if it is not someone one wants to accuse of blindspots, hypocrisy, or stupidity, like Kant.

In 1775 in "Von den verschiedenen Racen der Menschen," Kant defined race in the following terms:

> Among the deviations, that is, among the hereditary dissimilarities that we find in animals that belong to a single line of descent are those called races. Races are deviations that are constantly preserved over many generations and come about as a consequence of migration (dislocation to other regions) or through interbreeding with other deviations of the same line of descent, which always produces half-breed offspring. (AA, II, p. 430)[5]

That Kant was a leading proponent of the concept of race when its scientific status was still far from secure is well established.[6] Indeed, Kant can legitimately be said to have invented the scientific concept of race insofar as he gave the first clear definition of it. When the concept of race was attacked first by Herder and then by Georg Forster, Kant immediately rushed to its defense by publishing two further essays on race, "Bestimmung des Begriffs einer Menschenrace" (1785) and "Über den Gebrauch teleologischer Principien in der Philosophie" (1788).[7] Once Kant's role in constructing a rigorous concept of race is recognized, it is a relatively easy matter to give Kant a place in the history of racism. Using an argument of the kind employed by Berlin, one can readily show that his ideas gave rise to by-products that he nevertheless would have repudiated (cf. *SR*, p. 244). George Mosse in *Toward the Final Solution* drew such a connection between Kant's novel insistence on the immutability and permanence of race and the racist policies of the National Socialists.[8] My question here, however, is whether Kant's contribution to racism is limited to this role. So far as the question of whether his racism and his views on race obtruded into the critical philosophy, I will argue elsewhere that Kant's understanding of race is at stake in the discussion of teleology in the *Critique of Judgment*.[9] Here I will focus only on Kant's original contribution within the history of racism, ignoring his subsequent use by racists, such as the National Socialists in Germany.[10] It might seem that Kant's reputation for cosmopolitanism is so long-standing that any attempt to sully it now can be understood only as another example of tabloid philosophy in which one attempts to bring a thinker down simply because they are exalted. However, I believe that studying how the classical works of the history of philosophy connect with the institutional oppression of their time is the best preparation for questioning the limitations of our own thinking. The still dominant tendency to reduce our understanding of classic philosophers like Locke, Hume, Kant, and, for that matter, Heidegger to the most narrow, abstract and defensible statements of their positions that we can formulate, might at first sight seem to protect them and us from those things we prefer they had not written, but this restriction of their thought ultimately diminishes philosophy. Not least, it fosters the pretense that the great philosophers were unmotivated in their research and withdrawn from concern for society.[11]

It is extraordinary that Hume's racism has received more attention than Kant's, even though Hume's racism is much less extensive than Kant's and far less integrated into his philosophy.[12] I cannot document here the full range of Kant's anti-Semitism and anti-Black racism, nor introduce the qualifications necessary to establish a balanced picture. Given my aims, it will not be necessary for me to rehearse, for example, the often cited comment in Kant's *Observations on the Sublime and the Beautiful*.[13] But consider this quotation from the *Physical Geography*, which documents Kant's ideas about racial inequality:

> Humanity is at its greatest perfection in the race of the whites. The yellow Indians do have a meagre talent. The Negroes are far below them and at the lowest point are a part of the American peoples. (AA, IX, p. 316)[14]

Or consider Kant's claim in an unpublished note that Whites "contain all the impulses (*Triebfedern*) of nature in affects and passions, all talents, all dispositions to culture and civilization and can as readily obey as govern. They are the only ones who always advance to perfection" (AA, XV/2, p. 878). I will often return to this note, number 1,520 in the Adickes edition of Kant's fragments on Anthropology. Because some of its most shocking statements appear to have no exact parallel elsewhere in the Kantian corpus, it has to be approached with caution. However, in this case there are supporting documents in the form of student notes for his lectures on Anthropology from 1781 to 1782, which correspond sufficiently closely to note 1,520 to suggest that the latter belonged to Kant's own notes for his lectures. Thus in his lectures Kant declared that Native Americans are lacking in culture (*Bildung*) and any driving force (*Triebfeder*) and that insofar as Negroes have a capacity for culture it is only for slave culture. By contrast, "the White race contains all impulses and talents in itself" (AA, XXV/2, p. 1,187). Furthermore, in a major essay, "On the Use of Teleological Principles in Philosophy," Kant acknowledged a hierarchy among the races. Commenting on Native Americans, he wrote:

> That their natural disposition has not yet reached a *complete* fitness for any climate provides a test that can hardly offer another explanation why this race, too weak for hard labor, too phlegmatic for diligence, and unfit for any culture, still stands – despite the proximity of example and ample encouragement – far below the Negro, who undoubtedly holds the lowest of all remaining levels by which we designate the different races. (AA, VIII, pp. 175–6; *R*, p. 48)[15]

Of course, Kant was not the first to maintain the existence of such a hierarchy. Rather it was for him a fact that needed explaining. But it is highly significant, given the impact he had on the science of his time, that these were the kinds of "facts" that he would address in his lectures and essays.

The sources from which Kant drew his portraits of Native Americans and Blacks need to be studied more rigorously. Erich Adickes did some initial work at the beginning of the twentieth century identifying those sources for his edition of *Physical Geography*, but Kant's use of those sources has not been subjected to critical review. My own research suggests that Kant deliberately chose his sources in order to develop a most unflattering picture of Blacks. For example, in "On the Use of Teleological Principles in Philosophy," Kant cited from Sprengel's *Beiträge zur Völker – und Länderkunde*, a German paraphrase of a pro-slavery tract, "Cursory Remarks upon the Reverend Mr Ramsay's Essay on the Treatment and Conversion of African Slaves in the Sugar Colonies," to make a point about how the races are no longer capable of adapting to new climates. This anonymous text, now known to be by James Tobin, set out to challenge James Ramsay's *An Essay on the Treatment and Conversion of African Slaves on the Sugar Islands* and from it Kant cited with approval the judgment that among the many thousands of freed Negroes that one meets in America and England, there is "no instance in which any one of them has ever pursued an occupation that one can really call *work*" (AA, VIII, p. 174n; *R*, p. 54, n. 4).[16] Kant extended this point on the basis of his own observation of gypsies in Germany: "Indians as well as Negroes bring with them and pass on to their offspring no more of this impulse [to work] when living in other climates than what they had needed in their old mother land, and that this inner predisposition might be extinguished, just so little as the outwardly perceivable predispositions" (AA, VIII, p. 174n; *R*, p. 55, n. 4). I shall show later that Kant's use of this evidence is governed by his desire to make a larger theoretical point about the permanence of racial characteristics once formed. But there is a question as to whether Kant should not have been more critical of pro-slavery literature as a source of objective information about Blacks.

What makes Kant's use of Tobin's essay particularly shocking is that in 1785, only three years before his essay on teleology, Kant wrote a review of the second volume of Herder's *Ideen* in which he showed himself to be well aware of the need to question the reliability of the descriptions provided by travelers. Indeed, the contradictory reports about the intellectual inferiority of Native Americans and Blacks is one of the examples he gave:

> One may prove that Americans and Negroes are races which have sunk below the level of other members of the species in terms of intellectual abilities – or alternatively, on the evidence of no less plausible accounts, that they should be regarded as equal in natural ability to all the other inhabitants of the world. Thus, the philosopher is at liberty to choose whether he wishes to assume natural differences or to judge everything by the principle *tout comme chez nous*, with the result that all the systems he constructs on such unstable foundation must take on the appearance of ramshackle hypotheses. (AA, VIII, p. 62)[17]

It was with just this kind of choice that Kant, who had, of course, little or no experience on which to base his judgment of Blacks or Native Americans, was faced when he read Sprengel's volume. He chose to take up Tobin's view of congenitally lazy Negroes rather than adopt Ramsay's presentation of African slaves as people, who worked harder the better they were treated, although both positions were available to him in the very same volume of Sprengel's *Beiträge*.[18]

Now that I have established a context for reading Kant's discussions bearing on racial issues, I want to focus on three of the specific areas in which Kant has been or can be associated with racism. I will first examine Kant's position or rather lack of a stated position on the trade in African slaves and their use in America. Although one would expect Kant to have recognized that the system of chattel slavery ran entirely counter to the principles of his moral philosophy, there is no record of his having expressly opposed it. This silence has to be assessed. I will then turn to the issue of colonialism. By contrast with his failure to speak out on the question of chattel slavery, Kant was vociferous in his condemnation of the colonial practices of the Northern European powers. Even so, it can be argued that certain aspects of Kant's philosophy may have lent themselves to a colonialist ideology. This allows one to speculate that Kant's role within the colonial project follows the model proposed by Berlin whereby Kant's philosophy may have been opposed to the more vicious forms of colonialism but perhaps contributed to them nevertheless. However, rather than exploring this historical thesis, I shall turn finally to the question of race mixing where Kant's main contribution to racism can be seen, even though his comments on this issue are not especially prominent. There was already a political opposition against race mixing, but Kant provided the epistemological framework that would subsequently help to sustain it. Kant's remarks on race mixing oblige us to revise the image of his philosophy as, in Berlin's phrase, "deeply rational and cosmopolitan."

2

Kant's anti-Black racism is more puzzling than that of many of his contemporaries because it was not directly put to the service of a defense of slavery, the issue of his day that can most readily be understood as necessitating the development of a racist ideology.[19] There were relatively few voices for or against chattel slavery in the late seventeenth century and early eighteenth century. Slavery presented certain practical problems – should slaves be baptized? Could they be freed by their masters? – which touched on issues central to the organization of a society built on slavery, but, as an institution, such justifications of slavery that existed were not subject to scrutiny, largely because it was not at that time subject to sustained attack. The early opponents of slavery, like Samuel Sewall of Boston in 1700, were isolated and largely ignored.[20] There were discussions of slavery in the standard works of seventeenth-century political philosophy, for example, in Pufendorf and Locke, based on the idea that captives from a just war can be legitimately enslaved. John Locke argued that, because one does not have power over one's own life, one cannot enslave oneself to anyone else, but one can forfeit one's life by committing an act that deserves death.[21] Locke's argument also clearly excludes chattel slavery, but there is a strong possibility that it simply did not occur to Locke, who was above all concerned with the rights of Englishmen, that the chattel slavery of Africans needed justification, even though he was well aware of how the system operated and indeed profited from it through his investments.[22] Although slave traders did on occasion appeal to the just war theory of enslavement, it is clearly an inadequate model to apply to the chattel slavery of Africans by Europeans, particularly the enslavement of women and their children in perpetuity. At what point it became widely known that application of this argument to enslave Africans was specious is not clear, but in 1735 John Atkins explicitly addressed the argument and exposed it as false.[23] Montesquieu was the first philosopher to challenge the use of African slaves by Europeans, but he did so in an ironic fashion so that even in our own century he was not always correctly understood.[24] The dispiriting fact is that philosophers as a group were slow to recognize the evils of the chattel slavery in Africans and that even Kant failed to speak out against it.[25] Kant's ethics would seem to be a perfect instrument with which to combat chattel slavery. His remarks against serfdom and other forms of slavery leave no doubt that his philosophy provided him with the resources for doing so. And yet he was virtually silent on this topic.

Kant's silence on the slave trade in Africans cannot be explained by the fact that German involvement in that trade was less than that of a number of other European countries. Even though Germany was not as intimately involved with the slave trade as some of the other European countries, especially England, Kant was well aware of the intense debate over slavery. Many of the more recent contributions to the travel literature with which he was familiar participated in the debate on one side or the other. Kant's use of Sprengel's paraphrase of Tobin's essay on Ramsay's discussion of the condition of slaves in the West Indies is a clear case in point. Kant was well aware of the debate on the African slave trade and the conditions under which the slaves were held in the Americas. In "Perpetual Peace" he complained about the treatment of the slaves on the Sugar Islands (AA, VIII, p. 359),[26] but this did not lead him to address the question of whether and how slavery might be abolished. Slavery was the institutional racism of that period, which helps to explain why many opponents of slavery nevertheless could not see their way to proposing its immediate abolition. But I am aware of no direct statement by Kant calling for the abolition of either African slavery or the slave trade, even if only in principle. Indeed, the fact that Kant, for example, in his lectures on *Physical Geography*, confined himself to statements about the best way to whip Moors, leaves one wondering if, like some of his contemporaries, he had apparently failed to see the application of the principle to this particular case (AA, IX, p. 313; *RE*, p. 61).

When in *The Metaphysics of Morals* Kant introduced the familiar principle that "every one is born free, since he has not yet committed a crime" (AA, VI, p. 283; *PP*, p. 432), he provided the basis for attacking chattel slavery. Kant wrote this as part of a brief discussion of the conditions under which it can be said that a man's wife, child or servant are among that man's possessions, which he has a right to retrieve if they run away (AA, VI, p. 284; *PP*, p. 432). Kant acknowledged in this context that slaves have fewer rights even than servants, but insisted that the children of someone who has become a slave as a result of committing a crime are nevertheless free. This, of course, does not describe the ownership of African slaves and their progeny in North America, as Kant was almost certainly well aware, but it suggests that Kant would have had no place for chattel slavery. Nevertheless, Kant did not explicitly make the connection to the debate already raging in Northern Europe.

Later in *The Metaphysics of Morals*, Kant returned to the topic of people who, as a result of a crime, had been judicially reduced to the status of a kind of slave, a bondsman (*Leibeigener*). A bondsman is the tool of his owner, who can "alienate him as a thing, use him as he pleases (only not for shameful purposes) and *dispose of his powers*, though not of his life and members" (AA, VI, p. 330; *PP*, p. 471). Kant contrasted such a bondsman with a person who has contracted himself out for work. In order to establish that there are some implicit but indeterminate limits in terms of the quantity of work the latter is obliged to perform, Kant wrote:

> For if the master is authorized to use the powers of his subject as he pleases, he can also exhaust them until his subject dies or is driven to despair (as with the Negroes on the Sugar Islands); his subject will in fact have given himself away, as property, to his master, which is impossible. (AA, VI, p. 330; *PP*, p. 472)

Although the passage seems to be straightforward at first sight, it turns out to present certain difficulties. Because a Black slave in the Sugar Islands is neither a bondsman as Kant defines the term, nor a contract laborer, it is hard to understand why Kant would introduce this case, unless he meant to imply that it is legitimate for a slave owner literally to work his slaves to death. Kant had already made the point that a bondsman can be used by his owner as he pleases, but not for shameful purposes and not at the risk of his life and members. Kant was, in the text just cited, arguing that the same must be true of someone who contracts to perform certain services. Because the reference to African slaves occurs in the context of a comparison between a contracted laborer and a bondsman and not specifically in the context of a discussion of slaves, it is perhaps possible to argue that Kant was not underwriting slavery but merely noting an empirical difference in the way different social arrangements are usually understood. It is even possible to argue that Kant was saying that to be a slave means that you can be worked to death whereas the same cannot be said of a bondsman or a contracted laborer. On such an interpretation the passage could still be reconciled with the hypothesis that Kant was against slavery: to explicate the concept of slavery is not to legitimate its existence.[27] Nevertheless, Kant's failure to condemn chattel slavery as equally "impossible" as a bondsman or a contractual servant giving up their personhood renders such a reconstruction implausible. Given that Kant elsewhere referred to Blacks as "born slaves" (AA, XV/2, p. 878), one is left wondering whether that phrase does not offer an easier way to interpret Kant's reference to the slaves on the Sugar Islands, albeit it means relying on a phrase drawn from Kant's manuscripts, the notorious note 1,520 of the *Reflexionen zur Anthropologie*. A few lines later in the same place, Kant wrote that "Americans and Blacks cannot govern themselves. They thus serve only for slaves" (AA, XV/2, p. 878). I have already shown that the basic idea that Blacks embrace the culture of the slave, but not free culture, like the idea that they are incapable of directing themselves, which is also in this same note (AA, XV/2, p. 877), was repeated in Kant's lectures (AA, XXV/2, p. 1,187). The idea of the born slave could also be introduced to clarify a difficult passage in the introductory section of the *Metaphysics of Morals*, where Kant wrote that the class of "beings that have only duties but no rights" is vacant for "these would be men without personality (serfs, slaves)" (AA, VI, p. 241; *PP*, p. 396). Although it is extremely speculative, it is perhaps possible that, rather than denying that there are slaves, Kant understood such slaves as there are to be slaves by nature and so not human in the full sense. Did Kant's failure to repudiate the chattel slavery of Africans, even though his ethical principles seem from our point of view clearly to exclude it, arise from a lack of specific concern for this issue or because he did not regard them as fully human in the sense that they did not possess all the talents and dispositions?[28] Kant was in full possession of the arguments to reject chattel slavery, but one is left with the impression that the enslavement of Africans had Kant's attention when he was writing on anthropology, but not when he was writing on ethics.

3

In contrast with his failure to condemn chattel slavery directly, Kant was outspoken in his attack on certain practices associated with colonialism. Kant respected the *possession* of the Hottentots and the Native Americans. In *Perpetual Peace* Kant complained at the injustices committed against the inhabitants of America, Central Africa, the Spice Islands, and the Cape by those he called civilized (AA, VIII, p. 358; *PP*, p. 329). Their lands were, he complained, improperly regarded as lands belonging to no one.

In two places in *The Metaphysics of Morals* Kant expressly rejected any attempt to justify colonialism in terms of its possible contribution to the spreading of civilization. Kant denied that civilizing a people, even a people one regards as "savages," could be used as an excuse to override their rights. This is especially important given how widespread such arguments would later become in other hands. In his discussion of property rights in the section on public right, he rejected the suggestion that it would be legitimate to found colonies in an effort to civilize such savages as the American Indians, the Hottentots, or the inhabitants of New Holland (AA, VI, p. 266; *PP*, p. 417). Kant also rejected the argument, somewhat Lockean in inspiration, that the populating of vast tracts of land that would otherwise have remained uninhabited by civilized people was sufficient justification. Recalling the fraudulent purchases of land as his example, he dismissed as "Jesuitism" any such appeal to a good end as a way of justifying any means whatsoever (AA, VI, p. 266; *PP*, p. 418).

Later in his discussion of Public Right, Kant acknowledged a right to settle. It is legitimate to take possession of newly discovered lands, even in the neighborhood of a people that has already settled in the region, so long as one remained distant from their settlements (AA, VI, p. 353; *PP*, pp. 489–90). However, he introduced an important caveat.

> But if these peoples are shepherds or hunters (like the Hottentots, the Tungusi, or most of the American Indian nations) who depend for their sustenance on great open regions, this settlement may not take place by force but only by a contract that does not take advantage of the ignorance of these inhabitants with respect to ceding their lands. (AA, VI, p. 353; *PP*, p. 490)

The fact that such arrangements might be to the world's eventual advantage was again judged to be no excuse (AA, VI, p. 353; *PP*, p. 490). Kant recognized in his "Idea for a Universal History with a Cosmopolitan Purpose" that it was through their "inevitable *antagonism*" that human beings abandon a "lawless state of savagery" and enter a federation of peoples (AA, VIII, p. 24; *PW*, p. 47). But this was no justification, even if it meant that the whole earth might still be in a lawless condition. This reminds us of his apparent acceptance of the dictum *Fiat justitia et pereat mundi*: "Let justice be done, though the world may perish" (AA, VIII, pp. 378–9; *PP*, p. 345).

Kant's attack on these specific justifications of colonialism did not mean that there were not other justifications of colonialism that he might have accepted. Kant conceded that one is not bound to refrain from encroaching on what someone else possesses if, as in the state of nature, the other person does not provide equal assurance that he or she will be similarly restrained (AA, VI, p. 307; *PP*, p. 452). And the rights of nations, which are what is at issue here, are only provisional because there is a state of nature among nations (AA, VI, p. 350; *PP*, p. 487).[29] Kant's cosmopolitanism is most evident in *The Metaphysics of Morals* in his introduction of the rational idea of a peaceful community of all nations (AA, VI, p. 352; *PP*, p. 489). He granted that perpetual peace is an unachievable idea (AA, VI, p. 350; *PP*, p. 487), but the fact that all nations stand in a community of possible interaction (*commercium*) led Kant to recognize a right of citizens of the world to try to establish community with all by visiting them (AA, VI, pp. 352–3; *PP*, pp. 489–90). Kant's cosmopolitanism was based not on the unity of the human race or on some idea of humanity, but on the fact that the earth is a sphere: "Since the earth's surface is not unlimited but closed, the concepts of the Right of a state and of a Right of nations lead inevitably to the idea of a *Right for all nations (ius gentium)* or *cosmopolitan Right (ius cosmopoliticum)*" (AA, VI, p. 311; *PP*, p. 455). Kant's cosmopolitanism broke thereby with the Lockean assumption that there will always be an excess of land.[30] It had another impetus. Kant's "Idea for a Universal History with a Cosmopolitan Purpose" arose from indignation at the childish malice and destructiveness that appears to govern human affairs (AA, VIII, p. 18; *PW*, p. 42). His solution was that Europeans would bring order to the chaos: "our continent . . . will probably legislate eventually for all other continents" (AA, VIII, pp. 29–30; *PW*, p. 52). This claim put Kant in direct confrontation with Herder who, at the same time, was working on his *Ideen zur Philosophie der Geschichte der Menschheit*. Herder not only denied the concept of race, but challenged the colonial mentality more strongly than Kant did.[31] Berlin's rehabilitation of Herder's position enables one to see that, however enlightened Kant's position on colonialism might seem in contrast to nineteenth-century conceptions, his approach lacked the sensitivity to the cultures of non-European peoples that Herder demonstrated.[32]

In a recent essay Tsenay Serequeberhan accuses Kant of a lack of candor in his critique of the imperialistic practices of European states on the grounds that Kant legitimated the European practice of colonial expansion through his low opinion of non-European peoples and his conviction that Europe would probably give law to the rest of the world.[33] Serequeberhan acknowledges Kant's criticism in "Perpetual Peace" of the way that "the civilized intruders . . . counted the inhabitants as nothing," but he complains that "Kant cannot be candid in his critique of the imperialistic practices of European states . . . since he himself thinks that the Tahitians in particular, are 'nothing,' i.e. mere sheep."[34] Because Serequeberhan's aim is the broad one of exposing the failure of contemporary philosophers to address the eurocentrism in philosophy, using Kant only as an example, he is concerned with the effects of Kant's thought. Serequeberhan does not develop the specific problem I am raising of how Kant's insistence on the permanence of race can be reconciled in practice with his cosmopolitanism, particularly given that he understood the diversity of races as the work of Providence. The practice of colonialism is only one context in which it emerges.[35] I shall now turn to the question of race mixing, as it offered a possible way in which Kant might have resolved the apparent tension through the disappearance of the races. But it was a resolution Kant refused.

4

There is no doubt that Kant was opposed to the mixing of races. A manuscript which, so far as I know, is not yet to be found in the Akademie Ausgabe, dismisses the possibility of progress through the development of new and better races. Kant wrote that nature has already long since stopped creating new forms appropriate to soil and climate. He also warned, with reference to Europeans breeding with either Native Americans or Blacks that race mixing degrades "the good race" without lifting up "the bad race" proportionately. Even if Alexis Philonenko, who cites this text, is right to understand Kant to mean races that are well or badly adapted to the environment, and not superior or inferior races, the manuscript still carries a strong condemnation of "cross-breeding" between the races. Kant was quite specific: "The Governor of Mexico has wisely rescinded the order of the Court of Spain favoring this mixing of race."[36] Over the preceding couple of centuries there had already been extended discussion of race mixing, particularly in the context of colonialism, which brought groups from different parts of the world in sustained contact with each other. In South America there had been widespread race mixing, and that between the Native Americans and the other races had sometimes received official endorsement. By contrast, in North America there had been legislation against race mixing in some states for a long time, although these laws were widely ignored. My claim is not that Kant contributed directly to debates about race mixing, but that through his concept of race he lent the taboo against race mixing a certain scientific legitimacy. There had already been extensive speculation about the biological effects of race mixing, as well as its social effects, but in the absence of any precise concept of race all such discussions lacked a clear frame of reference. Kant's definition of race, which proved influential for Blumenbach and others, strengthened the resistance against what later came to be called miscegenation by providing a scientific or pseudo-scientific justification for the already widespread view that race mixing was contrary to nature. However, this was an effect of Kant's definition of race, not its main purpose.

Kant advocated the value of the scientific concept of race for natural history primarily as a support for monogenesis against the assault of Voltaire, Henry Home, and others.[37] That also places a clear distance between Kant and some of the worst proponents of racial segregation in the United States in the second half of the nineteenth century, who drew on polygenesis to strengthen the argument against race mixing.[38] Kant accepted from Buffon the idea that two creatures belong to the same species if they "perpetuate and conserve the similarity of the species by means of copulation."[39] He also recognized that Buffon's rule for determining species provided the resources to maintain the biological unity of humanity (AA, II, p. 429; *IR*, p. 8). Kant overlooked the fact that Buffon was himself already recognizing exceptions to his rule,[40] just as Kant also ignored the fact that color would not serve as an adequate determinant of race. By positing the existence of seeds or germs (*Keime*) which the original human beings shared, but which developed to produce skin color under specific climatic conditions, and which once developed were not subject to further modification, Kant recognized he had at his disposal the resources to explain, as Buffon could not, why race characteristics were permanent (AA, II, pp. 435 and 442; *IR*, pp. 14 and 21). Observers had long noticed that Blacks did not become white, nor Whites black, in the way that a simple climatic explanation would suggest they should, but theorists had had difficulty explaining this phenomenon and had sometimes confused the lighter skin of mulattos as support for the environmental thesis.[41] Kant in his lectures on *Physical Geography* took part in the debate:

The Europeans who live in this hot belt of the world do not become Negroes after many generations but rather retain their European figure and color. The Portuguese on Cape Verde, who should become Negroes in 200 years, are Mulattos. (AA, IX, p. 313; *RE*, p. 60)

Kant's view was that, although Whites and Blacks have a common parentage in an original pair, which just happened on his account to be White (AA, II, p. 441; *IR*, p. 20), and although some of the descendants of their pair became black by settling in Africa, Whites will not now become Blacks, no matter how many generations they stay in Africa.

The issue of race mixing is at the heart of the concept of race as Kant first developed it in 1775 in "On the Different Human Races." First, because a pair drawn from different races can produce fertile offspring, it is established, by the application of Buffon's rule for determining species, that all human beings belong to the same species. Together with the application of a version of Ockham's razor which precludes the multiplication of the number of causes beyond necessity, this suggests to Kant that all human beings derive from a single pair, thereby saving monogenesis scientifically (AA, II, pp. 429–30; *IR*, p. 9). Secondly, racial mixing is introduced, along with an appeal to a people's incomplete adaptation to the climate in which they find themselves, to account for the variety of different types that far exceeds the number of races. Kant did not deny that history was full of racial intermixing. He acknowledged in his first essay on race that race mixing produced peoples of a certain ethnic character (AA, II, pp. 432–3; *IR*, p. 11). Thirdly, what defines racial characteristics for Kant is the fact that the offspring of two different races share those characteristics equally (AA, VIII, p. 165; *R*, p. 41). Hence skin color was Kant's privileged example of a racial characteristic. A child of mixed race would, according to Kant, have a skin color in between that of his parents. It was different for "varieties" and "variations." Kant used the term "variety" to cover those cases where characteristics, like hair color, remain part of the stock and may reappear in later generations (AA, II, p. 430; *IR*, p. 9). Kant reserved the name "variations" (*Spielarten*) for those cases where characteristics are preserved, but where mixing with groups that do not possess those characteristics does not produce hybrids. In other words, races are in large measure defined by the production of hybrids.

The question for Kant is whether race mixing is desirable or not. In his 1775 essay, Kant discussed an early form of eugenics. He introduced Maupertuis's proposal that it would eventually be possible, through careful selection of the deviant births from the conformant births within a stable family strain, to produce from nature a noble strain of human beings in which understanding, ability, and uprightness would be hereditary (AA, II, p. 431; *IR*, p. 10). But Kant rejected Maupertuis's suggestion that the virtuous and productive people of society should be discouraged from breeding with the less worthy. Two years later, in the second edition of his essay, Kant explained that, while it was possible to pursue such a course, nature proceeds differently. It is by the mixture of evil with good that humanity develops all its talents and approaches perfection (AA, II, p. 431; *IR*, p. 10).[42] Nature did not need the kind of assistance proposed by Maupertuis. Left undisturbed across many generations, nature produces stable strains that give rise to recognizable peoples that would be called races, if the characteristics did not seem so insignificant and were not so difficult to describe. Kant explained that by leaving nature undisturbed he meant "without the effects of migration or foreign interbreeding" (AA, II, p. 431; *IR*, p. 10). In other words, to avoid race mixing was merely to act in conformity with nature. For Kant, the present division of races was permanent and indissoluble, so long as all race mixing was prevented (AA, VIII, p. 105). It seems to have been Kant's view that if Providence introduced the division of races, that meant that they should be retained.

Kant returned to the discussion of race mixing in his *Anthropology from a Pragmatic Standpoint*. He closed the section on "The Character of Nations" with these remarks: "This much we can judge with probability: that a mixture of stocks (*Stamme*) (by extensive conquests), which gradually extinguishes their characteristics, is not beneficial to the human race – all so-called philanthropy notwithstanding" (AA, VII, p. 320).[43] In the following section, "On the Character of Races," Kant explained that it is in the mixing of races that there is an extinction of characteristics. Kant continued:

> In fusing different races, nature aims at assimilation [*Verähnlichung*]; but here [with varieties and variations] it has made the exact opposite its law: that is, nature's law regarding a people of the same race (for example, the white race) is not to let their characters constantly and progressively approach one another in likeness – in which case there would finally appear only one portrait, as in prints taken from the same engraving – but instead to diversify to infinity the members of the same stock and even of the same clan in both their bodily and spiritual tracts. (AA, VII, p. 320; *AP*, p. 182)

Races were defined in such a way that it is only in the case of race mixing that the diversity at which nature usually aims is frustrated. Kant took this as confirmation that nature opposed race mixing.

Kant had explored the difference between races and varieties more fully in 1788 in "On the Use of Teleological Principles in Philosophy":

> The variety among human beings even from the same race was in all probability inscribed just so purposively in the original line of descent in order to establish, and in successive generations to develop, the greatest diversity for the sake of infinitely diverse purposes, just as the differences among races establishes fewer but more essential purposes. (AA, VIII, p. 166; *R*, p. 42)

Kant speculated that nature permitted this fusing of characters with respect to races because the conformities that constitute a given race, corresponding to the purposiveness of nature, are to be understood primarily in terms of suitability to a climate. Kant could see that through hybridity a human being could be produced that would be well adapted to several climates. Nevertheless, he persisted in regarding race mixing as contrary to nature: "nature, at least permits, even if she does not encourage, the fusing together of characters with respect to racial differences, because through this the progeny will be suited for several climates, although none of those produced by such fusing are suited for several climates to the same degree as was the first variant form" (AA, VIII, pp. 166–7; *R*, p. 42). The problem arose only because racial characteristics, once formed, were not on Kant's view open to further modification except by race mixing. The impossibility of such changes looked like lack of foresight on the part of nature, particularly in a context where Whites were becoming involved in activities for which their color did not suit them, such as international commerce, which Kant favored, and colonialism, about which, as we have seen, he had more reservations. That is why Georg Forster had objected to Kant that by making each race suitable primarily only for one climate, nature had placed limits on human adaptability.[44] By arguing that the original human stem contained the seeds which would enable human beings to become a race adapted to the climate in which they initially found themselves without any possibilities for further change, Kant seemed to have identified a lacuna in nature's largesse. In other words, Kant showed why race mixing would serve a purpose but at the same time he rejected it as a course of action. Why?

To arrive at an answer that goes beyond the hypothesis that Kant could not apparently conceive why from a single pair nature provided four races, if they were eventually to be reduced to a mixture, so negating the very differences of race, it is necessary to recall the extent of what Kant understood by race. Race in Kant is not only about physical adaptation to a climate, but also, continuing the tendency of earlier researchers like Linnaeus, about natural dispositions (AA, II, p. 431; *IR*, p. 10).[45] If all racial characteristics, including natural dispositions, are as permanent as skin color, this would place severe limits on the civilizing process which some Europeans had adopted as their task or mission. Kant wrote: "The Negro can be disciplined and cultivated, but is never genuinely civilized. He falls of his own accord into savagery" (AA, XV/2, p. 878). This prejudice found its way into his essay "On the Use of the Teleological Principle in Philosophy," where, on the basis of Sprengel's essay, he claimed that with the formation of the races further capacity for adaptation was lost. Africans, having adapted to a climate where nature's bounty did not require them to work, were now no longer capable of working except when forced to do so by others. This means that whatever Kant said in his "Idea for a Universal History with a Cosmopolitan Purpose" about seeds that through unsociability develop to reveal human purposefulness (AA, VIII, pp. 21–5; *PW*, pp. 43–9), Africans, Native Americans, and Indians would at best remain imitators, dependent on European discipline. One might imagine that race mixing provided a way by which other races might come to share in White perfectibility, but there is no reason to suppose that Kant believed that history would bring the races together and break down the biological divisions nature had set up. Indeed, Kant insisted on the separation of races, not their fusion, just as Kant favored the separation of states over their fusion (cf. AA, VIII, p. 367; *PP*, p. 336).

Any gain that hybridity might bring to Whites with respect to possible physical adaptation to less temperate climates would be at the price of compromising the capacity of Whites to contain "all impulses and talents" (AA, XXV/2, p. 1,187). Kant was explicit that natural dispositions were also subject to hybridization through race mixing (AA, II, p. 431; *IR*, p. 10). That provides a possible explanation of why Kant was so opposed to race mixing:

> Should one propose that the races be fused or not? They do not fuse and it is also not desirable that they should. The Whites would be degraded. For not every race adopts the morals and customs of the Europeans.[46]

Kant had defined races as opposed to varieties by the fusion of those characteristics that defined a race. If he now said there was no fusion, it was because he recognized a hierarchy between the races in which Whites were the most favored race. What might look like fusion would, from the point of view of Whites, be a degradation.[47] This underlines Kant's decisive statement of his disdain for race mixing. Kant was saying more than that Providence established the permanence of race and that one should not try to undo it by what in the late nineteenth century came to be known as miscegenation. Kant saw race mixing as leading to a degradation or pollution of Whites, a loss of some of their talents and dispositions. That suggests an alternative interpretation to Philonenko's as to why Kant applauded the Governor of Mexico for rescinding the order of the Court of Spain favoring the mixing of race, when he declared that it degrades "the good race" without lifting up "the bad race" proportionately. It also suggests that Kant has an additional argument against colonialism that he did not articulate directly: it is possible that he was concerned not only that it would lead to people being in a climate for which they were not suited, but that it might lead to race mixing. Whether or not Kant's fear of race mixing impacted on his concerns about colonialism, his belief that race mixing would lead to a weakening of the White race is more than speculation. It is at the heart of his racial theory. However, by opposing race mixing on the grounds that it would diminish the White race, Kant seemed to have excluded the best means left open to him for explaining how non-Whites, especially Native Americans and Blacks, might come to play an equal part in the cosmopolitan ideal. Kant wrote enough about race and was sufficiently committed to a defense of the concept for one to have a reasonable expectation that he should have addressed these problems. Did Kant simply not think sufficiently hard about these issues? Or did he retreat in fright at a possible solution?

The question arises as to what kind of cosmopolitanism Kant envisaged that would leave the races intact, especially given that each of the races was to a greater or lesser extent assigned a climate or part of the world to which they were best suited.[48] In "Perpetual Peace" Kant had remarked that the desire of every state to dominate the whole world is frustrated by the fact that nature wills it otherwise. The intermixing (*Vermischung*) of peoples is prevented insofar as linguistic and religious differences remain intact (AA, VIII, p. 367; *PW*, pp. 113–14).[49] Kant said nothing in this place about the fact that on his view nature also does not will mixing the races. Nevertheless, he was aware that through conquest mixing had taken place. Kant's own model of cosmopolitanism seems to have been focused on trade rather than on conquest or colonialism, but a phrase from note 1,520 of the *Reflexionen zur Anthropologie* suggests another, more sinister, resolution. Kant wrote: "All races will be extinguished . . . only not that of the Whites" (AA, XV/2, p. 878). Kant, who had presented the races as products of the foresight of nature, and wanted them to retain their integrity, seems to have reversed himself by suggesting that only Whites would survive. It is a scenario opened up perhaps by the knowledge, already available to him, of how non-White civilizations collapsed, by conquest or disease, on contact with Whites. We should beware overdetermining the meaning of Kant's note, but it suggests that, faced with two ways in which the foresight of Providence that had produced the races might be frustrated, Kant was more ready to contemplate the extinction of all the races except that of the

Whites, rather than see the disappearance of all the races through race mixing. Kant himself did not explain how the races apart from the Whites would be extinguished, nor does he repeat this thought elsewhere to the best of my knowledge. Rather than finding an attempted resolution to the problems of reconciling cosmopolitanism with a philosophy of racial inequality, what one finds in Kant is a dead end that, contrary to the impulse governing his idea of a universal history, suggests the destructiveness of human affairs.

This idea of the extinction of whole races would be used a century later to uphold White purity and comfort those who could not imagine a world in which people of all races could live in close contact together in peace. Kant's note shows that as soon as the idea of race is juxtaposed with the new discipline of a philosophy of history, it invites "solutions" that involve wholesale extermination. The fact that Kant did not solve the problem of how, within the framework of a universal history, cosmopolitanism can be reconciled with a view of White superiority meant that he left to posterity a dangerous legacy. Kant's note had no historical impact, but he was at very least an articulate spokesman for a framework that had disastrous consequences. One would expect both philosophical and political problems to arise from a view in which all human beings are divided into discrete groups, but where the members of one of the groups alone is in possession of all the qualities and talents necessary to flourish, so that the members of the other groups have no genuine contribution to make.[50] If, as in this case, procreation between the allegedly superior group and any of the other groups leads to a loss of the qualities that distinguish the former group, then matters are much worse. But this was the view that Kant sought to legitimate from a scientific perspective.

There is a widespread tendency within contemporary studies in the history of philosophy to focus on reconstructing and reformulating the so-called central arguments employed by major philosophers to the exclusion of all else. If a position is no longer attractive to current sensibilities, whether it be Kant's opposition to race mixing or his rejection of lying, it is enough to show that the central arguments do not rely on them and they can in effect be written out of the work. "Kant" is no longer the name of a historical thinker, nor is it shorthand for his written works, even the main works. The proper name "Kant" becomes a choice of what each generation regards as essential. I am not denying that there are ways in which a Kantian might negotiate the questions I have raised, while leaving certain central tenets of Kant's philosophy intact. But I am arguing that by abridging the works of a philosopher to suit our own interests, we are in danger of excluding what is most challenging.

The temptation of continuing the practice of editing Kant's philosophy to make it appear more wholesome will remain for some people, but the dangers can readily be illustrated by considering the analogous case of Kant's discussion of women. Kant held that women exhibit inclination rather than understanding (AA, VII, p. 309; *AP*, p. 172). The question has been raised whether this simply calls for a correction to Kant's anthropology while leaving his moral theory intact.[51] In response, Pauline Kleingeld has addressed the clear tensions between Kant's gender-specific views and his use of a generic language that suggests that many of his theories apply to everyone, in spite of the fact that his account of women does not always allow this.[52] She persuasively argues that dismissing Kant's discussion of women as mistaken so as to concentrate on what are perceived to be the more important philosophical achievements can lead to certain genuine problems being overlooked such as the socio-economic inequalities of the sexes.[53] Kleingeld therefore proposes that rather than rewriting Kant's thought in a gender-neutral language, which would not be true to the tensions within his thought, one should strive to retain the tension, thereby marking the work of re-evaluation that is still to be done. Although the problems are not exactly the same, similar issues arise in reference to Kant's discussions of the different races. Kant characterizes Blacks, Native Americans, and to a certain extent other races as well, in ways that suggest that they lack the autonomy to count as full moral agents. In other words, there is not only a question of how Blacks and Native Americans are regarded within Kant's moral theory, but also a question of whether he thought about them in such a way that compromised the universality of his universal moral theory. Again this can be dismissed as the results of bad anthropology, but we should beware doctoring the Kantian corpus so that race disappears from it. Kant's privileging of the White race and his conviction that racial differences are permanent created unresolved tensions for his cosmopolitanism, particularly given his opposition to race mixing. We will learn more about the difficulties of sustaining a genuine cosmopolitanism by focusing on these tensions than by pretending, for example, that it is always obvious in specific cases what is cosmopolitanism and what is simply a front for a project in which the White race legislates for all other races.

In this paper I have focused on trying to establish that Kant's racism presents a philosophical issue that should not be dismissed or side-stepped. I do not claim to have resolved how his racism and his cosmopolitanism can be combined, but I have also not sought to make the problem disappear by ignoring those passages that do not fit with our image of him, as so many Kant scholars have chosen to do. There are tensions within Kant that need to be recognized. On the one hand, Kant was obsessed with racial diversity in general, as is reflected in his effort to collect and disseminate knowledge of the races in his lectures on *Physical Geography*, and with Blacks in particular, as is reflected in his attempts to explain their skin color. On the other hand, Kant seems to have been able to forget about the ethical issue raised by the existence of Black slaves, introducing them only in the passing in *The Metaphysics of Morals* as part of his discussion of the bondsmen, but not stopping to comment. Kant's opposition to polygenesis set him against some of the more extreme forms of racism, but as Georg Forster pointed out in an essay, addressed to Kant, advocating polygenesis, the belief in monogenesis did not stop Whites from enslaving and exploiting Blacks: "Let me ask whether the thought that Blacks are our brothers has ever anywhere even once meant that the raised whip of the slavedriver was put away. Does he not torment the poor long-suffering creatures with an executioner's rage and a devilish delight in the full conviction that they are of his blood?"[54] In his reply to Forster, Kant did not respond to this point directly. He was again silent about slavery and the role monogenesis might play against it. Instead, he chose to make the comments cited earlier about the laziness of Blacks and their unwillingness to work except when forced to do so. We may like to remember Kant for the great innovations in the study of ethics, but if we are going to acknowledge the role philosophers play in society, we should also reflect on another of his contributions: his role in the development of the scientific concept of race with its power to legitimate prejudices against race mixing and against non-Whites generally.

Notes

1. Isaiah Berlin, *The Sense of Reality*, ed. Henry Hardy (New York: Farrar, Straus and Giroux, 1997), pp. 232–48. Henceforth *SR*.
2. See Thomas Jefferson, *Notes on the State of Virginia*, in *Writings* (New York: Library of America, 1984), pp. 264–7.
3. This problem is, of course, not confined to the Enlightenment period, and I have attempted to address this issue as a phenomenological question in "The Invisibility of Racial Minorities in the Public Realm of Appearance," in *The Phenomenology of the Political*, ed. Kevin Thompson and Lester Embree (Dordrecht: Kluwer, 2000), pp. 169–87.
4. Compare M. Horkheimer and T. W. Adorno, *Dialektik der Aufklärung* (Darmstadt: Wissenschaftliche Buchgesellschaft, 1997), p. 210; tr. John Cumming, *The Dialectic of the Enlightenment* (New York: Seabury Press, 1972), p. 185.
5. References to the Akademie Ausgabe of Kant's works (Berlin: Walter de Gruyter, 1902–) will be given in the standard way by employing the abbreviation AA followed by the volume number and then the page number. I have cited the translation of Kant's "On the Different Human Races" by Jon Mark Mikkelsen in *The Idea of Race*, ed. Tommy L. Lott and R. Bernasconi (Indianapolis: Hackett, 2000), p. 9. Henceforth *IR*.
6. This seems to have been widely recognized in the nineteenth century and first half of the twentieth century and seems to have been forgotten only in the last fifty years and then primarily by philosophers. I argue that Kant, and neither Buffon, nor Blumenbach, invented the scientific concept of race in a paper "Who Invented the Concept of Race?," in *Race*, ed. R. Bernasconi (Oxford: Blackwell, 2001), pp. 11–36. Henceforth *R*. For a recent expression of Kant's importance for race thinking, see Emmanuel Chukwudi Eze, "The Color of Reason: The Idea of 'Race' in Kant's Anthropology," in *Postcolonial African Philosophy*, ed. E. C. Eze (Oxford: Blackwell, 1997), pp. 103–40.
7. AA, VIII, pp. 89–106 and 157–184. When in 1775 Kant accompanied the announcement of his lectures on Physical Geography with the publication of his first essay on race, he described them as more a useful diversion than a toilsome occupation (AA, II, p. 429). Kant's subsequent investment in the concept of race as evidenced by his 1785 and 1788 essays confirms that this description was not meant to be extended to the essay on race itself. Susan Shell argues that Kant abandoned his attempts at an archaeology of human races and that his theory of race loses its pivotal status, but there seems little or no basis for doing so and her claims that in "On the Use of Teleological Principles in Philosophy" Kant's treatment of the history of the species shifts from race to variety and that Kant makes no mention there of the physical superiority of Whites are simply false. *The Embodiment of Reason. Kant on Spirit, Generation, and Community* (Chicago: University of Chicago Press, 1996), pp. 203, 258, 387 n. 23, and 418 n. 53. I am especially puzzled by Shell's thesis that "What removes race from the forefront of Kant's anthropological interest may be, in part, a new understanding of human history emphasizing the cultural advances introduced by European peoples" (ibid., p. 387). It seems to me that it was precisely Kant's focus on those "advances" that led Kant and those who, either directly or indirectly, follow him on this topic, to the dangerous obsession with the central role of race in the philosophy of history.

8. George L. Mosse, *Toward the Final Solution* (Madison: University of Wisconsin Press, 1985), pp. 30–1 and 73.

9. There is a long history of readings of Kant's writings on race in which their connection with the Critique of Teleological Judgment has been clearly drawn. See, for example, Christoph Girtanner, *Über das Kantische Prinzip für die Naturgeschichte* (Göttingen: Vandenhoefund Ruprecht, 1796), esp. pp. 17–30, and Theodor Elsenhans, *Kants Rassentheorie und ihre bleibende Bedeutung* (Leipzig: Wilhelm Engelman, 1904), esp. pp. 40–52.

10. One finds frequent references to Kant, including some to his essays on race, in National Socialist literature, particularly during the early years before Nietzsche took his place. See, for example, Olga Nippert, "Einiges über Kants Ansichten von Naturgaben, Vererbung und dem Zusammenhang zwischen Körper und Seele," *Volk und Rasse*, 7, 2 (1932), pp. 80–6. However, the fact that National Socialists made use of Kant does not, of course, show that they did so legitimately.

11. This is a problem with the current debate on racism in philosophy. See, for example, Stephen T. Asma, "Metaphors of Race: Theoretical Presuppositions Behind Racism," *American Philosophical Quarterly*, vol. 32, no. 1 (January 1995), p. 21.

12. David Hume, "Of National Characters." See especially Richard Popkin, "Hume's Racism Reconsidered," *The Third Force in Seventeenth-Century Thought* (Leiden: E. J. Brill, 1992), pp. 64–75 and Robert Palter, "Hume and Prejudice," *Hume Studies*, vol. 21, 1 (April 1995), pp. 3–23. Hume was against slavery but not on the ground of equality; as is well known, he clearly believed Africans inferior. For his remarks against Blacks, Hume was attacked by Beattie, but Beattie did not call for the immediate abolition of slavery either. There has been a certain refusal on the part of some Kant scholars to acknowledge this issue, believing apparently that reference to Kant's cosmopolitanism is sufficient response. See the anecdote of Alex Sutter, "Kant und die 'Wilden.' Zum impliziten Rassismus in der Kantischen Geschichtsphilosophie," *Prima Philosophia* 2, 2 (1989), pp. 258–9.

13. The remark referred to is to be found at AA, II, p. 253; tr. John T. Goldthwait, *Observations on the Feeling of the Sublime and the Beautiful* (Berkeley: University of California Press, 1973), pp. 110–11.

14. I have cited the translation by K. M. Faull and E. C. Eze in *Race and the Enlightenment*, ed. E. C. Eze (Oxford: Blackwell, 1997), p. 63. Henceforth *RE*.

15. Translations from "On the Use of Teleological Principles in Philosophy" are by Jon Mark Mikkelsen. The translation appears in R. Bernasconi (ed.), *Race*. Note Kant's remarks on the great chain of being of Leibniz and Bonnet in the *Critique of Pure Reason*. Kant observed that "the steps of the ladder" are much too far apart to enable us to state the law of the continuous gradation of created beings in an objective assertion. Nevertheless, Kant granted it is as "a legitimate and excellent regulative principle of reason" (*Critique of Pure Reason*, tr. Werner S. Pluhar (Indianapolis: Hackett, 1996), pp. 637–8 (A 668; B 696).

16. [James Tobin], *Cursory Remarks upon the Reverend Mr Ramsay's Essay on the Treatment and Conversion of African Slaves in the Sugar Colonies* (London: G. and T. Wilkie, 1785), p. 117: "In the year 1773, . . . it was pretty accurately determined, that there were at that time in England at least fifteen thousand negroes; and that they have greatly increased since then is beyond a doubt. A very small proportion of this number are females; it may, therefore, be fairly presumed, that there are ten or twelve thousand able negro men in England. Out of all this number, I will ask Mr Ramsay whether he ever saw a single one employed in any laborious task?" Cf. "Anmerkungen über Ramsays Schrift von der Behandlung der Negersklaven in den Westindischen Zuckerinseln," *Beiträge zur Völker- und Länderkunde*, vol. 5 (Leipzig: 1786), p. 287. For a survey of the various stages of Tobin's debate with Ramsay, see Falarin Shyllon, *James Ramsay. The Unknown Abolitionist* (Edinburgh: Canongate, 1977), pp. 59–70.

17. Translation by H. B. Nisbet in *Political Writings*, ed. Hans Reiss (Cambridge: Cambridge University Press, 1991), p. 217. Henceforth *PW*.

18. James Ramsay, *An Essay on the Treatment and Conversion of African Slaves in the British Sugar Colonies* (London: James Phillips, 1784), pp. 52–125; tr. "Behandlung der Negersklaven in den Westindischen vorzüglich der englischen insel St Kitts," *Beiträge zur Völker- und Länderkunde* (1786), 5, pp. 1–74. Sprengel published a translation of only parts of the first two chapters of Ramsay's *Essay*. Even though he omitted, for example, the chapter which argued for "the natural capacity of African slaves," there was still enough material included to enable Kant to argue again Tobin's view of Africans and African slavery generally, had he been of a mind to do so. Indeed, it is noteworthy that, in pages passed over by Sprengel, Tobin did not maintain the inferiority of Africans, nor did he think that their slavery depended upon it. *Cursory Remarks*, pp. 140–1.

19. Henri Grégoire acknowledged that much of the discussion of Blacks was no more than a pretext to justify slavery. See *De la littérature des Nègres* (Paris: Maradan, 1808; Kraus-Thompson reprint, 1977), p. 40; tr. Graham Russell Hodges, *An Enquiry Concerning the Intellectual and Moral Faculties, and Literature, of Negroes* (Armonk, NY: M. E. Sharpe, 1997), p. 16.

20. Samuel Sewall, *The Selling of Joseph. A Memorial*, ed. Sidney Kaplan (Amherst, MA: University of Massachusetts Press, 1969).

21. John Locke, *Two Treatises of Government*, ed. Peter Laslett (Cambridge: Cambridge University Press, 1988), p. 284.

22. Locke, of course, was not only familiar with the use of African slaves in North America, but helped to formulate the severe code whereby the freemen of Carolina had absolute power and authority over such slaves. See R. Bernasconi, "Locke's Almost Random Talk of Man: The Double Use of Words in the Natural Law Justification of Slavery," *Perspektiven der Philosophie*, vol. 18 (1992), pp. 293–318.

23. John Atkins, *A Voyage to Guinea, Brazil, and the West-Indies* (London: Caesar Ward and Richard Chandler, 1735), pp. 176–80.

24. Montesquieu, *De l'esprit des loix* (Paris: Société Les Belles Lettres, 1950), pp. 220–1; tr. Ann M. Cohler, B. C. Miller and H. S. Stone, *The Spirit of the Laws* (Cambridge: Cambridge University Press, 1989), p. 250.

25. Among Kant's contemporaries Granville Sharp was perhaps the foremost philosophical opponent of African slavery, but his argument was sustained by an appeal to the law of nature buttressed by appeal to Scripture. See *Tracts on Slavery and Liberty* (Westport, CT: Negro Universities Press, 1969), and *A Tract on the Law of Nature, and Principles of Action in Man*, (London: B. White and E. and C. Dilhey, 1777).

26. For a translation see I. Kant, *Practical Philosophy*, tr. Mary J. Gregor (Cambridge: Cambridge University Press, 1996), p. 330. Henceforth *PP*.

27. This possible interpretation has been suggested to me by Joshua Glasgow.

28. There are, of course, other possible explanations. One lies in what Husserl called "normalcy." When, for example, humanity at large is that horizon of one's reflections, a specific idea of a mature normal humanity is privileged. On Husserl's view, one's idea of humanity tends to focus on adults rather than children, the sane rather than the mad, Europeans rather than Chinese. In this way a certain empirical determination or modification of the idea infects the essence to establish a norm of humanity. See, for example, Edmund Husserl, *Die Krisis der europäischen Wissenschaften und die transcendentale Phänomenologie*, Husserliana VI (The Hague: Martinus Nijhoff, 1962), pp. 369–70; tr. David Carr, *The Crisis of European Sciences and Transcendental Phenomenology* (Evanston: Northwestern University Press, 1970), pp. 358–9.

29. Kant seems to have recognized a flaw or incoherence in the standard contractarian account insofar as the agreement that secures acquisition is only among a specific people (*Stamm-volk*): "such acquisition will always remain only provisional unless the contract extends to the entire human race" (AA, VI, p. 266; *PP*, p. 418).

30. Locke's phrase was "enough and as good." Laslett (ed.), *Two Treatises*, p. 288.

31. Both issues emerge clearly in Kant's review of the first two volumes of Herder's *Ideen* (AA, VIII, pp. 45–66; *PW*, pp. 201–20).

32. Isaiah Berlin, "Herder and the Enlightenment," *Vico and Herder* (London: Hogarth, 1976), pp. 145–216. See also R. Bernasconi, " 'Ich mag in keinen Himmel, wo Weisse sind.' Herder's Critique of Eurocentrism," *Acta Institutionis Philosophiae et Aestheticae*, vol. 13 (1995), pp. 69–81.

33. Tsenay Serequeberhan, "Eurocentrism in Philosophy: The Case of Immanuel Kant," *The Philosophical Forum*, vol. 27, no. 4 (Summer 1996), pp. 333–56. See also a revised version of the essay under the title, "The Critique of Eurocentrism and the Practice of African Philosophy," in *Postcolonial African Philosophy*, pp. 141–61.

34. Serequeberhan, "Eurocentrism in Philosophy," p. 343.

35. The extent to which Kant fails to clarify the relation between the biological and moral senses of the concept of mankind's basic unity or how his views on the diversity of human beings relate to his conception of a universal civil society, thereby leading to an uncertainty about how Kant's writings on race connect with his writings on history, has been brought out by Nathan Rotenstreich. See his *Practice and Realization* (The Hague: Martinus Nijhoff, 1979), pp. 100–110.

36. Alexis Philonenko, *La théorie Kantienne de l'histoire* (Paris: Vrin, 1986), p. 178. The same passage is cited by Léon Poliakov, who records that the title of the text is "Worin besteckt das Fortschreiten zum besseren Menschengeschlecht." See *The Aryan Myth*, tr. Edmund Howard (New York: Barnes and Noble, 1996), p. 353 n. 59. A similar thought is found in note 1,520 where Kant wrote: "It is not good that they intermix. Spanish in Mexico" (AA, XV/2, p. 878).

37. Voltaire, *Essai sur les moeurs et l'esprit des nations, Oeuvres complètes*, vol. 11, ed. Louis Moland (Paris: Garnier Frères, 1878), p. 12. Henry Home, Lord Kames, *Sketches of the History of Man* (Edinburgh: W. Creech, 1774), vol. 1, pp. 38–9.

38. I have examined this prejudice in "The Logic of Whiteness," in a special issue, "Outing Whiteness," ed. Phyllis Jackson and Darrell Moore, of *The Annals of Scholarship*, vol. 14, no.1, pp. 75–91.

39. Georges-Louis Leclerc, Comte de Buffon, "Histoire des animaux," *Histoire Naturelle, Générale et Particulière*, vol. 2 (Paris: De l'imprimerie royale, 1771), p. 18.

40. Georges-Louis Leclerc, Comte de Buffon, "De la dégénération des animaux," *Histoire Naturelle, Générale et Particulière*, vol. 14 (Paris: De l'imprimerie royale, 1766), pp. 337–8.

41. For a survey of the debate see Winthrop Jordan, *White over Black. American Attitudes Toward the Negro 1550–1812* (Baltimore: Penguin, 1969), pp. 11–20, 239–52, and 513–17.

42. See also John H. Zammito, *The Genesis of Kant's Critique of Judgment* (Chicago: University of Chicago Press, 1992), pp. 394–5.

43. I have modified the translation by Mary J. Gregor found at I. Kant, *Anthropology from a Pragmatic Point of View* (The Hague: Martinus Nijhoff, 1974), p. 182. Henceforth *AP*.

44. Georg Forster, "Noch etwas über die Menschenrassen," *Werke*, vol. 8, ed. Siegfried Scheibe (Berlin: Akademie, 1991), pp. 150–3.

45. For a speculative reconstruction of Kant's position see Mark Larrimore, "Sublime Waste: Kant on the Destiny of the Races," *Canadian Journal of Philosophy. Supplementary Volume*, 1999, pp. 99–125.

46. Arnold Kowalewski (ed.), *Die philosophischen Hauptvorlesungen Immanuel Kants nach den neu aufgefundenen Kollegheften des Grafen Heinrich zu Dohna-Wundlacken* (Munich: Rösl, 1924), p. 364.

47. Gobineau would call this a "degeneration," but in Kant's time this term was still used neutrally. *Oeuvres*, vol. 1, ed. Jean Gaulmier and Jean Boissel (Paris: Gallimard, 1983), pp. 161–2.

48. Pauline Kleingeld has shown that it is important to distinguish between different senses of cosmopolitanism, not just within the period under discussion, but also within Kant himself. Here the "moral" cosmopolitanism of citizens of a supersensible world is most important (AA, VIII, p. 350n; *PW*, p. 99n), but "international federative," legal, cultural, market, and romantic cosmopolitanism are also relevant. See "Six Varieties of Cosmopolitanism in Late Eighteenth Century Germany," *Journal of the History of Ideas*, vol. 60, 1999, pp. 505–24.

49. However, in a footnote Kant remarks on the peculiarity of the phrase "religious differences" likening it to the peculiarity of the notion of "different moralities" (AA, VIII, pp. 367n; *PW*, p. 114n). Kant's insistence that "there can only be *one* religion which is valid for all" represents a limit to the extent that he was willing to see the idea of different races translated into what we today could recognize as a philosophy of human differences.

50. Kant on more than one occasion raises the question of why certain peoples – the people of Tahiti or the New Hollanders – exist. See AA, VIII, p. 65; *PW*, pp. 219–20 and AA, V, p. 378. It is a genuine question from his perspective.

51. See, for example, Sally Sedgwick, "Can Kant's Ethics Survive Feminist Critique?" *Feminist Interpretations of Kant*, ed. Robin May Schott, (University Park, PA: Pennsylvania State University Press, 1997), pp. 89–90.

52. Pauline Kleingeld, "The Problematic Status of Gender-Neutral Language in the History of Philosophy: The Case of Kant," *The Philosophical Forum*, vol. 25, no. 2 (1993), pp. 134–50.

53. Ibid., pp. 144–5.

54. Georg Forster, "Noch etwas über die Menschenrassen," p. 154.

CHAPTER 9

"The Great Play and Fight of Forces": Nietzsche on Race

DANIEL W. CONWAY

As a people of the most monstrous mixture and medley of races, perhaps even with a preponderance of the pre-Aryan element, as "people of the middle" in every sense, the Germans are more incomprehensible, comprehensive, contradictory, unknown, incalculable, surprising, even frightening than other people are to themselves: they elude definition *and would be on that account alone the despair of the French.*

Friedrich Nietzsche, *Beyond Good and Evil*, Section 244

These high-falutin and haughty hucksters of ideas, who imagine themselves infinitely exalted above all national prejudices, are thus in practice far more national than the beer-quaffing philistines who dream of a united Germany. They do not recognize the deeds of other nations as historical: they live in Germany, to Germany, and for Germany; they turn the Rhine-song into a religious hymn and conquer Alsace and Lorraine by robbing French philosophy instead of the French State, by Germanizing French ideas instead of French provinces.

Karl Marx, *The German Ideology*

Scholars are now generally agreed that the Nazi appropriation of Nietzsche's writings is largely a misappropriation. Virtually no one honors the proprietary claims made on Nietzsche by his sister, Elisabeth, who willfully misrepresented his philosophy in order to curry the favor of the nascent Nazi regime.[1] Her strategy was both simple and effective: she brazenly offered her brother's philosophy as the theoretical foundation for the rabid nationalism and anti-Semitism espoused by her late husband, Bernhard Förster, with whom she founded the Aryan colony of Nueva Germania in South America.[2] Here it must be said that Frau Förster-Nietzsche was devoted even more fervently to the logic of political opportunism than to the principles of Aryan eugenics.[3] She and her cronies knew so little of her brother's work that charges of "distortion" and "misinterpretation" miss their mark. As early as 1941, in fact, Crane Brinton wondered what might become of Germany if young Nazis actually happened to read the books composed by *Der Führer*'s favorite philosopher.[4]

It must also be said, however, that the fraud perpetrated by Elisabeth was possible only because Nietzsche himself regularly uttered careless remarks about race, eugenics, and politics. He naïvely adopted the standard pseudo-scientific beliefs of his day about racial characteristics and types, and he issued baseless pronouncements on the heredity, descent, origins, character, and destiny of various peoples and races. For example, he often described cultural advancement in terms of the "breeding" of superlative races and castes. More famously, he traced the advance of "noble" peoples to the residence within them of what he calls "the splendid *blond beast*" (*GM*, I:11),[5] a designation that pro-Aryan agitators were happy to adopt. Finally, both he and Zarathustra exhorted thriving cultures to accelerate the demise of those misbegotten creatures who are unlikely to contribute to the extant complement of human perfections. In the hands of anti-Semites and Nazi propagandists, this careless rhetoric proved to be both inflammatory and explosive.[6]

Nietzsche's complicity in his sister's fraud thus illuminates an expansive middle ground that has not yet been adequately explored. Indeed, if the Nazi appropriation of his writings is neither entirely faithful nor completely outlandish, then a fuller accounting of his views on race is warranted. My primary concern in this essay is to investigate the ease with which he grafts popular prejudices about race on to his evolving philosophical system of thought. This ease is attributable, or so I contend, to his supposedly scientific treatment of races as reservoirs of disposable vitality, from which lawgivers under his tutelage might productively draw in their efforts to rejuvenate the decadent peoples and nations of nineteenth-century European culture.

In particular, his mechanistic model of racial cultivation readily lends itself to distortion and prejudice. This model reduces all races to the status of contingent, transient assemblages within "the great play and fight of forces" that characterizes the Nietzschean cosmos. His plan to preside over a reintegration of European culture requires him (or his disciples) to enter this *agon* and arrange these contesting "forces" into more desirable configurations. As it turns out, the projected victors in this "great play and fight of forces" are none other than the Germans, whom Nietzsche hopes to rescue from their besetting decay. His treatment of race thus enables him to present his Germanocentric prejudices as if they were substantiated by reliable scientific evidence, which in turn emboldens him to sketch his blueprint for European reintegration.

I

Nietzsche's concept of race is unusually broad and ill-defined. He sometimes means to refer to what we might call a "tribe," "people," "nation," or "culture," while at other times he apparently means to refer to a social class or caste. On still other occasions, he adverts to the cultivation of a distinctly *European* race, which presumably will comprise (some of) the more familiar peoples and nations of Europe (*D*, 272; *BGE*, 62). His explicit use of the term "race" (*die Rasse*) is predictably slippery. At times he uses the term descriptively, to refer indiscriminately to any number of identifiable peoples or nations, such as the Germans, Poles, Jews, Russians, Celts, French, and British. At other times he uses the term prescriptively, to refer with approval to those select peoples and nations that have earned the lofty status of racehood. I will be concerned in this essay primarily with an exploration of this prescriptive use of the term "race." In the course of this exploration we will not only examine his account of how races are made and unmade, but also discover the pre-philosophical prejudices that inform this account.

Nietzsche's prescriptive use of the term "race" boldly reverses the popular wisdom of his day. Most deserving of the designation of "race" are the Jews, while most egregious in their misplaced claims to this distinction are the Germans, the self-appointed guardians of Aryan purity. He thus asserts that

> The Jews . . . are beyond any doubt the strongest, toughest, and purest race now living in Europe; they know how to prevail even under the worst conditions (even better than under favorable conditions), by means of virtues that today one would like to mark as vices – thanks above all to a resolute faith that they need not be ashamed before "modern ideas"; they change, *when* they change, always only as the Roman Empire makes its conquests – being an empire that has time and is not of yesterday – namely, according to the principle, "as slowly as possible." (*BGE*, 251)

Nietzsche's juxtaposition of Germans and Jews is both unconventional and disarming. It is also largely responsible for the ambivalence recorded by scholars with respect to his complex relationships to racism and anti-Semitism. Never before has a philosopher spoken so highly of the Jews and so disparagingly of his own people. Never before has a philosopher praised the Jews for their spirit, strength, and culture, while ridiculing his own people's pretensions to the same. And although his praise for the Jews and criticism of the Germans should not be underestimated, we should also be careful not to overestimate the moral content of these sentiments. As we shall see, he praises Jews and chastises Germans only against the background of his larger plan to orchestrate the unification of Europe and the development of a new ruling caste.

Nietzsche's startling juxtaposition of Jews and Germans is in large part the consequence of his understanding of the dynamics of racial cultivation. In the passage that follows, he observes that some European "nations" do not yet (and may never) deserve the honorific designation of racehood:

> What is called a "nation" ["*Nation*"] in Europe today, and is really rather a *res facta* [something made] than a *res nata* [something born] (and occasionally can hardly be told from a *res ficta et res picta* [something contrived and depicted]) is in any case something evolving, young, and easily changed, not yet a race [*noch keine Rasse*], let alone such an *aere perennius* [more enduring than bronze] as the Jewish type . . . (*BGE*, 251)

This dense passage reveals two important components of Nietzsche's understanding of the dynamics of racial cultivation: 1) he observes a hierarchical gradation of the stages of racial development; and 2) he believes that genuine races are made, not born. Let us consider each component in order.

Nietzsche's comparisons in this passage imply his reliance on an ascending scale comprising four distinct gradations of racial designation. There are the so-called "nations" of contemporary Europe, which are callow, variable, and not yet sufficiently developed to warrant the designation they claim for themselves; then there are the true (*res facta*) nations of contemporary Europe (of which this passage provides no examples), which might someday become genuine races; then there are those unnamed peoples and nations that constitute genuine races, each possessing a unique racial identity and heritage; and finally there are the Jews, whom he considers the race *par excellence*.

Nietzsche's reliance on this ascending scale of racial designations indicates that he is relatively unimpressed with the more familiar, quantifiable indices of the modern nation-state, e.g., its military capacities, economic advantages, natural resources, geographical boundaries, and population distributions. He is far more impressed with the native endowments of a people or nation in cultural and spiritual resources, such as history, tradition, acculturation, education, religion, history, cuisine, art, music, and letters. Holdings in *these* resources, he believes, indirectly attest to the native strength, perseverance, and adaptability of the people or nation in question. As a result of his appreciation for these undervalued cultural and spiritual resources, he is able to distinguish between those nations that are likely to warrant the future of humankind and those "nations" that will spend themselves in pursuit of transient victories in military, political, and economic skirmishes. His ascending scale of racial designations is therefore positively related to the contributions made (or likely to be made) by representatives of each grade to the advancement of human civilization. Races contribute more than nations (and, *a fortiori*, more than "nations") to this worthiest of causes, and no race presently contributes more to the advancement of civilization than the Jews.[7]

Nietzsche's title for Part 8 of *Beyond Good and Evil*, "Peoples and Fatherlands," conveys in a somewhat different parlance his reliance on this hierarchy of racial gradations. Contesting the popular claim that Germany constitutes both a people *and* a fatherland, he proposes that "people" [*Volk*] and "fatherland" [*Vaterland*] designate two contrasting outcomes of racial development. By means of protracted cultivation, a tribe or community can become a *people*, a designation he treats as honorific. Bereft of the spiritual advancement wrought by cultivation, a tribe or community instead becomes a *fatherland*, a designation he treats as pejorative. A "people" is a positive result of racial cultivation, denoting the self-transformation of a nation or tribe by means of self-imposed disciplines of spiritual elevation. Nietzsche thus identifies a "people" as a proto-race, whose success thus far at consolidating its own racial identity promises further consolidation in the future. A fatherland is a negative result, whereby a "nation" remains unbred and uncultivated by dint of its stubborn attachments to nationalistic hatreds and hostilities.[8] He thus describes nationalism as the *"névrose nationale* with which Europe is sick, this perpetuation of European particularism" (*EH*, cw, 2).

Nietzsche's distinction between *Volk* and *Vaterland* recalls his more famous distinction between "master" and "slave" moralities (*BGE*, 260).[9] Just as "the noble human being honors himself as one who is powerful, also as one who has power over himself" (*BGE*, 260), so a genuine *Volk* derives its sense of identity from a sober accounting of its own accomplishments, values, traditions, and history. Conversely, just as the slavish human being defines himself in opposition to others, especially those "powerful" and "dangerous" others who "inspire fear" (*BGE*, 260), so a *Vaterland* derives its sense of identity from its defining campaign to protect itself from imaginary enemies, both internal and external. The toll exacted by this constant vigilance is so great as to ensure that a *Vaterland* will not, and cannot, devote its resources to the cultural development that is emblematic of a *Volk*. Indeed, whereas a *Volk* can be viewed from the perspective of cultural advancement as a race-in-progress, a *Vaterland* appears from the same perspective to be a dead end. Remarking on the much celebrated concentration of military power in the new *Reich*, Nietzsche warns,

> One pays heavily for coming to power: power *makes stupid*. The Germans – once they were called the people of thinkers: do they think at all today? The Germans are now bored with the spirit, the Germans now mistrust the spirit; politics swallows up all serious concern for really spiritual matters. *Deutschland, Deutschland, über alles* – I fear that was the end of German philosophy. (*TI*, 8:2)

Let us turn now to consider the second component of Nietzsche's understanding of the dynamics of racial cultivation. As his distinction between *res facta* and *res nata* indicates, he believes that races are fashioned over time.[10] Nature itself usually provides only a chaotic array of diverse racial types and characteristics. If something is to be made of this diversity, if its latent power and energy are to be harnessed, then a race must be fashioned. This means that form must be applied to matter, a single system of acculturation imposed upon an amorphous aggregation of diverse peoples and tribes. Nietzsche's hierarchy of racial gradations is thus predicated on his heterodox belief that races are made, not born. This belief is also the source of his prescriptive use of the term "race," e.g., as an honorific designation, for not every people or nation becomes a race. According to Nietzsche, a race always emerges from something that is not yet a race (e.g., a loose collection of tribes, nations, and/or peoples) and eventually disintegrates into its constituent elements. Racial purity, he believes, is always achieved only as the result (and on the condition) of an antecedent racial impurity. He consequently displays no patience for specious appeals to aboriginal progenitors, uninterrupted descent from whom supposedly ensures racial purity. Indeed, before racial purity can be meaningfully established and preserved, a race must first be summoned into existence, fashioned from a diverse collection of tribes, communities, and peoples.

Nietzsche's understanding of race as a *res facta* marks the distance that separates him from the anti-Semites of his day. If race is a *res facta*, something which the German "nation" only crudely resembles, then the concern of the anti-Semites to preserve the blood purity of the Aryan race is misplaced.[11] In the following passage, in fact, he not only alludes ominously to the Aryan race as a *res facta* (as evidenced by its probable degeneration), but also denounces the primitive tribalism that would soon take the form of National Socialism in Germany:

who can say whether modern democracy, even more modern anarchism and especially that inclination for *"commune,"* for the most primitive form of society, which is now shared by all the socialists of Europe, does not signify in the main a tremendous *counterattack* – and that the conqueror and *master race*, the Aryan, is not succumbing physiologically, too? (*GM*, I:5)

In Nietzsche's eyes, the likely decline of the Aryan race confirms his theory that races are continually made and unmade over time. If he is correct, then the anti-Semites' campaign to protect the blood purity of the Aryan race is strategically flawed. As he insists elsewhere, the only hope for those who stake their claim to the Aryan legacy lies in interbreeding with stronger, purer races. The prohibition of interbreeding with other races (which, for the Aryans, means *lesser* races) is not so much a defense against racial degeneration as an unmistakable symptom of it.

As Nietzsche's praise for the Jews demonstrates, a genuine race is characterized by its possession of a cluster of virtues – including constancy, perseverance, endurance, self-determination, adaptability, and maturity – that are acquired only over a very long term of concerted effort and incremental development. A people or tribe or nation becomes a race only over centuries – perhaps millennia – of self-imposed discipline and sacrifice, and only under the aegis of a self-perpetuating system of acculturation. He thus explains that "The beauty of a race or family, their grace and graciousness in all gestures, is won by work: like genius, it is the end result of the accumulated work of generations" (*TI*, 9:47). As he indicates by means of his metallurgical metaphor for the Jews, moreover, a nation or people becomes a race only when tempered in the forge of hardship by the flames of opposition and animosity. He thus explains that

> The people who had some value, *attained* some value, never attained it under liberal insti-
> tutions: it was great danger that made something of them that merits respect. Danger
> alone acquaints us with our own resources, our virtues, our armor and weapons, our *spirit*,
> and *forces* us to be strong. *First* principle: one must need to be strong – otherwise one will
> never become strong. (*TI*, 9:38)

Nietzsche provides a fanciful example of this thesis in his considerations of the future of Europe. In order that Europe might acquire a single will and purpose, he speculates, the threat of external pressure may be necessary:

> I do not say this because I want it to happen: the opposite would be rather more after
> my heart – I mean such an increase in the menace of Russia that Europe would have to
> resolve to become menacing, too, namely, *to acquire one will* by means of a new caste that
> would rule Europe, a long, terrible will of its own that would be able to cast its goals
> millennia hence – so the long-drawn-out comedy of its many splinter states as well as its
> dynastic and democratic splinter wills would come to an end. The time for petty politics
> is over: the very next century will bring the fight for the domination of the earth – the
> *compulsion* to large-scale politics. (*BGE*, 208)

Nietzsche thus cleaves to a strongly (though not strictly) formal account of race and racehood. A race becomes and remains what it is by virtue of the successful imposition of form upon matter. The consolidation of a single, overarching form of acculturation allows for the making of a race; the dissolution or disintegration of this form spells the unmaking of a race. The material composition of a race (as determined, for example, through descent or blood purity) is far less important to him than the formative processes responsible for creating it. Genuine races, in fact, are fashioned from a welter of disparate customs, traditions, histories, characteristics, and mores. Nietzsche's beloved Greeks, for example, originally belonged to any number of tribes, peoples, and nations scattered throughout the greater Mediterranean-Adriatic-Ionian region. They became "the Greeks" only as a result of their common formation under a unique, galvanizing array of cultural practices and disciplines.[12] They ultimately became what they were, moreover, only upon importing an extra-pantheonic deity from Asia Minor: Dionysus. Every race originates amongst the "rabble" (*BGE*, 61), only to return there when its organizing principle of acculturation finally disintegrates. The formerly noble Germans are now "a people of the most monstrous mixture and medley of races," and this general fate is now shared by most European peoples (*BGE*, 244).

We may safely conclude, then, that Nietzsche is far more interested in "spirit" than in "blood" as a determinant of racial purity and cultural advancement.[13] Racehood and racial identity secured not (simply) through birth, but through cultural practices conducive to the production of "spirit." This means not merely that Nietzsche attaches little importance to the so-called "purity" of blood, but also that he openly applauds the cultural advancements achieved by Jews, Poles, and other allegedly "inferior" races. Indeed, immediately after praising the "splendid *blond beast*" that resides in all "noble races," he explicitly mentions the Roman, Arabian, and Japanese cultures as (non-Aryan) examples of racial nobility (*GM*, I:11).[14] So whatever it is that makes this noble beast "splendid" and "blond," it cannot be blood alone – Aryan or otherwise.

At the same time, however, Nietzsche's treatment of race is neither as "spiritual" nor as benign as his contemporary champions occasionally suggest. He may not be interested in linking cultural advancement to the preservation of blood purity, but he *does* acknowledge blood as a significant determinant of cultural advancement. His account of race, therefore, is not quite strictly formal; the material composition of a race is not entirely unimportant. Even the most sublime apparatus of culture cannot ensure the emergence of a genuine people or race. As he explains in his notebooks, for example, "[S]pirit alone does not make noble; rather there must be something to ennoble the spirit. – What then is required? Blood" (*WP*, 942). His continued interest in blood as a determinant of cultural advancement is also evidenced in his selective adoption of the biological jargon and theories that dominated the study of race in his day. In response to the ethnographical findings of Rudolf Virchow, for example, he cautions that

> [I]t is wrong to associate traces of an essentially dark-haired people which appear on the more careful ethnographical maps of Germany with any sort of Celtic origin or blood-mixture, as Virchow still does: it is rather the *pre-Aryan* people of Germany who emerge in these places. (*GM*, I:5)

Although he ridicules the anti-Semites' appeal to blood as a foolproof guarantor of racial purity, he does not abjure outright the biologistic assumptions that shape their thoughts on race. For Nietzsche, that is, racial identity is neither reducible to blood nor independent from it.

Compounding this concern are his occasional references to determinants of cultural advancement other than "blood" and "spirit." In a passage in which he explicitly addresses "the problem of race" [*das Problem der Rasse*], he explains that

> It is simply not possible that a human being should not have in his body the qualities and preferences of his parents and ancestors, whatever appearances may suggest to the contrary. If one knows something about the parents, an inference about the child is permissible: any disgusting incontinence, any nook envy, a clumsy insistence that one is always right . . . that sort of thing must as surely be transferred to the child as corrupted blood; and with the aid of the best education one will at best deceive with regard to such a heredity. (*BGE*, 264)

In what is widely interpreted as a Lamarckian gesture,[15] Nietzsche distinguishes these unnamed acquired traits from "corrupted blood," but he insists that they "must as surely be transferred" to the next generation. They are not to be dismissed or taken lightly, moreover, for their heredity defies even "the best education."

"That sort of thing" is therefore inherited, but it is not necessarily transmitted via blood descent. Here Nietzsche would appear to have in mind a set of defining traits and tendencies that reside in the body of a human being but not (simply) in his blood. These acquired traits and tendencies are thus associated with a constellation of habits, customs, and instincts that no longer serve the best interests of the bodies in question. This is an oblique reference, that is, to the problem of decadence, which dooms generations to come with a degenerate set of bodily habits – or "instincts" – that even the best education can at best disguise. Hence the importance of form in the cultivation of a race: the wrong kind of acculturation – including degenerate versions of the right kind of acculturation – can poison a family or tribe or people for years, even centuries, to come. Nietzsche thus fears the debilitating effects of decadence far more than the relatively harmless problem of miscegenation. No system of education can counter or reverse the descensional spiral of decadence, whereas interbreeding often contributes to the consolidation of a race by introducing novel and diverse racial characteristics. "The problem of race," one might be tempted to conclude from this passage, is the problem of *decadence*, i.e., the problem of identifying those acquired habits and customs that are neither reducible to blood nor amenable to spiritual elevation – for such traits could frustrate even the best-framed plans for racial cultivation.

Regardless of its scientific merit and plausibility, Nietzsche's emphasis on the inheritance of acquired traits remains problematic. As long as he acknowledges the possibility that some acquired traits are simply inimical to cultural advancement, his treatment of race bears a strong family resemblance to that of his avowed enemies. The failure of a promising system of acculturation could be conveniently traced to these acquired traits, and the decadent race in question could be reasonably excluded from future efforts to restore the circle of culture. In such an event, Nietzsche's "Lamarckian" sympathies could conceivably support race policies that resemble those endorsed by his supposed enemies. Under the quasi-scientific aegis of his theory of decadence, in fact, he endorses political views that are more commonly associated with anti-Semites, Aryan supremacists, and Nazi sympathizers. Having diagnosed most of contemporary Europe as decadent, for example, he may then with good conscience ignore most European peoples and nations in his discussions of the future of Europe. As we shall see, in fact, he treats these decadent peoples and nations as the raw materials to be fashioned into a new, improved European union.

II

Let us grant that Nietzsche plausibly identifies race as a *res facta*. How, then, is a race fashioned from a collection of disparate tribes, nations, and/or peoples? For the most part, he observes, races are produced by accident, as "lucky strikes" on the part of an indifferent nature (*AC*, 4). What nature more typically provides is a chaotic welter of racial types, traits, and characteristics, which occasionally and accidentally cluster themselves as distinct tribes or peoples. Nietzsche thus assigns no metaphysical index – divine, teleological, or otherwise – to those races that have in fact successfully emerged over time. But he unabashedly admires and celebrates them for having done so.

An overarching theme of Nietzsche's philosophy is that human beings can/should assume greater control over some processes that have heretofore been left to accident and chance, e.g., the process of producing exemplary human types. This overarching theme also governs his specific treatment of race. He believes that humankind has reached a point in its development such that it need (and should) no longer consign the cultivation of races to accident and chance. Because "nature is a bad economist" (*SE*, 7), indifferent to the judgments and evaluations that determine the proper course of human affairs, a people or nation bent on racehood must eventually assume some control over its own development and destiny. The superlative races, in fact, are those that have responded to the accident of their emergence by designing laws, traditions, mores, and institutions that will both commemorate their racehood and ensure the continuation of their ongoing process of cultivation. Nietzsche endorses this response in general, and he advocates (for himself and others) a more involved role in the cultivation and preservation of races.

His metallurgical metaphor for the Jews – *aere perennius* – not only conveys the strength and constancy of a well-formed race, but also alludes to the role of the unnamed smith who forges and tempers the metal in question. The role reserved for the smith thus represents the opportunity for human design to continue (and improve upon) the racial cultivation accidentally initiated by nature. By merit of the smith's founding labors, a race might consolidate its diverse resources and thereby provide for its continued development and growth. Whereas all tribes, peoples, and nations display some measure of internal order, the superlative races are those whose forms of internal order have become *self*-regulated. Applying *nomos* to the task of perfecting *physis*, a race can partially and temporarily defy the rule of accident and chance. Such races thereby achieve the fullest measure available to them of autonomy or self-determination. Explicitly addressing the dynamics of racial cultivation, Nietzsche submits that

"Asceticism and puritanism are almost indispensable means for educating and ennobling a race that wishes to become master over its origins among the rabble and that works its way up towards future rule" (*BGE*, 61).

Nietzsche's respect for the Jews confirms that the most enduring races are those that refuse the blind impresses of historical contingency and seize control of their own ongoing cultivation. As we have seen, he honors the Jews by comparing them, in terms of strength, constancy, and self-determination, to the Roman Empire (*BGE*, 251). In fact, his avowed shift in allegiance from Greek to Roman antiquity (*TI*, 10:2) can be traced in part to his belief that the Romans better exemplify this general principle of subjecting to human design what formerly was left to chance and accident. Although he never ceases to appreciate the Greeks for their unrivaled vitality and originality, he comes to admire the Romans for their imperial vision and perseverance.[16] On his reading, the Romans diligently improved upon their relatively modest natural endowments to rival the cultural extravagance bestowed upon the Greeks. Whereas the Greeks *became* a race of world-historical import, the Romans *made themselves into* a race of equal or greater significance. On several occasions, he conveys his admiration for the grandiose design and relentless efficiency of the Roman Empire, and he expressly models his own plan for pan-European integration on its founding principles. Indeed, he believes that he inherits from the Romans their unwavering commitment to the capacity of human design to attend to the task of perfecting nature.[17] As madness descended, he even posted a letter to Strindberg under the imperial signature "Nietzsche Caesar."[18]

As we have seen, Nietzsche does not link cultural advancement to the preservation of blood purity (Aryan or otherwise). Even a perfunctory genealogical investigation will reveal the checkered history of any race whose blood purity is claimed to be worthy of preservation.[19] Yet the goal of racial purity is nevertheless central to his larger political project. In a passage entitled "The Purification of the Race," he observes that

> There are probably no pure races but only races that have become pure, even these being extremely rare . . . The Greeks offer us the model of a race and culture that has become pure: and hopefully we shall one day also achieve a pure European race and culture. (*D*, 272)

As this passage suggests, Nietzsche understands racial purity, like race itself, as a *res facta*. The racial purity that he values is not guaranteed as a chaste bequest from a primal horde of aboriginal progenitors, as the anti-Semites wishfully maintain, and it is therefore not vulnerable to subsequent pollution through miscegenation. In fact, a prime index for Nietzsche of racial purity is the sheer wealth of diverse peoples, nations, and tribes that a single race can collect under a single, unifying system of acculturation. No race is born pure, but some races are able to become pure, by dint of an apparatus of acculturation that expresses *one* will, *one* direction, *one* goal. The "purity" of a particular race thus refers to the identity and integrity that accrue to it by virtue of its regnant system of acculturation. The "purest" race in nineteenth-century Europe, Nietzsche boldly asserts, is none other than the Jews (*BGE*, 251).

Races are thus made through the imposition and consolidation of a single apparatus of acculturation. We should be careful, however, not to confuse Nietzsche's idea of *Bildung* with more familiar models of education. Critical throughout his career of the deteriorating state of education in Europe (and especially in Germany), he recommends a system of acculturation that is both thorough and pervasive. The goal of *Bildung* is nothing short of a training of the whole human being, a goal that involves the installation of a coherent, unified set of "instincts." Education on the model of Nietzschean *Bildung* thus begins with the body, in which the proper habits, customs, mores, and other pre-reflective dispositions of corporeality must be carefully inculcated. Nietzsche thus explains that

> It is decisive for the lot of a people and of humanity that culture should begin in the right place – not in the "soul" (as was the fateful superstition of the priests and half-priests): the right place is the body, gesture, diet, physiology; the rest follows from that. (*TI*, 9:47)

As we shall see, beginning the acculturation of a people in "the right place" also involves forcibly divesting this people of the complex apparatus of embodiment under which it has heretofore operated. The violence transacted in the institution of any such educational program should not be underestimated.

If races are not born, but made, then they are also unmade – witness (Nietzsche's account of) the degeneration of formerly noble races. The cultural task of achieving racial purity thus begets the political task of protecting the integrity of a proven system of acculturation. As we have seen, a people becomes strong, becomes a race, only if it *needs* to become strong (*TI*, 9:38). The development of a people into a race thus presupposes historical and material conditions conducive to this development; the arrangement of these conditions is (almost) exclusively a matter of accident and chance. Having become strong, however, a race must continue to cultivate its holdings in strength and spirit, and it cannot rely solely on historical contingency to deliver the requisite impetus toward further development and growth. Having become a race, that is, a people must now assume direct control of its continued growth and development. Even if human design has played no role in the (accidental) formation of a race, its exertions are absolutely essential to the preservation of the purity of a race.

Once a genuine race has been bred from a motley collection of peoples and tribes, the purity of this race must be preserved through the founding of appropriate political institutions. To Nietzsche's mind, no political regime is better suited to this task than the pyramidal aristocracy, or "caste" system, that he regularly praises.[20] As he succinctly (if melodramatically) opines,

> Every enhancement of the type "man" has so far been the work of an aristocratic society – and it will be so again and again – a society that believes in the long ladder of an order of rank and differences in value between man and man, and needs slavery in some sense or other. (*BGE*, 257; cf. *AC*, 57)

A pyramidal hierarchy fosters the continued growth of a people or race by creating the internal conditions of productive contest and conflict. As he explains, a pyramidal hierarchy stimulates the *"pathos* of distance" that is indispensable to cultural advancement:

> Without the *pathos of distance* which grows out of the ingrained difference between strata
> . . . that other, more mysterious *pathos* could not have grown up either – the craving for
> an ever new widening of distances within the soul itself, the development of ever higher,
> rarer, more remote, further-stretching, more comprehensive states – in brief, simply the
> enhancement of the type "man," the continual "self-overcoming of man," to use a moral
> formula in a supra-moral sense. (*BGE*, 257)

Indeed, one way to appreciate Nietzsche's unusual emphasis on the hygienic stratification of aristocratic political structures is to link this emphasis to his interest in preserving the purity of race.

Nietzsche's commitment to "great politics" thus reflects (and complements) his understanding of the dynamics of racial cultivation. Just as an individual race takes shape through its coalescence around a single, unifying will, so, Nietzsche hopes, Europe itself can *"acquire one will* by means of a new caste that would rule Europe" (*BGE*, 208). As he explains, the acquisition of a single will is necessary if Europe is to throw off the debilitating influence of Christianity. His contribution to "great politics" is thus meant to fight fire with fire, with the future of Europe hanging in the balance:

> And yet when they gave comfort to sufferers . . . how much more did they have to do
> besides, in order to work with a good conscience and on principle, to preserve all that
> was sick and that suffered – which means, in fact and in truth, to worsen the European
> race? . . . Doesn't it seem that a single will dominated Europe for eighteen centuries –
> to turn man into a sublime miscarriage? . . . [S]uch men have so far held sway over the
> fate of Europe, with their "equal before God," until finally a smaller, almost ridiculous
> type, a herd animal, something eager to please, sickly, and mediocre has been bred
> [*herangezüchtet*], the European of today – (*BGE*, 62)

III

Nietzsche's general explanation of racial development centers around the imposition of order onto chaos. A race is formed through the imposition of cultural order onto a diverse collection of peoples, tribes, and nations that cohabitate a particular (if imperfectly defined) geographical region. As we shall see, however, the motif of "imposing order onto chaos" shelters the prejudices – many of them pernicious – that inform his thoughts on race.

The imposition of order onto chaos is a familiar motif of Nietzsche's philosophy.[21] It ranks among his favorite descriptions of the activity of the will to power, which, according to one note, finds its "supreme" expression in its capacity "to impose upon becoming the character of being" (*WP*, 617). This motif also serves as a model for his twin projects of soulcraft and statecraft. Commentators often cite with approval his formula for "giving style to one's character," whereby the imposition of order ("the constraint of a single style") onto chaos (*"free* nature: wild, arbitrary, fantastic, disorderly, and surprising") yields a soul that is "tolerable to behold" (*GS*, 290).[22] Commentators are far less sanguine about the political articulation of this motif, however, for it would seem to countenance violence, injury, exploitation, and usurpation. Witness, for example, his account of the origins of the "state":

> [S]ome pack of blond beasts of prey, a conqueror and master race [*eine Eroberer- und Herren-Rasse*] which, organized for war and with the ability to organize, unhesitatingly lays its terrible claws upon a populace perhaps tremendously superior in numbers but still formless and nomadic. (*GM*, II:17)

This account, which apparently glorifies the violence perpetrated by a "conqueror and master race," becomes even more disturbing against the background of Nietzsche's attempt to identify this violence as the "essence" of life itself. In an oft-cited and oft-reviled passage, he avers that

> [L]ife itself is *essentially* appropriation [*Aneignung*], injury, overpowering of what is alien and weaker; suppression, hardness, imposition of one's own forms, incorporation [*Einverleibung*] and at least, at its mildest, exploitation [*Ausbeutung*] . . . "Exploitation" does not belong to a corrupt or imperfect and primitive society: it belongs to the *essence* of what lives, as a basic organic function; it is a consequence of the will to power, which is after all the will of life. (*BGE*, 259)

Advancing this motif of the (political) imposition of order onto chaos, he identifies the "modern soul" as "a kind of chaos," which reflects "that enchanting and mad semi-barbarism into which Europe had been plunged by the democratic mingling of classes and races" (*BGE*, 224). Europe now stands in desperate need of order, and Nietzsche's political musings are typically concerned to satisfy this need. It is his belief that "an age of disintegration that mixes races indiscriminately . . . owes [its] origins to the same causes" that produce "those magical, incomprehensible, unfathomable ones" who, like Caesar, are "predestined" to impose order onto chaos (*BGE*, 200).

Nietzsche's distinction between order and chaos reproduces the more basic distinction between form and matter. As we have seen, he treats racial cultivation as a predominantly formal process, and he is surprisingly (although not altogether) indifferent to the material components of this process. He thus views the dynamic cultivation of a race on the model of an imposition of general, universal form onto a specific, local mass of matter or stuff. In the following passage, for example, he characterizes decadence in terms of the scarcity of "materials" for building a genuine society:

> To say it briefly (for a long time people will still keep silent about it): What will not be built any more henceforth, and cannot be built any more, is – a society [*Gesellschaft*] in the old sense of that word; to build that structure [*um diesen Bau zu bauen*], everything is lacking, above all the material [*Material*]. All of us are no longer material for a society. (*GS*, 356)

He also cleaves, moreover, to the familiar value judgment that traditionally attends the philosophical distinction between form and matter: he treats the formal process of acculturation as more essential to the development of race than the material to which it is applied. This value judgment in turn reinforces the troubling conviction that the human recipients of acculturation are uncultured, uncivilized, anonymous, disposable, and not quite fully deserving of human sympathy and respect. Although it may be helpful (or at any rate not inaccurate) to treat a system of culture as a "form," "order," or "mold," it can be misleading and morally corrupt to treat a collection of people simply as the "matter" or "stuff" onto which a system of acculturation is forcibly imposed. Indeed, this motif tends to mask and diminish – and so to justify – the violence involved in statecraft.

The violence implicit in this motif is perhaps most visible in Nietzsche's habit of referring to the process of cultural advancement as a series of exercises in *breeding*. He often draws his references to racial cultivation from the practices and vocabulary of animal husbandry, and the verb he customarily employs in these references, *züchten*, is more commonly found in accounts of the cultivation of plants and animals. As these references suggest, the project of acculturation requires for its success an abundant breeding stock of uncultivated human beings, who stand to the political lawgiver as animals stand to their trainer. (This "trainer" thus plays a structurally similar role in the development of race to that of the "smith," as discussed above.)

Although it may be tempting to treat "breeding" as merely a careless synonym for "cultivation" or "acculturation," there are larger problems with this terminology. If races are fashioned through the implementation of techniques borrowed from the practice of animal husbandry, then it becomes all-too-easy to view (and to treat) the recipients of cultivation as mere animals. Prior to their cultivation at the hands of their appointed breeders, animals are often described as "wild," "savage," and "uncultivated." Many of the techniques that breeders employ in the cultivation of these "wild" animals are painful, uncompromising, and, presumably, indispensable to the process of domestication. In the case of "breeding" superlative peoples and races, this distinction between "wild" and "cultivated" is even less plausible than in the case of animal husbandry, and the violence it shelters is even more insidious. The recipients of human cultivation may be animals of some kind, as Nietzsche allows, but they are neither "wild," nor "savage," nor "uncultivated." The breeding they involuntarily receive always replaces an already functioning system of acculturation, which the breeders in question have deemed inadequate or inefficient. As we have seen, moreover, Nietzsche's particular account of acculturation is hardly unobtrusive. Culture begins "in the body," and its aim is to equip the body with a new, improved complement of instincts. His notion of "breeding" thus serves to render invisible the pre-existing cultures of the individuals slated for domestication, and it thereby countenances the violence involved in furnishing these individuals with a new system of acculturation.

Even if it were plausible to posit a mythical Alpha node in the historical evolution of the human animal, at which point wild hominids (Nietzsche calls them *Halbthieren*) received an originary dose of culture (*GM*, II:16), it is certainly not plausible to suggest that the human recipients of "breeding" are wild, uncultivated animals. Rather than tame wild hominids, techniques of human "breeding" in fact replace one regnant system of acculturation with another, and at enormous cost to the recipients of the imposed "breeding." Their lives are turned upside down and inside out, as they are forcibly wrenched from their familiar context of traditions, practices, beliefs, mores, and habits. And even if it was necessary at one time in the dim pre-history of the species for this "breeding" to comprise torture, vivisection, and other disciplines of enforced cruelty, as Nietzsche's philosophical anthropology fancifully suggests (*GM*, II:13), it does not follow that similar disciplines are now either necessary or desirable. As Nietzsche himself well knows, the origin of these techniques and their current utility are two separate matters (*GM*, II:12). Hence the greatest danger involved in pursuing the imagery of "breeding": it becomes much easier to mistreat human beings if they appear under the aspect of the animal, and Nietzsche's recourse to the jargon and imagery of animal husbandry places *all* human beings under this aspect. The imagery of "breeding" is therefore potentially dangerous, for it suggests that the human recipients of "breeding" are antecedently lacking in culture and cultivation. Even if Nietzsche himself does not misunderstand the precise sense in which human beings are also animals, his readers have not always been so discerning.

In keeping with his aspirations to political realism, Nietzsche does not pretend that these various peoples are either innocent of culture or devoid of identities – though some such pretense might very well serve as the basis for the sort of "noble lie" that he claims to admire. He is well aware that any "morality of breeding," the "most magnificent example" of which he finds in the "law of Manu," must proceed by virtue of strictures and practices that he deems *"terrible"* (*TI*, 7:3). Although these peoples are to be treated like raw materials in the creation of a race, there is nothing raw about them. They are not noble savages who will be humanized by the institution of a social contract. Nor does Nietzsche claim for himself a moral obligation to "enlighten" races stalled in their protracted nonage or to envelope their primitive breeding grounds within the civilizing environs of European culture. Yet he nonetheless arrogates to himself the prerogative to determine their identities and destinies. This means that the imposition of a new cultural order will require them to relinquish many of the customs, traditions, and characteristics from which they have heretofore derived their sense of identity. Nietzsche is not so naïve as to imagine that these peoples should welcome the imposition of a new cultural order, but he also does not pretend that we (*his* "we") should care if they do not.

Nietzsche's reliance on the imagery of breeding thus illuminates his commitment to the active, participatory role that (some) human beings might now play in determining the future of particular races, and even of humankind as a whole – a role that modern writers on politics generally tend not to address. As Nietzsche sees it, the unique historical conditions of late modernity have created both the possibility and the desirability of the intervention of a lawgiver, who might oversee the future development of humankind. If his diagnosis of late modernity is even vaguely accurate, that is, then *someone* must play the role of the "animal trainer" who oversees the breeding of the new human type, lest the development of humankind continue to languish under the rule of accident.

Even if we set aside the familiar moral objections to his "realism," however, Nietzsche's reliance on the imagery of "breeding" remains problematic. He may wish to elide the traditional distinction between humans and animals (*GM*, II:16), but his analogy between animal husbandry and human acculturation is faulted by the importance he attaches to the activity of the "breeder." Although his express intention in returning humankind to the animal kingdom is to exorcise the metaphysical specter of humanism (*BGE*, 230), he continues to attribute to (some) human beings a legislative capacity that separates them from all other animals. The metaphor of "breeding" thus implies the activity of a breeder who stands apart from his livestock, who enforces disciplines to which he does not subject himself, and who knows better than his subjects what is best for them. He is, by virtue of his intellect, insight, *phronesis*, or evolved state of consciousness, different from and other than those whom he breeds. The metaphor of "breeding" thus suggests an unbalanced, non-reciprocal relationship between "breeder" and "animal," which in turn recalls some of the pernicious binarisms that have traditionally nourished the development of Western philosophy. For example, the unbalanced relationship between "breeder" and "animal" reproduces the familiar ontological divide that has traditionally separated humanity from animality, higher humanity from lower humanity, superior races from inferior races, freemen from slaves, men from women, and adults from children. In Nietzsche's own writings we witness similarly unbalanced relationships between Nietzsche and his readers and between Zarathustra and his auditors. That this metaphor affords Nietzsche the opportunity to rehearse his own credentials as "breeder" should only pique our suspicions of its applicability to the politics of racial cultivation.

IV

As we have seen, Nietzsche's reliance on the motif of an imposition of order onto chaos yields some troubling political views. In order to see why this is so, let us turn now to consider in greater detail his understanding of the dynamics of racial cultivation.

Nietzsche's attention to the dynamics of racial cultivation does not generally yield acute, nuanced interpretations of particular peoples and races. In fact, he regularly relies on racial typologies that appear to be as brute and simplistic as those employed by the anti-Semites and nationalists whom he means to oppose. Although he claims to treat race as a product of development and acculturation, as a *res facta*, he is generally able to document only two basic types of race: the "strong" type and the "weak" type. "Strong" races, like the Jews, are characterized by their demonstrated capacities for growth, constancy, and adaptation, whereas "weak" races, like the Germans, are marked by their stagnation, inconstancy, and inertia.

Regardless of its intuitive appeal, this binaristic presumption cannot help but exert a leveling influence on Nietzsche's analyses of various races. If he is predisposed to discuss instances of only two types of race, then he is unlikely to discover any races that would trouble the Procrustean categories of his typology. If all instances of either type are relatively indistinguishable, moreover, then they may easily be treated as roughly interchangeable; instances of the "weak" type of race may even be ignored altogether. To complicate matters further, his analysis of race is dominated by his conviction that the pandemic of European decadence has reduced most races to an insignificant status – hence his utter silence about most European races and peoples.

He consequently claims to find very few instances of the "strong" type of race. The following passage is representative of the way in which he maps Europe in the late nineteenth century:

> Russia [is] the *only* power today which has endurance, which can wait, which can still promise something – Russia, the concept that suggests the opposite of the wretched European nervousness and system of small states, which has entered a critical phase with the founding of the German *Reich*. (*TI*, 9:39)

As this passage suggests, his reliance on the binaristic typology of "strong" and "weak" races both enables and limits his attempts at racial analysis. He may gain thereby the simplicity of vision that galvanizes political activity, but he forfeits the complexity of analysis that might grant him access to the uniqueness of all races and peoples. How can he help but elide important differences between races, thereby trivializing the cultural achievements he supposedly wishes to document?[23]

As we might expect, in fact, Nietzsche's reliance on this typology regularly obliges him to traffic in racial stereotypes. His favorite stereotypes are neither novel nor benign. Throughout his writings we find multiple references to a familiar cast of stock characters: the constipated German, the priggish Englishman, the licentious Frenchman, the lusty Italian, the brooding Russian, the spiritually evolved Hindu, the wandering Jew, the frigid northerner, and the sensuous southerner.[24] Even his silences are typical of the leveling influence exerted by his binaristic typology. For the most part, in fact, he lumps together and then ignores the various "splinter" nations of Europe. We read little or nothing about the Dutch, Danes, Swedes, Norwegians, Finns, Portuguese, Spanish, Irish, Welsh, Belgians, Czechs, Slovaks, Slavs, and Turks, not to mention the diverse peoples and nations of North America, South America, Africa, and Asia.[25] When he does comment on the customs and traditions of exotic peoples, he typically relies more readily on popular legend than on current ethnographical research.[26]

The problem here is not simply that Nietzsche employs brute dichotomies, which are far too blunt to serve as instruments of careful racial analysis. These dichotomies in turn issue forth from a dynamic model of racial cultivation that he neither fully articulates nor adequately defends. As we have seen, he treats race as a *res facta*, as something fashioned over time under auspicious conditions of acculturation. As we have also seen, he understands acculturation as a project of bodily cultivation, whereby the individuals in question are (forcibly) equipped with a new set of instincts, habits, customs, and other patterns of pre-reflective corporeality. In fact, when he describes the actual micro-processes responsible for the acculturation of a race, he generally prefers the mechanistic language of *growth, assimilation, digestion, adaptation, selection, absorption, expenditure,* and *elimination*. As we have already seen, he identifies the mechanical process of "exploitation" [*Ausbeutung*] (which is itself the "mildest" form taken by such processes as "appropriation," "injury," "overpowering of what is alien and weaker," "suppression," "hardness," "imposition of one's own forms," and "incorporation") as "the *essence* of what lives, as a basic organic function . . . [as] a consequence of the will to power, which is after all the will of life" (*BGE*, 259). Availing himself liberally of this terminology of mechanical processes, he explains that

Purity is the final result of countless adaptations, absorptions, and secretions, and progress toward purity is evidenced in the fact that the energy available to a race is increasingly *restricted* to individual selected functions, while previously it was applied to too many and often contradictory things: such a restriction will always seem to be an *impoverishment* and should be assessed with consideration and caution. In the end, however, if the process of purification is successful, all that energy formerly expended in the struggle of the dissonant qualities with one another will stand at the command of the total organism: which is why races that have become pure have always also become *stronger* and *more beautiful*. – (*D*, 272)

As this passage indicates, Nietzsche views the achievement of racehood as enabling a productive concentration of the latent energies possessed by the peoples and tribes who compose the race in question. The achievement of race thus allows the constituent peoples and tribes (or their regents) to harness the untapped power resident within their collective diversity of racial types and characteristics. He thus treats the achievement of race as the fashioning of disparate peoples into an efficient (and potentially self-regulating) mechanism or system. He apparently believes that the mechanical processes responsible for the formation of a race also galvanize its native resources, thereby transforming a mature race into a supercharged receptacle of disposable energy. As he remarks in a section entitled "What the Germans lack,"

In the end, no one can spend more than he has: that is true of the individual, it is true of a people. If one spends oneself for power, for power politics, for economics, world trade, parliamentarianism, and military interests – if one spends in *this* direction the quantum of understanding, seriousness, will and self-overcoming which one represents, then it will be lacking for the other direction. (*TI*, 8:4)

He consequently describes races as "factors in the great play and fight of forces [*Faktorum im grossen Spiel und Kampf der Kräfte*]," and he implies that "a thinker who has the development of Europe on his conscience" must be prepared to enter this fray and lend order to its constitutive chaos – even if this intervention involves the making and unmaking of entire races (*BGE*, 251). As this passage suggests, he thus views race as a transient, contingent constellation of forces regulated by a particular regime of mechanical processes. Whereas some of these processes are initiated and maintained by nature – that is, amorally and indifferently – others are amenable to human design and regulation. Here we see that the lawgivers responsible for overseeing the advancement of culture are literally social engineers: they must understand fully the mechanical processes that govern the dynamics of racial cultivation, and they must be prepared to enter the "great play and fight of forces" to arrange these forces into superior configurations.

This "great play and fight of forces" thus serves as the cosmological background against which Nietzsche develops his understanding of the dynamics of racial cultivation. Wishing to eschew the humanism and folk psychology that typically dominate discussions of politics, he attempts to substitute a strictly naturalistic and thoroughly amoral cosmology of contesting forces. The more standard discussions of "Europe's *democratic* movement," he explains, point merely to "moral and political foregrounds," behind which, he claims, "a tremendous *physiological* process is taking place and gaining momentum" (*BGE*, 242). The type of human being produced by this "physiological process" is best distinguished not by its "'civilization,' or 'humanization' or 'progress',", but, "physiologically speaking," by its possession of "a maximum of the art and power of adaptation" (*BGE*, 242). Continuing (ominously) along this mechanistic line of explanation, he presents the Jewish question as if it were a simple matter of efficient digestion:

> That Germany has amply enough Jews, that the German stomach, the German blood has trouble (and still will have trouble for a long time) digesting even this quantum of "Jew" – as the Italian, French, and English have done, having a stronger digestive system – that is the clear testimony and language of a general instinct to which one must listen, in accordance with which one must act. (*BGE*, 251)

This dynamic model of racial cultivation meshes neatly with the larger mechanistic trends that inform Nietzsche's later philosophy. Especially in his post-Zarathustran writings, he regularly treats races (and ages) as if they were reservoirs or vessels of transfusable stuff, which can be tapped and harnessed by the canny lawgiver for purposes of creative redistribution. He thus presents his binary typologies as if they were derived from a quasi-empirical inventory of the relative stores each respective race holds in, alternately, "energy," "force," "strength," "spirit," "will," or "vitality." "Strong" races are treated as repositories full, even overfull, of vital stuff, whereas "weak" races are regarded as depleted or empty repositories. In the case of each type, the relative stores of vital stuff are attributed to the efficiency of the resident mechanism in processing, reserving, and discharging this stuff. "Strong" races are relatively efficient at generating and preserving spirit, assimilating (or eliminating) desirable (or undesirable) racial traits and characteristics, and expending resources in creative expressions of self-externalization. Conversely, "weak" races are typically inefficient in their management of these internal processes. Comparing the Germans to the French on this point, he explains that

> Culture and the state – one should not deceive oneself about this – are antagonists: "*Kultur-Staat*" is merely a modern idea. One lives off the other, one thrives at the expense of the other. All great ages of culture are ages of political decline: what is great culturally has always been unpolitical, even *anti-political* . . . At the same moment when Germany comes up as a great power, France gains a new importance as a *cultural power*. Even today much new seriousness, much new *passion* of the spirit, have migrated to Paris . . . (*TI*, 8:4)

These two types of race furthermore attest to a natural cycle of growth and decay: "strong" races must eventually weaken and contract, while "weak" races, under the proper conditions, can acquire strength and spirit. The aim of "great politics" is to control if possible the periodicity of this natural cycle, lengthening its ascensional trajectory while minimizing its descensional trajectory. Although Nietzsche is convinced that the timely intervention of lawgivers can in fact manage these natural cycles – his favorite example here, as elsewhere, is the enduring reign of the Roman Empire (*AC*, 58) – he offers little evidence that this is the case.

Whatever its ultimate explanatory power, this mechanistic model of race complements Nietzsche's ongoing studies of contemporary science. Especially in his post-Zarathustran writings, the labels he uses to designate these two types of race confirm his interest in science. His workhorse distinction between "strong" and "weak" races gradually yields to the more overtly biologistic distinction between "healthy" and "decadent" races. He thus presents the relative "health" of a race or people as empirically verifiable, as a measurable function of its native "vitality" – hence his avowed capacity to diagnose and classify entire peoples and races. In fact, he seems to take great pride in these periodic demonstrations of his currency with the cutting-edge scientific debates of his day.[27] Far from abjuring biologistic theories of race, he apparently wishes instead to deliver an improved, updated theory of race, one that better reflects the most current status of scientific research.[28]

For all of Nietzsche's interest in science, however, his mechanistic model of race would seem to defy empirical confirmation. Despite his enthusiasm for a mysterious "dynamometer" that can supposedly measure the native vitality of an organism (*TI*, 9:20), he can provide no credible evidence that his diagnoses involve anything beyond his own subjective evaluations of the races in question. "Strong" races are strong and "weak" races are weak in no empirically verifiable sense, even if these diagnoses possess for some readers an irresistible intuitive appeal. His diagnoses tend not only to caricature entire races, reducing complex issues of racial identification to simple, empirical questions of measurable vitality, but also to describe individual representatives of particular races in radically anti-subjective terms. Individual representatives of particular races are summarily reduced to involuntary representatives of these larger racial economies; they are regarded as mere symptoms of the underlying health or sickness of the people in question.[29]

We might conclude, in fact, that his mechanistic model of racial development is not only unscientific, but also anti-scientific. His scientific pose masks his failure both to define a defensible method for ethnographical research and to found a bank of credible empirical data. What is worse, however, is that his mechanistic model of race lends a patina of scientific respectability to his untutored reflections on race. He speaks confidently and authoritatively about mechanical processes of selection, assimilation, absorption, etc., without ever establishing the relevance of these processes for the dynamics of racial cultivation. His mechanistic model of race furthermore boasts no reliable predictive power. It is used to explain after the fact what general processes are underway and why his judgments of these processes are valid. That the result of these processes invariably confirms his prejudices about various races should be sufficient in itself to give us pause.

Rather than provide a credible account of racial development, Nietzsche's model in fact allows him to treat all races of either type as roughly interchangeable. By figuring all races as mechanistic repositories of disposable stuff, he lumps together all "strong" races on the one hand and all "weak" races on the other hand. He thereby reduces all races to the status of blank screens, onto which he projects his most basic racial prejudices. Owing to his unexamined presuppositions about race and politics, he is apparently unable to consider a race on its own merits or to evaluate it on its own preferred terms. In no event is he prepared to assign an intrinsic, non-instrumental value to the integrity of racial identity, especially if the race in question might contribute to some greater good through (further) assimilation. In his reflections on the future of Europe, in fact, he does not even mention most European peoples and nations; they have apparently become anonymous elements to be mixed and matched in the proposed rejuvenation of European culture. His (nearly) exclusive attention to the formal characteristics of race thus affords him the opportunity to add his own "content" after the fact, or none at all; as we have seen, the "content" he supplies often reflects little more than his own prejudices about the race(s) in question. That these racial analyses strike some readers as either intuitively accurate or astutely rendered should not distract us from their lack of empirical basis and their origin in prejudice.

V

The ambit of Nietzsche's discussion of "Peoples and Fatherlands" sheds some clarifying light on the prejudices that contour his racial analyses. This discussion is dominated by his unflattering portrait of the Germans, who, despite their fatherlandish follies, are to play a leading role in the ruling caste that he envisions for his pan-European empire. (One may fairly wonder why this should be so, especially if his ridicule of the Germans is even remotely warranted.) After the Germans in order of importance for the new European order comes a race that Nietzsche does not even consider European: the Jews, whom he introduces into his highly Christianized utopia much as a cosmopolitan chef adds an exotic spice to an otherwise bland stew. He recruits the Jews to infuse into an enervated, dispirited Europe the spirituality that will galvanize its cultural regeneration. In return, he graciously offers to support the nomadic Jews in their efforts to secure the European home they have long desired – which he claims to know to be their wish (*BGE*, 251).

Next in order of importance in "Peoples and Fatherlands" come the French and British, who are acknowledge, respectively, for their "*noblesse*" and "vulgarity" (*BGE*, 253).[30] As this distinction suggests, the French will play a greater role than the British in the new European order. It is likely, in fact, that he regards the French (and perhaps the French alone) as comprising a genuine nation. Apart from the Germans, only the French stand to benefit directly from the racial analyses that inform his political thinking. Indeed, although his rhetoric of pan-European integration might lead us to believe that he values the cultural advancements of *all* European peoples, most of these peoples merit little or no mention. He makes no mention of the anticipated contributions of the Dutch, Spanish, Portuguese, Belgians, and Poles. Nor does he enumerate the potential contributions of the Scandinavian, Baltic, and Balkan nations. The Greeks, from whom he traces the descent of European civilization, merit no consideration in the new European order. The Italians, from whom his beloved Roman Empire received its original shape and direction, are similarly absent from this discussion. He mentions Russia only in passing, and he does not even consider the potential contributions of the various peoples huddled under the umbrella of the Austro-Hungarian Empire. Presumably, his pan-European culture need incorporate nothing of note from these nations, of which, not coincidentally, he has very little first-hand knowledge.

Here we can gain even greater precision: the "Europe" that Nietzsche envisions is really an alternative version of the German *Reich* – a *Reich*, that is, whose primary influence is cultural rather than military. Whereas Nietzsche himself may "have been merely *sprinkled* with what is German" (*EH*, wise, 3), the new European order he envisions will be more recognizably Germanic than anything else. He explains, in fact, that "in the history of European culture the rise of the *Reich* means one thing above all: a displacement of the center of gravity" (*TI*, 8:4). The restoration of this "center of gravity" thus requires that Germany accede once again to a position of European pre-eminence; there are no alternative centers of gravity to be explored or installed. If Europe is to thrive once again, moreover, then "in what matters most – and that always remains culture," the Germans must become once again "worthy of consideration" (*TI*, 8:4). Hence the seemingly undeserved emphasis that Nietzsche places on the future of Germany: the future of Europe, and of a distinctly European race, rests in the balance.

This Germanocentric view of Europe partially explains Nietzsche's persistent efforts to cultivate a readership in his fatherland, despite his low regard for the Germans' reading skills. At one point he expressly poses to himself the question his readers have long since formulated – namely, why does he continue to write in German, presumably for a German public he openly despises, if "nowhere [he is] read worse than in the fatherland" (*TI*, 9:51)? If he has been "discovered" by readers "in Vienna, in St Petersburg, in Stockholm, in Copenhagen, in Paris, in New York" – "everywhere," in short, but "in the shallows of Europe, Germany" (*EH*, gb, 2), then why does he not express himself in a language more readily available to these discerning readers? His "answer," which rehearses his familiar ambitions to approximate "the forms of 'eternity',", only begs the question, for his aspirations to immortality could presumably have been nourished by any number of languages and cultures.

Perhaps more revealing is his boast to be "the first among the Germans" to "master . . . the aphorism, the apothegm" (*TI*, 9:51). The weight of this accomplishment (and the bite of the boast) would require the continued relevance of the German language – and, *a fortiori*, the German people – for the new European order he envisions. In fact, despite his many objections to the Germans – which ultimately exert a force more enduringly rhetorical than philosophical – he nevertheless believes that the animating spirit of German culture can and should be preserved as the core of the new European order.[31]

But whence this stubborn allegiance to the cultural relevance of the German people, especially in light of his unflattering prognosis for Bismarck's *Reich*? Why is Nietzsche, of all philosophers, not willing to consider the possibility that the march of European advancement must circumvent the Germans and proceed in spite of them? In Nietzsche's own terms, this allegiance to the Germans can amount to nothing more than a *prejudice*, a pre-judgment from which his philosophy draws its energy and momentum. If we continue to read Nietzsche against Nietzsche, we see that this prejudice in turn betrays "the moral (and immoral) intentions" his philosophy has been designed simultaneously to mask and to execute (*BGE*, 6). His plan for European integration emerges not so much from an empirical inventory of the cultural resources scattered throughout Europe in the final quarter of the nineteenth century, as from his unshaken commitment to the nobility of the German spirit. His guiding motive is to rescue Germany from its corrosive nationalism while reserving for it a prominent role in a new European order.

We should not be overly surprised by Nietzsche's *sotto voce* rendition of *"Deutschland, Deutschland über alles."* "Philosophy," he tells us, "always creates the world in its own image" (*BGE*, 9), and his image, like the new world order he creates, is unmistakably Germanic. Let us not be misled by his anti-German tirades, his travels throughout Italy and France, or his admiration for French psychologists, Russian novelists, and Italian composers. This is a thinker who never strayed far from either his *Vaterland* or his *Muttersprache*.[32] This is a philosopher whose criticisms of Germany are matched in their passion only by his admiration of its past and his despair for its future. I would furthermore speculate that it is the subterranean presence of his Germanocentric prejudices – and not his more familiar philosophical teachings – that attracts to him the pre-reflective sympathies of anti-Semites, Aryan supremacists, and Nazi ideologues. It is not implausible that they see in him a kindred Germanophile and fellow traveler along the path toward a German domination of Europe. That he clearly prefers cultural to military domination may not be as important a difference to them as it is to him. He too hopes to establish something like a *Reich*, and his opposition to Bismarck may not overly concern his pro-German readers.

At one point, in fact, he candidly admits to his besetting "Germanomania," and he does so immediately following his proposal of intermarriage between Jews and Germans (*BGE*, 251). "Germanomania" is an apt diagnosis of the illness that afflicts him, for his allegiance to Germany as the cultural center of Europe is so strong that he is apparently willing to cancel or submerge all other European racial identities in order to save the Germans from themselves. Yet he remains remarkably calm and cheerful about his mania, as if he were in full control of it (or wished us to believe this about him). Having acknowledged his affliction, in fact, he declares that

> [H]ere it is proper to break off my cheerful Germanomania and holiday oratory; for I am beginning to touch on what is *serious* for me, the "European problem" as I understand it, the cultivation of a new caste that will rule Europe. (*BGE*, 251)

Proper, yes; but possible? Are we to believe that Nietzsche is sufficiently in command of his "cheerful Germanomania" to execute such a decisive transition? Especially since he acknowledges that his affliction "touches on" what is *"serious"* for him, might we not fairly conclude that *his* Germanomania, like that of the other Germans whom he so adeptly diagnoses, is not so easily "broken off"? Wagner, for example, to whom he admits an enduring kinship (*EH*, cw, *P*), is German through and through – but somehow Nietzsche is not? How are we to know – other than to take his word for it – that what follows is not *also* "holiday oratory," contaminated by the author's "Germanomania"? What he plausibly intends as a joke may also, even simultaneously, be serious, and vice versa.

Nietzsche has toiled mightily to distance himself from the dispirited, fatherlandish Germans and to convince his readers of his disgust with all things German, all the while claiming the unique, privileged perspective of an insider outside.[33] But perhaps he protests too much? His professed distaste for the Germans need not be understood as deviating from, or competing with, his Germanomania. He, too, is a decadent (*EH*, wise, 2), and he, too, fits his own profile of the Germans as "a people of the most monstrous mixture and medley of races," as "more incomprehensible, comprehensive, contradictory, unknown, incalculable, surprising, even frightening than other people are to themselves" (*BGE*, 244). Would Nietzsche not say of Nietzsche that his "Germanomania" strikes very deep, coaxing his thought to develop along planes and vectors unknown to him?

In fact, Nietzsche's "Germanomania" betrays the racial prejudices at work in his philosophizing. He sincerely wishes to contribute to the rejuvenation of European culture, but he cannot seriously consider for this culture a ruling caste that is not recognizably Germanic. So although his political thinking promises an eclectic pan-European culture, his racial analyses specify the Germans as the rightful heirs and arbiters of European culture. And although it may be true that we cannot ultimately fault him for his Germanomania, it is at least equally true that we need not mistake it for scientific objectivity.[34]

Notes

1. Macintyre (1992) points to Elisabeth's friendship with Dr Wilhelm Frick, later Reich Minister of the Interior, as decisive in her decision to marry her brother's legacy with the political agenda of National Socialism (pp. 176–80).
2. See Macintyre (1992), pp. 119–48.
3. See the excellent discussion by Macintyre (1992), pp. 176–201. I am also indebted to Aschheim's (1992) erudite treatment of "Nietzsche in the Third Reich," pp. 232–71.
4. Brinton (1948), pp. 221–31.
5. With the exception of occasional emendations, I rely throughout this essay on Walter Kaufmann's translations/editions of Nietzsche's writings for Viking Press/Random House, and on R. J. Hollingdale's translations for Cambridge University Press (see Bibliography for full citations). Numbers refer to sections rather than to pages, and the following key explains the abbreviations I employ: *AC*: *The Antichrist(ian)*; *BGE*: *Beyond Good and Evil*; *D*: *Daybreak*; *EH*: *Ecce Homo*; *GM*: *On the Genealogy of Morals*; *GS*: *The Gay Science*; *SE*: *Schopenhauer as Educator*; *TI*: *Twilight of the Idols*; *WP*: *The Will to Power*; *Z*: *Thus Spoke Zarathustra*. The abbreviations "cw," "wise," and "gb" refer to the chapters in *Ecce Homo* entitled "The Case of Wagner," "Why I am so Wise," and "Why I Write Such Good Books."
6. Oehler (1935) maintains, for example, that "To wish to give proof regarding Nietzsche's thoughts, to establish that they agree with the race views and strivings of the National Socialist movement, would be carrying coals to Newcastle" (p. 86) (cited by Kaufmann, 1974, p. 290).
7. As Simon (1997) observes, the accuracy of Nietzsche's remarks about the Jews may be confirmed in part by the spread of anti-Semitism through the *Reich*: "Thus the Jews become somewhat offensive to those 'nations' that are searching for their identity, for the Jews make it clear with their example that these attempts to become a 'nation' can lead only nowhere" (p. 110).
8. This point is made succinctly by Simon (1997): "This 'nihilistic' will to become a nation is dangerous; instead of having (in a transcendental sense) its own identity, this will must *define* itself by delineating itself from others. Such delineations must be asserted and defended; they are genuinely 'polemic' and can never be 'absolutely' certain" (p. 109).

9. Nietzsche presents his distinction between "noble" and "slave" moralities in *On the Genealogy of Morals*, which he drafted just after finishing *Beyond Good and Evil*. On its title page, Nietzsche introduces the *Genealogy* as "A Sequel to My Last Book, *Beyond Good and Evil*, Which It Is Meant to Supplement and Clarify." And, indeed, he derives his famous distinction in the *Genealogy* between "noble" and "slave" moralities from his distinction between "master" and "slave" moralities in *Beyond Good and Evil* (*BGE*, 260).

10. Although he does not explicitly identify race as a *res facta*, it is clear from this passage that he understands a "nation" as a work-in-progress that may someday become a genuine race. So if a "nation" is a *res facta*, then presumably a race is as well, since all races were at one time in their respective evolutions identifiable as (or similar to) what nineteenth-century Europeans call a "nation."

11. Speaking specifically of the law of Manu, Nietzsche alludes to the problematic nature of appeals to blood purity: "These regulations are instructive enough: here we encounter for once *Aryan* humanity, quite pure, quite primordial – we learn that the concept of 'pure blood' is the opposite of a harmless concept" (*TI*, 7:4). I cannot see that in this section of *Twilight* "Nietzsche denounces '*Aryan* humanity',," as Kaufmann (1974) claims (p. 297). His reference to "Aryan humanity" is at best neutral, and his juxtaposition of "Aryan" and "Christian" values might suggest a degree of sympathy with the Aryan "morality of breeding."

12. Hubert Cancik (1997) persuasively argues that Nietzsche's plan for a new European order is modeled on his earlier account of the origin of the Greeks as an identifiable race or nation. As Cancik explains, this account denies the popular myth of a progenitory race of "pure" Greeks, claiming instead that the various peoples and tribes who eventually acquired a Greek identity did so only when they came to Greece and developed under the discipline of Greek culture and custom (pp. 55–8). Cancik thus traces the racism inherent in Nietzsche's plan for a unified Europe to this earlier account of the "origin" of the racial identity of the Greeks (pp. 59–60).

13. The influential distinction between "blood" and "spirit" is attributable to Kaufmann (1974), pp. 284–94. In Kaufmann's hands, however, this distinction is not optimally effective, for he antecedently understands "race" as a biologistic, blood-based concept. He is therefore unable to appreciate fully Nietzsche's theory of racial development through spiritual elevation. Witness the following passage: "Even in the context of Nietzsche's early philosophy . . . it was perfectly clear that Nietzsche looked to art, religion, and philosophy – and not to race – to elevate mankind above the beasts, and some men above the mass of mankind . . . If the value of a human being – and one should note that for Nietzsche all value is derivative from that of the individual and his state of being – were a function of race or indeed of anything purely biological, the consequences would be momentous: the chasm between the 'powerful' elite and those others who are doomed to mediocrity would be fixed and permanent, even hereditary – and large masses of people, possibly whole nations, might be reliable determined to be inferior and possibly worthless 'vessels of wrath fitted to destruction' (Rom. 9:22)" (p. 285).

14. According to Kaufmann (1974), "[T]he 'blond beast' is not a racial concept . . . [I]t specifically includes the Arabs and the Japanese . . . [I]t is an ideogram Nietzsche used to symbolize the people who have strong animal impulses that they have not yet learned to master" (p. 297).

15. Kaufmann (1974), for example, cites this passage as evidence of Nietzsche's Lamarckian sympathies (pp. 294–7). For a charitable interpretation of the role of these Lamarckian sympathies in Nietzsche's philosophy, see Schacht (1983), pp. 334–8.

16. He thus explains that "To the Greeks I do not by any means owe similarly strong

impressions; and – to come right out with it – they *cannot* mean as much to us as the Romans. One does not *learn* from the Greeks – their manner is too foreign, and too fluid, to have an imperative, a 'classical' effect. Who could ever have learned to write from a Greek? Who could ever have learned it *without* the Romans?" (*TI*, 10:2).

17. One of the earliest, and most powerful, statements of this position appears in Nietzsche's *Untimely Meditation* on "Schopenhauer as Educator": "It is the fundamental idea of *culture*, insofar as it sets for each one of us but one task: *to promote the production of the philosopher, the artist and the saint within us and without us and thereby to work at the perfecting of nature*" (*SE*, 5).

18. Nietzsche (1986), vol. 8, pp. 567–8. Bergmann (1987) offers an illuminating account of Nietzsche's "Caesarism" (pp. 180–7), which he links to the "defeatism" that characterizes Nietzsche's later thought. As Bergmann explains, "Defeatism cut closer to the bone by accepting the either/or of militarism – either giving battle or shameless capitulation – and opting for the latter" (p. 180).

19. In a genealogically inflected passage that clearly distinguishes him from the anti-Semites of his day, Nietzsche avers that "The German soul is above all manifold, of diverse origins, more put together and superimposed than actually built: that is due to where it comes from. A German who would make bold to say, 'two souls, alas, are dwelling in my breast,' would violate the truth rather grossly or, more precisely, would fall short of the truth by a good many souls" (*BGE*, 244).

20. See Cancik (1997), p. 60. For a sustained treatment of Nietzsche's defense of aristocratic political regimes, see Conway (1997), ch. 2.

21. See Kaufmann (1974), pp. 287–95.

22. See, for example, Nehamas (1985), pp. 185–99.

23. A similar line of criticism is pursued by Schutte (1999), pp. 68–70, to whom I am indebted for her problematization of Nietzsche's notion of the "good European."

24. Witness this familiar pronouncement by the self-styled author of the revaluation of all values: "We would no more choose the 'first Christians' to associate with than Polish Jews – not that one even required any objection to them: they both do not smell good" (*AC*, 46).

25. Krell and Bates (1997) record a similar observation of Nietzsche's apparent eurocentrism: "He did not open his eyes to Africa or the Orient; Venice was as close to China as he ever got, and German translations are as close as he came to Huckleberry Finn" (p. 1).

26. As Krell and Bates (1997) explain, for example, Nietzsche's fascination with Oaxaca and its hospitable climate is attributable to stories told to him by "a group of Swiss colonists on vacation in Sils[-Maria]" (p. 149). Nietzsche speaks longingly of "the highlands of Mexico, near the Pacific" in his letter of 14 August 1881 to Köselitz (Nietzsche, 1986, vol. 6, letter 136, p. 113).

27. Müller-Lauter (1999) makes a compelling case for the seriousness of Nietzsche's study of science, and especially his study of the theories of the biologist Wilhelm Roux (pp. 161–82). Roux's influence on Nietzsche is also helpfully illuminated by Ansell Pearson (1997), pp. 93–100.

28. Nietzsche's continued interest in biologistic theories of race is evidenced in the following parenthetical remark: "The Celts, by the way, were definitely a blond race [*eine blonde Rasse*]; it is wrong to associate traces of an essentially dark-haired population [*Bevölkerung*] which appear on the more careful ethnographical maps of Germany with any sort of Celtic origin or blood-mixture, as Virchow still does: it is rather the *pre-Aryan* population of Germany who emerge in these places. (The same is true of virtually all Europe: the suppressed race [*die unterworfene Rasse*] has gradually recovered the upper hand again, in coloring, shortness of skull, perhaps even in the intellectual and social instincts" (*GM*, I:5).

29. For example, he boldly exposes "Socrates and Plato [as] symptoms of degeneration, tools of the Greek dissolution, pseudo-Greek, anti-Greek" (*TI*, 2:2).

30. Lampert (1999) suggests that the genuine addressees of Nietzsche's intermarriage proposal are the French, "a mothering people of genius involuntarily prey to the suitors of a fathering people" and the Germans, whose philosophical opposition to this "fathering people," *viz.*, the imperial British, make them a much better match for the French (p. 55).

31. Speaking of himself and his fellow "good Europeans," Nietzsche identifies the precise "sense" in which he is not German: "we are not nearly 'German' enough, in the sense in which the word 'German' is constantly being used nowadays, to advocate nationalism and race hatred and to be able to take pleasure in the national scabies of the heart and blood poisoning that now leads the nations of Europe to delimit and barricade themselves against each other as if it were a matter of quarantine" (*GS*, 377). As this passage indicates, Nietzsche is far more eager to identify the "senses" in which he is *not* typically German than to identify the "senses" in which he remains thoroughly – even stereotypically – German.

32. As Krell and Bates (1997) remark, Nietzsche "never left the continent of Europe. Nor did he see many of the places a good European would find 'essential' to his or her culture. He never made it to Paris or Barcelona, St Petersburg or Copenhagen, London or Brussels or Prague. Moreover, Nietzsche was by no means a master of modern European languages: his Italian was execrable and his Russian nonexistent, although Dostoevsky made him want to learn; his English too was poor, and not even Sterne or Twain or Emerson could convince him to make the effort; only his French was passable" (p. 1).

33. The following passage is typical both of Nietzsche's animosity toward the Germans and his attempt to establish his critical distance from them: "It is part of my ambition to be considered a despiser of the Germans *par excellence* . . . – the Germans seem impossible to me. When I imagine a type of man that antagonizes all my instincts, it always turns into a German . . . I cannot endure this race among whom one is always in bad company, that has no fingers for nuances . . . The Germans have no idea how vulgar they are; but that is the superlative of vulgarity – they are not even ashamed of being merely Germans" (*EH*, cw, 4).

34. For their instructive suggestions on earlier drafts of this essay, I would like to thank Rachana Kamtekar, Jackie Scott, and Julie Ward.

References

Ansell Pearson, Keith 1997: *Viroid Life: Perspectives on Nietzsche and the Transhuman Condition*. London: Routledge.

Aschheim, Stephen E. 1992: *The Nietzsche Legacy in Germany 1890–1990*. Berkeley: University of California Press.

Bergmann, Peter 1987: *Nietzsche, "The Last Antipolitical German."* Bloomington: Indiana University Press.

Brinton, Crane 1948: *Nietzsche*. Cambridge, MA: Harvard University Press.

Cancik, Hubert 1997: "Mongols, Semites and the Pure-Bred Greeks': Nietzsche's Handling of the Racial Doctrines of his Time. In J. Golomb (ed.), *Nietzsche and Jewish Culture*, London: Routledge, 1997, 55–75.

Conway, Daniel W. 1997: *Nietzsche and the Political*. London: Routledge.

Kaufmann, Walter 1974: *Nietzsche: Philosopher, Psychologist, Antichrist*, 4th Edn. Princeton, N.J.: Princeton University Press.

Krell, David F. and Bates, Donald L. 1997: *The Good European: Nietzsche's Work Sites in Word and Image*. Chicago: University of Chicago Press.

Lampert, Laurence 1999: "Peoples and Fatherlands": Nietzsche's Philosophical Politics. In Jacqueline Scott (ed.), *Nietzsche and Politics. The Southern Journal of Philosophy*, vol. XXXVII, Supplement, 43–63.

Macintyre, Ben 1992: *Forgotten Fatherland: The Search for Elisabeth Nietzsche*. New York: Farrar, Straus and Giroux.

Müller-Lauter, Wolfgang 1999: *Nietzsche: His Philosophy of Contradictions and the Contradictions of his Philosophy*. Tr. David J. Parent. Urbana: University of Illinois Press.

Nehamas, Alexander 1985: *Nietzsche: Life as Literature*. Cambridge, MA: Harvard University Press.

Nietzsche, Friedrich 1967: *The Birth of Tragedy* and *The Case of Wagner*. Tr. Walter Kaufmann, ed. Walter Kaufmann. New York: Random House/Vintage Books.

Nietzsche, Friedrich 1968: *The Will to Power*. Tr. Walter Kaufmann and R. J. Hollingdale, ed. Walter Kaufmann. New York: Random House/Vintage Books.

Nietzsche, Friedrich 1974: *The Gay Science*. Tr. Walter Kaufmann. New York: Random House/Vintage Books.

Nietzsche, Friedrich 1980: *Sämtliche Werke: Kritische Studienausgabe in 15 Bänden*. Ed. G. Colli and M. Montinari. Berlin: dtv/de Gruyter.

Nietzsche, Friedrich 1982a: *The Antichrist*, in *The Portable Nietzsche*. Tr. and ed. Walter Kaufmann. New York: Viking Penguin.

Nietzsche, Friedrich 1982b: *Daybreak: Thoughts on the Prejudices of Morality*. Tr. R. J. Hollingdale. Cambridge: Cambridge University Press.

Nietzsche, Friedrich 1982c: *Twilight of the Idols*, in *The Portable Nietzsche*. Tr. and ed. Walter Kaufmann. New York: Viking Penguin.

Nietzsche, Friedrich 1983: *Untimely Meditations*. Tr. R. J. Hollingdale. Cambridge: Cambridge University Press.

Nietzsche, Friedrich, 1986: *Sämtliche Briefe: Kritische Studienausgabe in 8 Bänden*. Ed. G. Colli and M. Montinari. Berlin: dtv/de Gruyter.

Nietzsche, Friedrich 1989a: *Beyond Good and Evil: Prelude to a Philosophy of the Future*. Tr. Walter Kaufmann. New York: Random House/Vintage Books.

Nietzsche, Friedrich 1989b: *On the Genealogy of Morals*. Tr. Walter Kaufmann and R. J. Hollingdale. And *Ecce Homo*, Tr. Walter Kaufmann. New York: Random House/Vintage Books.

Oehler, Richard 1935: *Friedrich Nietzsche und die Deutsche Zukunft*. Leipzig: Armanen.

Schacht, Richard 1983: *Nietzsche*. London: Routledge and Kegan Paul.

Schutte, Ofelia 1999: Nietzsche's Cultural Politics: A Critique. In Jacqueline Scott (ed.), *Nietzsche and Politics. The Southern Journal of Philosophy*, vol. XXXVII, Supplement, 65–71.

Simon, Josef 1997: Nietzsche on Judaism and Europe. In J. Golomb (ed.) *Nietzsche and Jewish Culture*. London: Routledge, 101–16.

CHAPTER 10

Liberalism's Limits: Carlyle and Mill on "The Negro Question"

DAVID THEO GOLDBERG

1

In 1849 *Fraser's Magazine*, the popular London literary periodical, published an anonymous attack on the nature of black people under the title, "Occasional Discourse on the Negro Question." The vicious essay turned out to be written by Thomas Carlyle. Outraged by the incivility of its language, if not distressed by the intransigence of the sentiment it expressed, literate liberals in Britain and the northern states in the American Union openly objected to the attack. Chief among the responses was a particularly impassioned essay published again anonymously in the following issue of *Fraser's* under the title, "The Negro Question." This time the author was England's leading public intellectual of the day, John Stuart Mill. Four years later, fueled no doubt by his increasingly acrimonious feud with his former mate Mill, Carlyle published in pamphlet form a revised and expanded version of the atttack under the more pointed title, "Occasional Discourse on the Nigger Question." And there the matter was left to stand until 1971, when the two essays were first brought together with an introductory commentary by the editor Eugene August.[1]

It is curious that from their initial appearance to August's edition, and indeed since, no commentary exists on this exchange which offers a particularly revealing window to the excesses and limits of nineteenth-century racialized discourse.[2] This semi-anonymous exchange, almost too sensitive to touch in their own names, exemplifies the parameters of Victorian racialized sentiment, explicitly racist in one direction, seemingly egalitarian in the other, as August hopefully has it. Indeed, while it exemplifies colonial racialization and racist derogation – colonialism's vicious recourse to neo-scientific racism, on one hand, and liberalism's polite racism, on the other – the exchange reveals at once the long reach of colonial discourse to elements of contemporary postcolonial racist expression. Carlyle on race was to mid-nineteenth-century Britain what Dinesh D'Souza is to late twentieth-century America, offering a totalizing rationalization of the sorry state of black folk in the most extreme, and thus eye-catching terms. By contrast, Mill's singular contribution to "The Negro Question" – just as his "On the Subjection of Women" was his seminal and remarkable contribution to "The Woman Question" – nevertheless marks the implicit limits to racialized egalitarianism for liberal Victorianism. This suggests at once the challenge facing liberalism on the question of race more generally.

The socio-historical background to the exchange concerned the fading prospects and conditions of the British plantation owners in the West Indies, though the questions of race addressed have to be understood in terms of the colonial condition more broadly. Emancipation of slaves in the British empire in 1833 curtailed the supply of desperately cheap labor and cut into the artificial profit margins enjoyed by the West Indies sugar planters. In 1846 the British parliament ended plantation subsidies, thus forcing plantation owners in the islands, those increasingly disaffected white British subjects, to compete unprotected on the world market. Carlyle's voice was that of the disenchanted colonial "aristocracy" abroad and (more ambiguously) the distressed English working classes and Irish peasants closer to hand, combined under the racialized aggrandizement of whiteness; Mill's by contrast was that of "enlightened" Victorian abolitionism. Here, then, are to be found the two prevailing pillars of nineteenth-century racial theory. Carlyle represented the bald claim to "the Negro's" inherent inferiority articulated by racist science of the day; Mill on the other hand was the principal spokesman for the European's historically developed superiority, though (as Afrocentrists like Molefi Asante and their critics like Mary Lefkowitz both should note) he temperately acknowledged the influence of ancient Egyptians on the Hellenic Greeks.

2

Carlyle's negrophobia is interesting intellectually only because its vituperative language directed at black people was an expression of more than just bald prejudice, though it was clearly that. Thus, his objectionable language (revealing of equally objectionable presumptions) regarding people of African descent was expressed against the background of, if not prompted by, a critique of the conditions of the working classes in Britain. Carlyle's negrophobia accordingly was tied up with a critique of *laissez faire* capitalist political economy prevailing at the time. The failure of the patato crop due to extended drought had devastated Irish peasants, and the mid-century recession had caused massive unemployment among the English working classes, represented in Carlyle's discourse in the forlorn figure of the "Distressed Needlewoman." Carlyle contrasted these desperately sad figures with the stereotype of the lazy, "sho 'good eatin'" Negro.[3] Carlyle assumed that the capitalism of his day somehow causally tied the alienation of working people in England and Ireland to the emancipation of shiftless and workless Negroes in the colonies. He thus predicated in this essay what might otherwise be deemed an insightful reading of unregulated capitalism that he had developed, for example, in *Past and Present* (1843) on a set of deeply racist premises. In the spirit of the early Marx, Carlyle criticized *laissez faire* capitalism for reducing *human* relationships (the paradigm for which he assumes to be between whites) to the "cash contract"[4] between employer and employee. Capitalist "Lords of Rackrent" (or landlords) lost all interest in the impoverished Irish peasant or English seamstress once the latter were unable to afford the rent. The latters' freedom, under *laissez faire* liberal capitalism, was reduced to the liberty to die by starvation. Carlyle accordingly predicted that the importation of English workers into the West Indies in response to planters' demands for workers who would work would render the Negro inhabitants as free to starve as their British counterparts.

Carlyle attributed the underlying cause of this general condition to the demise of paternalistic control by the British, superior on all counts, over the inherently inferior natives of the islands. Those in a situation of superiority had a paternalistic obligation to effect the wellbeing of the inferior for whom the former were responsible. Carlyle insisted that the feudal serf was (materially) better placed than the Irish peasant, English needleworker, or "Negro" of his day. He concludes that "the Negro Question" was to be answered by turning "Negroes" into a relationship of loyal serfdom to the benevolent feudal-like lordship of their white masters. White men, wisest by birth (right), were destined by nature and God to rule, Negroes to serve; whites ought to try and convince Negroes to asume their God-given role as servants, failing which masters would be obliged to turn to "the beneficent whip."

Likely unaware first hand of any black people, Carlyle's "Nigger" of the "Nigger Question" was the stereotypical figure of "Quashee," a polygenic form of black lowlife – lazy, laughing, rhythmic, musical, dance-loving, language defective (p. 12). "Horse-jawed and beautifully muzzled" (p. 4), "Quashee" was the Carlylean equivalent of "Sambo," etymologically linked to squash and so to pumpkin. Carlyle characterized "Quashee" as working only at eating pumpkin – Carlyle's mean metaphor for any juicy tropical fruit like watermelon, cantaloupe, mango, or papaya – and drinking rum. Yet Carlyle insisted on finding "the Negro," "alone of wild-men," kind, affectionate, even lovable, and pointedly not the object of his "hate" (p. 12). The abundance of tropical fruit in Carlyle's view reduced the need on the part of West Indian natives to work. Carlyle's solution was to compel "the Negro" in the Islands to work by restricting to the laborless the right to own fruit-producing land or to enjoy its abundant products (p. 9).

In order to sustain this degraded image of the inherently inferior "Nigger," Carlyle (like his counterpart D'Souza a century and half later) was driven to reduce the debilitating effects of slavery's experience for people of African descent. Carlyle accordingly insisted that the debilitations of slavery were "much exaggerated" (p. 13). Slavery, and so mastery too, were considered "natural" conditions; slaves, as Aristotle once put it, are slaves by nature. Blacks are born to be servants (Carlyle's euphemistic bow to the abolitionists, p. 22) of whites who "are born wiser . . . and lords" over them (p. 32). Indeed, Carlyle insisted that there is a slavery far worse than that of "Negroes" in the colonies, "the one, intolerable sort of slavery" (as though enslavement of black people is not): this, he remarked without a hint of irony, is the "slavery" throughout Europe of "the strong to the weak; of the great and noble-minded to be the small and mean! The slavery of Wisdom to Folly." (p. 14) Thus Carlyle diminished the horrible experience and effects of *real* slavery historically by reducing them to less than the "platonic" manifestations of a metaphorical servitude of the strong and wise to the weak and ignorant. Of course, it says little for the strength and wisdom of the European wealthy and wise that they should be so constrained by the weak and witless, a point to which Carlyle in all his critical power seems oblivious.

Carlyle emphasized that it was Europeans who developed the colonies from their supposed prehistory of "pestilence . . . and putrefaction, savagery . . . and swamp-malaria" (p. 28) through their creativity, ingenuity, and productivity; that it was the English (or "Saxon British," p. 27) who supposedly made the West Indies flourish and without whom the islands would reduce to "Black Irelands" (p. 33) or "Haiti" with "black Peter exterminating black Paul" (p. 29). Yet Carlyle repeatedly contrasted the conditions of "Negroes," those "Demarara Niggers," with the conditions of English laborers, white working women, and Irish peasants. Fat from the abundance of land, the consumption of fruit, and lack of labor, the character of the Negro was measured against, if not silently considered the cause of, working peoples' plight in the mother country and the colonies. Carlyle's discourse nevertheless reveals beneath the racialized overlay of this contrast a class-induced ambivalence. Thus he identified also the Distressed Needlewomen, Irish peasants, and English working classes through a nineteenth-century version of the discourse of an underclass (or lumpen) poverty of culture with "the Nigger" of the West Indies (pp. 20–1). Most of the 300,000 Distressed Needlwomen, he objected, were really "Mutinous Servingmaids" unable "to sew a stitch," and defying their inherent need for a master: "Without a master in certain cases, you become a Distressed Needlewoman, and cannot so much as live" (p. 21). Indeed, Carlyle further reduced this equation of posing seamstress and free "nigger" to the infantilized condition of babies and the animalized conditions of dogs and horses (pp. 23, 12), all of whom needed accordingly to be cared for, looked after, mastered by "philanthropic Anglo-Saxon men and women" (p. 23). Equal in quantity to an entire English county, black West Indians "in *worth* (in quantity of intellect, faculty, docility, energy, and available human valor and value)" amounted to a single street of London's working-class East End.

In Carlyle's view, the working classes and particularly Negroes were born to serve, to have masters. With little wit of their own, they would flourish only in servitude, in being told what to do and looked after. Carlyle concluded from this claim of inherent servility that the "Black gentleman" be hired "not by the month, but by a very much longer term. That he be 'hired for life'." That, in other words, he be the slave he was to "Whites . . . born more wiser than [he]" (pp. 21–2, 33, 34–5). Ironically, and against the naturalist grain, such lifelong servitude was to be enforced through might and fright (pp. 26–7, 29, 31), for if "the Saxon British" failed to assert their dominance, some other colonial power would (p. 35). The colonial imperative was as much about relations of power, domination, and "the education of desire"[5] internal to Europe as it was straightforwardly about imposing European will upon its Other.

3

It was Carlyle's call to reinstitute slavery to which Mill principally objected in his response. This perhaps is predictable, given Mill's longstanding and well-known commitment to abolition. Mill's critical concern with Carlyle's racist sentiment was only secondary and much more understated. Moreover, not only did Mill not object to colonial domination, he insisted upon it ablbeit in "benevolent" form. After all, Mill worked for the better part of his working life administering colonialism. Thus Mill opened his letter to the editor of *Fraser's* by emphasizing that abolition was "the best and greatest achievement yet performed by mankind" in "[t]he history of human improvement" (pp. 38–9). Slavery was wrong for Mill on utilitarian grounds in that it produced much more pain than would liberty and equal opportunity, and it is for this reason that Mill considered slavery inherently inhumane (pp. 48–9), a view derided by Carlyle under the mocking title of the "Universal Abolition of Pain Association" (p. 2). In contrast to Carlyle's critique of *laissez faire* capitalism, Mill offered a defense of *laissez faire* principles as embodying economic freedom and underpinning a liberal social order. Mill, however, qualified these *laissez faire* principles by insisting that all people, black and white, enjoy equal opportunity: "[Carlyle] . . . will make them work *for* certain whites, those whites *not* working at all . . . Does he mean that all persons ought to earn their living? But some earn their living by doing nothing, and some by doing mischief . . ." (pp. 42–3). Mill continued:

> [L]et the whole produce belong to those who do the work which produces it. We would not have *black* labourers [in the West Indies] compelled to grow spices which they do not want, and *white* proprietors who do not work at all exchanging the spices for houses in Belgrave Square [an expensive neighborhood in London]. . . . Let them have exactly the same share in what they produce that they have in the work. If they do not like this, let them remain as they are, so long as they . . . make the best of supply and demand." (pp. 44–5, my emphases)

Mill's quiet qualification of class by race – black laborers, white proprietors – was tied to his denial that every difference among human beings is inherent, a "vulgar error" he rightly imputed to Carlyle (p. 46). In objecting to Carlyle's racist hierarchical naturalism, however, Mill inscribed in its place, and in the name of *laissez faire* and equal opportunity, an imputation of the historical inferiority of blacks. Mill implied that this assumption of inferiority, because historically produced and contingent, was not always the case (Egyptians influenced Greeks) and might one day be overcome. Yet Mill's superficial bow to what has become an Afrocentric cornerstone barely hid beneath the surface the polite racism of his Eurocentric history. Contingent racism is still a form of racism – not so usual, not so bald, not so vituperative, and polite perhaps, but condescending nevertheless even as it is committed to equal opportunity. Equal opportunity among those with the unfair, historically produced inequities of the colonial condition will simply reproduce those inequities, if not expand them.

The very title of his response to Carlyle – "The Negro Question" – indicates Mill's presumption that (to use Du Bois's terms) blacks are a problem, rather than that people of African descent in the New World faced problems – least of all that those problems were imposed by their masters – and that such problems might best be resolved through the utility calculus. This interpretation is borne out by placing Mill's response to Carlyle in the context of Mill's views on development, modernization, and race. These were views he developed most fully in terms of India and his experience in the English East Indies Company but which he generalized to Africa and the West Indies also. So to confirm that these premises indeed underpin Mill's liberal egalitarianism, it is necessary to turn to his views on the colonies.

Mill worked as an examiner for the English East Indies Company from 1823 until 1856 and then, like his father, as chief examiner until his retirement to politics in 1858. Thus he was central in, and ultimately responsible for, all bureaucratic correspondence between the British government and its colonial representation in India. (Mill was involved in writing 1,700 official letters to India over this period.) It was in the context of India (and the Asiatic countries more generally), then, that he worked out his views on colonial intervention in those "underdeveloped" countries which he considered stagnant and inhibiting of progress, and he generalized from this context to other areas.

In *The Principles of Political Economy*, Mill wrote that "Colonization – is the best affair of business, in which the capital of an old and wealthy country can engage."[6] It would do so in order to establish:

> [F]irst, a better government: more complete security of property; moderate taxes, and freedom from arbitrary exaction under the name of taxes; a more permanent and more advantageous tenure of land, securing to the cultivator as far as possible the undivided benefits of industry, skill, and economy he may exert. Secondly, improvement of the public intelligence: the decay of usages or superstitions which interfere with the effective employment of industry; and the growth of mental activity, making the people alive to new objects of desire. Thirdly, the introduction of foreign arts, which raise the returns derivable from additional capital, to a rate corresponding to the low strength of the desire of accumulation: and the importation of foreign capital, which renders the increase of production no longer exclusively dependent on the thrift or providence of the inhabitants themselves, while it places before them a stimulating example, and by instilling new ideas and breaking the chains of habit, if not by improving the actual condition of the population, tends to create in them new wants, increased ambition, and greater thought for the future.[7]

Mill picks out for application of these principles India, Russia, Turkey, Spain, and Ireland. The West Indies and African countries were not recognized as having the capacity for self-development at all.[8]

The difference between a developed and undeveloped country, between those more or less civilized, was defined by Mill in terms of the country's capacity to enable and promote representative self-government and individual self-development. In short, in terms of its capacity for autonomy and good government. "Good government" would enable a society, as Mill once said of himself, "to effect the greatest amount of good compatible with . . . opportunities"[9] with a the view to maximizing wellbeing and so happiness. Mill attributed the success of such promotion fundamentally to economic development which apparently would enable opportunities. Civilized countries like Britain limited government intervention in individuals' lives; those less civilized he thought should be ruled by those more so with the view to promoting their capacity for self-development. Liberal individualization was consonant with economic, political, and cultural modernization. This would require greater restriction in the ruled country on people's freedoms and so more government regulation. Progress was considered a function of education and enlightened institutions but also of people of "similar civilization to the ruling country," of Britain's "own blood and language. The latter – Mill mentioned Australia and Canada – were "capable of, and ripe for, representative government." India, by contrast, was far from it, for India had stagnated for many centuries under the sway of Oriental despotism.[10] In India's case, and even more perpetually in the case of the West Indies and African colonies, "benevolent despotism" – a paternalistic "government of guidance" imposed by more advanced Europeans – was the rational order of the day.[11]

Thus, for Mill, the justification of colonization was to be measured according to its aid in the progress of the colonized, its education of superstitious colonial subjects in the virtues of reason, and the generation of new markets for capital accumulation through the fashioning of desires. The purpose of education was to inform: both to provide the informational basis to make rational decisions and to structure the values framing practical reason in ways conducive to the colonial ends Mill deemed desirable. Mill considered progress to consist in being socialized in the values of liberal modernity, that is, in the sort of social, political, economic, cultural, and legal commitments best represented by the British example. As a colonized country exemplified such progress, the colonizing country progressively would give way to the colonized's self-governance. So Mill's "benevolent despotism" amounts to a colonialism with a human face. The world was to be directed by the most developed and capable nations whose self-interests nevertheless would be mitigated and mediated by the force of utilitarian reason.

Mill was blind to the internal tensions in his indices of progress. The ideal conditions for the generation of new markets and the fashioning of new desires for the sake of capital accumulation are likely inconsistent with genuine self-determination, autonomy, and self-governance. Colonization is straightforwardly consistent with developing new markets and desires – it is after all a central part of the historical *raison d'être* for colonialism – in a way in which it is historically, if not conceptually, at odds with self-determination. Mill thought different socio-economic imperatives face the "advanced," and "backward" nations: improved distribution of goods (not wealth) for the "advanced," better conditions of production for the "backward" countries.[12] So before worrying about distribution of goods among the people of the "backward countries," improving production was paramount, and in any case (re)distribution of wealth was never an issue.

Mill's "benevolent despotism," relatively benign and masked by humane application perhaps, neverthless sought "to make provision in the constitution of the government itself, for compelling those who have the governing power, to listen to and take into consideration the opinions of persons who, from their position and their previous life, have made a study of Indian subjects, and acquired experience in them."[13] Thus Mill recognized the relation between knowledge and power, specialized information and administration, as the underlying imperative of colonial governments. Knowledge of the Native was instrumental to establishing the conditions for developing the colonies in a way that would continue to serve the interests of the colonial power. It may seem curious that Mill implied that the Natives themselves would not be consulted in accumulating knowledge about local colonial conditions, for he did insist that qualified Natives be appointed to all administrative and governmental positions "for which they are fit," though without "appointing them to the regular service." Mill's utilitarian reason for this restriction was that Natives were not to be "considered for the highest service" for "if their promotion stooped short while that of others went on, it would be more invidious than keeping them out altogether." And as Europeans, rationally superior, were to be the appeal of last resort, Natives' ascension was naturally delimited.[14] James Mill seemed to project onto the Natives of the colonies the same utilitarian paternalism with which he treated his son, and John Stuart never managed to shake this paternal(istic) framing.[15]

However, even in their administrative advance, the Natives (here Indian) were to be "Indian in blood and colour, but English in tastes, in opinions, in morals and in intellect."[16] Blood may run thicker than water, but it was to be diluted by a cultural solution. Cultural colonialism mediates racial inferiority, culture replacing biology as the touchstone of racial definition. Accordingly, English was to be the language of administration, the local vernacular to be used only to convey rules and regulations to the local population. Far from "creating the conditions for the withering away of their rule,"[17] Mill (even if inadvertently) was instrumental in identifying and administering the sort of conditions that would perpetuate indirect rule, postcolonial control from afar without the attendant costs.

4

Mill's argument for benevolent despotism failed to appreciate that neither colonialism nor despotism is ever benevolent. Benevolence here is the commitment to seek the happiness of others.[18] But the mission of colonialism is exploitation and domination of the colonized generally, and Europeanization at least of those among the colonized whose class position makes it possible economically and educationally.[19] And the mandate of despotism, its conceptual logic, is to assume absolute power to achieve the ruler's self-interested ends. Thus colonial despotism could achieve the happiness of colonized Others only by imposing the measure of Europeanized marks of happiness upon the Other, which is to say, to force the Other to be less so. Mill's argument necessarily assumed superiority of the despotic, benevolent or not; it presupposed that the mark of progress is (to be) defined by those taking themselves to be superior; and it presumes that the ruled will want to be like the rulers even as the former lack the cultural capital (ever?) quite to rise to the task. Mill's ambivalence over the inherent inferiority of "native Negroes," event as he marked the transformation in the terms of racial definition historically from the inescapable determinism of blood and brain size to the marginally escapable reach of cultural determination, has resonated to this day in liberal ambivalence regarding racial matters.

Liberalism's racially mediated meliorism and commitment to a moral progressivism translates into an undying optimism that its racist history will be progressively overcome, giving way ultimately to a standard of nonracialism. Yet this standard nonracialism (sic) is imposed upon the body politic at the cost of the self-defined subjectivity of the traditionally dominated. Liberalism's response to matters of race in the face of the fact that race matters amounts to denying or ignoring race, paternalistically effacing a self-determined social subjectivity from those who would define themselves thus without imposing it on others. This erasure in the name of nonracialism rubs out at once the history of racist invisibility, domination, and exploitation, replacing the memory of an infantilized past with the denial of responsibility for radically unequal and only superficially deracialized presents. Divested of a historically located responsibility, the relatively powerful in the society are readily able to reinstate the invisibility of the subject positions of the presently marginalized: savages become the permanently unemployable, the uncivilized become crack heads, the lumpenproletariat the underclass, Distressed Needlewomen become sweated labor, poor Irish peasants turn into distressed defaulting family farmers and, well, "Niggers" become "Negroes" or blacks scarcely disguised beneath the seemingly benign nomenclature. For every Mill of yesteryear there is today a William Bennett or a Gary Becker, and for every Carlyle a Dinesh D'Souza.

Between Mill's "Negro" and Carlyle's "Nigger," then, lies the common thread of racist presumption and projection, bald and vicious on the one hand, polite and effete on the other, but both nevertheless insidious and odious. Better in utilitarian terms to have a Mill, perhaps, for at least one gets the sense that it is possible to enlighten and thus transform such a person. With a Carlyle one knows clearly and openly what resistance to racisms is up against, what it has to confront and in some circumstances to avoid; with a Mill, a promoter of abolition is at once a barrier to it. This exchange between two leading English public intellectuals of their day reveals in the final analysis, then, that structural and discursive transformations necessary for resisting racisms are deeply related to subjective expression. Ultimately, it makes abundantly apparent that a combined commitment to changing minds and to changing conditions is crucial.

Notes

1. August (1971). All parenthetical page references in the text are to this edition.
2. August includes in his little volume an editorial in a London newspaper of the day, *The Inquirer*, protesting Carlyle's claims.
3. This is Fanon's cutting characterization: (1970b), p. 79.
4. August (1971), p. xvii.
5. Laura Anne Stoler (1995).
6. John Stuart Mill (1990), p. 971.
7. Mill 1848, pp. 189–90.
8. Gyozo Fukuhara (1970), pp. 67–8.
9. Mill (1924), p. 72.
10. Mill (1977), p. 563.

11. See Bearce, Jr (1954); S. V. Pradhan (1976), p. 16.
12. Mill 1848, p. 749.
13. Mill 1852–3, pp. 313–4.
14. Mill 1852–3, pp. 324–5.
15. Cf. Pradhan (1976). p. 6.
16. Mill, quoted in Sharp (1920), p. 116. See Harris (1964), pp. 195ff.
17. Harris (1964), p. 201.
18. See Henry Sidgwick (1981), p. 239.
19. See Fanon (1970a), p. 17.

References

August, E. (ed.) 1971: *Carlyle, The Nigger Question and Mill, The Negro Question.* New York: Appleton Century Crofts.

Bearce, Jr, George D. 1954: John Stuart Mill and India. *Journal of the Bombay Branch of the Royal Asiatic Society*, 29, 5, 74–5.

Fanon, Frantz 1970a: *A Dying Colonialism.* London: Pelican Books.

Fanon, Frantz 1970b: *Black Skin White Masks.* London: Paladin.

Fukuhara, Gyozo 1959: "John Stuart Mill and the Backward Countries." *Bulletin of University of Osaka Prefecture.* Series D: Sciences of Economy, Commerce and Law, 3, 64–75.

Harris, Abraham L. 1964: John Stuart Mill: Servant of the English East India Company. *Canadian Journal of Economics and Political Science*, 30, 2 (May) 195ff, pp. 185–202.

Mill, J. S. 1924: *Autobiography.* Ed. Harold Laski. London: Longmans.

Mill, J. S. 1977: *Considerations on Representative Government*, pp. 371–577 In *Collected Works*, vol. 19, Essays on Politics and Society. Toronto: University of Toronto Press.

Mill, J. S. 1852–3: *Parliamentary Papers*, 30, 313–4.

Mill, J. S. 1900: *Principles of Political Economy.* London: Longmans.

Pradhan, S. V. 1976: Mill on India: A Reappraisal. *Dalhousie Review*, 56, 1 (Spring) 16, pp. 5–22.

Sharp, H. 1920: *Selections from Educational Records*, 1. (1781–1839) 116.

Sidgwick, Henry 1981: *The Methods of Ethics*, 7th edn. Indianapolis: Hackett.

Stoler, Laura Annel 1995: *Race and the Education of Desire.* Durham: Duke University Press.

CHAPTER 11

Heidegger and the Jewish Question: Metaphysical Racism in Silence and Word

BEREL LANG

Is a metaphysics of race more or less serious than a . . . biologism of race?
Jacques Derrida[1]

My title invites an immediate objection: why, this late in the day, return to the archaic formula of the "Jewish Question" – a phrase which on the rare occasions that we now encounter it almost always comes framed by the quotation marks of obsolescence? Put quite simply, there *is* no Jewish Question today, at least as the phrase at one time immediately and unmistakably brought to mind a single question about the Jews, evidently the one that mattered. To recall the currency of the Jewish Question in the nineteenth and the first half of the twentieth centuries is to establish the historical contrast, for during that time it appeared in a constant variety of linguistic and ideological appearances: as the *"Judenfrage"* that Marx and Herzl (agreeing on that one provocation) sought to answer; in the French of Bernard Lazare, the Hebrew of Ahad Ha'am, the English of Justice Brandeis – and by innumerable other writers in those or other languages: a common title or marker for both Jewish and non-Jewish writers, used without prejudice (at least *that* far) by philosemites and antisemites alike. The term or phrase was understood by anyone who thought about the Jews because there *was* a (that is, the) Jewish Question whose formulation was accepted by all sides however they disagreed after that: the question, that is, of how the Jews were to live among the nations – or, conversely, from the perspective of "nations," how the nations were to live with the Jews.

But the phrase and the Question itself have now lost that currency, and there are two main reasons for this displacement. The first of these explains the disappearance of the Jewish Question by claiming its resolution: the Jewish Question ceased to exist

205

– so the contention holds – because it was answered, in 1948, by the establishment of the state of Israel. With that event, Jews, wherever they were and willingly or no, entered a relationship with a country that resembled other countries in political definition; thus, the most obvious source – or cause – of the Jewish Question disappeared, and so also the Question itself. There *was* a Jewish country; Jews living outside it would accordingly be addressed in similar terms to those characterizing other people who had historical or ethnic ties to a nation other than the one they happened to inhabit. No longer was it a question for European or Asian or American governments of how to classify this group of people who until then, although insisting they were more than just a religion, had been unable to point to any other visible means of support. Governments understand governments; and so Jews around the world – Zionists, anti-Zionists, non-Zionists alike – benefited from the fact of Israel's existence, if only to the extent that they could stop hearing references to the Jewish Question. Even the fact that most Jews chose not to "return" to Israel was incidental; Israel was the answer to the Jewish Question as a *question* even if, for many Jews individually, it did not answer the question of how or where they should live individually, indeed even if the question itself had never occurred to them. (But then the Question had not been addressed to them as individuals either.)

Israel's existence, however, is only a partial (both incomplete and tendentious) explanation for the disappearance of the Jewish Question; it is one in any event that hardly touched Martin Heidegger one way or the other. Any scruples about that reaction, however, are slight when measured by Heidegger's response to the second reason for the obsolescence of the Jewish Question, which involved an event that occurred several years before the declaration of Israel's independence; like the Jewish Question itself, this event was named by having the definite article attached to a common, not a proper noun. I refer, of course, to "the Holocaust" and the stop *it* put to the Jewish Question. For in the aftermath of the Nazi genocide, it became clear to almost everyone that *now* to ask the traditional question of how Jews might live (or not) among the nations must be at least an occasion for embarrassment, at most, a moral offense. And this for the obvious reason that the answer the Nazis had proposed for the Question – how *they* thought to resolve it – disabled the Question itself; this was the case even though their intention was realized only in part. It was, after all, the Jewish Question as a question for which the "Final Solution" was designed as a solution – "*Frage*" eliciting "*Lösung*." And if it is unfair to ascribe responsibility for the answer given to a question to the question rather than to those who answer it, it is nonetheless evident that answers are not given unless questions make them possible; thus a necessary, if not a sufficient condition.

From this twofold perspective, furthermore, the genealogy of the Jewish Question, the sources of its history, appear no more mysterious than do the causes of its demise. It was the Enlightenment – or just as euphemistically from the viewpoint of Jewish history, the Emancipation – that made the Jewish Question a question; and it is the inheritors of the Enlightenment – we – who even at this distance, otherwise stirred by the inclusiveness of its fraternal principles, look back now with like measures of awe and disbelief at the conflicting answers that the Question evoked. To be sure, we are not obliged to decide exactly what we would have been willing to forego in the

Enlightenment in order to avoid a question to which the "Final Solution" was an answer – but the very possibility of such a connection casts a shadow both backward and forward: backward to the origins of the Jewish Question, forward to its present discussion as that has now to be justified retrospectively, through the framework of quotation marks.

The justification for recalling the Jewish Question here – that is, as the "Jewish Question" – begins in an expanded version of my title which discloses itself as a thesis: For Martin Heidegger, there was no Jewish Question retrospectively in the post-Holocaust era (when it would be the "Jewish Question"); and the reason for that absence is that there had been no Jewish Question for Heidegger even when the Question existed, that is, before the Holocaust.

The possible confusion of the two appearances of the Jewish Question in this thesis (once as the "Jewish Question," once as the Jewish Question)[2] will, I hope, be soon cleared up. Certainly the first appearance – the Jewish Question seen retrospectively, framed by quotation marks – can be rephrased in terms that are well known; these are the terms of Heidegger's post-Holocaust silence or, on the few occasions when he broke that silence, what was arguably still more evasive and in this sense no less "silent," the combination of what he omitted to say and of what, even in speaking, he formulated in unreachable abstraction – the refuge, in sum, that he found in obliqueness and avoidance. I shall elaborate on this representation mainly by reassembling here the now-familiar evidence of those few overt expressions of Heidegger's post-Holocaust response to the Holocaust as they serve to underscore his *more* overt – louder – silence.[3] The conclusion at which this evidence points is, at any rate, clear and concise: even after the Holocaust was over and its consequences known, fully in the public domain, Heidegger, who had met certain manifestations of the Holocaust at first hand and was well aware of many others, remained silent. There was for him no "Jewish Question," no issue of what it was that had happened to the Jews among the nations (not even within or at the hands of *his* nation),of why what happened to them happened or how to assess that occurrence in moral terms – or of what any of these implied for future conduct (including his own). In the thirty post-Holocaust and otherwise prolific years of his life, about these matters there was silence.

For many commentators, including some who find in Heidegger's writing during those thirty years the most valuable elements of his work, this silence is more troubling than anything Heidegger did or said while the Nazis (and for a year, he himself) were in power. Even the excuses sometimes made for this absence reflect the concession they more explicitly deny: lame and rhetorical, on the one hand ("what if he *had* spoken of Auschwitz? Would this change anything in our appreciation of other aspects of his work – except perhaps to make that work easier to ignore for those who wished to do so anyway?") – or, on the other hand, tendentious and unverifiable. ("His writing and lecturing after 1934 were through and through oppositional, he was speaking out virtually *all the time*; to see this, one has only to read him subtly, supply, correctly.")

Well, for the latter claim, there is the test of reading itself; for the former, the more accessible measure of common sense. And prior to either of these, the challenge posed by Heidegger's *ostensive* silence and the few interruptions of it that he ventured.

Together, it seems to me, these disclose the apologias that have been offered as specious, since in the end they are committed to denying that the silence was indeed silent notwithstanding the loud sound by which that silence announced itself. They are, moreover, also bound to ignore the evidence that provides an explanation of origins: if there was no silence, then there would be no reason why the silence occurred. And yet I should argue exactly the opposite: Heidegger's post-Holocaust silence mirrors – *follows* from – his silence before that. There was no "Jewish Question" after the Holocaust for Heidegger, in other words, not because of the Holocaust but because the Jewish Question had not existed for him before then either. Indeed, one might argue that it would have been factitious, in bad faith, for Heidegger to agree to a question in retrospect that he had earlier denied or ignored, at a time when it *was* real. And in fact – or so I would claim – he made no such pretense. Thus the fulcrum of my thesis overall is also the fulcrum of Heidegger's position: there was no Jewish Question for Heidegger even when the Jewish Question existed – and that is why there would also be no "Jewish Question" for him retrospectively, after the Holocaust marked a stopping point in the history of the Question.[4]

In this way, my second and conceptually more basic concern (to which the first, although later chronologically, serves as preface) reaches farther back historically, asking how it was that even when there was a Jewish Question, it did not exist for Heidegger. I provide a more detailed account of the latter point elsewhere,[5] but its general outline can be stated concisely: what precludes acknowledgment of the Jewish Question for Heidegger is the metaphysical status he ascribes to the concept of the "*Volk*" – and within that general concept, the privileged role he assigns specifically to the German *Volk* – in relation to Being (to both *Sein* and *Dasein*) and to Truth. As he construes the concept of the *Volk* in its history and destiny, there is, quite simply, no place for the Jews in Heidegger's thinking – not as a matter of prejudice (although also *that* was a part of his denial) but as a matter of categories. In establishing this, we also learn as much as we can about Heidegger's relation to the Jews (and by inversion, about Heidegger's relation to one central theme of Nazi Germany, its campaign against the Jews).

In this rejection of the Jewish Question and in the reconstruction that I do present here of Heidegger's denial, retrospectively, of the "Jewish Question," I shall be attending to what Heidegger did not say and what he might have said as much as to what he in fact did say; considering, that is, the matters he would have had to address if indeed the Jewish Question, early or late, existed for him. The two topics of "Heidegger and the 'Jewish Question'" and "Heidegger and the Jewish Question" can, I believe, be represented quite impersonally and even, up to a point, nonjudgmentally. Indeed, one might argue that this twofold formulation itself impedes any later assessment: supposing that he *did* deny or ignore the "Jewish Question" and/or the Jewish Question; well, what then? Surely there were many other questions (and "questions") that he (like any other writer) also failed to acknowledge; and surely no one can dictate to someone else the order of questions they "ought" to consider. Interests, to say nothing about caring or concern, cannot be commanded; why then call attention to either a "Question" or a Question that Heidegger, as it happened, chose not to ask?

But Heidegger cannot leave the room so easily or impersonally – for there remains yet another issue that makes its presence known just at the point where accounts of his denial of the Jewish Question – whatever interpretations they give that denial – end; namely, the matter of his antisemitism. To be sure, the importance of this matter should not be exaggerated. It is no doubt possible that the main theses asserted here – that there was no "Jewish Question" for Heidegger, and that this was the case because there had been for him no Jewish Question – could be sustained even if antisemitism were not uncovered as a later factor in the causal chain. In this sense, antisemitism is not necessary as an element in Heidegger's rejection of both the "Jewish Question" and the Jewish Question. (I suggest in fact that there had been no Jewish Question for Heidegger *first* because of his attitude toward the Germans, not toward the Jews.) But if – on independent grounds – there is *also* evidence of antisemitism in any of its traditional kinds, a philosophical circle would have been completed: there would then be a concrete ground in experience itself that motivated the denial of those two questions. There is, I believe, sufficient evidence of this, too – that is, of Heidegger's antisemitism.[6] And in this sense, his not-thinking about the Jewish Question (or about the Holocaust) appears as a form of thinking from the ground up, absence as denial, omission as assertion. Thus, a connection between "merely" psychological or personal dispositions – the minimal grounds of antisemitism – and philosophical reflection also announces itself as a factor in Heidegger's own history. Exactly how the two considerations of personal predisposition and theoretical reflection are related systematically – the logic of their relationship – is a separate issue; whatever position one takes on that issue in general, however, the *specific* conjunction in Heidegger speaks for itself.

There was then – thus part of my general thesis – no post-Holocaust "Jewish Question" for Heidegger, certainly nothing in or around the "Question" that he found worth talking about. The few intimations he gives of admitting even the possibility of that Question are oblique – subordinated to other, larger (in his view) concerns, or concluding, even when provoked by direct challenge, in denial; thus, their effect is to intensify rather than to overcome the silence. This absence cannot be attributed to a lack of information in or after 1945 or to the speed with which events moved around him: the nature and extent of the Nazi genocide against the Jews were widely known (the Nüremberg trials ensured the availability of this information if by unlikely chance other sources had failed), and Heidegger himself, with the leisure forced on him because of his (as it turned out, temporary) exclusion from the University of Freiburg as a result of the "denazification" hearings in 1945, if anything increased his already remarkable productivity during those and later years.

Even aside from such specific evidence, moreover, it seems impossible on prima facie grounds to find explanations for Heidegger's silence in ignorance or inadvertence. Unaware he *could* not have been; preoccupied he is unlikely to have been: is there evidence of any subject that Heidegger wished to write about but did not get around to? And since the act of "thinking" is a keystone in his own philosophical architectonic, there seems no alternative here to a conclusion of active rejection: Heidegger *refused* to think about the Holocaust, let alone to think it, with the refusal itself having been thought. (I echo here Hannah Arendt's tribute to Heidegger on his eightieth birthday:

"Heidegger never thinks 'about' something; he thinks something."[7]) What this amounts to, one might say, is an act of "post-meditation" at least equal in moral weight to what premeditation adds to other evidence of agency. (We could speak here of weight added to weight: The most extreme Holocaust-"revisionists" – Faurisson, Rassinier, Butz[8] – do not deny that *if* the Holocaust had occurred, it would have been a moral enormity warranting reflection and judgment; they only deny that it *did* occur. Heidegger does not deny that the Nazi genocide against the Jews took place – only that, having occurred, it does not warrant thinking or talking about.)

Let me first summarize the evidence for claiming that for Heidegger there was no "Jewish Question" – his view, that is, that there was nothing to be thought or said about the Holocaust as such, let alone as he himself stood in relation to it. Since the argument here claims Heidegger's deliberate or thoughtful refusal to think about the Holocaust, the primary evidence for this ought to appear in his most "thoughtful" work, that is, from his writings that would ordinarily be classified as philosophical rather than popular or public or personal.[9] To be sure, there occurs here the same problem of ambiguity that any claim to interpret "silence" encounters – not only of deciding whether or not the silence at issue (once *that* is demonstrated) was calculated and deliberate (it might be no more than an expression of indifference or ignorance), but then also, assuming such calculation, of determining what its rationale was. For silence is at least as ambiguous, certainly no less open to interpretation, as the spoken word: the silence of horror – announcing the unspeakable – posed against the silence of consent: silent agreement or even pleasure as an alternative to suffering in silence; at times (and this, I believe, has a special relevance to Heidegger and the Jewish Question) silence may come from a decision not to say what one has in mind – in contrast to the silence that reflects indifference or the absence of opinion. And there might of course be still other unspoken reasons that have to do less with the occasion of a particular silence than with the state of the respondent: psychic causality, after all, does not always mirror the connections of the external world. None of these possibilities can be ruled out a priori as explaining Heidegger's silence on the Holocaust, and although he himself would point us toward the last option mentioned (more of this below), I shall be claiming that it is the earlier and more substantive reasons that put their mark on his silence.

Again: the problem of interpreting Heidegger's silence does not depend only on either the fact or content of what he did not say, since he did mention or allude to the Holocaust on a few occasions. But these references, too, in the context of the whole, only reinforce the louder impression of silence. That is, Heidegger's silence becomes more intense because of what he says on the few occasions when he breaks it. Admittedly, the passages in question are as slight as they are well known (they are well known in part *because* they are so slight). It is not even certain, in fact, that some of them do refer to the Nazi genocide against the Jews – and we have then to qualify even these statements with a caveat: they come as close as Heidegger ever does to referring to the Holocaust in his formal writings or teaching. There are in fact but two such statements, from the second and third of the so-called Bremen Lectures (1949) respectively:

Agriculture is now a mechanized food industry, in essence the same as the manufacture of corpses in the gas chambers and extermination camps, the same as the blockade and starvation of the countryside, the same as the production of the hydrogen bombs.

And then:

Hundreds of thousands die en masse. Do they die? They perish. They are cut down. They become items of material available for the manufacture of corpses. Do they die? Hardly noticed, they are liquidated in extermination camps. And even apart from that, in China millions now perish of hunger.[10]

The lecture in which the first of these statements appeared was later revised and published as *"Die Frage nach der Technik"* ["The Question concerning Technology"]. In its later appearance the statement quoted here is radically emended;[11] the lecture in which the second statement appears (titled *"Die Gefahr"* – "The Danger") has not been published at all.

Especially the former reference has drawn comment for the likeness it finds between the mechanization of agriculture and the "manufacturing" of corpses. To be sure, the fact of that likeness is part of the point that Heidegger is asserting *against* one likely outcome (and, in his view, abuse) of technology. But even making allowance for this purpose does not relieve Heidegger of the onus which that statement imposes; namely, the moral disproportion between the two forms that he asserts are essentially alike. It is Heidegger himself who is asserting about the consequences of an abusive technology that there is to be found in them no essential difference between the mechanized food industry and extermination camps: the likeness is what *he* is claiming.

Now of course analogies are always possible; they can be drawn between *any* two objects or practices. But it is not this truism that is pertinent to Heidegger's words that have been cited but the fact that analogies are also open to evaluation. They are, after all, intended to make – to come to – a point, to establish continuity between two ostensibly and otherwise dissimilar things. Thus, any likeness proposed is meant to be a significant feature in each of the two things (or events or practices) compared – and that common feature is also required to warrant consideration in a larger context that finds the feature itself to be of consequence. And it is on both these points that Heidegger's comparison is open to challenge – as ignoring the overriding *difference* between the mechanization of farm labor (presumably for the purpose of raising food) and the mechanization of killing (in fact for the purpose of genocide) – as well as in the unmediated abstraction of the concept of technology that he both applies and finds in his analogy. A related objection applies to the second statement which is even loftier than the first in its reach for abstraction. The focus here is on what Heidegger distinguishes as two varieties of dying – the one referring to an individual and authentic process (where dying virtually becomes an *act*), the other ("perishing") which is done en masse, mechanically, something that has been "manufactured." The latter qualities Heidegger assigns to death in the "extermination camps" – implying that death in those circumstances has less character, is less real or genuine than it would be under the other conditions referred to. The distinction, as Heidegger asserts it, is *meant* to be invidious – and thus what is at issue here is the forced abstraction that Heidegger imposes on the concepts of death and technology: the distance assumed in his distinction between them as ideas and in practice.

Even putting aside certain literal-minded questions that bear on the two statements (why, for example, does Heidegger speak of "hundreds of thousands" dead in the extermination camps and "millions" in the famine of China? Is this a challenge to the supposed number of victims in the extermination camps? And which Chinese famine is he speaking of – or is the reference only a figure of speech? etc.), we return to the issue of their substance: what they leave out and what is left out around them as well as what they assert. Let us assume for the moment that these are indeed references to the genocide against the Jews (perhaps not only to that, but to that as well as to other instances of victimization; the vagueness is itself part of what is being asserted): is it that all the groups of victims are alike? Is it that in respect to what is being asserted the groups of victims are "in essence" alike? But what does it mean to claim this and then not to consider the question of how those victims came to be victims, of who they were, and still more incisively, who *made* victims of them? Even in the unlikely event that all the victims indeed were "in essence" alike, these questions would not yet have been answered or even articulated. A reader of the two passages who did not know that Heidegger had written them after living through, in, the twelve years of Nazi rule, might reasonably imagine their author as inhabiting a distant land, perhaps in another age, as having at most second- or third-hand knowledge of the events he refers to, and caring (at most) academically about their histories (including the question of responsibility, of *whose* extermination camps they were: for all we know – and revisionist historians would later make just this claim[12] – there would be little or nothing to distinguish the Nazi death camps from Stalin's Gulag, with the latter even serving as a provocation and model for the former).

This is indeed as close as Heidegger comes to the "Jewish Question" in his formal writings from 1945 on. And few references can be added to this brief list even if one moves beyond the "Jewish Question" to the Nazi regime as a whole, whose crimes extended, after all, to millions of non-Jews, including tens of thousands of German non-Jews. There is, of course, the widely cited passage in the *Introduction to Metaphysics* (first presented as lectures in 1935, published in 1953) in which Heidegger speaks of "the inner truth and greatness of this movement [i.e., National Socialism]."[13] The dispute over whether the parenthetical comment that in the 1953 text immediately qualifies the claim of Nazism's "inner truth and greatness" ("namely, the encounter between planetary technology and modern man") was or was not present in the original version[14] hardly seems to matter. Indeed, it could be argued that the parenthetical phrase underscores the willful and malicious abstraction that the other phrase would represent if it appeared by itself. Certainly the two, taken together, have the effect of articulating the *specific* memory that Heidegger would transmit of National Socialism, bring into the post-Holocaust present; the feature of Nazism that it approvingly recalls – Nazism's solution to the "technology-question" – is apparently sufficient to justify omitting reference to everything else that occurred in the course of National Socialism. Those other events or acts are by implication reduced to accidents or mistakes,

212

the merely "external." Thus, National socialism is to be remembered for its potential "greatness" on the overriding issue of technology – and then also, regretfully, for its failure to realize that potential, to make external its "inner" truth. Once again, then, silence about the "Jewish Question."

But there remain the putatively non-philosophical writings or statements as well, those which are more informal (whether they were initially conceived with an eye to publication, as in the case of the *Spiegel* interview) – or not (as in Heidegger's letter to Herbert Marcuse). These too, after all, are statements in which Heidegger has a specific opportunity to address the "Jewish Question" and once again declines to, or comes so close to declining to as only, once again, to underscore that impression. I add this last qualifying clause specifically in reference to his response to Herbert Marcuse who in the opening letter of his post-War correspondence with Heidegger (August 28, 1947) challenged the latter's silence about Nazism in general and about the "Jewish Question" in particular (". . . You are still identified with the Nazi regime [that . . . killed millions of Jews – merely because they were Jews]. Many of us have long awaited a statement from you . . . that would clearly and finally free you from such identification. . . .").[15] To this formulation of the "Jewish Question" Heidegger then responds (January 20, 1948):

> To the serious legitimate charges that you express "about a regime that murdered millions of Jews . . ." I can merely add that if instead of "Jews" you had written "East Germans", then the same holds true for one of the allies, with the difference that everything that has occurred since 1945 has become public knowledge, while the bloody terror of the Nazis in point of fact had been kept a secret from the German people.[16]

Heidegger's reference here to the "bloody terror of the Nazis" is, I believe, the strongest expression of condemnation to appear in his writings, public or private; this, together with his acknowledgment of the "legitimate" charges Marcuse had made in respect to the millions of Jews murdered, accounts for the qualification in my own comment above, about the *"virtual"* (not complete) silence he maintained even in the face of Marcuse's direct challenge.

It may be objected that the words of Heidegger thus cited deserve more credit than I grant them, that they *do* break the silence. And had they appeared by themselves and without qualification, I would agree. But the context in which they are set makes a crucial difference to the force of the words. In his own subsequent response to Heidegger, Marcuse contends that to equate what the Nazis had done to the Jews with the fate of the the East Germans after the War's end (presumably on the responsibility of the Russians) raises the question of how "a conversation between men is even possible" – and to assess that equation more than forty-five years later can hardly lead to any other response. Should we say rather that in conceding the "Jewish Question" Heidegger was only adding to it an "East German" Question? But then we would still have to ask what the "Jewish Question" amounts to if Heidegger is instructing us to view it in the same terms as the expulsion of Germans from the East (the issue, obviously, is not about justifying the latter, but about its *equation* to genocide). One way to attempt to make something disappear is to place it – like a grain of sand in the desert – in the midst of a mass of supposed likeness; this is how Heidegger makes the "Jewish Question" invisible for himself and so sustains the silence. The collective *murder* of the Jews is bluntly equated with the deportation of the ethnic German populace – and it is Heidegger's emphasis on this *as* an equation that leads Marcuse to his claim that there could be little else to speak about with someone for whom no difference was evident there. One proof of antisemitism, after all, is the failure to recognize it when it occurs; in some cases, this failure may loom as large as the act itself.

Two other documents add significantly to our assessment of Heidegger's post-Holocaust stance; unlike his letter to Marcuse, Heidegger formulated these with the understanding that they would eventually be published, and this fact, together with the issues they address, places them on the boundary between Heidegger's personal or informal discourse and his more professional writings. The first of these – a memorandum written in 1945 and then given to his son, Herman Heidegger, for use as he saw fit – was not published until 1983; the second – the *Spiegel* interview – was recorded in 1966 and then published, in accordance with Heidegger's stipulation, after his death, in 1976.[17] The two statements are autobiographical in character; they are evidently intended to represent Heidegger's own view of his Nazi associations, partly in response to the charges made against him about those associations, partly as a more general reflection on that period of his life which began – formally, at least – with his assumption of the Rectorship of the University of Freiburg in April, 1933.

Here again, our interest in the two statements which speak also of other matters is with the "Jewish Question." Both are "post-Holocaust," written after the Jewish Question had encountered the "Final Solution." And also on these two occasions which are intended specifically to reflect on and even to judge the past, Heidegger meets the "Jewish Question" with silence. This does not mean that he does not utter the words "Jewish" or "Jew": he does – six times in more than forty pages of printed text, four of these times in citing by its informal title the "*Judenplakat*" or "Jewish Notice" (whose message was "*Juden nicht erwunscht*" – "Jews not wanted"), the other two occasions as the terms pertain to single events or persons, not to the Jewish Question. So in the *Spiegel* interview, he mentions the "so-called Jewish Notice" which his predecessor as Rector had refused to post and to which, he emphasizes, he added his own refusal (although not, as he leaves unmentioned, his refusal to enforce what it proclaimed: it is as if he is here concerned with what is *posted* on University walls more than on the policy advocated by the Notice itself);[18] he denies the charge that had been made against him of having removed books by Jewish authors from the Philosophy Library; in response to a question asked by his interviewers about his Jewish students, he speaks of one student (Helene Weiss), who, when she later received her doctorate from Basel ("this was no longer possible at Freiburg"), included an acknowledgment to Heidegger; he avoids a direct answer to the question of how the breach between him and Karl Jaspers developed, although denying that it occurred (only?) because of Jaspers' Jewish wife; he offers an explanation on philosophical grounds for the end of his relationship with his one-time teacher Husserl and a confession of "human failing" in having ignored him and the Husserl household at the time of Husserl's last illness and death (1938), for which, he says, he subsequently apologized to Husserl's widow (a claim that she herself subsequently disputed).

Heidegger makes other references to National Socialism in general, but the allusions mentioned are the only ones to the terms "Jew" or "Jewish" – and in neither the former *nor* the latter references as they together constitute what we might think of as Heidegger's "Last Will and Testament" concerning the "Jewish Question" – his last words (or silence) on the subject – is there the glimmering of a general reflection on the consequences of the policies of National Socialism for the Jewish Question or of his own relation to those policies. Admittedly, his interlocuters do not force that issue, although they question at some length Heidegger's general views on other topics, including the "condition of the world." Even after they remind Heidegger of his extraordinary assertion in 1933 that "the Führer and he alone *is* the present and future German reality and its law" (does any statement ever made by a serious philosopher – whether off-duty or on-duty – approach this usurpation of metaphysics by ideology?),[19] they do not question his rejoinder that these words appeared in a "local Freiburg student paper," that as Rector he knew he would have to make certain "compromises," that he "would not write those words today [1966!]" and that already in 1934 he "did not say them."

In "The Rectorat 1933/34: Facts and Thoughts," the document that he entrusted to his son, Herman, Heidegger also alludes to his resistance to posting the "Jewish Notice" and mentions the spontaneous silence with which a group of which he was part responded to a lecture on race by a Nazi official.[20] He mentions at some length his Rectoral Address of 1934 and other more professional writings from the same period and after his resignation as Rector, emphasizing what he alleges was the hostile reaction to them by Nazi orthodoxy. (That alleged reaction bears a considerable weight here and elsewhere in his apologia, as apparently intended to demonstrate the *difference* between him and other Nazis, a difference which Nazi officialdom itself thus supposedly recognized.) But once again, about the "Jewish Question" either during the 1933/34 period he is specifically considering or in its subsequent outcome, nothing more than what has been indicated.

One last document that has quasi-official standing should be cited here – this in a letter, dated November 4, 1945, in which Heidegger requested of the then Rector of the University of Freiburg his own reinstatement to the faculty. This personal formulation has a more specific purpose than the other two cited above in the second category I have distinguished, and perhaps this makes the absence of any general reference in it to the "Jewish Question" less egregious. In fact he calls attention here as he does not in the others to his early (and presumably continuing) dissent from the orthodox version of Nazi biological racism. Glossing a passage in the Rectoral Address which asserts that "The greatness of a *Volk* is guaranteed by its spiritual world values," he contends that "For those who know and think, these sentences express my opposition to Rosenberg's conception, according to which, conversely, spirit and the world of spirit are merely an 'expression' . . . of racial facts and of the physical constitution of man;" in a later passage of this same letter, he reiterates his (then) opposition to "the dogmatism and primitivism of Rosenberg's biologism."[21] As I argue elsewhere and contrary to what has often been held (including by Heidegger himself), this passage or others in the same spirit do not by themselves defuse the charge of antisemitism against Heidegger – since even for Nazi antisemitism and certainly for the older traditions of antisemitism, its biological ground was only one of its constitutive elements. More-over (and this too requires more elaboration than can be given it here), Heidegger's endorsement in these passages of the principle of the *Volk* on spiritual grounds reflects a basic and consistent line in his thinking, one which is in the end responsible, I would argue, for his denial of the Jewish Question even at a time when the Question itself was quite real. Also in this same context, his emphasis is on the alleged reaction of the Nazi hierarchy to his views, not to the consequences that followed historically from the Nazi concept of the "*Volk*" of which the biological ground was but one, albeit an important, element and to whose *other* grounds, the evidence shows, Heidegger himself was fully committed.

In other words, Heidegger here identifies antisemitism in *one* of its major strands; that is, as rooted in biological racism which defined Jewish identity as a genetic trait. And certainly this view of Jewish identity was held by some, although by no means all, members of the Nazi hierarchy (most prominently by Hitler himself). In pointing to his own rejection of *this* justification of antisemitism as exonerating him from *all* charges of antisemitism, however, Heidegger – whether consciously or not – it's difficult to know which would be more objectionable – ignores both the no less common source of what might be called "cultural antisemitism" and the much more basic source of what I call here "metaphysical" antisemitism. The evidence of Heidegger's cultural antisemitism closely resembles its other common manifesta-tions: the identification of the Jews as rootless, identified with the rise at once of capitalism (and urbanization) and socialism – all of which Heidegger persistently criticized, although without adding anything new to those quite conventional anti-semitic claims.

By contrast, his "metaphysical racism," although it too has historical precedents, bears his distinctive mark. For it is here that Heidegger at once establishes the concept of the "*Volk*" as something more than an empirical category: not merely reflecting geo-graphical location or even linguistic identity (although the German language, in his view, together with Greek affords a privileged opening to Being), but as a transhis-torical entity – one which seems more fundamental than the predicates attributed to individual persons or to *Dasein*. "The uppermost rung of Being will be attained if a *Volkisch* principle, as something determinative, is brought into place for historical *Dasein*."[22] Just how Heidegger establishes the role he ascribes to the "*Volk*" or the pri-ority he ascribes to the *German Volk* cannot be fully addressed here. So far as either the Jewish Question or the "Jewish Question" is concerned, however, what is crucial in these terms is that the Jews who, as he conceived of them, do not qualify as a *Volk* then – having been denied its benefits – are also less than equal to other groups which *have* achieved that status. (It is not that Heidegger provides a full list of those who are and are not, but he is clear both about some that do qualify and others that do not.) To be sure, this kind of racial (that is, racist) hierarchy might be interpreted as simply an instance of bad (empirical) science. But it is evident that Heidegger does not *think* that he is "doing" science in his elaboration of the concept or the rankings of the *Volk*. At least he no more thinks of that as empirically or scientifically grounded than he does of such other basic categories for him as *Sein* or *Dasein*.

There may be other documents in the second category of evidence (i.e., of "public" – vs. professional – writings or personal letters written by Heidegger himself) that I have missed or that will yet become known (almost certainly the still-closed Heidegger archives at Marbach include material in this category). But both in what they say and what they omit, the documents mentioned seem sufficient, when added to the more strictly "philosophical" statements, to justify the claim that for Heidegger, the "Jewish Question" – that is, the Jewish Question seen through the lens of the Holocaust – did not exist.

An objection might be raised to this summary of the evidence concerning "Heidegger and the 'Jewish Question'" that combines two points of his previously cited defense or apologia. The first point echoes Heidegger himself, contending that much of his philosophical writing was oppositional, posed against Nazi doctrine, even if it did not say *that* explicitly. This is, again, his own explication of his (implied) rejection in the Rectoral Address of Rosenberg's biological racism; in the same letter (1945) in which he asks for reinstatement at the University, he recalls his writing and lecturing on Nietzsche also as a gesture of dissent:

> It is unjust to assimilate Nietzsche to National Socialism, an assimilation which – apart from what is essential – ignores his hostility to anti-Semitism and his positive attitude with respect to Russia. But on a higher plane, the debate with Nietzsche's metaphysics is a debate with nihilism as it manifests itself with increased clarity under the political form of fascism.[23]

Again, the detail of this passage raises questions about what constitutes a defense (Heidegger never, early *or* late, disguised his antagonism to communism and Russia; thus his work on Nietzsche represented no retraction on *that* count. Why then should we believe that Nietzsche's attacks on antisemitism were an aspect of Nietzsche's writing that Heidegger demonstrated approval of by emphasizing Nietzsche's more general significance?) But more importantly: Even if one accepts Heidegger's construal of his own writings as tacitly oppositional, the evidence he adduces for this comes from the period of Nazi rule itself. If, however, he understandably felt obliged at *that* time to write obliquely – in effect joining the philosophical tradition that Leo Strauss characterizes under his title of "Persecution and the Art of Writing"[24] – he faced no similar danger after the War's end when he openly called his audience's attention to his earlier opposition. Why, one might ask in this connection, if he had earlier lectured tacitly in opposition, did he not speak out explicitly in the new present, during the thirty years of productive writing when he faced no such threat of punishment or censure? (And this, of course, leaves out the question of how much weight to attach to Heidegger's reading of his own texts; in fact, his glosses on his own writing seem at times no less contestable than certain of his glosses on other writers.)

The second point joining this first one is in its own terms imponderable; this is (again) the question of how silence is to be interpreted. For even if we provisionally accept the thesis I have been asserting – that after taking into account everything Heidegger says explicitly about the "Jewish Question," we find that this amounts to a denial, in effect to silence — there remains the fact that silence is itself ambiguous, that it may represent a variety of motives or principles. What, in other words, do we know even if we agree that for Heidegger there *was* no "Jewish Question?" The finding that he does not confront the "Question" does not mean by itself that he denied or chose to exclude it: the issue might more simply not have occurred to him — or he might have avoided it not because of what *it* entailed, but because in addressing it, he would have been obliged to speak on other matters that he preferred to avoid.

I have already suggested that we can usefully advance on these issues by considering those moments, public or private, when intimations of the "Jewish Question" do in fact arise for him; a number of these moments we have considered, and I have argued that they too affirm the predominant silence. An important additional source is to look at what Heidegger *was* thinking and writing about *other* questions (or even "questions"). He was not, after all, silent through and through; he spoke and wrote largely and widely — and surely the absence of some one matter or question can often be understood by seeing what else *was* present. We might find in these other words, for example, a basis for his exclusion of what is excluded — or we might find there a clue which forces us to revise our sense of that exclusion. In any event, silence by itself, here as elsewhere, is inconclusive.

Well, perhaps. And indeed in explaining elsewhere how Heidegger's silence on the Jewish Question is a source for his silence on the "Jewish Question," I make broader reference to what Heidegger *was* saying at the same time that he was not speaking about these topics. It is certainly arguable, in any event, that the more crucial test of Heidegger's views will be there, in the pre-Holocaust texts, without the pressure that his knowledge of history (of both Nazi history and his own history) then inevitably exerted on what he was saying by indirection. Putting those earlier references aside, however, one might grant all the possibilities mentioned and yet insist that the nature of what is absent must weigh heavily *no matter what* else is or may yet by said — that is, no matter how the silence is framed or hedged. When Heidegger writes in his letter to Marcuse, that "a confession after 1945 was impossible for me, because the Nazi partisans announced their change of allegiance in the most loathsome way; and I, however, had nothing in common with them," we have some idea of what he saw as his own motives for silence. Presumably, if he had spoken against the genocide against the Jews (as against any other Nazi crime), he might have been misunderstood as identifying himself with those other "partisans" who had none of the solid basis for a commitment to "true" Nazism that he had; they could much more easily deny their earlier allegiance because for them the allegiance itself had been easier, more superficial. Yet even if we accept Heidegger's contention here as credible, a question forces itself forward that is at least as obvious as the ground that Heidegger claims for himself. Is it not true that about *some* matters the risk of silence outweighs the risk of being misunderstood or misrepresented? But also about the latter question, Heidegger is silent. He is evidently willing to run the risk of silence, whatever the consequences — and since he implies also this claim in silence, we can only speculate about whether he recognized the risk of silence as a risk at all. It is at least possible — *probable*, I would contend — that for him the loss would be entirely on the other side. That is, only if he were to break the silence; that is, to speak.

Notes

1. Jacques Derrida, *Of Spirit: Heidegger and the Question*, tr. G. Bennington and R. Bowlby (Chicago: University of Chicago Press, 1989), p. 74.

2. The issues raised here have seemed to have evoked a "rhetoric of quotation marks": so, for example, Jean-François Lyotard's *Heidegger and "the Jews"*, tr. Andreas Michel and Mark S. Roberts (Minneapolis: University of Minnesota Press, 1990), and Derrida's Of Spirit, in which the analysis revolves around the difference between Heidegger's references to "*Geist*" and to "*Geist*" respectively are obvious precedents. To be sure, the issues at stake in these several accounts (and in mine) differ significantly – also on the question of what conclusions follow from the several uses of quotation marks.

3. At least at the most obvious and explicit level of that silence, there is little disagreement about the fact itself which has been the focus of numerous discussions. (Cf., e.g., Derrida, *Of Spirit*; Victor Farias, *Heidegger and Nazism* (Philadelphia: Temple University Press, 1989; Luc Ferry and Alain Renaut, *Heidegger et les Modernes* (Paris: Grasset, 1988); "Symposium on Heidegger and Nazism," ed. Arnold Davidson, *Critical Inquiry*, XV (1989), pp. 407–88; Gunther Neske and Emil Kettering, *Martin Heidegger and National Socialism*, tr. Lisa Harries (New York: Paragon House, 1990). What subsequently divides the accounts of Heidegger's silence, of course, is the question of what elements constitute that silence and how they are to be interpreted.

4. For purposes of the account given here, I set the date of the dividing line – between pre- and post-Holocaust – at 1945. Obviously, the Holocaust had been going on during the four years before that; I use the 1945 date because after Germany's formal surrender not only did the systematic extermination cease, but there can also be no doubt of Heidegger's awareness of the occurrence and extent of the genocide against the Jews.

5. In "Heidegger and the Jewish Question," in *Heidegger's Silence* (Ithaca: Cornell University Press, 1996).

6. This evidence has a positive form – in statements by Heidegger himself (e.g., his denunciation in *1929* of the "*Verjudung*" ["Jewification"] of German culture; cf. Ulrich Sieg, "Die Verjudung des deutschen Geistes," *Die Zeit*, December 22, 1989, p. 50, and in statements reported by others (his reference, according to Karl Jaspers, to the "dangerous international fraternity of Jews" (Karl Jaspers, "Philosophical Autobiography," in P. A. Schilp (ed.), *The Philosophy of Karl Jaspers*, 2nd edn (LaSalle, Ill.: Open Court, 1981,) p. 75). And it has a negative form – in Heidegger's denials, for example, in his own variation on the cliché that "Some of my best friends [for him, students] are [i.e, were] Jews." A more significant (because less persuasive) version of his denial of antisemitism is the emphasis he puts on his rejection of biological racism – as though by this rejection, the charge of antisemitism would be conclusively refuted. (So, for example, his own reading of his Rectoral Address.) That the pre-Darwinian history of antisemitism *and* Nazi antisemitism reflected numerous sources and themes quite independent of genetic theory was something that he evidently was unwilling to consider.

7. Hannah Arendt, "For Martin Heidegger's Eightieth Birthday," reprinted in Neske and Kettering, *Martin Heidegger*, p. 210.

8. See Robert Faurisson, *Memoir en defense* (Paris: La Vieille Taupe, 1980); Paul Rassinier, *Drame des juifs européens* (Paris: Les Sept Couleurs, 1964); Arthur Butz, *The Hoax of the Twentieth Century* (Torrance, CA: Noontide Press, 1977).

9. I introduce this distinction provisionally and for the sake of argument – mainly because it would be easier (if the evidence warranted this) to take it back or overrule it later than to

introduce it for the first time retroactively. The distinction represents in itself a substantive issue: what *is* the relation between Heidegger's "public" or exoteric statements and his more deliberately and technically philosophical texts? That the two were (at least at times) intended for different audiences (and thus, presumably, for different "implied readers") suggests an obvious point of difference – but neither this nor other stylistic factors entails incongruity or a sharp discontinuity between the two forms (although this position has been proposed, most radically by Richard Rorty). I believe to the contrary that the stylistic and substantive evidence argues for continuity and indeed often identity between the two forms; but since that is rather a separate issue from the central one raised here, I treat the evidence in the two categories separately (although the distinction is very sharp even when one *tries* to sustain it).

10. Quotations taken from "Bremen Vorträge," in Martin Heidegger, *Gesamtausgabe*, vol. 79 (Frankfurt am Main: Klostermann, 1994).

11. "Agriculture is now the mechanized food industry. Air is now set upon to yield nitrogen, the earth to yield ore, ore to yield uranium, for example; uranium is set upon to yield atomic energy, which can be released either for destruction or for peaceful use" ("The Question Concerning Technology," in *The Question Concerning Technology and Other Essays*, tr. William Lovitt (New York: Harper & Row, 1977)).

12. Cf. Ernst Nolte, *Das Vergehen der Vergangenheit: Antwort an meinen Kritiken in sogenannten Historikerstreit* (Frankfurt: Ullstein, 1987).

13. *An Introduction to Metaphysics* (New Haven: Yale University Press, 1959), p. 199.

14. If it was not – and the balance of evidence seems to point in that direction (see Rainer Martin, "Ein rassistisches Konzept von Humanität," in *Badische Zeitung*, December 19–20, 1987; see also Fred Dallmayr, "Heidegger and Politics," in *The Heidegger Case*, eds Tom Rockmore and Joseph Margolis (Philadelpha: Temple University Press, 1992), p. 292) – then there seems no alternative to assessing Heidegger's claims to the contrary (in the *Spiegel* interview) at least as mistaken and at most as a lie. For the present discussion, at any rate, the parenthetical expression is no less significant in respect to Heidegger's silence than the assertion about National Socialism would be if it appeared *without* the parentheses.

15. Reprinted in Richard Wolin, *The Heidegger Controversy* (Cambridge, MA: MIT Press, 1992), p. 161.

16. For the Heidegger – Marcuse Correspondence, see Farias, *Heidegger and Nazism*, pp. 283–7.

17. The 1945 memorandum, together with Heidegger's Rectoral address of 1933, was published as "The Rectorate 1933/34: Facts and Thoughts," tr. Karsten Harries, *Review of Metaphysics*, 38 (March, 1985), pp. 481–502. The *Spiegel* interview appeared under the title "Nor noch ein Gott Karn was retten" in *Der Spiegel*, May 31, 1976. Heidegger gave a television interview after the *Speigel* interview, on the occasion of his eightieth birthday (broadcast on September 24, 1969), but in the preparatory discussion for that interview, he made clear to Richard Wisser, the interviewer, that he would not address questions concerning his own political past or, by implication, about the Nazi period more generally. (He mentions to Wisser that these are taken up in the *Spiegel* interview.) See Richard Wisser, "Afterthoughts and Gratitude," in Neske and Kettering, *Martin Heidegger*, pp. 89–124.

18. The "Law for the Restoration of the Professional Civil Service," which called for the expulsion of the Jewish faculty, had been issued before Heidegger took office; thus he knew what he would be obliged to implement. This task was made easier because a number of Jewish faculty had been forced out of the University before he became Rector (cf. Hugo Ott, *Martin Heidegger: Unterwegs zu seiner Biographie* (Frankfurt: Campus Verlag, 1988), p. 171).

19. The statement appeared in the *Freiburger Studentenzeitung*, November 3, 1933, as part of an appeal by Heidegger as Rector for student support of Hitler's withdrawal of Germany from

the League of Nations in the November 12 plebiscite on that matter. It is perhaps about these lines that Heidegger, in his letter to Marcuse, writes: "A few sentences in [the statement] I regard today as a slip ["*Entgleisung*"]. That is all."

20. Farias gives a conflicting account of that meeting. See Farias, *Heidegger and Nazism*, p. 131.
21. Cited in Wolin, *The Heidegger Controversy*, pp. 62, 64.
22. *Beiträge zur Philosophie*, in *Gesamtausgabe*, vol. 65 (Frankfurt am Main: Klostermann, 1988), pp. 42–3.
23. Letter to Rector of University of Freiburg, November 4, 1945; cited in Wolin, *The Heidegger Controversy*, p. 64.
24. In Leo Strauss, *Persecution and the Art of Writing* (Glencoe, Ill.: Free Press, 1952). Heidegger himself does not make this association – either with the tradition or with Strauss.

CHAPTER 12

Sartre on American Racism[1]

JULIEN MURPHY

Jean-Paul Sartre, the famous French existentialist, visited America twice at the end of the War and was a sharp critic of American racism. His most famous writing on the topic was his play *The Respectful Prostitute* (1946). This play, his only one set in America, was about a racial lynching motivated by a trumped-up race charge. Sartre is believed to have based his play on the famous Scottsboro case in which two white prostitutes accused nine black men of raping them on a freight train traveling through Alabama in 1931. The nine men were sentenced to death for criminal assault and though one of the women issued a retraction and the Supreme Court twice rejected the verdict, the men were not freed for many years (Carter, 1969, Goodman, 1994).

The Respectful Prostitute is Sartre's most famous, but not his only, condemnation of America racism. In his first trip here in 1945, he was part of a group of French journalists invited by the US State Department and flown around the country on a B52 bomber. Sartre was sponsored by two French newspapers, *Le Figaro* and *Combat*. He returned to America on his own for several months in 1946 to visit friends he had met here and supported himself by writing for a number of American literary magazines. Although his travel writings during his 1945 and 1946 visits were generally about white America, he did notice and was shocked by the extent of segregation and the situations of black Americans.[2] He wrote two articles on race for *Le Figaro* in 1945 that remain untranslated, "Le quie j'ai appris du problème noir" (1945a) that contained a biting indictment of American racism, so harsh that one biographer called it a "declaration of war" (Cohen-Solal, 1987), and "Le problème noir aux États-Unis" (1945b), where he describes racism in terms of the proletarian culture. During this time, Sartre also began a philosophical essay, "Revolutionary Violence," on the evolution of racist consciousness beginning with slavery for his promised *Ethics*. A short excerpt appears as "Le Noir et le Blanc aux États-Unis," in *Combat* (1949). As is evident from the titles of his French newspaper writings, Sartre's focus was primarily on anti-black racism.[3]

While Sartre took up the topic of American racism in the late 1940s as part of his responsibility to speak out against injustice in his writing, he did not give it the sort of attention that it deserved. There is no sustained analysis of American racism like that of anti-Semitism found in *Anti-Semite and Jew*, also published in 1946. It is somewhat disheartening to know that, while it is in this period that America figured most prominently in his work, (he also published work by Richard Wright in his journal *Les Temps Modernes* (1946), and the same year devoted a special issue of the journal to the United States), his writings on race are scant and largely undeveloped. His piece on revolutionary violence is unfinished and was posthumously published as an Appendix to his *Notebooks for an Ethics* (1992). There is hardly any mention of racism in his other writings about America that he published during this time. There is no record of his public criticism apart from his newspaper pieces for the French press that, despite Sartre's growing popularity in America, were largely ignored by the American press. Although well known, his play is short, not regarded as particularly well written, and seldom performed after its initial debut; it became his public statement for Americans on racism. Little wonder that scholars have largely ignored Sartre's responses to American racism during the late 1940s.[4]

In order to construct Sartre's views of race relations in America, we need to piece his views of racism in *The Respectful Prostitute* together with comments about race in his newspaper writing, his unfinished political essay, "Revolutionary Violence," and a related political essay, "Materialism and Revolution" (1955a). When taken together, his views about American race relations privilege a class analysis. In this paper I will argue that Sartre is guilty of what I call *class profiling* in his early writings on American racism. The term, "class profiling" borrows its meaning in part from a related term, *racial profiling*, prevalent in American practices of suspect identification in law enforcement. Racial profiling uses race as a major clue to criminality. It involves not merely building race into the composite of criminal suspects, but making race the primary characteristic of suspect profiles. Recent attention has been paid to race-based profiling practices of police officers who assume that people of color are more likely to be criminals than are whites. In police districts where race profiling is practiced, people of color are stopped much more frequently than whites in order for police to search for criminal suspects and illegal drugs.[5] By "class profiling" we mean prioritizing class over all other factors, including race, gender, and ethnicity.

Certainly, class is an important feature of any analysis of racism, but it should not eclipse non-economic factors. Sartre treats racism, for the most part, as just another form of class struggle. Sartre notices and emphasizes class in his writings to emphasize class struggle and critique classism. For him, class oppression is the dominant form of oppression. By prioritizing the material conditions of black Americans, their proletarian status, over other dimensions of racism for the sake of solidarity between black and white workers, he obfuscated the specificity of race and its influence on material conditions, minimizing its effects while favoring a socialist revolution. We see evidence of Sartre's emphasis on class over race first in his famous American play, secondly, in his travel writings for American magazines and French newspapers during his visits here, and thirdly, in his political philosophy written during this period.

The American Play

The Respectful Prostitute was first performed here in 1948, two years after its French opening. It was quite controversial. Its successful New York run garnered it votes for the Critics Circle Award for the best foreign play of the year.[6] Critics were shocked by its topic of lynching, its anti-American sentiments, and sexual material. After New York, it was scheduled to open in Chicago, but censors in the city's government temporarily banned the play. They claimed it was immoral and feared it "would disturb racial relationship" and bring protests from black leaders. In fact, the National Association for the Advancement of Colored People (NAACP) supported the play. The American Civil Liberties Union (ACLU) also came to Sartre's defense and the ban was eventually lifted. Still, police were ordered to the opening (*New York Times*, 1948a,b, 1949, Calta, 1949a,b). Even the original French production in 1946 had led to complaints and calls for censorship. French critics feared Sartre was showing disloyalty to their American Allies. They claimed that Sartre's play was "a gross defamation of American democracy" and that he had "abused American hospitality" (Brown, 1946). Others claimed that Sartre had no business writing about an American problem in the first place, or after spending such a short time here, and having been hosted by the American government. These criticisms were neutralized by the endorsement of a famous black American writer, Richard Wright (Fleurent, 1946). Knowing that race was an explosive issue, Sartre took political risks with his emerging status as a major playwright and philosopher in writing the play.

The Respectful Prostitute borrows heavily from Sartre's American experiences. It is a story of racial violence and an alleged rape on a train and features a velvet-tongued Southern Senator Clarke, based in part on the powerful and racist Senator Theodore G. Bilbo. The play is about the efforts of a prominent family to free their son from punishment for killing a black man. The family accomplishes this by coercing a white prostitute, Lizzie McKay, to give false testimony. Sartre uses the play to depict the complexities of racism, including prolonged effects of institutional racism, for ordinary people. We see this in his construction of the plot. In the play, Thomas, a young white industrialist from a prominent family, and three friends board a train drunk after a football game and start a fight with two black men whom they feel do not belong on "their" train. Lizzie McKay, a white prostitute from the North, is riding the same train to relocate to a small Southern town. She sees the fight and sees Thomas pull out a pistol and kill one of the black men. The other black man escapes. In the opening scene, he finds Lizzie's new apartment and shows up there pleading with her to save his life. Thomas's cousin Fred, already at Lizzie's, having hired her for sexual services the night before, and Fred's father, the distinguished Senator Clarke, who arrives at the apartment later, try to coerce Lizzie to sign a false statement. They want Lizzie to testify that the two black men were attempting to rape her and that Thomas shot one of the men to defend her. They even circulate their story around town inciting a manhunt for the other innocent black man. Another black man, mistaken for the one from the train, has been lynched already for the alleged rape, but this does not stop the pursuit.

It is hard to deny that the play, with its timely anti-lynching message, is about race, even though some audiences of the time, like the Communists, took issue with the role of the innocent black man about to be framed as a rapist whose lines are confined to pleading for his life. In his own defense, Sartre would probably say that this is appropriate for a desperate, hunted, innocent man. Even so, Thomas's family is desperate too, but allowed various manipulative strategies that display developed characters. Still, Sartre's play is credited by Richard Wright and others for its accurate portrayal of characters. It is also curious that Sartre's play does not indicate that there were any organized confrontations with racism by the left or liberals at the time. This is ironic given that there was a federal anti-lynching law under debate at the time and the efforts of the NAACP on Sartre's behalf. Indeed, in the year of the play's opening in America, Truman will issue the order to abolish racial segregation in the military. We must remember, in Sartre's defense, that his setting is a small Southern town. His exclusion of these large political responses to racism portrayed the privileging of local politics over national progressive politics.

What is significant are the ways in which Sartre brings to the stage the influence of class on racism. The class disparity between Lizzie, the working-class prostitute new to the Southern town, and Thomas, the young industrialist, creates the dramatic tension in the play. Sartre makes a striking departure from the Scottsboro case, which involved no prominent citizen, by making the character of Thomas from the upper class. While Lizzie immediately assures the black man who shows up at her apartment to plead with her that she will tell the truth if asked to testify, the class pressure asserted on her by Thomas's family is overpowering. Thomas's cousin Fred sleeps with her for the night in order to entrap her in a prostitution charge, then Fred's father, Senator Clarke, visits her and makes persuasive appeals for her to collude with his family, and Fred reappears to offer her financial security as his mistress. It is not surprising that Lizzie signs the false statement. Sartre portrays her as detached from the racist politics of the Southern town she finds herself in, but also unattached to family or friends. Her main concern is to pay her bills and support herself. A larger goal is to be respected by mainstream society.

With his emphasis on exposing class conflict, Sartre gives the most convincing lines to Senator Clarke, the white character with the greatest social standing, who stands in sharp contrast to Lizzie. The senator presumes the legitimacy of the white middle class when he appeals to white America, the government, and the justice system (so obviously corrupt in this small Southern town). He reframes the truth, at least temporarily for her. It is not a question of did Thomas murder the black man, he proclaims, but rather the consequences of clearing Thomas of any charges especially when weighed against those of sparing the life of the black man, who remains nameless through the play. Thomas's guilt, he pejoratively declares, is a truth, but a common truth, or truth of the first degree. The more significant question is which life is more valuable. As Senator Clarke continues the ethics lesson, he instructs Lizzie to imagine Uncle Sam standing before her weighing the value of each of the two lives using a class standard. On such a scale, Thomas, Harvard-educated, an officer, an anti-communist (also an anti-Semite), and a major white employer in the area, is the clear winner. This confuses Lizzie. The senator encourages her to adopt the morality of the town, which is surely in agreement with him, and promises, in turn, that she will be embraced by the whole town. When she signs the prepared statement, he thanks her not only in behalf of his family but in behalf of white people everywhere, "in the name of the seventeen thousand white inhabitants of our town, in the name of the American people, whom I represent in these parts" (1955b, p. 265). In bearing false witness, she becomes aligned with the upper class, the white race, a "true" patriot.

Sartre uses the play to critique American class politics as much as to condemn anti-black racism. However, class looms larger in the play and eclipses revelations about race. In the final scene, when Fred offers Lizzie, an unremarkable white prostitute, the promise of a higher social standing – she would be kept in style as his mistress – the injustice of betraying the black man is all but forgotten. She has been coerced to betray her principles, and although she is insulted by the small sum of money Thomas's family gives her in return, her choice to give false testimony does not weigh heavily on her. With the character of Lizzie McKay, and the choice she makes, Sartre suggests the difficulty of making authentic choices within a capitalist society.

A final bit of evidence that the play emphasizes class over race is the changed ending for the Soviet production and the film version a few years later. For the Soviet production, the play was renamed *Lizzie McKay*, Lizzie's role was made heroic, and an optimistic ending added with Lizzie defending the honor of the black man. One critic claimed "the leading character seemed almost pure enough to join the Soviet Youth League" (*New York Times*, 1995). If the play were primarily about American race relations, why the new ending for the Soviets? When Sartre was asked about the changes for the Soviet performance, he admitted authorizing them, explaining, "I didn't see the production, but I agreed to an optimistic ending, as in the film version, which was made in France. I knew too many young working-class people who had seen the play and had been disheartened because it ended sadly. And I realized that those who are really pushed to the limit, who hang on to life because they must, have need of hope" (Sartre, 1976, p. 102). Yet, the changed ending represents a choice of loyalty that elevates the interests of the disheartened white working class over those of black Americans. Its optimism represents an extraordinary action on Lizzie's part; in choosing to tell the truth about the fight on the train, she gains respectability through her heroic choice. But heroic acts and optimistic endings did not reflect the reality of anti-black racism in America in the 1940s. An important aspect of racism is the failure on the part of many whites in defense of class standing or in pursuit of class mobility, to be authentic witnesses to racism. The changed ending neither affirms this nor challenges the working class to condemn racism.

Travel Writing

To profile classism over racism, race must be seen as less important than class, if not also caused by capitalism. Sartre claims that racism is a secondary effect of capitalism. We find this view even in his scattered remarks about race. For instance, in his essay,

"American Cities," for *Le Figaro*, Sartre criticizes the squalid housing conditions of black Americans. He refers to segregated housing, the inequality it manifests, the ways whites regard black neighborhoods, and the racial transformations of neighborhoods as whites move out, black families move in, and the neighborhood is regarded as "polluted." Sartre is outraged by these housing conditions. He comments,

> If you walk about there, you come upon tumble-down houses that retain a pretentious look beneath their filth . . . These were formerly aristocratic homes, now inhabited by the poor. Chicago's lurid Negro section contains some of these Greco-Roman temples; from the outside they still look well. But inside, twelve rat- and louse-plagued Negro families are crowded together in five or six rooms. (1955c, p. 110)

Although Sartre noticed the horrid housing conditions of black Americans, in a later piece, again referring to segregated housing, we see racism subsumed by class politics. When he returns to the topic for a piece on American novelists in *The Atlantic Monthly*, he compares the housing conditions of black Americans with that of French white workers, profiling class as the common problem in both cases. "Yes, the Negroes of Chicago are housed in hovels. That is neither just nor democratic. But many of our white workmen live in hovels that are even more miserable" (1946, 117). It is hard to know exactly what to infer from his claim here that white French workers, like American blacks, have horrible, even more horrible living conditions. Both situations are unjust and undemocratic, he believed. But in drawing the comparison, Sartre misses the point about race. Why was it that the housing conditions of American blacks, rather than simply Americans, stood out even to the casual observer? Was it not because race, not simply class, was an important factor in determining material conditions in America? Without an analysis that identifies the differences between race and class oppression, Sartre has no way of explaining many aspects of racism that class alone could not account for. Take, for instance, the execution of black veteran George Dorsey, his wife and two friends on a secluded road in Walton County Georgia by a white mob shortly after Sartre's second visit, (*New York Times*, 1946a,b) or incidents of burning crosses across America, like the one planted by the Klan at an African American housing project in New Jersey (Goldstein, 1945), or the Scottsboro case. It is not that Sartre ignores mob violence, but when he addresses it, once again, the unique aspects of racism are lost in his account.

Sartre briefly mentions mob violence in his piece for *The Atlantic Monthly*. Again, what is telling in that article is the comparison Sartre draws between the situation of black Americans and French whites. Only that this time, it is not white workers but white collaborationists that come to mind. In 1944, he notes, while Fritz Lang's movie *Fury*, depicting a Chicago lynching, was being shown in a movie theater in Paris, "Frenchmen in the Midi were hanging and shooting, without much discrimination, such members of the 'militia' and collaborationists as they were able to capture. They were shaving the heads of women in our provinces." Sartre concludes, "Thus, when we saw on the screen the adventures of Spencer Tracy, we did not think about your lynchings, but of ours – we took the lesson to ourselves" (1946a, p. 116). But what were the lessons to be drawn from mapping the Midi lynchings onto racist lynching of black

Americans? How was anti-black mob violence, by the Klan and other groups, mindful of white on white violence in postwar France? How was an innocent black American like a white French collaborationist? Sartre does not stop to explain the lesson, perhaps because his point is to show the importance of American writers and culture on occupied France. Still, it is a troubling comparison that might make some sense if he were a pacifist or even against capital punishment, but Sartre held neither belief.

Sartre's strongest statements on anti-black racism in America are in two of his articles for *Le Figaro*. In both of these pieces on racism, while describing race relations, he asserts a common socialist view, that blacks are the proletariat, a view shared by the American Communist Party that came to the defense of the Scottsboro men, but Sartre also deviates from it in places, offering an existential approach that recognizes but fails to analyze important differences between race and class.

Class is the dominant form of oppression and American racism is a problem of capitalism. Racism, Sartre claims, is "an almost inextricable situation resulting from the suppression of slavery and the economic structure of the land," a "class based problem" of the superstructure (1945a,b). He repeatedly says that American blacks are the proletariat; at one point he calls them the real proletariat, for the majority live in poverty, constitute a cheap labor force, and call themselves third-class citizens. He depicts America as "a democracy of luxury" that relies on the "semi-slavery" of black Americans (1945b). To understand racism, he believes, is to conceive correctly the effects of altered economic conditions. The Southern landowners are relatively poor, he explains, an oppressed class themselves, who need black workers to be a cheap work force and who exploit them because the South is afraid of being ruined. Hence, in the South, a cheap black work force is constituted that is "an essential rural proletariat." In the North, blacks are more likely to hold semi-skilled jobs, but still receive low wages. Segregation is less strict, with mixed schools, for example; and housing problems abound from the exclusion of black tenants by highly organized white landlords, to dilapidated, rat-infested housing that whites have abandoned. This gives rise to illness, epidemics, and a higher mortality rate for blacks than for whites. Also, there is widespread price gouging, with an informal practice of over-charging blacks for goods and services, including housing (1945a). All of this points to racial inequality and Sartre condemns it. When he goes on to reflect on why it is so, he attributes racism exclusively to the "conflict of an agricultural economy based on slavery with an industrial one based on the existence of a proletariat" (1945b). He is not wrong to point out the economic aspects of slavery or of racism since Emancipation. Rather, it is his assumption that the primary basis of racism is economic and that a change in the economic system alone could eradicate racial injustice that is hard to defend. Certainly there could be other structures (e.g., psychological, cultural, nationalist) that might support racism apart from a capitalist regime.

Class profiling does not make Sartre ignore the political manifestations of racism: "In this country, so justly proud of its democratic institutions," he writes, "one man in ten is deprived of his political rights; in this land of freedom and equality there live thirteen million untouchables: that is the fact" (1945a). However, he sees the political dimensions of racism primarily as controlled by economic factors and calls for the development of class consciousness among black Americans. He notes that some organizing has already begun; he mentions the formation of black unions such as The Brotherhood of Sleeping-Car Porters with ten thousand members (1945b). The difficult problem, he claimed, was uniting the black and white proletariat, who have common cause. "The Negro problem is neither a political nor a cultural problem: the Blacks belong to the American proletariat and their cause is the same as that of the White workers" (ibid.). And he repeats it, "Neither political nor cultural, it can be resolved only through the fusion of the black and white proletariat in the struggle for the recognition of their rights" (ibid.). While recognizing that whites would not easily see it in their interests to rally the cause of blacks, Sartre chose to ignore evidence of black and white solidarity that existed among liberals and those on the left.

Sartre is so convinced of the need for a socialist solution to racism that he claims black Americans cannot attain equal status with whites in capitalism. "In the most optimistic hypothesis, they can hope, within the capitalist framework, a certain improvement of their condition, but not total equality with the Whites" (ibid.). (Does he mean to suggest that capitalism *requires* racism or merely that once racism becomes entrenched in a capitalist system it cannot be eradicated? He defends neither interpretation.) Sartre never elaborates on his belief in the inevitability of racism within capitalism. Instead, he argues that it is in the interests of black workers to join with white workers, even though he knew the war was ending and it was likely that promises made to black communities, such as an increase in new housing, might be disrupted by the economic effects caused by the soldiers coming home.

Having collapsed much of American racism into class oppression, Sartre is left with a major problem of creating solidarity among a segregated proletariat. This is particularly perplexing given the divisive problems of racism among black and white workers. And it is precisely here that an understanding of the unique features of anti-black racism would be helpful for forging a political analysis inclusive of race *and* class issues. Before asking how solidarity might come about, we can ask what Sartre meant by his claim that black and white workers have the same cause? This implies a model of coalition politics that need not erase other differences but merely attempts to build solidarity around common rallying points. But there is no evidence in Sartre's race writings to suggest this interpretation. Rather, the more obvious interpretation is one using the exclusive sense of "their cause is the same." That would mean that no other causes (or differences between racism and classism) are important. Equally surprising is his claim that racism cannot be alleviated within a capitalist system. He is on the mark with his claim that solidarity among workers, black and white, is the real stumbling block to forming a powerful American proletariat. Would that he had explored this further. If racism is primarily an economic problem, then solidarity is in the interests of both black and white workers. So why do white workers resist? Sartre fails to acknowledge the competition over jobs between white and black workers that would arise if racial segregation were dismantled. The larger issue of how to address multiple forms of oppression (e.g., race and class oppression), or the extent to which a theoretical analysis of one oppression can apply to another oppression, goes unanswered. Even so, racism is not enough like class conflict to assume a class analysis of race, tempting as that might be. As Sartre noticed in his comments about housing conditions, blacks were not simply poor but regarded as "polluted" in segregated America. Yet, he has no way to account for non-economic aspects of racism that shape the situations of blacks.

Sartre's politics assume one oppressive system must be dominant. All sorts of havoc result from this hypothesis: he is unable to account for other oppressions, such as racism, being endemic to capitalism, or to concretely understand the barriers to solidarity among groups of workers who experience other forms of oppression, even though he is convinced that the abolition of his primary oppression, capitalism, is the solution. The overthrow of capitalism, then, becomes a vital but formidable project. But Sartre overlooked many issues here. What is needed instead is a politics that would allow for the comprehensive manifestations of oppressions people experience. This would require an emphasis on factors marginalized in Sartre's account. Cultural identity is one such factor. Sartre fails to address the importance of cultural differences and identities. Oppressors assumed that American blacks had no cultural identity and, even after several generations in America, could not be true heirs to American culture. This was the belief of Eugene Talmadge, a nominee for Governor of Georgia, who said at the time of the Dorsey massacre, "Nothing can be gained by giving equal rights to someone with an artificial civilization that has been forced upon him only one hundred and fifty years ago" (Staff, 1946a). Sartre exposes this sort of racist thinking in the senator's speech in his American play, and while he does not identify the cultural heritage of black Americans, he will recognize cultural identity for black Africans in his later writings on the decolonization of Algeria.

Nevertheless, Sartre recognized some ways in which a strict class analysis did not neatly fit racism. For instance, he claimed that blacks are not necessarily the proletariat. Though most live in extreme poverty, some gain professional positions but that is not enough to guarantee greater social standing. Black lawyers, physicians, professors, newspapers editors did not have any rights, "they do not count any more in the eyes of the Whites than the elevator operator or the shoe shiner" (1945a). Others pursue professional training but that is not sufficient for attaining professional jobs. Sartre mentions black porters with law degrees or bellmen who are studying medicine (1945b). If the problem were purely economic, a change in professional status or education would alter not only one's economic conditions but one's social status as well. Hence, race is not perfectly subsumed by class. The widespread segregation in the South, less so in the North, presents another difference between race and class oppression. Blacks were allowed access only to segregated or separate public accommodations, inferior to white ones. Even the factories had separate areas for black workers. Still Sartre argues that the major struggle should be about capitalism. But how can socialism address these forms of racism? He could have mentioned organizations such as the NAACP, the ACLU, and others, that not only protested the appalling conditions of black schools, poll taxes, and segregation, but also helped to establish local anti-lynching laws. Instead, Sartre offers us no clues about how to forge a link between the existential situations of blacks and whites and economic forms of oppression.

To his credit, Sartre identified some of the social effects of racism with his account of the averted gaze by blacks toward whites. On the streets in the American South, he finds "the look," introduced in *Being and Nothingness*, carried the burdens of racial prejudice. And there is no analogue in classism in America.

These untouchables, you meet them on the street at any hour of the day, but you do not meet their eyes. Or if by chance, they look at you, it seems to you that they do not see you and it is better for them and for you that you pretend not to have noticed them. They serve you at mealtimes, they shine your shoes, they run your elevator, they carry your suitcases into your compartment, but they do not deal with you, nor you with them: they deal with the elevator, the suitcases, the shoes; and they carry out their tasks as if they were machines. Not one of their words, not one of their gestures, not one of their smiles are for you; it is dangerous to enter at night the sections of town reserved to them; if along the way you stopped them, if you showed them some attention, you would catch them off guard without pleasing them and you would risk the displeasure of the other Americans. (1945a)

What is striking about this passage is the ways Sartre describes the assumed invisibility of black Americans in service jobs for whites. Bell hooks, in her writing on American racism, explains that "one mark of oppression was that black folks were compelled to assume the mantle of invisibility, to erase all traces of their subjectivity during slavery and the long years of racial apartheid, so that they could be better, less threatening servants" (1995, p. 35). At the same time, whites often assume that they are invisible to black people, she contends, "since the power they have historically asserted, and even now collectively assert over black people, accord them the right to control the black gaze" (ibid, p. 35). Sartre, though unfamiliar with the lived reality of race relations in the American South, is clearly uncomfortable with the racist politics controlling the black gaze. He is surprised that the black workers he encounters in hotels and restaurants, and on city streets refused to acknowledge him ("not one of their smiles are for you"), and that social practices quickly teach him not to acknowledge, even though it seems to him impolite, black men carrying his bags, running the elevator, and providing other services for him. There is no evidence he has encountered a similar system of racial segregation in such a direct way and he is appalled at how whites vigorously maintain it in the South. Sartre observes that even if he were to defy these racist conventions by addressing someone black who was performing a service for him, he would risk the disapproval of whites and create discomfort for the black person ("if along the way you stopped them, if you showed them some attention, you would catch them off guard without pleasing them and you would risk the displeasure of the other Americans"). He did not comment on how these practices forbidding the usual interactions in social exchanges would apply to friendships between whites and blacks such as those Sartre had with black intellectuals, writers, and musicians during his two American trips.

When he describes the existential dimensions of racism in passages such as the one quoted above, he fails to notice how they cut a sharp contrast with class relations. Negrophobia, Sartre claims, is a deep fear of blacks by whites. Although the upper class may have a fear of losing their class status, there are no counter terms for class oppression. The irrational fear of blacks, a terror of American society becoming black (Sartre uses the term "negrification" to describe this terror), gives rise to "an obsessive and emotional concern to avoid all contacts with Blacks" (1945b). Blacks are the untouchables, taboo, contaminated, "their race is a contagious disease which could infect the whole White population" (ibid.). He mentions white people who have their black servant wipe off the telephone receiver before handing it to them, soldiers who boast they would kill their sister on the spot if they found she had been with a black man, and an otherwise broad-minded physician who supported a newspaper campaign to block the Red Cross from accepting black donors, explaining to Sartre, "It is not good for Black blood to run in our veins" (1945a). Racist arguments defend discriminatory behavior by assuming not only that blacks are inherently inferior to whites, but that blacks will soon outnumber whites. The fear that blacks will be the new majority in America produces a "horror inspired by the mere idea of a sexual commerce with the Black race" (1945b). Sexual commerce between classes, by contrast, went unmentioned but was not feared. In fact, prostitution commonly occurs across classes (as we find in Sartre's play). These layers of oppression, based more on psychological fears than on economic status, are not neatly addressed by challenges to capitalism. If Sartre wants to maintain the primacy of class oppression he must show how and why certain "secondary" oppressions, like racism, are generated in all their psychological dimensions.

Political Philosophy

We find the key to understanding Sartre's class profiling in his 1946 essay, "Materialism and Revolution," published in *Les Temps Modernes*. There Sartre suggests that while black Americans are the proletariat, they cannot be revolutionaries. He accepts the Marxist claim that revolutions require a change in the material conditions brought about by transformations in the economic system. He sought an alternative to the usual choice between a philosophy of materialism and idealism, and this marked the beginnings of his vision of an existential socialism he would develop later and publish as the *Critique of Dialectical Reason*. He begins by accepting historian A. Mathiez's view that revolution requires institutional change along with major changes in the property system (1955a, p. 207). This is the socialist project. It means that oppressed people who do not advocate for changes in the property system are excluded from being revolutionaries. Hence, black Americans, to the extent that they wish to become equal participants in American social and political life, are not revolutionaries. As Sartre explains it,

> We cannot call . . . the American Negroes revolutionaries, though their interests may coincide with those of the party which is working for the revolution. They are not completely integrated into society. . . . What the American Negroes and the bourgeois Jews want is an equality of rights which in no way implies a change of structure in the property system. They wish simply to share the privileges of their oppressors, that is, they really want a more complete integration. (Ibid., p. 210)

What is needed is to sort out how racism, in various forms, complicates a class analysis. Nancy Fraser has argued for combining a politics of recognition that would validate important ethnic and racial differences with a politics of economic distribution as a "postsocialist" strategy. As she notes, race has cultural dimensions in addition to economic ones. "A major aspect of racism is Eurocentrism: the authoritative construction of norms that privilege traits associated with 'whiteness'" (Fraser, 1997, p. 22). Fraser includes cultural racism, such as "demeaning steroeotypical depictions in the media, as criminal, bestial, primitive, stupid, and so on; violence, harassment . . . exclusion from and/or marginalization in public spheres and deliberative bodies; and denial of full legal rights and equal protections" (ibid., p. 22). Had Sartre moved in this direction, he would have been able to acknowledge the importance of a racial identity for understanding one's heritage and wariness of assimilation while still emphasizing the necessity of class solidarity and economic injustice.

Instead, Sartre primarily emphasizes that the oppressions of blacks and Jews are contingent on capitalism. He accepts the binary assumptions of Mathiez, that one must either be an integrationist or a radical revolutionary but not both; integration cannot be a legitimate path to revolution. The reason for this is his belief that revolutionaries must be true outsiders, not partaking in the privileges of class. This is the only way, presumably, to destroy or transform the class system; and class, for Sartre, is the fundamental form of oppression. While black Americans, particularly those in the South, might seem like true outsiders, Sartre believes that their oppression is not the most fundamental form of oppression. Anti-black racism and anti-Semitism are spin-off effects of class oppression. He claims, "This means that oppression is not, like that of the Jews or the American Negroes, a secondary and, as it were, lateral characteristic of the social regime under consideration, but that it is, on the contrary, a constituent one" (1955a, p. 210). For Sartre, the revolutionary finds a future and goes beyond his or her given situation by questioning the economic basis of his or her social standing. His example here is that of a worker,

> in so far as he demands his liberation *as* a worker, he knows perfectly well that it cannot be brought about by a simple integration of himself with the privileged class . . . what he hopes for . . . is that the relationships of solidarity which he maintains with other workers will become the very model of human relationships. He hopes, therefore, for the liberation of the entire oppressed class. (Ibid., p. 211)

And here Sartre shows there is little place for black revolutionaries who privilege a racial identity over a class identity. This is all the more perplexing given that he describes the revolutionary as in need of a philosophy that would provide a "total explanation of the human condition" (which would have to include race politics) and describes revolutionary thinking as thinking within a situation (which would make it neatly include race) and that this would be "born of a historical enterprise" (he sketches out the historical enterprise of American slavery in 1955a, p. 211).

Sartre seems to assume that the worker, who springs to mind so easily in his example of the true revolutionary, is a white worker, hence one who has no contested racial identity and need not emphasize anti-racist struggles. Yet, Sartre has identified the segregation of black workers in the factories in America. This racial division of labor suggests that whites did not consider black workers to be fully legitimate workers. Hence, blacks lose out on Sartre's revolutionary plan on two accounts: first, they might foreground a racial identity, and second, in virtue of their race, as segregation practices in the factories already suggested, they are not regarded as equals of white workers. Not to be seen as a full member of the category "worker," Sartre's one legitimate political category, would make it extremely difficult, if not prohibitive, for blacks to wage revolutionary action by Sartre's criteria. It is the bad faith of white oppressors that he analyzes in his final work.

We find a different approach in Sartre's last work on American racism, intended as part of his promised *Ethics*. Although "Revolutionary Violence" is structured as a comparison between American slavery and modern capitalism, Sartre leaves aside much of the class-based analysis permeating his informal newspaper writings. There is no call for black and white solidarity as in the pages of *Le Figaro* or appeals to anti-capitalist revolutionaries as in his essay "Materialism and Revolution." Instead, Sartre provides the beginnings of a phenomenology of white oppressor consciousness. It is a loosely historical sketch of the constitution of racist consciousness, with some hints about what is necessary for its dissolution. We see Sartre struggling with the differences between class and race oppression, testing the limits of a class analysis to see if it can adequately account for institutionalized racism. This struggle is evident in his opening question: What are the differences, he asks, from the point of view of a phenomenology of the oppressor, between the oppression of blacks in American slavery and the oppression of workers in capitalism? Sartre quickly identifies slavery as a form of institutional oppression. Slavery is not violence, he argues, because violence challenges the system, whereas slavery was supported by laws. Capitalism, on the other hand, is para-institutional, affecting the superstructure of society. Sartre intends for capitalism to be not merely an institutional practice that, like slavery, could be demolished, but integral to the larger social framework shaping institutions.

Searching for a way to explain the evolution of oppressor consciousness, Sartre starts with the origins of slavery in America and projects it out three or four generations to a time when whites regard slave ownership as a natural (God-given) right. In order for slavery to become institutionalized, Sartre explains, a number of events needed to take place, among them the development of a bad conscience among slave holders. Steeped in bad faith, slave holders became not just the oppressors of black Americans, but oppressors who denied they were oppressing. Their bad faith was, in part, influenced by their historical situations. After three or four generations, slave holders were born into a world, quite distant from the original violence that established slavery, a world in which all major institutions (religion, economics, politics, social science) supported it. Slavery was legal, it had been legal for generations: this became a mantra of bad faith. And these views of white superiority were reinforced in relation with other dominant views in society. Slavery effected a sense of identity among white oppressors. "A type of relation between men gets established among the Whites, which is the recognition of one master by another. Each greeting indicates that one is a man by divine right and that one belongs to the privileged race" (1992, p. 569). White identity, as Sartre describes it, masks its dependence on segregation and the ways in which the lives of white and black people are forever linked. For Sartre, whiteness becomes a value, its value derived "precisely from the fact that he [a white person] is not treated as a Black" (ibid., p. 569). These ideas have a violent expression in the Klan and other racist mobs. The belief in white superiority extended even to poor whites, Sartre claimed, so that "the myth of the equality of the higher classes is maintained to the point that poor Whites do not perceive the exploitation of which they are the victims, fully occupied as they are in thinking that they belong to the higher class" (ibid., p. 569).

The centerpiece of Sartre's phenomenology of white oppressor consciousness is its development in American society, first as institutionalized oppression and later, after the collapse of some institutional racist structures, as racial violence. Again and again in his newspaper writing, Sartre had commented how little black Americans gained nearly a century following Emancipation. Here he suggests a partial explanation: bad faith on the part of whites persisted. White oppressors maintained institutional practices of racism such as poll taxes, voter exams, and segregated public accommodations. These same institutional structures that Sartre cites in his newspaper writing would be struck down when later challenged. In addition, there were organized practices of racial violence, such as lynchings, that were illegal (even Truman publicly condemned the Dorsey massacre). Federal anti-lynching legislation that would have provided the strongest denouncement was in debate for over a decade but was never passed. Lastly, practices of convention, such as the averted gaze and social norms, reinforced the bad faith of white oppressors and the inequality of black Americans.

Sartre finds that a conceptual scheme, born of abstraction and grounded in the belief of white superiority, is used to maintain the bad faith supporting racial inequality. Those who put forth racist views were not even aware of themselves as oppressors. Sartre uses an example of Rollin Chambliss, a Southern journalist, who writes that he was in college before ever reading a black author and then felt "that there would be something physical to show that this was done by a Negro" (ibid., p. 570). Chambliss's belief that race, or at least the black race, so permeated one's being, that the writing of a black author would indicate his or her race in a physical sense is hard to comprehend because it is illogical. White oppressor consciousness appeals to a hierarchy of values that could justify slavery in one century and segregation in the next. W. T. Couch, a Chapel Hill sociologist, is an example of this. He argues in his 1944 publisher's introduction to *What the Negro Wants*, which Sartre cites, that the inferiority of blacks is supported by a solid ethical belief in the universality of values. For Couch, nothing is worse than relativism. We must assume that some values are universal, and a handy belief he offers up in this regard is that some groups of human beings are innately superior to others (1992, p. 570). What troubles Sartre is Couch's appeal to a hierarchy of values to measure the worth of human beings. Such an assumption violates Sartre's existential philosophy.

Existentialism is a powerful weapon for the dissolution of white oppressor consciousness. This is so because Sartre's existentialism assumes freedom as a core human value. He was critical of any view that suggested human beings are completely trapped by their situation (as he found in Faulkner's novels) (Sartre, 1955d) or determined by history (the fact that black Americans were once regarded as inferior does not mean that they were inherently inferior). Bad faith upheld by bad arguments masks the hidden causes of slavery as well as the hidden causes for the situations of black Americans. There were always reasons, grounded in racist ontology or a misuse of history, to defend white superiority. Existentialism, on the other hand, presents a counter view.

235

People are never completely determined by history or even material conditions but are free to act, Sartre insisted. If white oppressor consciousness is to be resisted, racist arguments used to defend white superiority must be seen for what they are. But this would require the displacement of oppressive forms of conceptualization.

In order to cease oppressing, Sartre returns to the phenomenology of the gaze, described in *Being and Nothingness* and above in his *Le Figaro* piece. Here he claims that the gaze, transformed, can be a radical form of seeing. Oppressors need a radical shift in their conceptualization of the world, Sartre insists. "And to see clearly in an unjustifiable situation, it is not sufficient that the oppressor look at it openly and honestly, he must also change the structure of his eyes. As long as he looks at it with a conceptualist apparatus, he will judge it to be acceptable and just" (ibid., p. 571). As bell hooks reminds us, Malcolm X later used similar words to urge a shift in consciousness among the oppressed ("We've got to change our own minds about each other. We have to see each other with new eyes. We have to see each other as brothers and sisters. We have to come together with warmth" (hooks, 1995, p. 96).[7] For Sartre, a critical consciousness would understand the masked causes of racism. However, he provides no clues for bringing about such a radical shift in consciousness. Simply reading Sartre's existential philosophy, or his preliminary analysis on American racism, would not be enough to see through long-defended white privilege.

It is not even clear that Sartre has completely "changed the structure of his eyes," for he failed to notice how some of his own comments in his newspaper piece about cross-breeding or the physical characteristics of black Americans reinforce oppressive stereotypes. In his first *Le Figaro* piece on race, he describes blacks in America, not as a pure race like blacks from the Sudan or the Congo. Blacks in America, he explained, were brought here by slave traders from all regions of Africa, and miscegenation was frequent, resulting in a mixing of African races and cross-breeding with Native Americans and Chinese. "And besides, since, as a rule the planters formerly took their mistresses among the Black slaves, hardly a quarter of American Negroes are from pure African descent" (1945a). As Renate Peters points out, Sartre assumes an anthropologist's tone when he describes the physical characteristics of black Americans, the differences in height, the color of lunules under the finger nail, the shape of their faces and noses, as if blacks were some unusual human form (1997). This easily shows the limits of Sartre's political consciousness about race at the time.

In addition, in Sartre's conceptual framework, racism is subordinate to class struggles. For Sartre, racism can only end with the destruction of white oppressor consciousness but this requires an end to capitalism. Sartre provides a partial sketch of the relationship between racism and class conflict in the final paragraph of "Revolutionary Violence." He sets out to compare slavery with capitalism, but the piece breaks off too soon before this project is developed and we are left with an account that exacerbates the conflict between his existential views and his socialist politics. Sartre claims that capitalism is para-institutional, neither sanctioned nor ensured by law. He tries to draw links between racism, in the aftermath of slavery, and class oppression, as when he argues that white oppressors (presumably like the bourgeoisie) sense they are champions of the current form of social organization. He then rushes to sketch a dialectical scheme in the final paragraph to explain the connections between violence and oppression. The first term in that scheme is exploitation on the individual level without any institutional structures. The second term is the abstract positing of rights; here, Sartre mentions as examples those found in capitalism and internationalism. This is the level of the superstructure. The third term is the concrete freedom of workers, not yet realized. He has outlined the movement from individual acts to larger social structures concretized as rights that, in turn, influence individual freedoms. He does not indicate whether the use of rights could ever be essential for liberation. One attempt was The Universal Declaration of Human Rights that was passed in Paris in 1948. Moreover, a glaring problem arises from Sartre's own critique of hierarchies of value. He cannot prioritize class over race, as class profiling demands, while maintaining an existential rejection of hierarchy of values.

If his existentialism forces him to reject external systems of value, including the hierarchy of values used to justify white superiority, then he would similarly need to reject a hierarchy of oppressions implicit in his views on American racism. For in order to rank oppressions as primary or secondary, as Sartre does, one must assume some external system of values. While we might differentiate major from minor acts of oppression by appealing to small and large infringements on liberty, we could not justify claims that one large historical form of oppression, (e.g., capitalism) is primary and others (e.g., racism and sexism) only derivative. This ordering presupposes a value-laden criterion that is not self-evident merely from an existential assumption of onto-logical freedom. All sorts of problems related to multiple readings and assessment of history abound if we were to pursue a ranking of oppressions. For instance, racism existed before capitalism. Should that matter in our assessment? As I have argued here, it is difficult to avoid diminishing other forms of oppression (e.g., racism) when one is intent on rank ordering large, historical oppressive systems.

In his writings on American racism (1945–9), Sartre offers a view of racism that, while advocating for its abolition, reflects class profiling. In the end, his assumption of a hierarchy of oppressions that justifies class profiling cannot be supported by his own existential beliefs. Even if it could, he still has not shown why racism is contingent on capitalism. He also does not see the ways his application of socialism conceals differences in oppression and fails to probe the depths of racism. His writings on American racism occur relatively early in the development of his own political consciousness. Why worry then about Sartre's views on American racism in his early writings? Some appear only in French newspapers, are never translated into English, and never find their way into collections of his writing. His play, bold for the time, is no longer performed here. The second of the two political essays we have discussed is unfinished and posthumously published. Sartre's American period, the period of 1945–9, encompassed the end of the War, the rebuilding of Europe, Sartre's two American visits, and revolutionary writing that preceded America's cold war politics. Much has changed since then. Socialist theory, for instance, has moved in new directions since the 1940s.

These factors would make Sartre's writings on race relations in America easy to dismiss were it not for the emergence of class profiling as a current conservative trend in American politics. Arguments asserting the primacy of class over all other consider-ations are used to strike down race preferences in university admissions policies, for example, with proponents arguing that poverty, not race, is the important considera-tion. The courts have overturned mandates for school busing, despite the fact that there continues to be fewer resources available for Southern black schools that are markedly unequal compared to white schools and trends point toward school resegre-gation. An analysis of arguments against civil rights remedies is beyond the scope of our project, but I do wish to point out that, whereas Sartre argued that classism is the real oppression, race is only secondary, political leaders now argue that poverty is the single mark of oppression for people of color, hence, race need not be considered. Some believe that "color-blindedness" is the best approach to achieving racial equality. Yet, race has more than a little to do with the material conditions of people of color, and that is why there is such a fuss about including race as part of the analysis. Further-more, if race is not a significant factor, why do we find eruptions of racial violence, its entrenchment in white supremacy groups, so disturbing? All this suggests the impor-tance of Sartre's work on racism in America, particularly, his sketch of white oppres-sor consciousness steeped in bad faith. While there are many differences between 1940s racism and racism today, white oppressor consciousness, a critical factor in maintain-ing racial inequality in America, persists in myriad forms of class profiling that now occur, not by prioritizing serious challenges to capitalism, but lacking any challenge to it at all.

Notes

1. My thanks to Linda Bell, William McBride, and Constance Mui, for their thoughtful comments on earlier version of this essay and to Joan Boggis for computer support. English translations of Sartre 1945a, 1945b, and 1949 cited in the text are by Marie-Jose Silver.
2. For instance, according to biographer Annie Cohen-Solal (1987), when traveling from Baltimore to Philadelphia by train, Sartre and the other journalists in his group noticed two black army officers were refused service in the dining car. The staff, embarrassed by the French journalists witnessing the incident, relented partially by seating the officers at a table in the back of the dining car and drawing a curtain.
3. The term, "anti-black" racism was popularized in philosophical writings by Lewis Gordon (1995).
4. One exception is Peters (1997, 1990). Gordon (1995) uses Sartrean philosophy for an analysis of race but doesn't analyze Sartre's work on American racism.
5. There are many examples of this. See Herbert (1999), Holmes (1999), Egan (1999), Goldberg (1999), Wilgoren (1999).
6. An adaption of *The Respectful Prostitute* by Eva Wolas was staged in New York on February 9, 1948 and became a hit with over 350 performances. Rattigan's *The Winslow Boy* actually won the award.
7. This visual metaphor for a transformed consciousness has been applied to women in the work of feminist poet, Adrienne Rich. For a comparison of Rich and Sartre on oppressed con-sciousness see my essay, "The Look in Sartre and Adrienne Rich," (Murphy, 1987).

References

Brown, John L. 1946: Jean-Paul Sartre Again Stirs Paris with Two New Plays. *New York Times*, December 22, 4.

Calta, Louis 1948a: Revocation of Ban Urged for Chicago: Local Stage Units Ask Mayor Kennelly to Act on Barring of the Sartre Play. *New York Times*, December 11, 12.

Calta, Louis 1948b: Sponsors Cancel Sartre Play Tour: New Stages Calls off Trip for "Respectful Prostitute," with Chicago Ban a Factor. *New York Times*, December 18, 14.

Carter, Dan T. 1969: *Scottsboro: A Tragedy of the American South*. Baton Rouge: Louisiana State University Press.

Cohen-Solal, Annie 1987: *Sartre: A Life*. New York: Pantheon Books.

Egan, Timothy 1999: The Trouble in Looking for Signs of Trouble. *New York Times*, April 25, section 4, 1.

Fleurent, Maurice 1946: Richard Wright in Paris. *Paru*, December 25. Also in Richard Wright, Keneth Kinnamon and Michel Fabre, *Conversations with Richard Wright*, Jackson: University Press of Mississippi, 1993, 113.

Fraser, Nancy 1997: *Justice Interruptus: Critical Reflections on the "Postsocialist" Condition*. New York: Routledge Press.

Goldberg, Jeffrey 1999: The Color of Suspicion. *New York Times Magazine*, June 20, section 1, 50.

Goldstein (Friedan), Betty 1945: Fiery Cross Burns Over Negro Housing Project Site in New Jersey. *The Federated Press*, cited in Daniel Horowitz, *Betty Friedan and the Making of the Feminine Mystique*, Amherst: University of Massachusetts Press, 1998.

Goodman, James 1994: *Stories of Scottsboro*. New York: Pantheon Books.

Gordon, Lewis R. 1995: *Bad Faith and Antiblack Racism*. New Jersey: Humanities Press.

Herbert, Bob 1999: Hounding the Innocent. *New York Times*, June 13, section 4, 17.

Holmes, Steven A. 1999: Both a Victim of Racial Profiling and a Practitioner. *New York Times*, April 25, section 1, 18.

Hooks, Bell 1995: *Killing Rage: Ending Racism*. New York: Henry Holt and Company.

Murphy, Julien S. 1987, 1989: The Look in Sartre and Adrienne Rich. *Hypatia*, 2, no. 2, 113–24. Reprinted in Jeffner Allen and Iris Young (eds), *The Thinking Muse: Feminism and Modern French Philosophy*, Bloomington: Indiana University, 101–12.

New York Times 1946a: Georgia Mob of Twenty Men Massacres Two Negroes, Wives; One Was Ex-GI. *New York Times*, July 27, 1 and 32.

New York Times 1946b: Kin Not at Rites for Mob Victims; Friends Ascribe Absence to Fear: Services Are Held Up for Two Hours on Word that Group Had Started from Farm. *New York Times*, July 29, 36.

New York Times 1948a: Sartre Play Condemned: Chicago Police Head Says Work Should Not Be Given Here. *New York Times*, December 5, 95.

New York Times 1948b: Sartre Play Ban Stands: Chicago Refuses to Allow "The Respectful Prostitute" to Go On. *New York Times*, December 7, 43.

New York Times 1949: Ban Off, Sartre Play Will Open in Chicago. *New York Times*, April 20, 31.

New York Times 1955: Sartre Play in Moscow. *New York Times*, September 5, 44.

New York Times 1999: 1946 Killing of Four Blacks is Recalled: Veteran is Honored in Georgia Service. *New York Times*, June 1, A16.

Peters, Renate 1990: From Illusion to Disillusion: Sartre's Views of America. *Canadian Review of American Studies*, vol. 21, 2, 173–82.

Peters, Renate 1997: Sartre, White America, and the Black Problem. *Canadian Review of American Studies*, vol. 27, 1, 21–41.

Sartre, Jean-Paul 1945a: Le quie j'ai appris du problème noir. *Le Figaro*, June 16, 2.

Sartre, Jean-Paul 1945b: Le problème noir aux États-Unis. *Le Figaro*, July 3, 1–2.

Sartre, Jean-Paul 1946: American Novelists in French Eyes. *The Atlantic Monthly*, 2, 117.

Sartre, Jean-Paul 1948: *Anti-Semite and Jew*. Tr. George G. Becker. New York: Schocken Books. *Reflexions sur la Question Juive*. Paris: Paul Morihien, 1946.

Sartre, Jean-Paul 1949: Le Noir et le Blanc aux États-Unis. *Combat*, June 16, 4.

Sartre, Jean-Paul 1955a: Materialism and Revolution. In Annette Michelson (tr.), *Literary and Philosophical Essays*, New York: Macmillan, 185–239. This is a translation of "Matérialisme et Révolution," in *Les Temps Modernes*, no. 9, June 1, 1946, 1537–67, no. 10, July 1, 1946, 1–32.

Sartre, Jean-Paul 1955b: *The Respectful Prostitute*. Tr. Kitty Black. In Stuart Gilbert (ed.), *"No Exit" and Three Other Plays*, New York: Vintage. *La Putain respectueuse*. Paris: Gallimard, 1946.

Sartre, Jean-Paul 1955c: American Cities. In Annette Michelson (tr.), *Literary and Philosophical Essays,* New York: Macmillan. This is a translation of "Villes d' Amérique," In Jean-Paul Sartre, *Situations, III*, Paris: Gallimard, 1949, 92–111.

Sartre, Jean-Paul 1955d: William Faulkner's *Sartois*. In Annette Mickelson (tr.), *Literary and Philosophical Essays*, New York: Macmillan, 78–83.

Sartre, Jean-Paul 1976: *Sartre on Theatre*. Documents assembled, edited, introduced, and annotated by Michel Contat and Michel Rybalka. Tr. Frank Jellinek. Pantheon Books: New York.

Sartre, Jean-Paul 1992: Revolutionary Violence. Appendix II in Jean-Paul Sartre, *Notebooks for an Ethics*, tr. David Pellauer, Chicago: University of Chicago Press, 555–60.

Wilgoren, Jodi 1999: Police Profiling Debate: Acting on Experience, or on Bias. *New York Times*, April 9, A21.

Wright, Richard 1946–7: *Black Boy*. Les Temps Modernes, nos. 13–18.

CHAPTER 13

Sartrean Bad Faith and Antiblack Racism[1]

LEWIS R. GORDON

As a limiting constant, the color of a person might be thought of as, in paradigm cases, an unalterable, objectively given absolute. However a distinctively black *Negro may think himself racially, it would seem that he cannot change the fact of his color. In physiological terms, he is a black man. In situational terms, the matter is far more complicated. . . . One thing is clear; race in some color-wheel sense has little to do with the reality of being black, white, or anything else in the present world. It is in the situation of the individual that race categories have significance, and that means that the definition of the situation by the actor on the social scene establishes the meaning which 'objectivity' and the constants have for social reality. Definition in this sense is a modality of choice.*

Maurice Natanson[2]

What Natanson is considering in this passage from *The Journeying Self* is that antiblack attitudes and some pro-black attitudes may be forms of bad faith. Natanson's conception of bad faith in that work is "That which threatens the self by fixing and desiccating the subject. . . . Bad Faith consists in the individual's moving from subject to object in social roles which have congealed consciousness into routine expectancy and which have made of intersubjectivity a masked and masking reality" (p. 45). Bad faith threatens every dimension of human reality, including the existential impact of history: "The binding of time in Bad Faith is a way of denying the possibilities of the self, of stripping the individual of his involvement in history" (p. 92).

The concept of bad faith and the difficulty of developing authentic social relationships from an existential-phenomenological perspective have played a major role in the development of Natanson's philosophical ideas. He first grappled with the concept in his dissertation on Jean-Paul Sartre's ontology in 1950. In his subsequent work, he continued to contribute to our understanding of the concept. What follows is an exploration of Natanson's insight in the above quotations through stressing the importance of the Sartrean concept of bad faith for the understanding of racism – particularly antiblack racism. Although Sartre will be the focus of the rest of our discussion, the underlying interpretation of bad faith takes advantage of Natanson's reminder of the self-deception involved in "stripping the individual of his involvement in history."

1

I should like to quote a passage from *The Words*, a passage which, I hope, will make clear a great deal of what Sartre is up to when he comments on the various ways in which human beings evade responsibility and in effect evade human beings. He writes,

> In the struggle between generations, children and old people often join forces: the former pronounce the oracles; the latter puzzle them out. Nature speaks, and experience translates: adults have only to keep their traps shut. Failing a child, one can take a poodle: last year, at the dogs' cemetery, I recognized my grandfather's maxims in the trembling discourse that runs from grave to grave: dogs know how to love; they are gentler than human beings, more faithful; they have tact, a flawless instinct that enables them to recognize Good, to distinguish the good from the wicked. . . . An American friend was with me. With a burst of indignation, he kicked a cement dog and broke its ear. He was right: when one loves children and animals *too much*, one loves them against human beings.[3]

The crucial term here is *human beings*. Sartre sets human beings in opposition to "children" and "animals." There is a sense in which a human being embodies a form of maturity for Sartre. He is, in effect, saying, "Oh, grow up!"

There are many ways to attempt not to grow up. These forms of evasion are generally characterized as forms of bad faith. The Sartrean conception of bad faith is that it is an effort to evade freedom and responsibility – an effort to evade living in situation, an effort to evade human beings. Fascination with children and animals suggests an effort to evade judgment – the Look, that is, of those who are aware of what we are up to. We can call this fascination a form of exoticizing and romanticizing of the Other in a way that denies his freedom to judge. In the language of subject–object dichotomies, we can speak of bad faith as a desire to be either purely a subject or purely an object.

The effort to become purely a subject carries the danger of eliminating both the social world and the world; it is an effort to protect oneself by a retreat to a form of solipsism, where one would, in effect, escape being seen by others by way of eliminating the presence of all other perspectives and consequently the very notion of perspectivity itself.[4] To become a pure object involves the elimination of one's own humanity in the presence of an Other. In both cases, the social world is threatened and misanthropy emerges.[5] Misanthropy and its many variations usually take the form of emphasizing abstract humanity over concrete human beings or of focusing upon the corporeality and facticity of human beings as though they were devoid of other possibilities.

Thus, a person in bad faith could love humanity in the abstract while torturing human beings in the flesh. Or a person who claims to hate all "isms" may choose to regard the materiality of the flesh to the point of living in a world best suited for the dead. Sartre identifies these tendencies in his discussion of the body.[6] His discussion can be regarded as a description of the body in bad faith.[7]

The body can be regarded through three dimensions: the body as lived, the body as seen by others, and the body realized as seen by others. Sartre regards the denial of embodiment, the denial that one has a perspective on the world that can be seen by others, as sadistic; it is an effort to deny the humanity of others. He regards as masochistic the denial that one has a perspective on the world; it is a retreat to the view that one is pure body in the sense of a corpse or wood floating on water. The correlated forms of bad faith attitudes towards the body are that the sadist regards the Other's body as mere physical body and the masochist regards the (subject) Other's body as if it were a chasm into which to fall.

Another feature of bad faith is a form of play on evidence. A person in bad faith may demand "perfect" evidence where adequate evidence is all that can be achieved and accept shady evidence where evidence of necessary and sufficient conditions being met is needed.[8] One example is the demand for the Other to justify his right to exist. A person may offer his deeds, his history, examples he has set by his actions, but the problem is that the *standard* by which they are judged belongs to him who makes the demand for justification. The questioner's right to make such a demand is presumed in the question, but the Other who is questioned is presumed suspect. No human being "is" existentially justified in virtue of the fact that no human being is a complete(d) reality or substance. His existence in itself is without justification. It is, in a word, absurd. The human being lives his justification as well as his lack of justification, his triumphs as well as his failures. If his deeds are excluded, if his history is of no consequence, all is left is his bare, existing body. Without appeal to other criteria, all he can offer on behalf of his existence is the fact that he exists. Since he cannot justify his existence beyond his own presentations of himself, the very demand ultimately sets him who makes the demand on the level of God – that is, a self-justified, substantiated standpoint on all reality – and the Other, ultimately, below human.[9]

2

Rather unexpectedly, the racist group points accusingly to a manifestation of racism among the oppressed. The "intellectual primitivism" of the period of exploitation gives way to "medieval, in fact prehistoric fanaticism" of the period of liberation.

Frantz Fanon[10]

A problematic demand on some liberation movements is the demand for ideal subjects of liberation. This demand relies on the thesis that to *deserve* liberation, an oppressed person or group must be without fault, must be morally pure, must be materially constituted as either pure virtue or pure innocence – in short, the ideal victim. This demand is an obvious form of bad faith in that it imposes a double standard on subjects; dominant groups are exempted from the criterion of innocence and idealness (if not falsely presented as innocent or ideal), whereas oppressed groups are judged by higher and perhaps unattainable standards. Among the oppressed group a different situation emerges, however, when ideal subjects of liberation are sought. Whereas a dominating or oppressing group may say that members of the oppressed group aren't worthy of compassion, are guilty of their own victimization, members of oppressed groups sometimes compete for victim status. The former claims to be holier than thou, whereas the latter claims to be (if not holier) more oppressed than thou.[11] The consequence of both forms is the spirit of seriousness that Sartre declares war on in *Being and Nothingness*.

The spirit of seriousness involves regarding values as material features of the world. For a serious person, people *are*, in their "essence," materially constituted as good or bad, innocent or guilty. We can regard this serious attitude as a demand that one be objectively valuable. Consider, for example, the problems raised by the demand or search for ideal agents of liberation in the supposed tension between gender and race categories.[12] This demand has been a source of tension between black and white feminists.[13] Black feminists have argued that white feminists have presented "woman" in ways that militate against the aspirations and womanness of black women.[14] But the problem goes deeper. Some black feminists have observed, for instance, that white feminists have been wont to objectify black men in stereotypical identities of rapists and violent criminals.[15] The tension between race and gender comes to a head here. This is because a consequence of making women "pure victims" is the mistaken notion that men cannot possibly be victims, that they are purely victimizers. The black male, the embodiment of the exploited or colonized male, is an obvious threat to this model, for such a model relies on rendering illegitimate his claim to being oppressed. The consequence is an evasion of wider categories of exploitation. Such a model locates women as fundamental subjects of liberation and ultimately glorifies black women, in virtue of their "double-victimization" status, as contemporary bearers of oppression and liberation.[16]

The irony of the *situation* of women and blacks (conspicuously presuming *white* women as women in the formulation) is that women who attempted to objectify black males as lustful and as rapists situated themselves on the oppressive end of seriousness. Although black women's criticisms of white women placed black women on the oppressed end, they have often also argued that black women have the claim to paramount oppression.[17] The demand for holy or morally "clean" black men betrays a false standard. Black women's demand for "truly oppressed" white women masked a criterion that no white woman could achieve as a *white* woman. No white woman could "be" a black one.

Before we go further, let us take a pause to address a concern that may be on the minds of some Sartre scholars. Wait, they might urge, how can we be looking into black liberation (and feminist) concerns from a Sartrean perspective when it is well known that Sartre's "early" philosophy, particularly his critical work on ontology, not only lacks a social theory, but is also vehemently antisocial?[18] Witness the very structure of his description of human reality as a reality built upon conflict and his relegation of subject–subject relationships – "we" relationships – to mere psychological phenomena.[19]

First, recall that it is a form of bad faith to deny facing either one's embodiment or the Other's freedom. If these are bad-faith relations to embodiment, what would be authentic relations to embodiment? In the case of the Sartrean sadist, it would be the recognition of his facticity or the possibility of his objectification and recognition of the Other's transcendence or subjectivity. In the case of the masochist, it would be recognition of his own transcendence and the Other's facticity. That the body is the perspective on others and is seen by others makes the body-subject here necessary for social experience.[20] But, second, there is a stronger argument, a *transcendental* one. Evasion of the body *cannot* be a form of bad faith without the social significance of recognizing humanity, or perhaps I should say human beings, in the flesh. That is to say, the concept of bad faith radically applied, unfolds into the social world of contextually significant forms of alienation and dignity. This transcendental move is not intended to serve as a proof of the existence of others. Instead, it is here presented as a line of argument that *Sartre* cannot avoid given his existential phenomenological critique of sociality in *Being and Nothingness*. Sartre later conceded a variation of this argument when he wrote, "The very fact that *Being and Nothingness* is an ontology before conversion takes for granted that a conversion is necessary and that, as a consequence, there is a natural attitude."[21] The world of the natural attitude is a social world.[22]

That the Sartrean conception of bad faith actually leads to a transcendental phenomenological move leads to the ironic conclusion that Sartre may have also set the groundwork for a transcendental existential phenomenology. The deeper structure of social reality and critical good faith is, as Natanson observed on more than one occasion, rich with Husserlian transscendental phenomenological significance.[23] The problem, properly understood, is how to be seen in the "right" way and how to see others in the "right" way. The wrong way is tantamount to not seeing human beings at all.

There are at least two kinds of "look" or ways of seeing others and being seen in *Being and Nothingness*. There is the immediate encounter in the flesh, where one actually looks at the Other or one is actually looked at. Then there is the symbolic Look, which is best developed in Sartre's discussion of the Third. The Third is the institutional super ego that influences factical identities along collective lines. Sartre identifies the bad faith implicit in the Third when he refers to it as the *anarchic consciousness*.[24] The Third is a variation of the futile effort of disembodiment, for it is ultimately a form of radical freedom that is regarded by itself as the perspective beyond which there is no other *perspective*. Thus, for example, the bourgeoisie's being the Third involves a form of denial on their part of the possibility of being seen as an "us," as an object. Frantz Fanon makes a similar observation on the powerful when he describes French settler's way of seeing Algerian natives: "In Algeria there is not simply the domination but the decision to the letter not to occupy anything more than the sum total of the land. The Algerians, the veiled women, the palm trees and the camels make up the landscape, the *natural* background to the human presence of the French."[25]

3

Our worthiest souls contain racial prejudice
Sartre[26]

There are obvious ways in which antiblack racism is a form of bad faith. One way of looking at antiblack racism is that of its being the institutional demarcation of the inferiority of black people. Another way of looking at it is the institutional demarcation of black people's being regarded as material embodiments of inferiority – objective antivalues in the world. Under this interpretation, which doesn't preclude the first, it is a form of spirit of seriousness and hence a form of bad faith. But Sartre argues that bad faith is a *choice*.[27] Thus as a form of bad faith, antiblack racism is also the choice of lying to oneself about one's superiority to black people. One ultimately chooses to be an antiblack racist – even when one is black. For example:

> "You, as a Negress –." "Me? A Negress? Can't you see I'm practically white? I despise Negroes. Niggers stink. They're dirty and lazy. Don't ever mention niggers to me."
> I knew another black girl who kept a list of Parisian dance-halls "where-there-was-no-chance-of-running-into-niggers."[28]

How can something institutional be a choice? It is this problem of antiblack racism and racism generally that Sartre touches upon in *Being and Nothingness* and grapples with here and there in his many post-*Being and Nothingness* discussions of race and racism. The philosophical discussion that emerges is a development of the existential significance of *situation*. Choices don't occur in themselves but in the midst of a world of institutional presentations and meanings. Choices are lived by virtue of social reality. Yet, social reality can be infected, poisoned, against the beings by whom it exists in the first place.

Recall that the demand for the Other to provide evidence of his right to exist is a form of bad faith that involves playing the role of being God. The racist usually demands members of the condemned race to provide evidence for their right to exist. But this demand conceals an impossible standard, for there is no evidence that can serve as justification for one's existence beyond one's existence "in itself." In one of his many discussions of the anti-Semite's attitudes towards Jews and the Jew's situation in face of such attitudes, Sartre makes this point clear when he writes, "The Jew had to be put to death wherever he came from not because he had been caught preparing to fight, or because he was taking part in resistance movements, but simply *because he was Jewish*."[29] The Jew is ultimately guilty of being Jewish. In *The Respectful Prostitute*, the same point is made regarding blacks: "A nigger has always done something."[30] To be black in an antiblack world calls for Natanson's observation of a factical existence of closed possibilities. To be black is to be *too black*; to have always done something means to be guilty. No amount of evidence can establish a black's innocence.

The Respectful Prostitute can be regarded as a study of the Manichæism of antiblack societies, where good and evil are regarded as material embodiments of white and black people.[31] When the character Fred looks at the bed in which he has spent the night with the prostitute Lizzy, he observes, for instance, that it "smells of sin." In a serious world, the "rational" route is obvious: clean the bed and wipe away the sin. The historical significance of "cleansing" the world hardly needs development here.

The Respectful Prostitute has often been criticized because of the seemingly politically incorrect portrayal of the black man in the play: he is not a protagonist and he is weak. But we should note that the character (1) has no name – he is simply referred to as *The Negro* – and (2) *his* fate is subject to the "choice" of a white woman who, within a purely white context, is regarded as pariah. The Negro's lack of a proper name exemplifies a fundamental feature of all antiblack societies: there is no difference between one black and a million blacks. Any *one* will do. Thus, as a principle of "justice" the lynching of *any* black would set the material balance of *dikaiosunê*, or (Platonic) cosmological justice, back on course. In The Negro is every Negro and in the lynching of *a* Negro is the symbolic death-wish on *every* Negro. The Negro is simultaneously a substance who can be represented and represents. But he is also an absence. As Fanon confesses,

> As a good tactician, I intended to rationalize the world and to show the white man that he was mistaken. . . . Reason was confident of victory on every level. I put all the parts back together. But I had to change my tune. That victory played cat and mouse with me; it made a fool of me. As the other put it, when I was present, it was not; when it was there, I was no longer.[32]

Wherever the black stands, rationality, logic, humanity are apparently sucked into the void, and the black soon comes to realize that wherever he is, the "standard" rules of the game no longer apply; where he is, they are not.

The Respectful Prostitute presents yet another dimension of racial dynamics. Lizzy stands to the Negro as the possibility of solidarity or betrayal. Since betrayal for Sartre is also self-betrayal, Lizzy faces herself when she faces the Negro. Lizzy, the white woman – desired, exploited, existing as the meaning of rape victim – may choose to prostitute herself to become a white man in relation to the Negro in virtue of her *de facto* power over his future or to liberate herself by showing that she does not have a price. I won't develop the existential psychoanalytic significance of Lizzy here, but I suggest that the infamous discussion of slime and femininity in *Being and Nothingness*[33] ultimately makes sense in regard, and perhaps *only* in regard, to white women and the underlying, gnawing sense that to be a white woman in an antiblack world, a world that was in fact Sartre's world and is in fact our own, is to live as the symbol of betrayal. Whatever solidarity she may have with The Negro on the level of "class," or perhaps even "the oppressed," Lizzy's situation comes to the fore in the fact that she needs only declare "rape." She knows who really has a "race problem."[34]

We now face a central theme of black liberation theorists from W. E. B. Du Bois to Cornel West, that antiblack racism is a "white problem." The expression "white problem" is loaded with equivocation. I here declare straight away that I reject the interpretation that the white problem excludes the possibility of a nonwhite problem. Fanon has shown in *Black Skin, White Masks* that, like it or not, oppressed people have special problems of their own. The white problem could mean that it is a white pathology. Or it could mean that it is a white responsibility. When Du Bois originally deployed it, it simply meant that antiblack racism betrays a white pathology: hatred of blacks. He observed this when he wrote his monumental tome *The Philadelphia Negro*, which was initiated by the University of Pennsylvania to spell out the "problem" with Negroes.[35] Du Bois' retort in *The Souls of Black Folk* and *Darkwater* was to shift the discussion to the "problem" of the powerful. Yet from an existential standpoint, there is a sense in which whites are responsible for the white problem.

Sartre's later writings represent a long meditation on his coming to grips with his bourgeois status in a world in which, at least from the standpoint of authenticity, losers win.[36] Only the oppressed, it seems, can have salvation. Sartre understood that although each individual bourgeois cannot change the relation of the bourgeoisie to the proletariat, each individual bourgeois is nevertheless responsible for such a relationship.[37] He can either stand out of the proletariat's way or work on behalf of the proletariat revolution or try to destroy it, but in either circumstance his project is bankrupt in virtue of the realization that the revolution is not *for him*. Similarly, there are whites who may fight on behalf of racial justice, and they may even develop interesting arguments premised upon either universal racism ("Everyone is racist") or moral self-interest, but in the end, there is the gnawing feeling that racial justice is not *for whites*.[38] The white problem is deeper than most of us – white, brown, or black – may be willing to admit. To be black may mean to suffer, literally and figuratively, on an everyday basis, but to be white may ultimately mean – at least when moral reflection is permitted to enter – to be condemned: ". . . it would be better for us to be a native at the uttermost depths of his misery than to be a former settler. . . . It is enough today for two French people to meet together for there to be a dead man between them."[39] Although it may appear that this exaggerated conclusion has its genesis in Plato's *Republic*, it is more likely based on a line of reasoning from the *Notebooks for an Ethics*, Appendix B. There Sartre observes that the "kind" master is regarded by the slaves as more responsible for their condition in virtue of the fact that he has let the cat out of the bag: to treat his slaves humanely is to admit, by virtue of action, that they should not be slaves. We can see the obverse in acts of lynching: to treat the victim as inhumanly as possible is to attempt to absolve the white man from moral condemnation.

The white problem, then, is that there doesn't seem to be any salvation for whites in an antiblack world once antiblackness is admitted to be oppressive (which is the reason why some whites may choose vehemently to deny that such a world is oppressive). This was certainly Sartre's conclusion in his preface to *The Wretched of the Earth* (p. 27):

> What a confession! Formerly our continent was buoyed up by other means: the Parthenon, Chartres, the Rights of Man, or the swastika. Now we know what these are worth; and the only chance of our being saved from shipwreck is the very Christian sentiment of guilt. You can see it's the end.

When the Rights of Man take up company with the swastika fulfillment of one's moral duty takes on a meaning that carries a degree of faith and commitment that dwarfs the most staunch Kantian and parallels Kierkegaard's Abraham's Faith.

4

Let us now focus on the problem of applying Sartre's analysis of Jews to blacks and focus on Fanon's criticisms of Sartre. These two concerns are of importance to us for two reasons. First, the problems raised by Sartre's discussion of anti-Semitism question the extension of phenomenology to history, or more appropriately, to whether there can be a phenomenology of history. Second, Fanon's criticisms of Sartre have been the most enduring criticisms among black liberationists and scholars and, as such, like the problem of history, poses the question of the limitation of existential phenomenology.

A great deal of Sartre's discussion in *Anti-Semite and Jew* is built upon the *anti-Semite*'s problem of anti-Semitism. Its major premise is that the Jew is fundamentally constituted as an object of the anti-Semite's sadistic look. Although it is true that the anti-Semite is The Third in anti-Semitic societies, Sartre's conclusion that it is the anti-Semite who makes the Jew is blatantly false. Those who adhere to Abraham's covenant have lived long before anyone decided to hate them. What the anti-Semite makes or, in phenomenological language, *constitutes* is the pejorative conception of being Jewish.

The black situation is different. Although Jews may have existed before anti-Jews, it is not clear that blacks existed before antiblack racism. The reasoning requires a separate work for a developed discussion, but in brief, it is possible that no African nor Aborigine had any reason to think of himself as black until Europeans found it necessary to define him so. This power of *defining* required specific conditions that were external to those people themselves. It is possible that, given the conditions emerging in Europe near the advent of slavery and exploitation on the basis of race, black people may have emerged even if there were no people morphologically similar to the people of Africa or Australia whom we have come to regard as "blacks." It is this aspect of the black condition that compelled Fanon to declare that there is noting ontological about antiblack racism:

> Ontology – once it is finally admitted as leaving existence by the wayside – does not permit us to understand the being of the black man. For not only must the black man be black; he must be black in relation to the white man.[40]

There is an interpretation, however, under which sense can be made of one of Sartre's more controversial claims. Sartre was rebuked for claiming that Jews have no history. Suppose we make a parallel claim about blacks: blacks have no history. The meaning of such a statement is obviously false – in a colloquial sense of having a history.[41] Let us demarcate this sense of history with a lower-case *h*. Suppose we adopt a Hegelian sense of History – distinguished with the upper-case *H* – where the "highest" embodiment of *Geist* is situated. According to Hegel, the place and the people of History in his epoch were European Christians.[42] Today, it might as well be "Americans." *Geist* is where the globally dominant culture is located.[43] In such a context, is it any wonder that historians of Africans and Afrocentric historians send their messages to deaf ears?

Would this not also be a meaningful sense of lacking History? How can one have History when one is invisible *to* History?

It should be noted that, in *The Journeying Self*, Natanson offers a phenomenological theory of being historical that falls outside of the framework of the two conceptions offered thus far. "It must be understood at once," he writes, "that microcosmic history is not written at all; it has no historian. We are speaking of the life of the individual in the mundane world, and the 'we' speaking is the participant himself, each of us who lives reflectively in the midst of the social world and seeks to transcend the limits of Bad Faith."[44] Every black person *faces* history – *his* or *her* story – every day as a situation, as a choice, of how to stand in relation to oppression, of whether to live as a being subsumed by oppression or to live as active resistance towards liberation or to live as mere indifference. This conception of history is rooted in daily life. As a consequence it has no "heroes." There is no question of elevating one's value beyond oneself into a realm of seriousness. There is, instead, the recognition of how one's *actions* unfold into one's identity in relation to the sociotemporal location of one's experience. Natanson adds,

> It is *his* [the individual's] career in the world which is at the center of the history of mundanity. To say that he is prejudiced or naive is to miss the point, for what is at issue is not disengaged observers. Action, not description, is the operative category here. . . . The 'history' which emerges is then an egological or 'first-person' report of the becoming of the person. If the 'history' of each one of us were nothing more than the story of what befell us, we would be left with the simple meaning of autobiography. . . . What distinguishes microcosmic history from autobiography is the typification of ordinary existence which the individual lives through and defines are constitutive of an intersubjective matrix of mundane reality, the public world which transcends autobiography. The history of the individual is then caught up inevitably in the history of sociality, a structure which phenomenologists called the 'life-world.'[45]

We have said that racial discrimination leads to a form of existential indiscrimination; from the standpoint of antiblack racism there is no difference between any of the following dyads – blacks versus *a* black, *the* black versus *a* black, *blacks* versus *this* black. In existential phenomenological language, this means that blacks are "overdetermined." In the eyes of antiblack racists, blacks suffer a hemorrhage in their facticity that permeates their existence into a colored totality. A consequence is that there is no black autobiography in antiblack worlds. To read Frederick Douglass' *Narrative of the Life of Frederick Douglass* or W. E. B. Du Bois' various "autobiographies" or Malcom X's "autobiography" means more than to look into the lives of these men. It is to stare the black situation and the life-world of the United States in the face. Their facticity is linked to the significance of the United States beyond the sphere of the Revolutionary War, the Emancipation Proclamation, the 13th and 14th Amendments, *Plessey v. Ferguson*, or *Brown v. Board of Education of Topeka Kansas*. Their facticity is linked to who they were in light of their choice to recognize their relation to those moments in History. Frederick Douglass' situation was that of once being a slave. But *Frederick Douglass* emerged out of a clear understanding of *his* situation and *his* facticity. The

Frederick Douglass of History is one figure. The man who made the decision to escape from Maryland was another. When he was making the decision, he was no hero. He simply knew the world that mattered to him in specific ways that limited his options but not his choices. His options were factical, mediated, and "objective" (Historical), but his choices were transcendent, immediate, and "situated" (historical). Impositions upon him may belong to a series of factors beyond his power, but his liberation could not be achieved without his taking account of his "role" in the process. It is bad faith to deny one's role in history.

I suspect this is what Sartre had in mind in "Black Orpheus" when he saw negritude as a dialectical negation into History qua the proletarian revolution.[46] He had reflected in the *Notebooks for an Ethics*, whose completion was abandoned during that period, that "In a word, for progress to be one of the meanings of History, it has to descend into History as lived, sought for, and suffered progress."[47] If what the authors of negritude wanted was progress on the fight against antiblack racism, then their plight had to be understood in its lived, willed, and suffered dimensions that ironically set the stage for their liberation (progress). The authors of negritude, Fanon observes in *Black Skin, White Masks*, needed not to *know* their Historical situation.[48] Fanon's conclusion affirms Sartre's verdict on the negritude-fortified black's relation to History – that if the black's cry were to be heard as a cry, it would not be a black one.[49] History (with upper-case *H*) already had and continues to have a "place" for the black man. "However painful it may be for me to accept this conclusion," Fanon confesses, "I am obliged to state it: For the black man there is only one destiny. And it is white."[50] That is a consequence of an earlier proposal: "I propose nothing short of the liberation of the man of color from himself."[51] There is no hope, from Fanon's point of departure, for the black man to gain another "place." For his blackness, recognized as such, renders such a feat no more than a *coup*.[52] What both Fanon and Sartre began to see in the late forties and ultimately saw by 1961 was that revolutionary considerations were needed for a *human* place in the story of self-consciousness that stands outside of white superiority and colored inferiority.

Yet Fanon provides an argument against the application of Sartrean ontology to antiblack racism. This is ironic since, as we will see, Fanon's revolutionary humanistic project is rooted in Sartrean ontology. As one of Fanon's commentators notes, ". . . it has to be said that a Negro is 'thrown into the world" in a total sense which escapes the white man, and therefore the testimony of a Fanon provides indispensable evidence for the wider and more complexly articulated system of a Sartre."[53] Before discussing Fanon's criticisms of Sartre's ontology, it may be fruitful to devote a few more words to "Black Orpheus," since I regard that work as suffering from a number of disturbing problems in spite of its political insight into the Historical invisibility of blacks.

"Black Orpheus" is a classic case of racial exoticism, where the proponent of the oppressed, in league with what Fanon calls "Negro baiters," slips into reductions of virtue and victimization. Sartre slips into the general racist, dyadic matrices of whiteness in the world of reason and blackness in the world of affect. It is not, as one might be inclined to think, that Sartre attempts to reduce blacks to the proletariat. It is instead that Sartre seeks to *elevate* blacks to such a level. Sartre appears to have been aware of the "under-class" status of blacks. Yet Sartre seems to have abandoned his general project of exposing the spirit of seriousness, for even though negritude reflected an under-class designation, it also reflected a form of Manichæism – the material anti-value of blackness in the face of whiteness. Even if it is pointed out that Sartre regarded negritude as a relative attitude instead of an objective value – which means that he was not to regard it as what the proponents of negritude considered it to be – it must be remembered that he also regarded the white working-class as an objective value, as in fact History. The same problem of seriousness re-emerges.[54]

Fanon's explicit attack on Sartrean ontology is this. Even if the white working class were to recognize black workers as workers, there was still the problem of the fact of blackness. For example, Fanon and Sartre were both formally French-educated men who would, but for their color, be considered members of the same class. But Sartre was addressed by his colleagues and strangers with the respectful French second-person pronoun "*vous*," whereas Fanon had to contend with the second-person pronoun "*tu*," a term that refers to personal acquaintances or strangers who are either children or one's inferior. The consequence is an attack in *Black Skin, White Masks* on Sartre's ontology as well as his interpretation of blacks' relation to History: "Though Sartre's speculations on the existence of The Other may be correct," Fanon writes, "(to the extent, we must remember, to which *Being and Nothingness* describes an alienated consciousness), their application to a black consciousness proves fallacious. That is because the white man is not only The Other but also the master, whether real or imaginary."[55]

Since Fanon rejects the ontological significance of alienation, his interpretation of alienation is here psychoanalytical and Historical. He accepts the psychoanalytical significance of Sartre's analysis, but he argues that the Historical reality shadows the hermeneutic of "Other" in black–white situations.

What would be the case, however, if we were to re-introduce the critical ontological significance of alienation, of unfreedom, in our interpretation of the Sartrean system and consider it in relation to antiblack racism? Fanon would have to show how the existential phenomenological description of bad faith does not operate in his criticism. He would have to show that *his* effort to liberate the black man from himself, to eradicate the black man as black skin with a white ego, can be explained without an appeal to the concept of bad faith. If he cannot do so, then he will have to show that existential phenomenological interpretations only contingently fit such phenomena. To be white may be to deny that race "really" matters, but Fanon shows that to be black is to know and to live every day the reality of how much race really matters. How different is (Fanon), "'Mama, see the Negro! I'm frightened!' Frightened! Frightened! Now they were beginning to be afraid of me. I made up my mind to laugh myself to tears, but laughter had become impossible," from (Sartre), ". . . it is as a No that the slave first apprehends the master, or that the prisoner who is trying to escape sees the guard who is watching him"?[56] How different is Fanon's analysis of white hypocrisy towards universal brotherhood from Sartre's claim that "the bourgeois makes himself a bourgeois by denying that there are any classes, just as the worker makes himself a worker by asserting that classes exist and by realizing through his revolutionary activity his 'being-in-a-class'"?[57] Fanon's own experience attests to Sartre's conclusion that we are responsible for the *way* we live our situations. First:

> "Look how handsome that Negro is! . . ." [Fanon's response:] "Kiss the handsome Negro's ass, madame!" Shame flooded her face. At last I was set free from my rumination. At the same time I accomplished two things: I identified my enemies and I made a scene. A grand slam. Now one would be able to laugh.[58]

Fanon regarded the situation of each man to be a constant struggle against the degradation of Man. "I find myself suddenly in the world and I recognize that I have one right alone: That of demanding human behavior form the other. One duty alone: That of not renouncing my freedom through my choices. . . . I, the man of color, want only this: That the tool never possess the man. That the enslavement of man by man cease forever. . . . That it be possible for me to discover and to love man, wherever he may be."[59] In his letter of resignation from his position as *chef de service* at the Blida-Joinville psychiatric clinic, he summarized the existential situation of the psychiatrist and the colonized neurotic:

> Madness is one of the means man has of losing his freedom. And I can say, on the basis of what I have been able to observe from this point of vantage, that the degree of alienation of the inhabitants of this country appears to me frightening. . . . For many months my conscience has been the seat of unpardonable debates. And their conclusion is that I cannot continue to bear a responsibility at no matter what cost, on the false pretext that there is nothing else to be done.[60]

The way Fanon lived his situation in 1956 was not only by resigning, but also by placing himself in the service of the revolutionary forces of Algeria.

Fanon issues a rejection of Sartrean ontology because, I suspect, he, like some of Sartre's critics, fails to appreciate fully the significance of the concept of bad faith. Bad faith is not simply a by-product or possibility of human reality. It is, as Sartre declares in *Being and Nothingness*, the "determined attitude which is essential to human reality and which is such that consciousness instead of directing its negation outwards turns it toward itself."[61] Sartre's ontology is a critical ontology premised upon the human being qua freedom as the being who can *deny* its own freedom. Fanon's criticism of ontology was qualified by the phrase "once it is finally admitted as leaving existence by the wayside" for good reason. Existential phenomenology stands outside of his criticism of ontology, though not his criticism of the Sartrean interpretation of I–Other relationships.

The very liberation project that Fanon seeks for blacks is possible in virtue of the fact that blacks are human beings. This is not only a historical realization. The black is also pre-reflectively aware of this at every moment he feels responsible for his oppression even though he is aware that he is being oppressed just as the rape victim feels responsible for what she knows is not her fault.

Fanon has shown that the white stands in front of the black as the master *in an antiblack world*, in the Historical world. Although he has not *shown* that the relation is contingent, he believes the relation is a consequence of a contingent Historical situation. We find ourselves in the epoch of an antiblack world, but other kinds of world have existed and *could* exist in the future. His liberation project demands that the relation of the white to the black be contingent.[62] Otherwise, how would "this [veiled Algerian] woman who sees without being seen frustrates the colonizer" make sense?[63]

Fanon declares that "[Society,] unlike biochemical processes, cannot escape human influence. Man is what brings society into being. . . . The black man must wage his war on both levels: Since [H]istorically they influence each other, any unilateral liberation is incomplete, and the gravest mistake would be to believe in their automatic interdependence."[64] To this we add that what is contingent need not be accidental. History (all three kinds) has shown that a subjugated black race was no accident. Two years later, in his analysis of the Antillean and the African, Fanon takes the existential phenomenological standpoint of analyzing racial phenomena from the standpoint of bad faith and, in effect, substantiates our criticism of his earlier position through admitting the importance of an analysis that differentiates contingency from "deeper" levels of philosophically significant phenomena: "I shall be found to use terms like 'metaphysical guilt,' or 'obsession with purity.' I shall ask the reader not to be surprised: these will be accurate to the extent to which it is understood that since what is important cannot be attained, or more precisely, since what is important is not really sought after, one falls back on what is contingent. This is one of the laws of recrimination and of bad faith. The urgent thing is to rediscover what is important beneath what is contingent."[65] This realization is often overlooked in contemporary, ultimately postmodern approaches to the study of Fanon and the study of race.[66]

5

Natanson's conception of philosophy, brought to fruition especially in *The Journeying Self* and the subsequent *Anonymity*, is that philosophy is fundamentally existential, phenomenological, social, therapeutic, and imaginative. It is the commitment and effort to stand as clearly and truthfully as possible before oneself, others, and the possibilities shared by such commitment. It is from such a standpoint that he considered the impact of race in the quotations that opened our discussion. He was one of the first professional philosophers to understand the *social* significance of Sartrean ontology. What he understands and I now affirm is that the common thread in the application of Sartrean existential phenomenology to problems of social role – a primary concern of black and I suspect all liberation theories – is this: that ontology sets the framework from which to be on guard against the reductionism or bad faith of demanding ideal, romantic, innocent, or exotic subjects on the one hand and the denial of responsibility for the liberation of humankind in the current epoch on the other. Instead of a dichotomy of the free and the determined, existential phenomenology reminds us that proper human categories are the free and the unfree, which calls for the dialectical resolve of the historically liberating.

Notes

1. I would like to thank Steven Crowell, Phyllis Morris, Martin Matustík, Gary Schwartz, and Eric Ramsey for their valuable, constructive criticisms of earlier drafts of this paper.

2. *The Journeying Self: A Study in Philosophy and Social Role* (Reading: Addison-Wesley, 1970), pp. 102–3.

3. *The Words: The Autobiography of Jean-Paul Sartre*, tr. Bernard Frechtman (New York: George Braziller, 1964), p. 30.

4. Natanson and Alfred Schutz have criticized Sartre for committing forms of methodological or practical solipsism. See Natanson, "The Problem of Others in *Being and Nothingness*," in *The Library of Living Philosophers*, vol. XVI, *The Philosophy of Jean-Paul Sartre*, ed. Paul Arthur Schilpp (La Salle, Ill.: Open Court, 1981), p. 341; and Schutz, *Collected Papers*, vol. 1, *The Problem of Social Reality*, ed. Maurice Natanson (The Hague: Martinus Nijhoff, 1962), p. 203. On this matter, see our discussion below of Sartre's ontology as an examination of human reality *from the standpoint of bad faith*. The methodological or practical solipsism of which Natanson and Schutz speak is a function of bad-faith attitudes towards human relationships. But such an attitude depends, ultimately, on the possibility of authentic attitudes – or a practice that is *not* solipsistic. The problem is comparable to Freud's problem of the scope of sexuality in the interpretation of human reality; he needed a non-sexual standpoint from which to make the sexual aspects meaningful.

5. See Sartre, *Being and Nothingness: A Phenomenological Essay on Ontology*, tr. Hazel Barnes (New York: Washington Square Press, 1956), pp. 533–4.

6. Ibid., Part 3, ch. 2.

7. For a developed discussion of this formulation of bad faith, see Lewis R. Gordon, *Bad Faith and Antiblack Racism* (Atlantic Highlands: Humanities Press, 1995), esp. Part I. For similar discussion, see also Debra Bergoffen, "Casting Shadows: The Body in Descartes, Sartre, De Beauvoir, and Lacan," *Bulletin de la Société Américaine de Philosophie de Langue Française*, IV, nos. 2–3 (1992), pp. 232–43.

8. *Being and Nothingness*, esp. p. 113.

9. Sartre argues that this is the ultimate implication of the standpoint of power. See his discussion of The Third, *Being and Nothingness*, esp. p. 547.

10. "Racism and Culture," in *Toward the African Revolution*, tr. Haakon Chevalier (New York: Grove Press, 1967), p. 37.

11. Ibid., pp. 25, 36–7.

12. The literature is extensive, but for general discussions of gender categories, see Carol C. Gould and Marx W. Wartofsky (eds), *Women and Philosophy: Toward a Theory of Liberation* (New York: Perigee Books, 1980), and for race categories, see David Theo Goldberg (ed.), *Anatomy of Racism* (Minneapolis: The University of Minnesota Press, 1990). For a study of the use of gender categories to undermine resistance to Western colonial/racist onslaughts, see Fanon, *A Dying Colonialism*, tr. Haakon Chevalier (New York: Grove Weidenfeld, 1965), ch. 1, "Algeria Unveiled."

13. During the infamous Mike Tyson rape trial, a number of my white female friends were outraged that their black sisters were reluctant to "believe" the prosecutrix's testimony that she was raped by Mike Tyson. This case hit the core of what I suspect is the key difference between what is sometimes caricatured as "white feminism" versus "black feminism." White feminism calls for the construction of women as victims. Black feminism argues that although women are oppressed, they are not victims. Thus white feminists purportedly invest a great deal of energy on the dynamics of rape and the rejection of the thesis that

when a woman says "no" she means "yes." But in this regard, their plight differs from black women. Black women live in a reality in which it simply doesn't matter whether they *say* anything. The consequence is that although it is a politically feasible route to reject ideal innocence of the victim in rape cases – for the obvious reason that it should be the rapist, not the woman on trial – black women are more willing to admit that women, like men, are neither ontologically nor morally neat. Both can not only say what they don't mean, but they can also lie to themselves about what they mean when they say what they say. Black feminism therefore doesn't deny the possibility of seduction, that a person can deny what he wants in order to deny responsibility for what he receives. But this doesn't entail that he who takes advantage of such a situation is not responsible as well. In this regard, black feminism is more in stream with Sartrean ontology. Because of his many observations on the role of seduction in human reality, Sartre has been the object of a great deal of white feminist attacks, and I would say for good reason, for without the possibility of seduction, sexual or otherwise, Sartrean ontology, premised as it is upon freedom, responsibility, and the ever-present threat of bad faith, loses all meaning.

14. See Angela Davis, *Women, Race, and Class* (New York: Vintage, 1983); bell hooks, *Ain't I a Woman?: Black Women and Feminism* (Boston: South End Press, 1981); and Jacqueline Grant, *White Women's Christ and Black Women's Jesus* (Atlanta: Scholars Press, 1989). The argument predates the feminist movements of the 1960s and 1970s and the Womanist movement in the academy in the 1980s. For example, women's causes on the part of colonizers in the supposed interests of colonized women took the form of European female identity and served as a means of breaking down the anti-European identity of colonized people – particularly in regards to their family structures. See Fanon's *A Dying Colonialism*, pp. 37–42.

15. See Davis, *Women, Race, and Class*, ch. 11, "Rape, Racism and the Myth of the Black Rapist." It should be noted that the maligning of black males is not indicative of feminism in general. It can be argued, for instance, as Davis does, that a strong feminist position is against the exploitation and stereotyping of females *and* males of all races, class, and creeds. Our discussion here is meant to illustrate how bad faith can be identified in cases where ideal subjects of liberation are sought.

16. An example of the exoticizing of black women is the mania around black female literature in the academy. For discussion, see Hazel V. Carby, "The Multicultural Wars," in *Black Popular Culture: A Project by Michele Wallace*, ed. Gina Dent (Seattle: Bay Press, 1992), pp. 192–3.

17. For example Grant, *White Women's Christ and Black Women's Jesus*, p. 220.

18. I describe Sartre's ontology as "critical" because it ultimately falls outside of the traditional interpretation of ontology as the study of Being or the Metaphysics of Presence. Sartre's claim that we encounter our own existence, which is a lack of being-in-itself, suggests that his is an ontology that is ultimately critical of traditional ontology.

19. *Being and Nothingness*, pp. 545–5.

20. This is, by the way, one of the contentions of Husserl's Fifth Meditation, in *Cartesian Meditations: An Introduction to Phenomenology*, tr. Dorion Cairns (Dordrecht: Martinus Nijhoff, 1960).

21. *Notebook for an Ethics*, tr. David Pellauer (Chicago: University of Chicago Press, 1992), p. 6.

22. Husserl, *Cartesian Meditations*, esp. section 57. See also Natanson, *The Journeying Self*, *passim*.

23. *The Journeying Self*, pp. 31–2; "The Problem of Others in *Being and Nothingness*," pp. 331–4, 342.

24. *Being and Nothingness*, p. 554.

25. *The Wretched of the Earth*, with a Preface by Jean-Paul Sartre, tr. Constance Farrington (New York: Grove Press, 1963), p. 250. Hereafter "Preface" will refer to Sartre's preface and *Wretched of the Earth* will refer to Fanon only.

26. Sartre, "Preface," p. 21.

27. *Being and Nothingness*, pp. 112–13.

28. Fanon, *Black Skin, White Masks*, tr. Charles Lamm Markmann (New York: Grove Press, 1967), p. 50. These two quoted examples present a rather startling challenge to conventional wisdom. An implication of these two black women's efforts to avoid places where there are blacks is a form of self-lie that involves the denial of their being black in a room in which any one of these two women is the only black. This challenges the thesis that the black becomes self-conscious of himself as black in virtue of the way he is seen by whites. In the absence of other blacks, these women are able to make themselves believe the lie of a coordination between their white masks and their skin – the lie of having both white masks and white skin. They confront the fact of their blackness through the eyes of *other blacks*.

29. *Between Existentialism and Marxism: Sartre on Philosophy, Politics, Psychology, and the Arts*, tr. John Mathews (New York: Pantheon Books, 1974), p. 67.

30. *The Respectful Prostitute*, in *"No Exit" and Three Other Plays* (New York: Vintage, 1955), p. 263.

31. For a discussion of Manichæism, see R. McL. Wilson's article, "Mani and Manichæism," in *The Encyclopedia of Philosophy*, vol. 5, ed. Paul Edwards (New York: Macmillan Publishing Company and the Free Press, 1967), pp. 149–50.

32. *Black Skin, White Masks*, pp. 118–20.

33. *Being and Nothingness*, pp. 772–82.

34. The literature on racists' identification of other races with sexual promiscuity and rape is extensive. Angela Davis and bell hooks have already been mentioned. Consider also Fanon's "The 'North African Syndrome," in *Toward the African Revolution*, esp. pp. 11–12; *Black Skin, White Masks, passim*; and Calvin Hernton, *Sex and Racism in America* (New York: Grove Press, 1965).

35. Du Bois provides a discussion of the history behind this work and *The Souls of Black Folk* in *The Autobiography of W. E. B. Du Bois: A Soliloquy on Viewing My Life from the Last Decade of Its First Century*, ed. Herbert Aptheker (New York: International Publishers, 1968), see especially ch. XII.

36. See "Preface," pp. 7–31; *The Words*, esp. pp. 247, 254. See also Simone de Beauvoir's account of his meeting with Fanon in Rome, where Fanon argued that Sartre is ultimately "guilty" of being French. Simone de Beauvoir, *The Force of Circumstances*, tr. Richard Howard (New York: Putnman, 1965), p. 592.

37. *Being and Nothingness*, p. 554.

38. This is the heart of the problem with so-called "reverse discrimination" arguments. They are based upon the assumption that racial justice is met when one fights for the interests of whites (as if the interests of whites weren't already a feature of the structure of the antiblack world). This is no doubt the seduction and foundation of the logic deployed by most white supremacists and the reason why their arguments, however loaded, have *some* appeal to their audience. White supremacists and the like argue that whites who seek the liberation of nonwhites are ultimately fighting for a cause that is "abnormal" because it is not their own. Fanon puts it this way, "The racist in a culture with racism is therefore normal . . . One cannot with impunity require of a man that he be against 'the prejudices of his group'." "Racism and Culture," p. 40. In 1961, he stated the situation of racial justice

in more succinct, biblical terms: "The last shall be first and the first last," *Wretched of the Earth*, p. 37.

39. Sartre, "Preface," pp. 29–30.

40. *Black Skin, White Masks*, p. 110.

41. For the significance of the relationship between the colloquial or everyday sense of having a history and the understanding of bad faith, see Natanson, *The Journeying Self*, p. 91. One's history is an aspect of one's facticity. To deny it is a form of bad faith.

42. See Hegel's *Philosophy of History*, tr. J. Sibree (New York: Dover, 1956), p. 107, and Part II; and Hegel, *Philosophy of Right*, tr. T. M. Knox (Oxford: Clarendon Press, 1967), esp. p. 51. See also Charles Taylor, *Hegel and Modern Society* (New York: Cambridge University Press, 1979), pp. 100–101.

43. We should note that for Hegel, this does not mean that might makes right. See *Philosophy of Right*, p. 216, paragraph 342, There is, however, a problem. In paragraph 343 he claims that *"Geist* is only what it does, and its act is to make itself the object of its own consciousness. In history its act is to gain consciousness of itself as *Geist*, to apprehend itself in its interpretation of itself to itself." Does this preclude black self-consciousness outside of the framework of a white conception of blackness? I don't see how an affirmative response can be made without being fallacious. Blacks would either become Historical through their own recognition of their own History, in which case there would be at least two Histories, or they would be Historical through recognizing themselves in a way that is equivalent to the History that has already emerged. The former affirms blackness, the latter marks its elimination. But if the former were asserted, I don't see how the following resort can be avoided: *Whose* History? An Hegelian would have to show that although blacks may make themselves objects of their own consciousness, and hence become self-conscious, this does not constitute, in their case, their embodying *Geist*. Such a resort is identical with the racist's credo that, ultimately, the problem with other races is the races themselves. Ordinary criteria of evidence for their equality to those who are the self-designated standpoint of all humanity are thereby rejected.

44. *The Journeying Self*, p. 94. In this regard, Natanson anticipated what has been described by Pauline Marie Rosenau as the "Affirmative Post-Modernist Subject": "a post-modern subject with a new nonidentity, focused not on the 'Great Men' of history, but rather, on daily life at the margins. This subject will reject total explanations and the logocentric point of view that implies a unified frame of reference, but s/he need not oppose all dimensions of humanism," *Post-Modernism and the Social Sciences: Insights, Inroads, and Intrusions* (Princeton: Princeton University Press, 1992), p. 57. It would not be correct to conclude, however, that Natanson is a "post-modern" philosopher. He *emphasizes* history versus History, but he doesn't reject the latter, and his philosophy of social role is firmly rooted in the Husserlian conception of the transcendental ego, which is a form of "unified frame of reference" (see esp. *The Journeying Self* and his more recent *Anonymity: A Study in the Philosophy of Alfred Schutz* [Bloomington: Indiana University Press, 1986]). Given his concerns with philosophical anthropology as well as phenomenological perspectives of the social sciences, his argument here should be considered no more post-modern than existential phenomenology itself.

45. *The Journeying Self*, p. 94.

46. "Black Orpheus," tr. John MacCombie, in *"What is Literature"? and Other Essays*, ed. Steven Ungar (Cambridge, MA: Harvard University Press, 1988), pp. 326–30.

47. *Notebooks for an Ethics*, p. 42. For a discussion of Sartre's conception of progress, see Ronald Aronson, "Sartre on Progress," in *The Cambridge Companion to Sartre*, ed. Christina Howells (Cambridge: Cambridge University Press, 1992), pp. 261–92. Sartre's efforts to articulate

history as lived took on more complex form in his discussion of the relationship between interiority and exteriority in the later *Critique of Dialectical Reason*, vol. 1, *Theory of Practical Ensembles*, tr. Alan Sheridan and ed. Jonathan Rée (London: Verso, 1991). passim. He writes, for example, "If History is totalisation and if individual practices are the sole ground of totalising temporalisation, it is not enough to reveal the totalisation developing in everyone, and consequently in our critical investigations, through the contradictions which both express and mask it. Our critical investigation must also show us *how* the practical multiplicity (which may be called 'men' or 'Humanity' according to taste) realises, in its very dispersal, its interiorisation" (p. 64).

48. *Black Skin, White Masks*, p. 135.
49. Ibid., p. 29.
50. Ibid., p. 10.
51. Ibid., p. 8.
52. Ibid., pp. 11, 30.
53. David Caute, *Frantz Fanon* (New York: Viking Press, 1970), p. 33.
54. This is not the place for a discussion of the meaning, and social-scientific and phenomenological validity of "class." The literature on the concept is vast, and here I only hint at some of Sartre's interpretations. But Sartre's most sustained analysis of the concept can be found in his *Critique*. For commentary, see William L. McBride, *Sartre's Political Theory* (Bloomington: Indiana University Press, 1991), esp. pp. 78–9, 164–6.
55. *Black Skin, White Masks*, p. 138 n. 24.
56. The first quotation is from *Black Skin*, White Masks, p. 112, and the second quotation is from *Being and Nothingness*, p. 87.
57. *Being and Nothingness*, p. 680.
58. *Black Skin, White Masks*, p. 114.
59. Ibid., pp. 229–31.
60. "Letter to the Resident Minister" (1956), in *Toward the African Revolution*, p. 53.
61. *Being and Nothingness*, p. 87.
62. In short, the *struggle* for racial justice requires such a possibility. In his discussion of class struggle in *The Critique of Dialectical Reason*, p. 679, Sartre makes a similar point: "But this serial, practico-inert statute [roughly, a stratified, oppressed group identity] would not lead to class *struggle* if the permanent possibility of dissolving the series were not available to everyone; and we have seen how a first, abstract determination of this possible unity emerges through class interest, as a possible negation of destiny."
63. *A Dying Colonialism*, p. 44.
64. *Black Skin, White Masks*, p. 11.
65. "West Indians and Africans," p. 18.
66. A recent example of interpreting Fanon in a post-modernist (post-structuralist or deconstructive) way is Homi Bhabha's "Interrogating Identity: The Postcolonial Prerogative," in *Anatomy of Racism*, pp. 183–209. Although Sartre and Fanon would agree that there is a postcolonial prerogative, I suggest that they would also add that to assert our contemporary neocolonial Historical situation as a postcolonial one is a form of bad faith. Postcolonial discourse in colonial and neocolonial times serves, ultimately, as sustenance for the *status quo*. Both Sartre and Fanon were aware that colonial categories of identity needed to be criticized with circumspection and a critical historical outlook – ultimately, critical good faith – for a revolutionary praxis to emerge.

CHAPTER 14

Beauvoir and the Problem of Racism

MARGARET A. SIMONS

In *The Second Sex* (1949) Simone de Beauvoir compares and contrasts the situations of women, Jews, American blacks, and the proletariat in analyzing women's oppression and the possibility of liberation. Racism and anti-Semitism are models of oppression for Beauvoir. Her theory of oppression, drawing upon Marxism and theories of racist oppression, challenges biological and psychoanalytic essentialism as well as economic reductionism to lay the theoretical foundations of radical feminism. The centerpiece of her theory is her social constructionism ("one is not born, but rather becomes a woman" [1949, II, p. 13]), the theory that apparently natural racial and gender differences in character actually reflect the *situation* of oppression. "[T]he biological and social sciences no longer believe in the existence of immutably fixed entities that would define given characteristics such as those of the woman, the Jew or the Black. They consider character to be a secondary reaction to a situation" (ibid., I, p. 12). Indeed for Beauvoir, "the body is not a *thing*, it is a situation . . . it is the instrument of our grasp upon the world, a limiting factor for our projects" (ibid., I, p. 72). Beauvoir does not deny the reality of stereotypes such as femininity or the black soul; she argues that oppressive ideologies and institutional structures shape the psyches and the bodies of the oppressed. Only with the dismantling of oppressive castes will stereotypes disappear and individual differences be allowed to develop freely.

Beauvoir's understanding of racism is central to her philosophical project in *The Second Sex*; but racism and ethnocentrism are also problems for her. Beauvoir was an anti-colonialist and, in the 1960s, was a vocal supporter of Algerians in their war for independence from France, but nonetheless *The Second Sex* is marred by ethnocentrism. In her study of women in history, Beauvoir elects to focus solely on the West, and more specifically France, dispensing with the rest of women's history in a footnote: "We will examine this evolution in the Occident. Woman's history in the Orient, in India, in

China was in effect that of a long and immutable slavery. From the Middle Ages to our days we will center our study on France whose case is typical" (ibid., I, p. 133). Furthermore, Beauvoir is popularly known as a writer of the French Resistance and a supporter of Israel, receiving the Jerusalem Prize in 1975. But critics, and the author of her popular 1990 biography, charge her with anti-Semitism and collaboration with the Nazi Occupation. How are we to understand these charges? How should they influence our reading of Beauvoir's philosophy in *The Second Sex*?

To examine the charges of anti-Semitism, we will begin by analyzing Beauvoir's unpublished diary from 1927. Then we will analyze her war diaries and correspondence with Sartre for the origins of her concept of "situation" and her postwar engagement in struggles against anti-Semitism. Finally, we will examine Beauvoir's account, in *America: Day by Day* (1948), of her experience of American racism and her search for an alternative to essentialist and nominalist explanations of race.

Beauvoir's personal struggle with the problem of racism began in her childhood dominated by an ardent Catholic mother and an atheistic, but virulently anti-Semitic, French nationalist father. In her biography, Deirdre Bair charges that Beauvoir's anti-Semitic legacy from her father prevented her friendship with a fellow Sorbonne philosophy student, Georgette Lévy, in the late 1920s.

> There were only two [girls] with whom she might have developed intellectual as well as personal friendships, but . . . Georgette Lévy was Jewish. Georgette's wealthy family lived in the fashionable Sixteenth Arrondissement, and Simone used the difference in their social background as a convenient excuse to end what might have been an interesting friendship. . . . Many years later Simone de Beauvoir insisted that she had never been anti-Semitic in her life, but when asked whether her attitude toward Georgette Lévy might have been influenced in some way by the harsh antipathy of her father toward Jews, she said curtly, 'Probably'. (Bair, 1990, p. 124)

Bair relied on interviews with Beauvoir and her published memoirs in charging Beauvoir with anti-Semitism. But it is now possible to investigate this charge more directly through a study of Beauvoir's handwritten diary from 1927, deposited in 1990 in the Bibliothèque Nationale by Sylvie Le Bon de Beauvoir, Beauvoir's adopted daughter and literary executor. Beauvoir's 1927 diary contains an account of her relationship with Georgette Lévy which challenges Bair's charge that Beauvoir's anti-Semitism ended a friendship that "might have been." In the opening pages of the diary, Beauvoir includes Georgette Lévy in a list of friends, "those beings for whom I am something" (Beauvoir, 1927, p. 8). But a legacy of anti-Semitism is apparent in an early diary passage, which contains an ethnic stereotype: "April 28. Saw G. Lévy again and held forth on the social self and the pure self, amusing discussions: she is very Jewish and too fond of juggling with words" (ibid., p. 16). Thus, the 1927 diary does provide some evidence of anti-Semitism. However, this is the only such instance in the diary, which contains over thirty references to Georgette Lévy, many of them describing a friendship of increasing depth and intimacy, which endures throughout the year despite the differences in their religious backgrounds.

A consistent theme in the references to Georgette Lévy is her contribution to Beauvoir's self-understanding, as in the following passage: "G. Lévy clarified for me what I experienced next to Barbier: when one loves beings as we love them, not for their intelligence, etc. . . . but for their soul, how to legitimate a choice?" (ibid., p. 44). Beauvoir's use of the word "we" is also interesting in this passage, suggesting a sense of her identification with Georgette Lévy. But a diary entry for May 13 describes their differing attitudes towards philosophy as a barrier to their friendship: "Georgette Lévy is indeed intelligent but very distant from me since playing is sufficient for her" (ibid., p. 50). Beauvoir's anguished spiritual and philosophical quest isolates her from most of her friends, not just Georgette Lévy: "G. Lévy revealed to me that deep down, happiness would be enough for her . . ." (ibid., p. 56).

But the passages also reveal Beauvoir's pleasure in her friendship with Georgette Lévy and a sense of regret at their different interests: "Georgette Lévy irritates me (although I have so much pleasure in seeing her) by this need to pose problems everywhere and to enclose herself in her indecision" (ibid., p. 61). But despite their differences, Beauvoir values Georgette Lévy's insights: "My heart sleeps under the weight of my philosophical meditations . . . G. Lévy is becoming almost a friend: I should have specified to her exactly the nature of my pain and understood on the basis of that how it would be necessary to live" (ibid., p. 67). The diary recounts Beauvoir's trust in her friend's judgments: "G. Lévy is right. . . . Nothing exists but me and the veiled and snickering monster that is named God, life, or reality. . . . It is there, it watches me. I'm afraid" (ibid., pp. 81–2).

In an entry from July, Beauvoir includes her friend in a list of persons to talk to during the next school year: "G. Lévy of course." Another entry on the list is a new acquaintance and fellow philosophy student, Maurice Merleau-Ponty, who shares Beauvoir's struggle with Catholicism that isolates her from Georgette Lévy. In July, as Beauvoir is emotionally shaken by the pressures of her success on the philosophy exams (where she has come in second, behind Simone Weil, and ahead of Merleau-Ponty), she turns to Georgette Lévy: "Once again, here I am stronger from the love that others have for me. Charming afternoon at G. Lévy's reading poetry together and handling beautiful books" (ibid., p. 87). She looks forward to continuing their friendship during the next year: "Certainly a friendship would be precious to me for support—neither Zaza, nor M. Blomart, nor any girl; maybe G. Lévy; . . . I can . . . discuss with her but she is too interested in herself to truly support me" (ibid., p. 89). Georgette Lévy, while she has her own interests, brings to the relationship with Beauvoir a shared interest in philosophy and the intimacy of female friendship. Indeed in another passage, Beauvoir ranks Georgette Lévy among her valued advisers, vowing to "confide in someone who criticizes and takes me seriously: [Jean] Baruzi [her philosophy professor at the Sorbonne], G. Lévy or Pontremoli [another student]" (ibid., p. 91).

During the summer, separated from her friends, Beauvoir thinks of "G. Lévy whom I miss more than I would have believed" (ibid., p. 93). Georgette Lévy has become a valued, intimate friend to Beauvoir, despite their differences. As Beauvoir struggles with her own Catholic heritage, her Jewish friend seems able to provide a helpful perspective. In an important July 10 diary passage, highlighted with a later marginal line, Beauvoir writes:

Mademoiselle Mercier is trying to convert me; she speaks to me of Abbé Beaussard who would like to see me and I think of G. Lévy saying "You will be tempted by that way;" it's true. This morning . . . I passionately desired to be the girl who takes communion at morning mass and walks in a serene certainty. (Ibid., p. 94)

Beauvoir's concern with Catholicism draws her to Merleau-Ponty, "Ponti [sic] says: 'there is this path (of Catholicism); I wish to see if it is possible.' I say: why this path. I believe it is impossible" (ibid., p. 110). For a time, references to Georgette Lévy and Merleau-Ponty appear together in Beauvoir's discussions of philosophy:

my dissertation where I deny substance contradicts this realism that I exposed to G. Lévy. I'm too easily satisfied with contradictions. But there's the explanation: I require all or nothing. Ponti [sic] says "it's better to sacrifice becoming than being;" I say that [when] I see a defect in a system, I want to sacrifice the entire system. (Ibid., p. 110)

But when Georgette Lévy begins to criticize the conservative Merleau-Ponty, the first signs of another rift between the friends appears: "Ponti [sic] has not experimented: he advances only when the route becomes clear – 'shades of Mauriac' [*Tête* Mauriac] said Georgette Lévy. . . . But I had no doubt that this would be a *friend*. How young, playful, intelligent, serious, nice he is!" (ibid., p. 123). Beauvoir continues to write Georgette Lévy with her philosophical concerns while on summer vacation: "Wrote to G. Lévy my will to call everything into question because I believe that a duty, to rethink every postulate, to renounce even that in which I believe" (ibid., pp. 142–3). She remembers fondly the past academic year: "the wonder at ourselves that Georgette and I maintained" (ibid., p. 143). Georgette Lévy is still a trusted adviser, as is apparent in the following passage, highlighted with a later marginal line, where she encourages Beauvoir to write: "To write . . . delicious temptation! . . . But I will not have the time to manage everything at once: exams, the search for the truth, and the expression of self. Georgette Lévy says that I should not fear splitting in two: to try?" (ibid., p. 146).

As the diary ends with the beginning of the fall term, Beauvoir is at first "pleased to see Georgette Lévy again" (ibid., p. 165). But as her intimacy with Merleau-Ponty grows, anchored by their shared interest in Catholicism, her affection for Georgette Lévy wanes: "Sweet pleasure of walks with Ponty. . . . We chat about . . . Claudel, Mauriac, Thomism. . . . And at times I think of him with a great tenderness. . . . I saw G. Lévy Wednesday. Without affection. . . . this necessity of being of her opinion. Not my friend, no" (ibid., p. 166). Since some of Georgette Lévy's opinions include an attack on Merleau-Ponty, Beauvoir's break with Georgette Lévy is predictable:

Saw G. Lévy again on Saturday morning and also the following Monday . . . Interesting talks like a "Proustian concierge;" the word suits her. How little disdainful she is basically in the importance that she gives to the least of her disdains! She does not know how to make herself loved because she understands only herself. Always justifying what *she* does! Well, she has certain qualities and lives quite according to her thought. (Ibid., p. 167)

Given the lack of anti-Semitic comments in this angry passage, Beauvoir's friendship with Georgette Lévy seems to have been cut short not by anti-Semitism but by Beauvoir's increasing intimacy with her Catholic friend, Merleau-Ponty, *"mon cher, cher ami"* (ibid., p. 169). If prejudice inhibited any of Beauvoir 's relationships in 1927, it may be a friendship that might have been with someone named Lagache, whose sexual behavior Beauvoir apparently found shocking: "I could not approach Lagache after what G. Lévy told me; how is she not revolted?" Beauvoir traces this reaction to her Catholic upbringing: "It is without doubt my Catholic heritage that lifts me up in this way" (ibid., pp. 85–6). A reference to Lagache appears also on the final page of the diary: "G. Lévy spoke to me of Lagache who is perhaps a lesbian" (ibid., p. 168), indicating that the prejudice inhibiting Beauvoir's friendship might be homophobia rather than anti-Semitism. The depth of Beauvoir's friendship with Georgette Lévy appears on a page summarizing the 1927 academic year and inserted into the 1928 diary. Beauvoir writes of her "friendship with Georgette Lévy," "who taught me to put into words [my] metaphysical pain" (ibid., n.p.).

The charge of anti-Semitism resurfaces in Beauvoir's life during the years of World War II and the Nazi Occupation. Beauvoir wrote a Resistance novel, *The Blood of Others* (1945) and in 1941, joined with Sartre in founding a Resistance group, "Socialisme et Liberté," that published a newsletter to engage the French people against the Germans. But the group, which failed to establish contact with the Communists or the Resistance in the Vichy zone, disbanded in October of 1941, having, as Eva Lundgren-Gothlin writes, "accomplished very little but at great risk to its individual members" (Lundgren-Gothlin, 1996, p. 35). Recently, however, critics have charged Beauvoir (and Sartre) with "a sort of intellectual collaboration" during the war, describing them as "opportunists who saw passive collaboration as the way to become rich and famous" (Bair, 1990, pp. 242, 280). The charge of passive collaboration refers to Beauvoir's signing of an oath required of all teachers that she was neither a Jew nor a Freemason, and continuing to write and publish under German censorship, often working in a Paris café frequented by German officers. A more serious charge of active collaboration levelled against her by Bair and taken up by Susan Rubin Suleiman (1992) is that, after being fired from her teaching job in 1943 by the German-controlled Ministry of Education for "corrupting a minor," Beauvoir actively collaborated with the Nazis by producing a radio-show for Radio-Paris, and tried to suppress the evidence of her collaboration by having the archives closed to the public (Bair, 1990, p. 640n).

According to Ingrid Galster, however, this charge includes serious factual errors. Galster, who made a meticulous study of six of Beauvoir's radio scripts on "The Origins of the Music-Hall," explains that the programs were produced for the French National Radio, popularly known as "Radio-Vichy," and not for Radio-Paris, "the microphone of the occupation force aided by a French woman of the ultra-right who shared the Nazi ideology and considered the Vichy government to be a reactionary and clerical gerontocracy" (Galster, 1996b, p. 113). Other critics disagree, however, including a veteran of the Resistance, Gilbert Joseph, who describes Radio-Vichy as "a formidable propaganda organization" (cited in ibid., p. 113). Beauvoir herself maintained a careful distinction between Radio-Vichy and Radio-Paris in her memoirs:

> Writers on our side had tacitly adopted certain rules. One could not write in the news-
> papers and magazines of the occupied zone, nor speak on Radio-Paris; one could work in
> the press of the Free Zone and for Radio-Vichy: everything depended on the sense of the
> articles and broadcasts. (Beauvoir, 1960, p. 588).

Galster agrees with Joseph that entertainment shows such as Beauvoir's were broadcast in an effort "to ensure the passivity of the French" (Galster, 1996a, p. 108). Furthermore, while "by and large the National Radio retained its cultural character," Vichy
propaganda increased in late 1943, and "Philippe Henriot – the Goebbels of France –
spoke on the radio twice a day" from January to June 1944, "in an attempt to cut the
Resistance off from the rest of the nation" (ibid., p. 109). "Did Beauvoir's name, which
was just beginning to become known in literary circles," Galster asks, "not lend credibility to the names of Henriot and other defenders of the National Revolution?" (ibid.,
p. 109). Galster arrives at an ambiguous conclusion. Beauvoir's choice of texts emphasizes "marginal individuals and rebels against the established order." She satirizes power
and defies the "virtuism" of the Vichy ideology, defining thieves' robbery as "work,"
for example. According to Galster, Beauvoir's scripts thus "do not favor the goals of
Vichy" – indeed, "the opposite is the case" (ibid., p. 110). Galster concludes that "it
would be difficult to group Beauvoir among the pure Resistants, or among the collaborationists, or even among the opportunists" (ibid., p. 110). Galster thus supports
those scholars who argue for a more complex, ambiguous understanding of the reaction of the French under the Occupation: "Beauvoir shared the ambiguity of her situation with the great majority of her compatriots, a fact she herself was well aware of
. . . writing in her memoirs: 'in Paris . . . the very fact of breathing implied a compromise'" (ibid., p. 110; Beauvoir, 1960, p. 549).

Beauvoir's war diary reveals a failure to recognize the reality of the war. Preparing
to flee Paris and the approaching German army, Beauvoir drinks with friends, "a bad
champagne abandoned by an Austrian woman sent to a concentration camp. It did
me some good" (Beauvoir, 1990a, p. 302). This cavalier attitude contrasts with her
reaction, later that month, to the grim news of the terms of the Armistice: "I passed
the Boulevard Grenelle in front of the former concentration camp for women – by the
terms of the Armistice one must give back to Germany all of the German refugees –
there are few clauses that look more sinister and implacable" (ibid., p. 313). On July
9, 1940, Beauvoir describes a pleasurable radio show as "cut off by alarming German
talk (against foreigners, Jews, for work, etc.)" (ibid., p. 345).

Beauvoir ambigous feelings and reluctance to acknowledge the realities of the war
are also evident in her accounts of her relationship with her young Jewish lover, Bianca
Bienenfeld. Beauvoir, who, in the fall of 1939, was increasingly jealous of Bienenfeld's
growing intimacy with Sartre, orchestrated the end of that relationship, expressing her
anger at Bienenfeld in anti-Semitic terms. Beauvoir describes her as "crying in front
of a wailing wall that she builds with her own diligent hands . . . Something of the
old Jewish usurer who cries from pity over the client whom he has driven to suicide"
(ibid., p. 193). In her own memoir, Bienenfeld, now Bianca Lamblin, recalls that
neither Sartre nor Beauvoir ever expressed any concern for her safety, breaking off their
intimate relations with her just as the Nazi threat was drawing near, a sign, for

Lamblin, of their egoism and political ignorance (Lamblin, 1993, pp. 71–2). Lamblin, who was shocked by the anti-Semitic remarks in Beauvoir's diary, recalls that "during the three years of our initial friendship, I never felt on the part of [Beauvoir] the least manifestation of a repugnance which could have been due to the fact that I was Jewish" (ibid., p. 83). That in her jealous anger Beauvoir would describe her in such anti-Semitic terms, Lamblin attributes to the tradition of anti-Semitism in Beauvoir's family background "that she was supposed to have totally condemned" and that contradicts "her conscious ideas, which were without doubt not anti-Semitic" (ibid., p. 86).

Susan Rubin Suleiman (1992) is also struck, in reading Beauvoir's diary, by her initial inability to grasp the reality of the war, finishing a novel, *She Came to Stay* (1943) and going skiing during the winter of 1940, only months before the Occupation began. After the Occupation begins, with Sartre in a prisoner of war camp, it still takes months, until January 1941, for Beauvoir to express a sense of solidarity that will feature in her Resistance novel, *The Blood of Others* (1945), written from 1941 to 1943. Suleiman asks if this novel might be a "compensatory fantasy" on Beauvoir's part – "she who signed the Vichy oath in 1940 with so few qualms that she didn't even bother to mention it in her diary? She who never, in fact, participated in any Resistance activity during the war and who accepted, a few months after finishing *The Blood of Others*, to work for the German-controlled Radio-Paris? Perhaps" (Suleiman, 1992, p. 15).

As we have seen above, Beauvoir did not work for Radio-Paris. But what about the Vichy oath, and Suleiman's interpretation of the absence of any mention of signing the oath in Beauvoir's diary? Actually, some of the most important and emotionally difficult events in Beauvoir's life, for example the death of her friend Zaza in 1929, are passed over in silence in Beauvoir's diary. Beauvoir writes only sporadically in her diary after the Occupation begins and Sartre is captured. So we should not conclude that Beauvoir had no qualms about signing the oath simply from the fact that it is not mentioned in her diary. Defending her action to Bair, Beauvoir said:

> "I signed it because I had to. My only income came from my teaching; my ration cards depended on it, my identity papers – everything. There simply was no other choice available to me. I hated it, but I did it for purely practical reasons. Who was I? A nobody, that's who. What good would it have done if some unknown teacher refused to sign a statement that had no meaning, no value, and certainly no influence or impact on anything? Refusing to sign such statement would have had only one significance: that I no longer had a profession or an income. Who, in wartime, in my circumstances, would have been so foolish as to risk such a thing?" (Bair 1990, pp. 242–3)

Suleiman concludes that Beauvoir's wartime writings "contain no revelations nearly as troubling as those that have recently come to light about certain other intellectual heroes like Martin Heidegger or Paul de Man," and that we should be grateful to her for "authorizing the publication, even posthumously, of writings that she surely knew would cast her in a less than heroic light" (Suleiman 1992, pp. 18–19). Thus Beauvoir's actions during the Occupation might be best described as neither Resistant nor collaborative, but rather an attempt at political disengagement. Indeed, in her memoirs Beauvoir writes that she continued to live "cut off from the world" throughout the war (Beauvoir, 1960, p. 604).

But given this evidence of Beauvoir's efforts to avoid the realities of the war and the dangers to Jews, how are we to account for the militancy of Beauvoir's postwar support for Israel and the struggle against anti-Semitism and racism? In *Force of Circumstance*, Beauvoir describes her friendship with a member of the radical Zionist Stern gang in the immediate postwar period. Later she would author prefaces to *Treblinka* and *Shoah*. What could account for this dramatic shift, unexplained by Beauvoir's biographers, which marks the beginning of a political engagement found in *The Second Sex*?

The key may be a harrowing experience that came only weeks before the liberation in June 1944 – the murder by the Nazis of a young Jewish man named Bourla, a member of Beauvoir's "family" of intimate friends. Although ignored by her biographers, this event is recounted by Beauvoir in detail in *Prime of Life* as well as her novel *The Mandarins*. In her memoir Beauvoir writes of her growing intimacy with Bourla, a former student of Sartre, who became the lover of Beauvoir's former student and lover, Natalie Sorokine in 1941. "He found me a bit too rational, but he loved me well. [Natalie] demanded at night that I tuck them into bed. I kissed her and he raised his face to me: 'And me? Aren't you going to kiss me?' I kissed him as well" (ibid., p. 605). Beauvoir describes Easter, 1944, when she learned that the Nazis had taken Bourla and his father away: "abruptly, the sky above our heads was covered with soot: Bourla had been arrested" (ibid., p. 659). Despite efforts to bribe the guards, Bourla and his father were eventually killed, an event which left Beauvoir profoundly shaken. "I was overwhelmed . . . many a death had already revolted me, but this one affected me intimately. Bourla had lived very near to me, I had adopted him into my heart, and he was only 19 years old" (ibid., p. 661). It is thus only near the end of the war that Beauvoir is personally touched by Nazi atrocities and the terror of anti-Semitism. The intrusion of the Nazi horror into her intimate circle means that she is no longer able to remain cut off from the world.

The result is a profound sense of guilt.

Sartre tried piously to convince me that in a sense life is complete, that it is no more absurd to die at 19 years of age than at 80: I didn't believe it. What cities and faces he would have loved, that he will not see! Every morning, when I opened my eyes, I stole the world from him. The worst is that I stole it from nobody; there was nobody to say: "the world is stolen from me." Nobody: and nowhere is this absence incarnated; no tomb, no cadaver, not one bone. As if nothing, absolutely, had taken place. . . . This nothingness left me distraught. . . . Why was it thus? . . . Why had the father thought himself safe, why did we believe it? . . . These were pointless questions, but they tormented me. . . . These four years had been a compromise between terror and hope, between patience and anger, between desolation and some recurrences of joy. Suddenly all conciliation appeared impossible, I was torn apart. . . . Never had I felt with such evidence the capricious horror of our mortal condition. . . . Because of his very death and all that it signified, the moments when I gave myself over to indignation, to despair took on an intensity that I had never known: truly infernal. (Ibid., pp. 661–2)

The intensity of Beauvoir's grief and her sense of responsibility and guilt for Bourla's death, her feeling that in living she "stole the world from him," echo her account of the sudden illness and death in 1929 of her close friend Zaza. In this earlier account, which concludes *Memoirs of a Dutiful Daughter*, Beauvoir describes Zaza's death as also accompanying the end of a war, the struggle to escape the oppressive confines of family and a woman's traditional role: "She often appeared to me in the night . . . and looked at me with reproach. Together we had struggled against the miry destiny that lay in wait for us and I thought for a long time that I had paid for my freedom with her death" (Beauvoir, 1958, p. 503). Scholars have long recognized the symbolic importance of the figure of Zaza in the theme of death, as well as the problem of the separation of self and other, in Beauvoir's texts. Beauvoir would make Zaza's death a subject in several of her early novels, before finally successfully recounting it in *Memoirs of a Dutiful Daughter*, with its concluding reference to Zaza's death haunting her. Bourla's death has a similar symbolic importance.

In the conclusion of the second volume of her autobiography, *Prime of Life*, Beauvoir returns to her nightmares of death, linking the death of Zaza to that of Bourla:

> There was Zaza; she still came to visit me at night; . . . and very near to me Bourla. Bourla disappeared into silence, into absence, and one day we knew that it was necessary to give to this absence the name of death. . . . Often, especially during the night, I said to myself: "Let's bury him, and not think about him any longer!" . . . What separation! What betrayal! With each beat of our hearts, we renounce his life and his death. (Beauvoir, 1960, pp. 691–2)

Bourla and Zaza are linked in Beauvoir's dreams, and by a haunting sense of betrayal and guilt. Reiterating the account of Bourla's death in the final pages of *Prime of Life*, and linking his death with that of Zaza, give Bourla's death a symbolic importance in the text. That Bourla's death shaped her writing she makes clear. In the "dialectic" at work in the "interior" of her postwar novel *All Men Are Mortal* (1946), Beauvoir addresses two problems central to her experience of Bourla's death: the dilemma of our responsibility for and impotence in our relations with others, and the problem of death, "the scandal of solitude and separation" (Beauvoir, 1960, p. 694). I would argue that Beauvoir's efforts to come to terms with her grief and sense of responsibility and betrayal after Bourla's murder by the Nazis also inspires the "dialectic" of Beauvoir's confrontation with, and condemnation of, racism in her two works that followed soon after: *America Day by Day* (1948) and *The Second Sex* (1949).

Beauvoir's linking of Bourla's death to that of Zaza in the conclusion of *Prime of Life* indicates its significance for Beauvoir. Both events mark turning points in Beauvoir's life and philosophy. Zaza's death became a symbol of society's threat to young women; Beauvoir was inspired to expose the "mystifications" of women in her novel written in 1937–9, *When Things of the Spirit Come First* (1979), as well as *The Second Sex*. Bourla's death at the hands of the Nazis became a symbol of racist violence, inspiring Beauvoir's postwar political engagement, which is reflected in her condemnations of racism and anti-Semitism in *The Second Sex*. According to *Force of Circumstances*, it was in

February 1945, only months after Bourla's death and the Liberation, that Beauvoir invited Misrahi, a member of the radical Zionist group, Stern, to accompany her to a seminar where she was to lecture on ethics. Beauvoir portrays Misrahi as legitimating her project to write an existentialist ethics which will convert the vain desire for being into an assumption of existence: "Write it then! He told me" (Beauvoir, 1963, I, p. 98). Beauvoir's narrative thus frames her project in existentialist ethics which argues that one must combat oppression by willing freedom absolutely, within the context of the Jewish struggle.

Beauvoir's diaries and correspondence are useful not only for investigating allegations of racism, but also for tracing the genesis of Beauvoir's understanding of racism and the key concept of "situation" in her philosophy. The importance of the concept of "situation" is evident in the original title of *The Second Sex*. Catherine Viollet, archivist at the Bibliothèque Nationale in Paris, reports that Beauvoir's manuscript is entitled, "Essays on woman's situation." In *Prime of Life*, Beauvoir argues that the originality of her thesis in *The Second Sex* lies in her concept of situation: "What distinguishes my thesis from the traditional thesis is that, according to me, femininity is neither an essence nor a nature: it is a situation created by civilizations from certain physiological givens" (Beauvoir, 1960, p. 417).

More to the point, in *The Second Sex* Beauvoir's analysis of femininity as a situation often draws upon an analogy with racism, applying the concept of "caste," which normally applies to race, to the situation of women:

> Whether it's a question of a race, of a caste, of a class, of a sex reduced to an inferior condition, the processes of justification are the same: "the eternal feminine" is the homologue of "the black soul" and "the Jewish character." . . . [T]here are profound analogies between the situation of women and that of Blacks: both are emancipating themselves from a same paternalism and the formerly master caste wants to keep them in "their place," that is to say in the place the master caste has chosen for them. (Beauvoir, 1949, 1, p. 24)

Thus, Beauvoir's concept of situation, in *The Second Sex*, is not applicable exclusively to sex, but also to race and caste, as well as to class. The question then arises as to whether, in developing her concept of situation, Beauvoir began with gender and sex, or with race. A careful study of the diaries and correspondence of Beauvoir and Sartre can provide some clues.

Beauvoir's earliest references to what she will later term her "situation" might be said to begin in her 1927 diary, where she reflects on her experiences as a woman entering the male world of philosophy. In one passage, for example, she defends herself when criticized by a male philosophy student, Merleau-Ponty, for her emotionality

> And so, my friends, you do not like girls but consider that not only do they have a reason to satisfy but a heavy heart to restrain – and in that respect I want to remain a woman, more masculine yet in the brain, more feminine in sensibility. (Besides everyone recognizes in approaching me that I am not like other girls. Oh Ponti [sic], as you told me so nicely. . . !) (Beauvoir, 1927, p. 107)

In response to another conversation with Merleau-Ponty, Beauvoir reaffirms the unique perspective that being a woman brings her: "Certainly, I have a more complicated, more nuanced sensibility than his and a more exhausting power of love. These problems that he lives with his brain, I live them with my arms and my legs. . . . I don't want to lose all of that" (ibid., p. 126). In these diary passages, Beauvoir seems to rely on a naturalized notion of femininity in contrast to her later concept of situation.

Beauvoir's 1927 diary also reveals her early struggle to come to terms with a future outside the comforts of women's traditional role of wife and mother. Forced by economic necessity to prepare for a career, since she lacked a dowry, Beauvoir takes pride in her abilities and academic success. But she also often feels isolated and afraid of a lonely future denied the warmth and intimacy of woman's role: "Yesterday how I envied M. de Wendel so pretty and unaffected! Without pride as without envy I cried in thinking of the lot which was reserved for me" (ibid., p. 107). "I would so like to have the right, me as well, of being simple and very weak, of being a woman; in what a 'desert world' I walk, so arid, with the only oasis my intermittent esteem for myself'" (ibid., p. 57). But despite her struggles with issues of gender identity as she prepared for a profession traditionally closed to women, Beauvoir was not interested in politics: "because for me what price could I attach to the search for the happiness of humanity when the much more serious problem of its reason for being haunts me? I will make no gesture towards this terrestrial realm; the interior world alone counts" (ibid., p. 66).

Nor had she thought deeply about the salience of race, as we've seen in her use of racial stereotypes in her diaries. In *Prime of Life*, Beauvoir recounts a conversation about race from the mid-1930s, when she was a philosophy teacher in Rouen. Beauvoir was asked by a student friend to explain exactly what it meant to be Jewish: "I responded with authority: 'Nothing. The Jews do not exist: there are only men.' She told me, much later, what a great success she had when she entered the violinist's room and declared: 'My friends, you do not exist! My philosophy professor told me so'" (Beauvoir, 1960, p. 191). As the memoir continues, Beauvoir explains the evolution of her thinking on race:

> On a large number of points, I was . . . deplorably abstract. I recognized the reality of the social classes; but in reaction against the ideologies of my father, I protested whenever one spoke to me of the French, the German, the Jew: only singular persons existed. I was right to refuse essentialism. I already knew what abuses followed from such notions as the slavish soul, the Jewish character, the primitive mentality, the eternal feminine. But the universalism to which I rallied carried me far from reality. What I lacked was the idea of "situation" which alone allows us to concretely define human groups [*ensembles*] without making them subservient to an intemporal fatality. But no one in those days furnished me with this idea, once one left the cadre of the class struggle. (Ibid., p. 191)

This passage suggests the importance of Marxism as a source for a concept of situation, and also Beauvoir's early interest in anti-Semitism in developing a concept of situation "outside the cadre of the class struggle." The passage also introduces the concept of situation as the solution to a problem with relevance to contemporary identity politics: the search for an alternative to both essentialism and universalism.

In the Introduction to *The Second Sex*, Beauvoir frames the problem of "what is a woman" similarly, with the concept of situation offering a solution to the dilemma of conceptualism or essentialism versus nominalism or universalism. Beauvoir rejects essentialism: rather than the reflection of a immutably fixed essence, character is "a secondary reaction to a *situation*." But she is not espousing nominalism:

> Assuredly woman is, like man, a human being: but such an affirmation is abstract. The fact is that every concrete human being is always singularly situated. Refusing notions of the eternal feminine, the black soul, the Jewish character is not to deny that there are today Jews, Blacks, and women. This negation does not represent a liberation for those concerned, but an inauthentic flight. It is clear that no woman can claim without bad faith to situate herself beyond her sex. (Beauvoir, 1949, I, pp. 12–13)

For Beauvoir, the situations of Jews, blacks and women are thus analogous, requiring a theoretical understanding that rejects both essentialism's mystification of difference and universalism's denial of difference. Authenticity entails that individuals recognize how they are "singularly situated" while rejecting the temptation to try to situate themselves "beyond" their gender or ethnicity. A difficulty comes in situations of oppression, when members of an oppressed caste are identified as the Other, defined as inferior and denied subjectivity. Neither universalism nor essentialism is an authentic alternative. Any attempt to cleanse oneself of a stigmatized difference and attain universal subjectivity is bound to fail, but accepting one's inferior identity as the Other is a mutilation, according to Beauvoir.

> It is a strange experience for an individual who experiences himself as subject, autonomy, transcendence, as an absolute, to discover inferiority in himself as a given essence: it is a strange experience for one who poses himself for himself as the One to be revealed to himself as alterity. That is what happens to the little girl when, serving her apprenticeship in the world, she grasps herself there as a woman.

To explain woman's experience of alterity, Beauvoir appeals to Richard Wright's description of the African-American experience of racism in *Native Son*:

> This situation is not unique. It is also the one known by American blacks, partially integrated into a civilization that, however, considers them as an inferior caste. What Bigger Thomas experiences with so much rancour at the dawn of his life is this definitive inferiority, this cursed alterity inscribed in the color of his skin. . . . The big difference is that the blacks suffer their lot in revolt. No privilege compensates for the harshness, while the woman is invited to complicity. (Ibid., II, pp. 46–7)

A young woman "knows that to accept herself as woman is to resign and mutilate herself; if the resignation is tempting, the mutilation is odious" (ibid., II, p. 43). Her only authentic alternative is to resist the temptation to complicity, and follow the model of American blacks in revolt.

How is authenticity possible in situations of oppression? Beauvoir's answer is complex. She rejects women's attempt to "be" a woman as an inauthentic flight:

271

"playing at being a woman is . . . a trap. To be a woman would be to be an object, the *Other*; and the Other remains subject in the heart of its abdication. The real problem for woman is refusing these flights in order to accomplish herself as transcendence" (ibid., 1, pp. 92–3). The quest for an identity as a woman, for a substantive self, is one form of the pursuit of being, the desire to alienate oneself in an object, and is thus an attempt to evade the hard demands of one's freedom. "Man attains an authentically moral attitude when he renounces *being* in order to assume his existence" (ibid., I, p. 233). Beauvoir clearly rejects a feminist politics based on a mystification of woman's difference: women's "demand is not to be exalted in their femininity; they want transcendence to prevail over immanence for themselves as for all of humanity" (ibid., 1, p. 222). "Those epochs that regard woman as the *Other* are those that refuse most bitterly to integrate her into society as a human being. Today she is becoming a fellow *other* only in losing her mystical aura" (ibid., 1, p. 120).

Authenticity for the oppressed entails refusal and defiance of their place and identity in society: "One manner of assuming the fact that she is poorly integrated into society, is to surpass its limited horizons" (ibid., II, p. 123). Defiance is one manner of assuming the ambiguous situation of being a transcendent subject in a world where she is denied "concrete possibilities for projecting her freedom into the world." Because freedom "remains for women abstract and empty, it can only be authentically assumed in revolt. . . . They must refuse the limits of their situation and seek to open paths to the future for themselves. Resignation is only an abdication and a flight. There is no other course of action for woman than to work for her liberation" which "can only be collective" (ibid., II, pp. 454–5). Thus, one authentically assumes a situation of oppression only by refusal and political action. Beauvoir models her concept of moral authenticity and feminist political action on the attitude of American blacks who "suffer their lot in revolt" (ibid., II, p. 47).

The concept of situation, as an alternative to essentialism or universalism, and as a vital component in her existentialist ethics, is thus central to Beauvoir's philosophy in *The Second Sex*. But what are its origins? In *Prime of Life*, Beauvoir writes that it was Sartre, during a military leave in February 1940, who provided her with the concept of situation and its moral implications (Beauvoir, 1960, p. 492). Galster, in her study of Beauvoir's wartime writings, uncritically repeats this account (Galster, 1996c, p. 4). But Beauvoir's and Sartre's war diaries and correspondence challenge this account, revealing a more complicated story. Beauvoir was interested in the concept of situation well before February 1940, and it was in a Beauvoir/Sartre dialogue where one sees the development of an ethics demanding that one assume one's situation. Beauvoir's interest in analyzing one's situation seems to have begun during the fall of 1939, after the mobilization of French troops and Sartre's departure for the front with women's shared experience of being left behind. Reading histories of World War I as the country waits for the fighting to begin, Beauvoir is struck by the contingencies of war, where periods of waiting were broken only by completely useless massacres (Beauvoir, 1990a, p. 69). But it's a personal relationship, the passion and jealousy she experiences with a young lover, Jacques Bost, whom she must share with another woman, which leads Beauvoir to deepen her reflections on the "contingent" situations shaping her life.

In a November 3, 1939 diary entry, Beauvoir rejects Sartre's efforts to convince her that she has chosen the relationship with Bost such as it is, refusing to be like those women who "make a pretense of choosing that to which they submit." Despite Sartre's ridicule, she is committed to analyzing the contingent, psychological dimensions of her situation:

> I used to have, above all, a moral attitude. I tried to believe myself to be what I wanted to be. Since this year, the presence of the contingent, the passionate due to Bost has been glaringly obvious. . . . Now it amuses me like a new domain. . . . It is one step towards a knowledge of myself that begins to interest me. I sense that I am becoming something well defined. . . . I feel myself to be a grown woman; I would love to know which one. Yesterday, I spoke at length with Sartre on a point which truly interests me in myself, that is my "femininity," the manner in which I am and am not of my sex. That must be defined, and also in general what I ask of my life, of my thought, and how I am situated in the world. (Ibid., pp. 124–6)

Thus, on November 3, 1939 Beauvoir is already on the path of seeking knowledge of herself and of her feminine situation that will lead to *The Second Sex*. The ambiguity of her experience of feminine identity and the element of refusal anticipate *The Second Sex*. Beauvoir continues her analysis in a diary entry from December 1939:

> Suddenly, awareness of my physique, and of my liaison with my parents, my milieu. . . . I feel myself French and provincial, a middle-class, déclassé bourgeoisie; . . . a state functionary and intellectual with links to Montparnasse; all of that is in my manner of dress and hairstyle. That must be studied as well, I desire more and more to do this study of myself. (Ibid., pp. 188–9)

So by December of 1939, Beauvoir is already interested not only in her femininity, but also in her economic class, her nationality, etc.

It is soon afterwards, in a January 2, 1940 diary entry, that Beauvoir reflects on the phenomenon of being "in situation" more generally, specifically to the situation of a German-Jewish refugee writer of an earlier era, Heinrich Heine: "I am reading the end of the Heine biography – it interests me because one can not be more 'in situation' than this guy, a Jew, German refugee, showing solidarity with the exiles in France, etc. – it's curious this German immigration of a hundred years ago, symmetrical to that of today" (ibid., p. 227). The origins of the cited phrase "in situation" are not specified.

In a January 8, 1940 letter to Sartre, cited by Suleiman, Beauvoir discusses the decision, in response to reading the Heine biography, which she has sent him, that he must assume himself as French:

> In part, yes, certainly, it seems to me that writing *Nausea* is in some ways assuming oneself as French. Didn't we talk about that one time at the "Rey"? That one could not be able to be in solidarity with persecuted German Jews as one would for French Jews, and that one must count borders in the fact of being "in situation"? . . . It's a question (or not?) in this case of attaining universal objects, ideas, works, etc., through a singular,

historical position. Now it would be necessary to define the position and limit it and see what commitments it entails – speak to me of this again; it interests me strongly: in my little novel [*She Came to Stay*] I put in a conversation where Pierre assumes himself as French precisely in refusing the idea of moving his theater to America. (Beauvoir, 1990b, II, pp. 25–6)

Thus, for Beauvoir, refusal – either Heine's refusal to remain in an anti-Semitic Germany, or Pierre's refusal to move his theater to America – is a key element in assuming one's situation. Beauvoir's argument that Sartre assumes himself as French in writing *Nausea* is also interesting for its element of individuality. Beauvoir's concept of situation refers to "a singular, historical position" rather than to nationality or ethnicity, and does not apparently entail political engagement, as it would in *The Second Sex*.

It is not until months later, in January of 1941, in the midst of the Nazi Occupation and with Sartre in a German prisoner-of-war camp, that, as Suleiman points out, Beauvoir discovers political solidarity. She has ceased to find comfort in "that historical infinite in which Hegel optimistically dilutes everything" and finds "a *metaphysical* solidarity that is a new discovery for me, I who was a solipsist" (Beauvoir 1990a, pp. 361–2; cited in Suleiman, 1992, p. 11).

I can not be a consciousness, spirit, among ants. I understand in what ways our anti-humanism fell short. To admire man as a given (fine intelligent animal, etc.), is imbecilic – but there is no other reality than human reality – all values are founded on it. And it is the "that towards which it transcends itself" which has always moved us and which orients each of our destinies. (Beauvoir, 1990a, p. 362)

Suleiman describes Beauvoir's discovery of solidarity with others reflected in this passage as "a major philosophical leap" (Suleiman, 1992, p. 12). On January 21, 1941 Beauvoir writes of her efforts to finish her solipsistic novel, *She Came to Stay*: "Haste to finish it. [It] rests on a philosophical standpoint that is already no longer mine. The next one will be about the *situation of the individual*, its ethical significance and its relation to the social. Importance of this metaphysical dimension" (Beauvoir, 1990a, p. 363).

At the end of the war, Beauvoir would bring her heightened consciousness of racist violence following Bourla's murder to her exploration of the social and political dimensions of the "situation of the individual." She continued to work on understanding her own situation, as a woman, while developing her understanding of racism. Beauvoir began work on *The Second Sex* in 1946, but interrupted it for a four-month lecture tour of the United States in 1947, which included a bus trip through the segregated South. Her encounter with American anti-black racism is a major theme of *America Day by Day* (1948), an account of her visit to the States. In this often overlooked text, recently retranslated in an edition that restores much of the material on racism deleted in the original translation, Beauvoir develops an analysis of the situation of blacks in America that has striking analogies with her analysis of women's situation in *The Second Sex*.

As I have argued elsewhere (Simons, 1999), Beauvoir's efforts to incorporate the political into her individualist philosophy drew her to the work of the African-American novelist Richard Wright, author of a bestselling novel, *Native Son* (1940), and an autobiography, *Black Boy* (1944), which was published in 1947 in several issues of *Les Temps Modernes*, the journal edited by Beauvoir, Sartre and others. Wright's influence on Beauvoir is apparent in *America Day by Day*, where Wright is portrayed as both her guide to Harlem and her intellectual mentor, leading her out of the dilemma posed by nominalism and essentialism. As a politically engaged author exposing the dire psychological effects of racism on blacks, Wright provides a model for Beauvoir of how descriptions of one's individual situation can disclose its political dimensions.

Beauvoir constructs *America Day by Day* not just as a chronicle of her visit, but as the dialectical working out of the nominalism versus essentialism dilemma. The book begins with nominalism, as Beauvoir describes herself upon arriving in New York as feeling "invisible to every gaze," like a "phantom" (Beauvoir, [1948] 1999, p. 7). The disembodied subject of modernism is evident as she ventures into Harlem, walking through neighborhoods that she has been warned by whites to avoid. Her response is a denial of difference: "these people . . . seem no more unlike the inhabitants of Lexington Avenue than the people of Marseilles seem unlike the residents of Lille" (ibid., p. 35). She interprets the alleged dangers of Harlem as a projection of white fears, "the reverse of hatred and a kind of remorse." With the focus on the white gaze, the subjectivity of blacks is invisible, and Beauvoir's descriptions are objectifying stereotypes: "there's a swarm of black children. . . . Blacks sit daydreaming on the doorsteps. . . . The open faces do not seem fixed on some invisible point in the future but reflect the world as it is given at that moment, under this sky" (ibid., p. 35). By privileging the white gaze, objectifying blacks, and denying their subjectivity, Beauvoir sets up the first horn of the universalism–essentialism dilemma. Beginning with universalist denial of difference, one ends up with the arrogant eye of colonialism.

Beauvoir's exploration of the second horn of the dilemma, essentialism, follows soon after, in her account of a visit to a famous dance hall in the company of Richard Wright. Instead of denying difference, this time Beauvoir mysticizes it, in a celebration of black music and dance:

> when you see these men dance, their sensual life unrestrained by an armor of Puritan virtue, you understand how much sexual jealousy can enter into the white American's hatred of these quick bodies. . . . What gaiety, what freedom, what life in that music and dancing! . . . They dance simply and quite naturally; you need perfect inner relaxation to allow yourself to be so utterly possessed by the music and rhythms of jazz. (Ibid., p. 38)

In this passage, mimicking the romanticism of the Harlem Renaissance, black music and dance are described not as cultural creations, requiring intellect and discipline, but as "natural" expressions of "unrestrained" bodies "possessed by the music."

As the passage continues, Beauvoir emphasizes epistemological essentialism, the sense that one has captured the true essence of an experience, with a level of spiritual insight that transcends ordinary knowledge:

> The Savoy is the biggest dance hall . . . in the world: something in this statement is sooth-
> ing to the spirit. And this jazz is perhaps the best in the world; in any case, there's no
> other place where it can more fully express its truth . . . When I used to go hear jazz in
> Paris or to see blacks dance, the moment never seemed enough in itself: it promised me
> something else, a more complete reality, of which it was merely a vague reflection. It was
> this very night that it promised me. Here I'm touching something that leads to nothing
> but itself; I've come out of the cave. From time to time in New York I've known the
> plenitude given to the surrendered soul by the contemplation of a pure Idea. That is the
> greatest miracle of this journey and it was never more dazzling than today. (Ibid., p. 39)

Essentialism is evident in the references to a truth being "fully" expressed, the satis-
faction of discovering "a more complete reality" in coming "out of the cave," an allusion to Plato's allegory of the cave, and finally, to the "plenitude" that comes to a
"surrendered soul" from the "contemplation of a pure Idea."

A challenge to both a universalist denial and an essentialist mystification of difference comes from Richard Wright following a visit to a black church, where Beauvoir
is struck by the political aspect of the service.

> You have to understand, [Wright] explains to me, that there isn't a minute in a black
> person's life that isn't penetrated by social consciousness. From the cradle to the grave,
> working, eating, loving, walking, dancing, praying, he can never forget that he is black,
> and that makes him conscious every minute of the whole white world from which the
> word "black" takes its meaning. Whatever he does, a black man is "committed." There
> is no black writer who can avoid the problem of commitment. It is resolved in advance.
> (Ibid., p. 58)

Wright has become Beauvoir's mentor, explaining the effects of racism. Wright rejects
nominalism, since he argues for the salience of race for blacks in a racist society, and
essentialism as well, since he argues that "black" takes its meaning not from an innate
essence in black people, but from their situation in a white racist world.

Immediately preceding this passage quoted above Beauvoir defends Wright against
those who dismiss his work as an "unaesthetic and superficial realism," which "tells
stories – that's all" (ibid., p. 54). Beauvoir's reply sheds light on her appreciation of
Wright:

> In France, we have intellectuals to spare, whereas the effort of writers to integrate life in
> its crudest form into literature was quite new to us and singularly enriching. . . . [I]n the
> American novels we like, the given is described through strongly felt convictions involv-
> ing love, hate, and rebellion. Life is revealed in its truth, that is to say that the hero's
> consciousness is present there. (Ibid., p. 55)

Wright's phenomenological approach thus offers an alternative to the subjectivity and
objectivity dichotomy, with "objective" reality disclosed through the consciousness of
the novel's protagonist, and the personal revealed as political.

That Beauvoir's interest is in political difference, and not more broadly in cultural
differences, is evident in her account of her visit to the Southwest, and her reaction to

Native American cultures. Alarmed by the rise of anti-Communism in America and the beginning of the cold war, Beauvoir ridicules the politically conservative aesthetes of Santa Fe and their fawning reverence for Native American culture, which she dismisses as either made for the tourist trade or simply uninteresting: "We get tired of this pottery" (ibid., p. 187). Beauvoir's attitude reflects her political concerns. But it also reflects the lack of anthropological or ethnographical perspective. Not until the last night of a three-day stay in the Santa Fe area does Beauvoir seem to glimpse a deeper reality while watching Indian women dancers: "They exert themselves with the passion of some deep faith; if this were not so, they would drop from fatigue" (ibid., p. 199). Beauvoir's lack of appreciation of non-industrialized cultures is also evident in the chapter from *The Second Sex* on "the primitive horde." The anthropologist, Nicole-Claude Mathieu (1999) observes that Beauvoir fails to recognize cultural creativity in the primitive horde, seeing pottery, which requires difficult technique, as mere domestic work. Beauvoir's lack of an anthropological appreciation of other cultures both reflects her Marxist perspective and helps explain the ethnocentrism of *The Second Sex*.

Beauvoir's experiences on the bus trip through the South with Natalie Sorokine confront her with the realities of American racism that challenge both the modern nominalist denial of differences and their mystification by essentialists. The nominalist position is undermined by Beauvoir's discovery of her embodiment and the subjectivity of black people. The disembodied subject is eroded as Beauvoir encounters segregation for the first time, in a Texas bus station:

> On the doors of the restrooms, one reads on one side "White Ladies," "White Gentlemen," and on the other, "Colored Women," "Colored Men." There are only whites in the large hall that serves as a waiting room; blacks are parked in a wretched little alcove. . . . This is the first time we're seeing with our own eyes the segregation that we've heard so much about. And although we'd been warned, something fell onto our shoulders that would not lift all through the South; it was our own skin that became heavy and stifling, its color burning us. (Beauvoir, [1948] 1999, p. 203)

The disembodied knowing subject who described herself as "invisible," a "phantom," earlier in the book, has discovered her embodiment as a white person. The meaning of her skin color is not biologically given, but is a result of her privileged situation as a white person in a white racist society.

As the previously disembodied knowing subject is disclosed as embodied, so is the subjectivity of the former objects of knowledge disclosed. Beauvoir no longer assumes that the hatred in the air emanates solely from whites. A French professor at Rice in Houston describes the blacks as

> indignant at being given no reward for the services they rendered during the war and the whites dreading that they might claim certain privileges and treating them even more arrogantly than in the past. . . . Since leaving the army, blacks have demonstrated a sense of racial solidarity and a will to revolt. (Ibid., p. 214)

While in New Orleans, Beauvoir wants to hear "real jazz played by blacks." But she is told by a club owner that: "the situation has been very tense between blacks and whites for some time now, and the blacks no longer want to perform for whites" (ibid., p. 221). As the bus travels from New Orleans to Jacksonville Florida, black hatred is as evident as that of whites:

> [T]hroughout the day the great tragedy of the South pursues us like an obsession. . . . From the time we entered Texas, everywhere there's the smell of hatred in the air – the arrogant hatred of whites, the silent hatred of blacks. . . . In the crowded line outside the bus, the blacks are jostled. "You aren't going to let that Negress go in front of you," a woman says to a man in a voice trembling with fury. (Ibid., p. 233)

This episode may explain Beauvoir's awareness in *The Second Sex* that, within women's situation, the loyalties of class and race undermine feminist solidarity.

As the bus travels across the South to Savannah, Georgia, Beauvoir is witness to the social force of institutionalized racism on individual lives in an experience that leaves her feeling powerless and ashamed.

> The blacks humbly crowd onto the seat at the rear of the bus, trying to make themselves inconspicuous. During the middle of the afternoon, in the heat and jolting of the bus, which are particularly rough in the back, a pregnant woman faints. Her lolling head knocks against the window at every jolt. We hear a college girl's shocked and jeering voice crying, "The Negress is crazy!" The driver stops the bus and goes to see what's happened; it's only a Negress who has fainted and everyone jeers – these women are always making trouble. . . . Someone shakes the woman a little and wakes her up, and the bus starts again. We dare not offer her our seats in the front; the whole bus would oppose it, and she would be the first victim of their indignation. The bus continues to roll along, the young woman to suffer, and, during a stop in town, she faints again. People go drink Coca-Cola without paying any attention to her; only one elderly American woman comes with N[atalie] and me to try and help her. She thanks us, but she seems worried and goes away quickly without accepting further aid: she feels guity in the eyes of the whites and she's afraid. This is only a small incident, but it helps me understand why, when we're travelling through the overcrowded black districts, the placid Greyhound gets such hostile looks. (Ibid., p. 233)

In a racist situation where black women are denied care, even simple gestures of kindness threaten to heighten the ridicule and abuse. Beauvoir feels trapped in a morally compromising situation where no individual action seems possible. The situation is a political one, as Beauvoir realizes during a walk through a black shanty-town neighborhood of Savannah:

> This is not Lenox Avenue or Harlem; there is hatred and rage in the air. . . . With every step, our discomfort grows. As we go by, voices drop, gestures stop, smiles die; all life is suspended in the depths of those angry eyes. The silence is so stifling, the menace so oppressive that it's almost a relief when something finally explodes. An old woman glares at us in disgust and spits twice, majestically, once for N[atalie], once for me. At the same moment, a tiny girl runs off crying, "Enemies! Enemies!" It seems a long way back to the squares with the flowering baskets. (Ibid., p. 236)

A young black law student seated next to Natalie on the bus explains with a "bitter passion" "why he so ardently wants to earn the right to plead cases in court: this is one of the only concrete ways to fight for the black cause." Beauvoir remarks that: "Behind all these docile faces – through discouragement, fear, or more rarely hope, revolt is always awakening. And the whites know it" (ibid., p. 234).

Beauvoir's encounters with racism convince her of the limitations of her own individual perspective on this social and political reality: "my experience is meager for such a vast subject" (ibid., p. 236). To understand her own experience, she must turn to other sources, notably *An American Dilemma*, the massive 1944 study of the American system of racial segregation under the direction of Gunnar Myrdal, which contains an appendix by Alva Myrdal on the parallel between the problems of blacks and those of women and children, whose status is also defined by "paternalism," as Beauvoir will argue in *The Second Sex*.

In *America Day by Day*, Beauvoir explains Myrdal's use of the concept of "caste" to describe the situation of blacks, a concept employed also by W. E. B. Du Bois and John Dollard:

> [I]t is noteworthy that the idea of "race" in the scientific sense is never applied precisely to "racial" questions. First of all, the African origin of American blacks is highly mixed; and above all, more than 70% of them have white blood, and about 20% Indian blood. A black person in the U.S.A. is an individual with a percentage, however small, of black blood in his veins. That's why sociologists use the word "caste" rather than "race" to designate this category of citizens. That on average certain defined physiological traits distinguish blacks from whites, is evident. But that these traits imply an inferiority is an unfounded claim. (Ibid., p. 238).

Beauvoir argues analogously in *The Second Sex* that women constitute an oppressed caste (see for example, 1949, II, pp. 561–2), and that inferiority is a result of her inferior position in society and not of her biology.

Beauvoir's extensive discussion of *American Dilemma*, much of which was deleted in the first English translation, shapes her understanding of how a shared situation of oppression can produce common psychological effects in different individuals. Gunnar Myrdal undermines the essentialist claim that the innate inferiority of blacks justifies their "place" in society, arguing instead the social constructionist position that blacks' inferiority is not innate, but the result of their oppressed situation: "their way of life is a secondary reaction to the situation created by the white majority" (Beauvoir, [1948] 1999, p. 237). "The faults and defects attributed to blacks are really created by the terrible handicaps of segregation and discrimination; they are the effect and not the cause of the white attitude toward black people" (ibid., p. 241).

> But many racists, ignoring the rigors of science, stubbornly declare that even if the physiological reasons haven't been established, the fact is that blacks *are* inferior to whites. You have only to travel through America to be convinced of it. But what does the verb "to be" mean? Does it define an immutable nature, such as that of oxygen? Or does it describe the moment in a situation that *has become*, like every human situation. That is

the question. And to fresh eyes it's clear that the second meaning is the correct one: "Blacks are uneducated." (Ibid., p. 239)

This passage anticipates the famous opening sentence of volume two of *The Second Sex*, "one is not born, but becomes a woman." Rejecting the essentialist explanation based on innate, biological differences, Beauvoir emphasizes the historical development of a situation which produces shared character traits reflected in stereotypes.

Anticipating her analysis in *The Second Sex* of how women's situation shapes their character, and following Wright's account of the effects of racism in *Black Boy*, Beauvoir explains various stereotypes of blacks as reflective of a shared situation of oppression:

> "They are lazy, lying, thieving . . ." I note in the margins of Myrdal's book that it is strik-ing how these stereotypes are found in the mouths of all oppressors with regard to all oppressed people: African blacks, Arabs, Indo-Chinese, Hindus, Indians seen through the eyes of the Spanish conquistadors, white workers back when the working class was defenseless. These "racial" defects are curiously universal. "Laziness" means that work does not have the same significance for the person who profits from it as for the person who executes it. Lying and theft are the defenses of the weak, a silent and clumsy protest against unjust power. Furthermore (as Richard Wright points out also in *Black Boy*), the white man encourages the black man to engage in petty larceny, because in that way he can prove that he does not aspire to the moral level reserved for whites. (Ibid., p. 240)

Given Beauvoir's lack of attention to black women in *The Second Sex*, it is notable that in *America Day by Day* she draws attention to their situation: "With even more flagrant bad faith, whites see all black women as loose and without virtue. But in the South it is impossible for these women to defend themselves against the sexual advances of white men, and it is impossible for black men to protect their families; the women are simply prey" (ibid., p. 240). In *The Second Sex*, Beauvoir emphasizes the importance of the denial of the right of self-defense in shaping the character of the oppressed:

> Violence is the authentic proof of each man's adhesion to himself . . . to radically deny it to someone is to deny them any objective truth, it is to enclose them in an abstract sub-jectivity. . . . In the American South, it is rigorously impossible for a Black to use vio-lence towards Whites. This order is the key to the mysterious "black soul"; the manner in which the Black person experiences the white world, the conducts by which he adjusts to it, the compensations that he seeks, his entire manner of feeling and acting are explained on the basis of the passivity to which he is condemned. During the Occupa-tion, those Frenchmen who had decided to not allow themselves any violent gestures against the occupation forces even in cases of provocation . . . felt their situation in the world profoundly overturned: the caprice of others could change them into objects; their subjectivity no longer having the means of expressing itself concretely, it was only a sec-ondary phenomenon. (Beauvoir, 1949, II, pp. 83–4)

This passage, included in Beauvoir's discussion of the psychological effects of the denial of the lessons of violence to a young girl, links in an interesting way the experience of American blacks and the French under the Occupation.

A central thesis in *The Second Sex* is that woman is the Other, forced to see herself as an object in the eyes of the men who oppress her. This concept has striking similarities to the description by W. E. B. Du Bois of the "double consciousness" of American blacks in *The Souls of Black Folk* (Du Bois, 1903, p. 3), which is quoted by Myrdal (1994, p. 809). Beauvoir does not refer to Du Bois in either *America Day by Day*, or *The Second Sex*, but the following passage points to Du Bois's indirect influence through the work of Richard Wright and John Dollard:

> As for blacks' famous laughter . . . It's often just a mask that the black person dons in the presence of whites because he knows it's expected of him. (Richard Wright and John Dollard in *Caste and Class in a Southern Town* both strongly insist on the black person's double face, one side of which is expressly meant for whites.) (Beauvoir, [1948] 1999, p. 242)

At the end of her bus trip, once again in New York, Beauvoir has become painfully aware of the subjectivity of black entertainers:

> This need to please is what makes me uncomfortable. I know too well how deeply it's resented. . . . For all those who smile for their supper, the customer is the enemy. But men who know that, in addition, their customers despise them, men who have been oppressed since birth and at every turn because of the color of their skin – they are not smiling deep down. (Ibid., p. 316)

Beauvoir is contemptuous of the romantic essentialism of a white audience at a black minstrel show, then undergoing a revival:

> The white public stared wide-eyed in wonder; they wanted to participate in the mysteries of the black soul, to be caught up in the whirlwind of its primitive violence, penetrated by its vibrant poetry. Well, they got what they wanted! The pianist jumped up and down on his stool, the guitarist and the bass player danced in place to a diabolical rhythm, and they all showed their teeth and rolled their eyes as if possessed. And all the white faces wore admiring and stupid grins. . . . I'm sure that among themselves they play in an entirely different way and that the pleasure of succeeding in a brilliant career is mingled with the pleasure of duping the public. Forgetting all the tragedies of racial discrimination – in the North they forget them rather easily – whites have opened their souls wide, and these appear soft and impressionable through the windows of their eyes, bathing innocently in the sophisticated music and the hatred. (Ibid., pp. 317–18)

In this passage deleted from the original English translation, Beauvoir shows her awareness of the subjectivity of the black entertainers and her contempt for the romantic essentialism of the white audience who refuses to acknowledge the realities and consequences of racial discrimination.

Richard Wright guides Beauvoir in a thorough rejection of essentialism, arguing against the romanticization of difference, and exposing its dangers:

> Wright deplores . . . the kind of attraction toward blacks felt by many whites in the North, especially in New York. These whites define blacks as the antithesis of American

civilization. Magnificently gifted in music and dance, full of animal instincts (including an extraordinary sensuality), carefree, thoughtless, dreamers, poets, given to religious feeling, undisciplined, childish – that's the conventional image of blacks that these whites readily construct. And they are "drawn to" blacks because they have projected onto them what they would like to be but are not. . . . Wright finds this attitude pernicious because it tends to maintain the gulf between blacks and whites. The obvious differences between the two castes come from differences in their historical, economic, social, and cultural situations, and these could – at least theoretically – be abolished. (Ibid., pp. 353–4)

Thus, Beauvoir, with the support of Myrdal and Wright, has employed the concept of situation in rejecting the essentialist horn of the dilemma that she defined in the opening pages of *America Day by Day*.

Beauvoir's experiences during her bus trip through the South have also provided her with the grounds for challenging universalism, the other horn of the dilemma. For if racial differences are not cast in stone, they are nonetheless salient features of individual lives in a racist society. The shameful discovery of her own embodiment as a white person ("my skin burns me") in a racist society, challenges the modernist illusion of her disembodied subjectivity, just as her discovery of the subjectivity of the black people she encounters challenges their objectification. The alternative that emerges is the concept of situation. For the racial gulf dividing whites and blacks to be abolished, the economic, political, legal, social situation of racial discrimination that engendered them must be eliminated – hence the need for political action.

In defining a political stance, Beauvoir turns to Richard Wright, rather than to Gunnar Myrdal, a paternalistic social engineer who sees whites, rather than blacks, as the agents of social and political change. Myrdal's strategy, defined before the violent onslaught of World War II, is a moral appeal to the consciences of whites. Beauvoir, hardened by the experiences of the Occupation and following Wright, takes a more radical approach, focussing on the rising tide of revolt among black Americans, and the resources for political change within the black community, including a new generation of black military veterans who returned from the war determined to achieve freedom and equality at home. Beauvoir "discusses with Wright" the questions of the political role of the black church where the sermons of the black preachers

> have immediate social resonance and help black people become conscious of their problems because they allude to the burning issues of justice and happiness. This is why many black intellectuals display a certain goodwill toward the Church, even as they deplore its submissive attitude. (Ibid., pp. 275–6)

Beauvoir finds a model of a politically engaged writer in Wright, "who because of his singular situation finds himself engaged and wants to be" (ibid., p. 345), much as Beauvoir will argue in *The Second Sex* that women must be. Anticipating her historical analysis of feminism in *The Second Sex*, Beauvoir describes the political attitudes among American blacks:

> As for the attitude of blacks, it is of course fundamentally one of protest and refusal, but they must also adapt themselves to the conditions they have been given, so their conduct

necessarily oscillates between revolt and submission. . . . For blacks, adaptation consists in modeling their behavior on whatever whites demand of them – an attitude that is widespread in the South, where they are more defenseless. Their most aggressive revolt is a kind of desperate anarchism that easily gives rise to crime (as with the hero of Richard Wright's *Native Son*). Between these two extremes, which are both harmful to the black cause, the black leaders try to invent a policy that is "adaptive" (therefore, partially submissive to white rules), and yet "progressive" (that is, capable of ignoring those rules). (Ibid., p. 248)

Beauvoir's admiration for the inventive politics of American blacks anticipates her praise in *The Second Sex* for both Gandhi and the British suffrage organization Woman's Social and Political Union: "During fifteen years they led a campaign of political pressure which recalls on certain sides the attitude of a Gandhi: refusing violence, they invented more or less ingenious substitutes" (Beauvoir, 1949, 1, p. 208).

Beauvoir's political commitment to combatting racism was not limited to the publication of *America Day by Day* and *The Second Sex*. *Les Temps Modernes*, with Beauvoir on the editorial board, was an early supporter of post-war French anti-colonialist struggles. During the Algerian War (1945–62), Beauvoir waged a successful campaign in defense of Djamila Boupacha, a young Algerian woman rebel who was tortured and raped by French soldiers (see Murphy, 1995). During the fifties and early sixties, Beauvoir spoke out internationally in defense of women's rights, becoming an active participant in the French women's liberation movement in the seventies. Thus, despite the often glaring limitations of her perspective, Beauvoir emerged from the anti-Semitism of her childhood family, through the intimacies of her student friendship with Georgette Lévy, and the horrors of Bourla's murder at the hands of the Nazis, to become an internationally renown politically engaged writer committed to exposing the devastating effects of situations of oppression on its victims and supporting the liberation of us all.

References

Bair, Deirdre 1990: *Simone de Beauvoir: A Biography*. New York: Summit.

Beauvoir, Simone de 1927: Cahier. Holograph manuscript. Bibliothèque Nationale, Paris.

Beauvoir, Simone de 1928: Cahier. Holograph manuscript. Bibliothèque Nationale, Paris.

Beauvoir, Simone de 1943: *L'Invitée* [She Came to Stay]. Paris: Gallimard.

Beauvoir, Simone de 1945: *Le Sang des autres* [The Blood of Others]. Paris: Gallimard.

Beauvoir, Simone de 1946: *Tous les hommes sont mortels* [All Men Are Mortal]. Paris: Gallimard.

Beauvoir, Simone de [1948] 1999: *L'Amérique au jour le jour*. Paris: Gallimard. *America Day by Day*. Tr. Carol Cosman. Berkeley, CA: University of California, 1999. This translation revised by me for citations in the text.

Beauvoir, Simone de 1949: *Le Deuxième Sexe*. 2 vols. Paris: Gallimard. *The Second Sex*. Tr. H. M. Parshley. New York: Knopf, 1952.

Beauvoir, Simone de 1958: *Mémoires d'une jeune fille rangée* [Memoirs of a Dutiful Daughter]. Paris: Gallimard.

Beauvoir, Simone de 1960: *La Force de l'âge* [The Prime of Life]. Paris: Gallimard/Folio.

Beauvoir, Simone de 1963: *La Force des choses* [Force of Circumstance]. 2 vols. Paris: Gallimard.

Beauvoir, Simone de 1979: *Quand prime le spirituel* [When Things of the Spirit Come First]. Paris: Gallimard.

Beauvoir, Simone de 1990a: *Journal de guerre: septembre 1939–janvier 1941*. Ed. Sylvie Le Bon de Beauvoir. Paris: Gallimard.

Beauvoir, Simone de 1990b: *Lettres à Sartre*. Ed. Sylvie Le Bon de Beauvoir. 2 vols. Paris: Gallimard.

Du Bois, W. E. B. [1903] 1989: *The Souls of Black Folk*. Introduction by Henry Louis Gates, Jr. New York: Bantam.

Galster, Ingrid 1996a: Simone de Beauvoir and Radio-Vichy: About Some Rediscovered Radio Scripts. *Simone de Beauvoir Studies*, vol. 13, 103–13; an abridged English version of 1996b.

Galster, Ingrid 1996b: Simone de Beauvoir et Radio-Vichy: A propos de quelques scénarios retrouvés. *Romanische Forschungen*, 108 (1/2), 112–32.

Galster, Ingrid 1996c: Simone de Beauvoir face à l'Occupation allemande. Essai provisiore d'un réexamen à partir des ècrits posthumes. *Contemporary French Civilization*, XX, 2 (summer–fall), 1–14.

Joseph, Gilbert 1991: *Une si douce Occupation . . . Simone de Beauvoir et Jean-Paul Sartre 1940–1944*. Paris: Albin Michel.

Lamblin, Bianca 1993: *Mémoires d'une jeune fille dérangée*. Paris: Éditions Balland.

Lundgren-Gothlin, Eva 1996: *Sex and Existence: Simone de Beauvoir's* The Second Sex. Tr. Linda Schenck. Hanover, NH: Wesleyan University Press.

Mathieu, Nicole-Claude 1999: La horde primitive. Paper presented at "Pour une édition critique du *Deuxième Sexe*," Eichstätt, Germany, 10–13 November.

Murphy, Julien 1995: Beauvoir and the Algerian War: Toward a Postcolonial Ethics. In Margaret A. Simons (ed.), *Feminist Interpretations of Simone de Beauvoir*, University Park, PA: Pennsylvania State University Press, 263–97.

Myrdal, Gunnar with Richard Sterner and Arnold Rose 1944: *An American Dilemma: The Negro Problem and Modern Democracy*. New York: Harper.

Sartre, Jean-Paul 1948: *Qu'est-ce que la littérature?*. Paris: Gallimard.

Sartre, Jean-Paul 1983: *Lettres au Castor et à quelques autres*. 2 vols. Paris: Gallimard.

Sartre, Jean-Paul 1984: *The War Diaries: November 1939–March 1940*. Ed. Arlette Elkaïm-Sartre. Tr. Quintin Hoare. New York: Pantheon.

Simons, Margaret 1999: *Beauvoir and* The Second Sex: *Feminism, Race, and the Origins of Existentialism*. Lanham, Maryland: Rowman & Littlefield.

Suleiman, Susan Rubin 1992: Life-Story, History, Fiction: Reflections on Simone de Beauvoir's Wartime Writings. *Contention: Debates in Society, Culture and Science*, vol. 1, no. 2 (winter), 1–21.

Wright, Richard [1940] 1993: *Native Son and How Bigger Was Born*. Introduction by Arnold Rampersad. New York: HarperCollins.

Wright, Richard [1944] 1993: *Black Boy (American Hunger)*. Introduction by Jerry W. Ward, Jr. New York: HarperCollins.

CHAPTER 15

Dewey's Philosophical Approach to Racial Prejudice

GREGORY FERNANDO PAPPAS

John Dewey[1] is the American Pragmatist who was most involved in speaking against racism, both in and outside of America.[2] However, there are very few places where he actually wrote about racial matters. It is only in a 1922 lecture that he gave in China entitled "Racial Prejudice and Friction" that Dewey explicitly addresses racial prejudice as a philosophical issue.[3] Yet a careful look at what we can find discloses a promising and interesting view of how an adequate investigation should be conducted, and about the role of the philosopher in this type of inquiry.

In this paper I will first make explicit the main tenets of Dewey's analysis of racial prejudice. I will then consider some possible objections to Dewey's analysis, and the general implications to be drawn from his approach to racial prejudice.

1

Dewey believed that mere "direct appeal and exhortation" (MW, 13, p. 242) usually does not take us very far in ameliorating a problem. Instead, with a problem like racial prejudice, we need to "analyze it and discover its causes" (MW, 13, p. 437). To try to banish racial prejudice by vigorous condemnation of its evil character, without trying to understand it and study the conditions for its occurrence, is "moral superstition" (MW, 13, p. 242).

What Dewey offered, in the few places where he discussed racial issues, was nothing more than a "rough and coarse analysis" (MW, 13, p. 243) that is concerned with the "generic," that is, with racial prejudice in general. His analysis suggested that we look at "some of the main elements" of racial prejudice in order to determine "the direction in which the solution is to be sought" (MW, 13, p. 440). He began by considering the nature of a prejudice and then proceeded to suggest the main causes or conditions (or "factors," as he calls them) of racial prejudice.

a. The Nature of prejudice in general

Dewey argued *against* the intellectualist's conceptions of the nature of prejudice, that is, against views that take prejudice in general to be "a defective, hasty judgment" or "an incomplete use of reason" (MW, 13, p. 243). For Dewey, prejudice is something that operates *prior* to judgment. Prejudice has more to do with "instinct," "emotion," and "habit" than with the kind of process we think of as "intellectual." Prejudices are biases that "originally spring from instincts and habits which are deep set in our natures. They influence without our being aware of it, all our subsequent reasonings" (MW, 13, p. 243). However, this does not presuppose the unprejudiced mind is "objective," in the sense of unbiased, impartial, and not influenced by emotional forces. For Dewey there is no thinking that is not guided by desire or emotion, and that is not slanted in a certain way. In *Human Nature and Conduct* he said, "We are always biased beings, tending in one direction rather than another" (MW, 14, p. 134).

Prejudice is experienced as a spontaneous like or aversion. Yet not all spontaneous aversions or likes operate as a prejudice. For example, for someone to have a spontaneous aversion toward what they either fear or distrust might be functionally important as "data" for subsequent inquiry. How then can we distinguish the "bias" that is prejudice from benign bias that can be used to advance inquiry?

Dewey considers a spontaneous bias to be a prejudice when the bias distorts the process of reaching a judgment. A prejudice, Dewey says, either "channels the direction of thoughts that arise subsequently toward the same direction of the prejudice" (MW, 13, p. 437) or "cuts it short" (MW, 13, p. 243). Prejudice is a force that can distort by either overwhelming any other tendency, and thereby monopolizing the direction of thought, or by simply truncating ongoing inquiry. In other words, an aversion becomes a prejudice when it is so strong in relation to other direct impulses or tendencies that it distorts or affects negatively the process of inquiry.

In the case of racial prejudice, the spontaneous aversion is not only distortive in its consequences, but it is itself "unreasonable" since it does not withstand the approval of intelligence in our more reflective moments. Hence, when the philosopher reflects on racial prejudice, she will likely be alarmed by the unreasonableness of, for example, the implication that someone cannot be worthy of equal treatment simply because of their color. Often, the actual reasoning of the racist defies paradigms of logical reasoning. Therefore, philosophers avoid the issue altogether by labeling racial prejudice as a "cognitive incapacity" (or irrationality) in order to move to more "tractable" concerns. For Dewey, however, this is an irresponsible way to ignore the complexity of an important issue. It is important to inquire about the conditions that continue to produce this recurrent and complex problem.

b. The generic conditions of racial prejudice

Dewey claims that racial prejudice originates from a more "general instinct" (MW, 13, p. 437), namely, "the instinctive aversion of mankind to what is new and unusual, to whatever is different from what we are used to, and which thus shocks our customary habits" (MW, 13, p. 243). Dewey's use of "instinctive" and "natural" needs to be understood in light of his philosophical psychology.[4] For Dewey these words do not presuppose claims about human nature in its genetic make-up or its essence. The "natural" aversion towards the new is a consequence of being creatures of habit.

The importance of habits in our lives is that they "form the standards of observation and belief . . ." (MW, 13, p. 244). Dewey said, "It is to our own ways of thinking, of feeling, of talking, of observing and expecting that the newcomer is foreign" (MW, 13, p. 244). Therefore, the "new" means what for an agent appears as foreign relative to her established habits. To illustrate this "instinctive" aversion, Dewey used the example of a real-life story he once had read of an Affrican traveler who returned to Europe after spending many years in Africa. "The sight of white faces was repellent to him. Although a white himself, white faces seemed sickly to him. And the sickness struck him not simply as a physical matter but as a kind of unnatural morbidity which aroused disgust and dislike" (MW, 13, p. 244).

To be sure, Dewey did not reduce racial prejudice to a natural antagonism towards that which is foreign. Such a view would have obvious difficulties. After all, as Dewey admits, the natural antagonism when "left to itself tends to disappear under normal conditions. People get used to what is strange" (MW, 13, p. 246). Instead Dewey claims that the natural antagonism is only "the original basis" (MW, 13, p. 245). "the primitive and fundamental foundation of the racial prejudice of today" (MW, 13, p. 438). Dewey could say this because in his *Logic*,[5] he presented the "postulate of continuity" and "emergence"[6] which allowed him to hold that a sociocultural phenomenon can develop out of the biological-instinctive plane without the reduction of one to the other. Dewey claimed that inquiry develops out of a biological and cultural matrix. He also believed that racial prejudice develops from the *same* matrix. Both inquiry and prejudice emerge from distinct factors that are connected in a process of continuous development. The basic "anti-foreign" feeling (which we have by virtue of being creatures of habit) is only one of the developmental conditions for today's racial prejudices. Furthermore, Dewey held that even though this natural antagonism "gets overlaid" (MW, 13, p. 246) by other elements, "it is the foundation upon which these other elements rest for their efficacy" (MW, 13, p. 246). Thus, natural antagonism is only one of the conditions that, in interaction with other elements, produces and helps perpetuate racial prejudice. What are these other "elements" or "factors," and what part do they play in racial prejudice?

c. Factors of human psychology

The first factors to be distinguished are those of human psychology that create a prejudice centered on the "myth" of a race. Race, for Dewey, was a "mythical idea" (MW, 13, p. 246). He anticipated the current skepticism about the validity of the concept of "race."[7] Nevertheless, Dewey claimed that "race" is a very useful fiction to center "a large number of phenomena which strike attention because they are different" (MW, 13, p. 246). Regarding physiological differences, Dewey said that despite being the most irrational element of racial prejudice, they are the most powerful, because they usually function as the "reliable symbols of race" (MW, 13, p. 438). Since they "do not wear off" they "serve as a nucleus about which many other things cluster" (MW, 13, p. 246). When marked physical differences coincide with cultural ones, prejudice can sometimes become more acute. Dewey thought this especially true when there are religious differences in doctrine, and, more visibly, in worship and rituals.

Dewey did not define a universal criterion about how many or which set of differences can "cluster" around physiological differences. The good investigator should be willing to consider many factors. Today, racial differences are identified or associated in everyday life not only with physiological differences but with differences in dress, manners, religion, language, custom, and style of living. Experience has shown that the tendency to cluster group differences around perceptible physiological differences, as well as the tendency to make unwarranted generalizations about social groups,[8] are factors in human behavior. When added to our instinctive aversion, these other psychological factors contribute to the development of racial prejudice.

d. Historical factors

Dewey indicated that two additional factors must be considered: the political and the economic. These are forces that are usually mixed and inseparable and that, even though they might not present themselves as the conscious object of racial prejudice, are operative as causes of social friction. Differences in political power can effect the relation between the groups that are classified as racially different. When the dominant group that rules is perceived to be racially different from the oppressed group that is "at great disadvantage economically and politically" (MW, 13, p. 248), racial prejudice and social friction bloom.

In an Address to the 23rd Annual Conference of the NAACP in May 1932, Dewey asserted that the fundamental difficulties of the black community in America "come from the fact that in a society which is economically and industrially organized as ours is, those who want the greatest profits and those who want the monopoly, power, influence, that money gives, can get it only by creating suspicion, dislike and division among the mass of the people" (LW, 6, p. 230). Dewey believed that many of the racial prejudices we have inherited today are historically rooted in political nationalism and in exploitative political relations. He says, "I was much struck by the remark made to me by a Chinese to the effect that if it had not been for Negro slavery in America and for British domination in India, prejudice based upon differences of color would not be at the present time a very influential force. There is I am sure great truth in the remark" (MW, 13, p. 247). Political domination can be responsible for creating and perpetuating the beliefs that are central to many forms of racism. In such a society, the dominant group, as a consequence of its oppression continues to produce the evidence that supports and reinforces the belief in its superiority and in the inherent inferiority of others.[9]

The economic factor is difficult to separate from the political, particularly when racial prejudice is a class conflict rooted in exploitation. In general, this factor points to all possible economic causes of antagonism between racial groups. Dewey mentions, for example, the antiracial sentiments that developed in the United States against immigrants who have come to compete economically. "When differences of color, of religion, of customs and manners and of political allegiance are added to this economic cause of antagonism, racial friction becomes acute, as for example in the case of the Japanese in the far-western American states" (MW, 13, p. 250).

Dewey searched for an operative relation between the several factors. He admits that most racial friction does not originate out of racial prejudice; instead, racial prejudice grows out of some actual social (political or economical) tensions and antagonism that are conveniently and effectively tied to racial differences. As Dewey says, "Race is a sign, a symbol, which bears much the same relation to the actual forces which cause friction that a national flag bears to the emotions and activities which it symbolizes, condensing them into visible-tangible form" (MW, 13, p. 253). But these factors are effectively associated, centered, and concealed behind racial differences because of other human psychological factors such as the natural antagonism toward that which is strange. The spontaneous negative reaction to the features that identify a group effectively replace and conceal the complex and contextual set of reasons for antagonism in the first place. Hence, the racist usually confuses (or unconsciously associates) the "real" reasons for his antagonism with the dislike for features that strike him as different and threatening.

Dewey's analysis entails that racial prejudice is only an instance of a much broader problem. Dewey's general claim is that the organic-psychological basis of racial prejudice is a native tendency that comes from being creatures of habit, namely, reacting against what is experienced as a threat to our habits, so that whether the object of racial prejudice happens to be different or new is not essential; the important thing is that it is experienced somehow as a threat. The implication is that racial prejudice develops out of a defensive response. So even if for the white racist the black person is not experienced as new or different, those features that identify blacks are or were at some point experienced as a threat and subsequently as antagonistic to one's habitual and comfortable experience of the world. Perhaps, in many racists, the protective response or aversion against those differences that identify blacks as a group, were, with time, transformed into the spontaneous experience of these differences as a sign of inferiority.[10] The spontaneous aversion to that which is strange does serve a positive role in the growth and self-preservation of an organism. Unfortunately, this aversion has been transformed and used by humans as an efficacious way of accentuating the antagonism between groups.

Even within very similar ethnic groups, there is the phenomenon of unconsciously selecting differences and making those differences (however minimal) the object of one's contempt and animosity. For example, the Puerto Rican prejudice towards Dominicans and Cubans can exhibit all the characteristics of racism while, to the outside observer, these groups are very much alike. The implication is that even if the capacity for the spontaneous aversion is eliminated, there would still be antagonism between groups. However, these antagonisms would not have the opportunity to center and to grow around racial, gender, or any other differences in the way they have.[11] Moreover, once the prejudice (as a psychological disposition) is present in individuals, "like other social effects it becomes in turn a cause of further consequences; especially it intensifies and exasperates the other sources of friction" (MW, 13, p. 253). Hence, the factors we have distinguished constitute forces that, in the process of the development of a racial prejudice, mutually reinforce each other. Therefore, no single factor is merely a cause or an effect of the other. Dewey conceives the problem as an "organic" whole.

2

Let us next consider some possible difficulties that Dewey's general account faces. The hypothesis that the anti-foreign feeling is a basis of racial prejudice does not explain why there is more prejudice (in quantity and quality) towards blacks than there is towards immigrants who are "more foreign." Yet this is a problem of *any* theory of racial prejudice. Even a theory that explains racial prejudice in terms of exploitation fails to explain why there is not equal prejudice against all exploited people. In any case, the "equal prejudice" objection is not applicable to Dewey because the objection implies a strict identity between racial prejudice and the "native antagonism." Dewey was not committed to the view that differences are going to be proportional to the prejudice. On the contrary, his analysis suggests that there can be so many intertwined and organically related factors that can cause racial friction that it will be difficult, if not impossible, to determine any general rule to explain why one racial prejudice and discord is more acute than another. Remember, Dewey is ultimately a contextualist.[12] We can compare racial prejudices at the general level of common-generic causes (as when we talk about economical and political causes), but each racial prejudice has its own particular history and unique set of causes.

A different kind of objection might be raised about the scope of Dewey's definition of a racist. One peculiar feature of Dewey's view is that he does not take the belief in the superiority/inferiority of a race as the starting point of his analysis. The implication of Dewey's view is that there are cases in which racial prejudice is operative only as a spontaneous repugnancy, a disgust of certain experienced difference. Dewey's view then should be distinguished from other views that limit racism to an ideology.[13] Many alternative views tend to assume that racist beliefs are the cause of the racists' experience, as if people first form their ideology and then, only as a consequence of that ideology, they experience the world differently from before. The implication of this last view is that if you get rid of the ideology (beliefs), you automatically get rid of the racial prejudice as a direct experience. For Dewey this would be simplistic. A racist ideology (as a set of beliefs) is not only a cause but also an effect of certain conditions that nurture, consolidate, and perpetuate the ideology. Some of these independent but related conditions are political and economic in nature, but there are also others that are a result of our being creatures of habit.

By accounting for racial prejudice in terms of deep-seated habits and a particular social environment, Dewey does not limit racist individuals to those who have a conscious belief in the superiority of their race. But is his account still too narrow? I will now consider different types of racists that may have been left out of Dewey's account.

What I will call the "straight-forward racist" is the individual who (1) believes as a racist (e.g., that blacks are inferior);[14] (2) behaves as a racist (i.e., makes decisions and

290

judgments that support racism and behavior such as discrimination); and (3) has an immediate spontaneous aversion to features that identify the victimized group. Someone who behaves as a racist and has the immediate spontaneous aversions yet does not believe he is a racist can be called a "naive racist." Can there be naive racists who have never had the aversion that Dewey refers to, that is, (3)? It is not uncommon to find someone who unknowingly practices racist behavior without ever having any kind of negative reaction towards the differences that identify the victimized social group. Moreover, thinkers like Martin Luther King have taught us that black racism is a collective problem. That is, racism is a problem of a "white power structure" that is perpetuated by individuals, whether they are in any way consciously aware of it or not.[15] But whether this is damaging to Dewey's analysis is questionable. He could argue that his analysis is primarily about racial prejudice (as a psychological phenomenon) and only by implication about racism. It is a separate but important issue whether all embodied forms of racism require a racial prejudice. Hence, Dewey could agree that, perhaps, not all racists exhibit racist prejudice.

To complicate the issue further, one could question whether there is a difference between an investigation about "racism" and an investigation about what it is to be a "racist." It might be that Dewey's account is only relevant to the latter but not to the former. Yet these last criticisms and concerns assume that Dewey's investigation is about the definition or conceptual analysis of certain terms. It is misleading to think that Dewey was concerned with the issue of determining the necessary and sufficient conditions of the concepts of "racist" or "racism." Instead, he is concerned with the causes of racism as a *problem*, so that we may intelligently approach it. Dewey could agree that the dispositional (psychological) factor might not always be present in particular cases of racism. All he has claimed is that this factor has been (and still is) one of the many forces that have served to originate, perpetuate, and reinforce racist practice.

Nevertheless, Dewey would not be troubled by the broad definition of racists as people who, through their everyday habits, perpetuate racist practices. Nor would he be troubled by the notion of racism as a collective problem (i.e., racism that is perpetuated by a society's political and economic institutions). Collective structural racism or "institutional racism" refers to institutionalized practices that have as their outcome the continued exclusion of a subordinate group regardless of intention or ideology.[16] If the practical purpose of reflecting and defining racism is to eradicate it, then one could argue that this purpose would be better served if we have a broad definition rather than a narrow one. If it serves the purpose of ameliorating the problem to count as racist everyone who in some way or another contributes to racism as a social practice, then why not to do so even at the risk of what Robert Miles called "conceptual inflation"?[17] This does not imply that definitions are arbitrary. In the pragmatist's reconstructive approach to political language the meaning of terms such as "racism" or "racist" evolves according to our understanding of the historical situation and our available means to solve it.[18] As social problems evolve, so should our conceptual equipment to face them. "Racism" is a term open for continuous modification. Hence Dewey would argue that we need to refashion a notion of racism and of a racist to reflect the present complexity of the problem.

The collective, structural character of black racism in America could lead one to doubt the *importance* of psychological factors. But for Dewey, there is no need to establish rules of importance or to decide whether racism in general is predominantly a collective problem or not. Dewey stresses the need to be contextualist. That is, the importance of each of the factors that Dewey distinguishes depends on the particular historical racism that is being considered. In the case of racism towards immigrants, there is little doubt of the presence of the psychological aversion that Dewey describes. In this case, a narrow definition of racist will suffice. However, when a long history of oppression yields a systematic kind of racism, such as with blacks in America, the psychological factor usually takes a "back seat." In order to correct (ameliorate) systematic and collective racism, we must broaden the definition of the racist to include anyone who, even if unconsciously, contributes to the sociohistorical system of oppression. One reason why collective racism is so pervasive is that it does not manifest itself in people's psychological reactions.[19] Yet the psychological-individual factors are still important to this kind of racism. They help perpetuate the conditions that foster racism. More importantly, it is not methodologically wise to reflect about present and future racisms by disregarding (a priori) the possible presence and importance of the psychological element. In 1922, Dewey's limited experience with racism resulted in an essay that may have overemphasized the role of the psychological. But to his credit, Dewey was able to avoid the philosophical "temptation" to define the problem as exclusively psychological or exclusively as a collective problem.

3

Dewey does not provide the careful conceptual analysis of Robert Miles, or the insightful analysis of racism in America by M. L. King and Du Bois. Yet Dewey did find a distinctive, though sketchy, approach to the problem. The fact that Dewey referred to his consideration of the topic as "philosophical" (MW, 13, p. 437) raises the issue of the role of philosophy (and of the philosopher) in the social inquiry about racial prejudice.

A careful reading of Dewey suggests several ways to treat the subject. Foremost, the philosopher should be concerned with the *method* of inquiry, that is, with how we should approach the problem. For Dewey the role of the philosopher is to detect methodological fallacies. Mistakes in method are obstacles to effective amelioration of a problem. Dewey noted the following fallacies:

1. The fallacy of "moral superstition": this is the assumption that mere "direct appeal and exhortation" ameliorates a problem. The energy used in disclosing the places where racial prejudice hides and in "vigorous condemnation" (MW, 13, p. 242) of its evil character are no substitute for inquiring into the conditions of the problem. Generating arguments that will dissuade the supporter or the practician of racial prejudice is a futile task. As Dewey says, "we need to change men's minds but the best way to change their minds is to change the conditions which shape them rather than go at it by direct appeal and exhortation" (MW, 13, p. 242).

2. Intellectualism: The treatment of racial prejudice simply as an ideology, or as a mistake in reasoning and belief, or as a cognitive aberration are instances of what Dewey calls mistakes of intellectualism.[20] Racism is a "deep-seated and wide-spread social disease" (MW, 13, p. 243) in part because it is deep-seated at the most habitual and emotional levels of character.

3. Reductionism: Dewey anticipated contemporary thinkers, like Gordon W. Allport,[21] who argue against the tendency of specialists in different fields to reduce racial prejudice to whatever factor is central to their theory. Reductionism would not be such an evil if it did not lead to over-simplified approaches to problems. Theoreticians would like to be able to argue that one factor is the foundation of all racial prejudice and racism while talk of any other factor is merely a verbal mask. Equally simplistic is the approach of those who argue that even though each of the factors under consideration is different and present, if we try to ameliorate the most basic factor, all of the other factors will be affected and will eventually disappear.

4. Universalism or Noncontextualism: Inquiring about the racist or about racism in general is a dangerous abstraction. We cannot forget that there are only particular racists embedded in unique historical and social circumstances. Racism varies from group to group, with time, and in expression. A contextualist holds that the relative importance of the psychological-individual factor and the collective causes (e.g., competition or oppression) are to be determined by the particular racism that is under consideration, not by a universal theory of racism.

Reductionisms are usually sustained by dualisms. Dewey's notion of the social and of the individual avoids the need to reduce racial prejudice either to a problem of individual psychology or to a social problem. It is one of his implicit assumptions that an adequate approach to racial prejudice can *distinguish* but not separate the dispositions developed in individuals from the causes of racial friction in their social environment. Dewey was aware of the tendency to reduce the problem to a matter of changing people's minds. Hence, he stressed the importance of the economic and political factors:

> . . . without the economic and political changes which are fundamental, these factors would not produce the effect of completely eradicating racial discord. (MW, 13, p. 439)

> . . . the cultivated person who thinks that what is termed racial friction will disappear if other persons only attain his own state of enlightment and emancipation from prejudice misjudges the whole situation. Such a state of mind is important for it is favorable to bringing about more fundamental changes in political and economic relationships. (MW, 13, p. 253)

However, for Dewey, it is equally mistaken to assume that the psychological-habitual factor is only a consequence, or a by-product, of any of these other factors. It is wrong to assume that we can ameliorate the problem of racism by changing only these basic factors. Moreover, we may be unable to ameliorate effectively the economic and polit-ical factors without modifying racial prejudice as a psychological disposition. Preju-dice continues to be a subconscious force in hiring practices. The problem of racism is a problem that must be engaged at *all* ends of the spectrum of factors that can be distinguished by reflection.

But is there anything that distinguishes Dewey's view from other multi-faceted (nonreductionistic) approaches to the problem? The difference is Dewey's "organic" conception of the problem. This can be contrasted with the pluralistic but "linear" approach to the problem, where racial prejudice is a "many sided" problem requiring simply a "multiple" or "eclectic" approach.[22] What is missing in the latter view is the interdependent relation among the many factors that are distinguished as a result of analysis. Dewey did not simply uncover multiple causes and factors in racial prejudice. He pointed out their mutually reinforcing "organic" relation. A complex "organic" problem requires an intelligent organic approach. That is, the approach requires not only that we ameliorate the problem from all sides but that we are alert as to how one side affects, sustains, and nourishes the other sides.

Philosophers can contribute to the inquiry about racism and racial prejudice by offering a comprehensive way of looking at the problem. One striking feature of Dewey's analysis is its universal scope, yet the universality of Dewey's analysis could be considered antithetical to the historical-contextualist thrust of his philosophy. Is it worthwhile to try to come up with an analysis of universal validity, given the varia-tion in types and instances of racial prejudice?

To answer to this last issue, we should reject the assumption that a pragmatist must be committed to the idea that the nonpractical character of a philosophy is propor-tional to its comprehensive, general, or speculative character. This is the same assump-tion that could lead one to believe that moral theory becomes of use for "practical" moral intelligence only if it becomes applied ethics, that is, if it addresses particular problems instead of general ones. However, there is no reason to think that, for example, a moral theory about the problem of abortion will better assist the particu-lar decisions about abortion than a theory that addresses the generic traits of moral problems. Dewey would be more suspicious of the former because it usually tries to replace individual-contextual reflection. When one views theories as tools, there is room for specialized tools as well as for tools that have a wide range of application and ref-erence. A tool can be either an obstacle or a vehicle to moral practice. Philosophy cannot be disregarded as a speculative waste of time simply because it is concerned with for-mulating hypotheses that have the widest possible range of reference. On the contrary, as indicated in his Introduction to *Reconstruction in Philosophy*, Dewey finds this to be one of the reasons why philosophy is important:

> It is designated "philosophy" when its area of application is so comprehensive that it is not possible for it to pass directly into formulations of such form and content as to be serviceable in immediate conduct of specific inquiry. This fact does not signify its futility; . . . Historical facts prove that discussions that have not been carried, because of their very comprehensive and penetrating scope, to the point of detail characteristic of science, have done a work without which science would not be what it now is. (MW, 12, pp. 263–4)

Of course, this is not to deny the futility of philosophical inquiries that are too abstract and detached from everyday experience. But usually the problem with these inquiries has nothing to do with being abstract or general per se. Problems stem from the tendency to reify theoretical abstractions over ordinary experience. Hence, Dewey can argue that so long as we understand the functional importance (as a general tool) and limitations of a general inquiry about racial prejudice, it can be a legitimate task. But let me suggest a reason that it might even be worthwhile to have such an inquiry.

It is the way of intelligence to study each racial prejudice in its contextual uniqueness. There are as many approaches to the problem as there are kinds of inquiry (in academic disciplines). However, attachment to one's own theoretical tools and their success in application to a particular context can tempt inquirers to forget their selectivity and the context-bound nature of what they are doing. This is why theoreticians are liable to reductionism, onesidedness, and oversimplification of concrete problems (such as racial prejudice). Hence, it might be a good idea to counteract this tendency by keeping the *method* of inquiry into racial prejudice generalized. This is not a theory that in some sense has to be true to all instances of racial prejudice, one that needs to be addressed in order to understand particular instances of racial prejudice. This general inquiry could serve as a reminder of the context-specific nature of our solutions in confronting particular prejudices. It would not be able to prescribe anything about the individual and the particular instances of prejudices, yet the general inquiry would be concerned with method and would be informed by insights gained in particular inquiries. It can preserve for future use those new elements or conditions that can be present in any racial prejudice, so that when a new racial prejudice appears, we are better prepared to approach its complexity. Perhaps it is the philosopher who is better equipped to take this standpoint on interdisciplinary generality – especially in the midst of the current wealth of intellectual expertise about a problem. The philosopher's role of a guardian against reductionism, onesidedness, intellectualism, and oversimplification in the inquiry about racial prejudice is small but critically important.

Dewey was aware that in a world that is becoming more and more interdependent, the opportunities for racial tensions and prejudice abound. He claimed that our century has brought an increase in the physical and commercial interaction of cultures and nations. These interactions are running ahead of corresponding political and mental habits. We are carrying old habits into new conditions. Our democratic ideal entails that we transform differences from sources of friction to sources of enrichment. For this we need to educate citizens to give them characters with suitable dispositions (e.g., open-mindedness and sympathy) that welcome and are nurtured by what is new and different in experience, yet these can be cultivated only by providing the conditions and environment for their development. There are also social, economic, and political factors that must be considered, and, if necessary, reconstructed. For example, we might have to improve the standards of living and political pariciption of certain groups, so that we can ameliorate unconstructive tensions. We should be skeptical of any simplistic solution. As Dewey says, "The difficulty of making any utterances upon this point which are not mere pious platitudes is indicated by the complexity of the facts as they are disclosed even by such an inadequate analysis as the foregoing" (MW, 13, p. 251).[23]

Notes

1. Citations of the works of John Dewey refer to the critical edition published by Southern Illinois University Press. Abbreviations I have used are: "MW" (*The Middle Works, 1899–1924*), and "LW" (*The Later Works, 1925–1953*); these are followed by volume and page numbers.

2. Dewey was acquainted with many kinds of racial prejudice throughout his life, such as the prejudice against Asians, blacks, and Jews. Dewey lived in a nation of immigrants where each wave of newcomers (Irish, Italians, and so on) was first the object of prejudice, and later these were the people responsible for prejudice. At the time of this lecture he had not encountered the Nazis. Dewey did not provide a substantive analysis of the situation of the Black community in America. But Dewey was one of the founding members of the NAACP and consistently spoke against racism. In 1909 he participated in a National Negro Conference (with W. E. B. Du Bois and other social leaders) to demand equal opportunity for all blacks.

3. This was a paper read before the Chinese Social and Political Science Association. It was first published in *Chinese Social and Political Science Review*, 6 (1922), pp. 1–17. In the critical edition it appears in MW, 13, pp. 242–54. In this same volume there is an appendix entitled "A Philosophical Interpretation of Racial Prejudice" (pp. 437–42). This small essay summarizes many of the same ideas published in the Chinese journal.

4. See "The Place of Impulse in Conduct," Part 2 of *Human Nature and Conduct* (MW, 14, pp. 63–118).

5. LW, 12.

6. See LW, 12, pp. 30–1. Dewey shared these postulates with George Herbert Mead.

7. Dewey did not write enough about this issue for us to know if his skepticism was a consequence of reading current science or just resulted from his own conceptual analysis of how people use the concept of "race." It has been suggested to me that the modern American anthropologist Franz Boas might have had an influence on Dewey in this regard. It would be interesting to see if there is any basis for this claim.

   For recent discussions of the mythical character of the idea of race see Robert Miles, *Racism* (London and New York: Routledge, 1989); Ashley Montagu, *Man's Most Dangerous Myth: The Fallacy of Race* (New York: Oxford University Press, 1974); Emanuel J. Drechsel, "The Invalidity of the Concept of 'Race', "in *Restructuring for Ethnic Peace* (Honolulu, Hawaii: Matsunage Institute for Peace, 1991).

   Even if "race" is a myth, racial prejudice (racism) is quite nonmythical, since it depends upon people believing (and acting) on the false assumption that race defines biologically discriminable groupings of people. That is, the social construction of groups as racial is quite real – and vicious.

8. Dewey makes reference to this psychological tendency in MW, 13, p. 247.

9. "For of course any people held in subjection and at great disadvantage economically and politically is bound to show the consequences" (MW, 13, p. 248). The situation is worsened by the fact that in this kind of political environment, racist beliefs are held in an insecure and divided manner. Sometimes the contempt and arrogance of the racist ruler is exacerbated by a latent fear or a "subconscious feeling that perhaps the subjected people is

not really so inferior as its political status indicates" (MW, 13, p. 248). This insecurity can be the source of a more violent hostility, or of the kind of concealed prejudices present in Dewey's example of gentlemen who "so far as their consciousness was concerned were fair and respectful in their treatment of women, nevertheless subconsciously believed in their inferiority because women as [a] class held an inferior political position" (MW, 13, p. 248).

10. This characterization of the racist experience of the "other" as a threat is in accord with Robert Miles's view of racism. Miles says, "it follows that such a naturally defined collectivity constitutes a problematic presence: it is represented ideologically as a threat" (*Racism*, p. 79).

11. Differences have been used to consolidate, rationalize, and conceal other causes of friction. When the differences are those that are usually associated with "race," it is racial prejudice. But we know that other differences, such as gender, can be the object of friction, hatred, and prejudice.

12. For an explanation of Dewey's contextualism, see "Context and Thought" (LW, 6, pp. 3–21).

13. A recent example of this view is found in Robert Miles, *Racism*, pp. 42–50.

14. I am assuming here the traditional narrow view of beliefs as cognitive apprehension of a proposition.

15. The meaning of racism has been expanded in this way by such authors as L. L. Knowles and K. Prewitt, *Institutional Racism in America* (Englewood Cliffs: Prentice-Hall, 1969). See also R. Blauner, *Racial Oppression in America* (New York: Harper & Row, 1972), and D. Wellman, *Portraits of White Racism* (Cambridge: Cambridge University Press, 1977).

16. For the history of the intellectual debates regarding "institutional racism" since the late 1960s see Miles, *Racism*, pp. 50–68.

17. See *Racism*, pp. 41–68. To evaluate the practical merits and possible dangers of "conceptual inflation" or to argue against Miles on this issue is not the main concern of this paper. In any case, I do not believe that Dewey's main concern in his essays on racial prejudice was to determine the exact scope of a concept.

18. For this view of political language, see James Campbell, *The Community Reconstructs: The Meaning of Pragmatic Social Thought* (Champaign: University of Illinois Press, 1992), pp. 59–70.

19. This is why, for example, Martin L. King was more worried about "the white moderate" than he was worried about the Ku Klux Klanner (see his "Letter to Birmingham City Jail," *Liberation*, June 1963, pp. 10–16).

20. See "Experience and Philosophical Method" (LW, 1, pp. 10–41), pp. 28–9.

21. Gordon W. Allport, *The Nature of Prejudice* (Cambridge, Mass.: Addison-Wesley Publishing Co., 1954).

22. Allport, *The Nature of Prejudice*, p. 514.

23. I am indebted to Peter Manicas, Jorge Garcia, and especially to Ronald Chichester for their valuable criticism of early versions of this paper.

Index